SOMETHING ABOUT THE AUTHOR

SOMETHING ABOUT THE AUTHOR

Facts and Pictures about Contemporary Authors
and Illustrators of Books for Young People

Anne Commire

VOLUME 11

GALE RESEARCH
BOOK TOWER
DETROIT, MICHIGAN
48226

Also Published by Gale

CONTEMPORARY AUTHORS:
A Bio-Bibliographical Guide to
Current Authors and Their Works

(Now Covers About 50,000 Authors)

Special acknowledgment is due to the members of the
Contemporary Authors staff who assisted in the prep-
aration of this volume, and to Gale's art director,
Chester Gawronski.

Associate Editor: Agnes Garrett

Assistant Editors: Linda Shedd, Rosemary DeAngelis Bridges

GRATEFUL ACKNOWLEDGMENT

is made to the following publishers, authors, and artists, for their kind permission to reproduce copyrighted material. ■ **ADDISON-WESLEY.** Illustration by Crockett Johnson from *The Little Fish That Got Away* by Bernadine Cook. Drawings copyright MCMLVI by Crockett Johnson. Reprinted by permission of Addison-Wesley Publishing Co. (Young Scott Books). ■ **ARTEMIS VERLAG.** Illustration by Monika Laimgruber from *The Adventures of Little Mouk* by Wilhelm Hauff. Copyright © 1974 Artemis Verlag. Reprinted by permission of Artemis Verlag. ■ **ATHENEUM PUBLISHERS.** Illustration by Jeff Cornell from *The Crows of War* by Steven Rayson. Copyright © 1974 by Steven Rayson./ Drawings by Milton Glaser from *Cats and Bats and Things with Wings*. Poems by Conrad Aiken. Text copyright © 1965 by Conrad Aiken. Illustration copyright © 1965 by Milton Glaser. Both reprinted by permission of Atheneum Publishers. **BEHAVIORAL PUBLICATIONS.** Illustration by Peter Landa from *The Man of the House* by Joan Fassler. Copyright © 1969 by Behavioral Publications, Inc. Reprinted by permission of Human Sciences Press, a division of Behavioral Publications, Inc. ■ **THE BOBBS-MERRILL CO.** Illustration by Ann Grifalconi from *Voices in the Night* by Rhoda W. Bacmeister. Copyright © 1965 by Rhoda W. Bacmeister./ Illustration by Nathan Goldstein from *Dan Morgan Wilderness Boy* by Bernice Bryant. Copyright © 1952, 1962 by the Bobbs-Merrill Co., Inc./ Illustration by Richard Rosenblum from *A Kidnapped Santa Claus* by L. Frank Baum. Introduction copyright © 1969 by The Bobbs-Merrill Co., Inc. Illustration copyright © 1969 by Richard Rosenblum./ Illustration by Nathan Goldstein from *Alvin C. York: Young Marksman* by Ethel H. Weddle. Copyright © 1967, The Bobbs-Merrill Co., Inc. All reprinted by permission of The Bobbs-Merrill Co., Inc. ■ **THOMAS BOUREGY & CO. INC.** Illustration by Edrien from *The Black Jade Filly* by Ethel M. Comins. Copyright © 1971 by Ethel M. Comins. Reprinted by permission of Thomas Bouregy & Co., Inc. ■ **CAROL-RHODA BOOKS.** Illustration by Joan Hanson from *The Giant Giraffe* by Eve Holmquist. Copyright © 1973 by Carolrhoda Books, Inc. Reprinted by permission of Carolrhoda Books, Inc. ■ **CAXTON PRINTERS, LTD.** Illustration by Dell J. McCormick from *Paul Bunyan Swings His Axe* by Dell J. McCormick. Copyright 1936 by The Caxton Printers, Ltd. Reprinted by permission of The Caxton Printers, Ltd. ■ **CHATTO & WINDUS, LTD.** Illustration by Mary Dinsdale from *The Summer of the Lame Seagull* by Iris MacFarlane. © Iris McFarlane. Reprinted by permission of Chatto & Windus, Ltd. ■ **CHILDRENS PRESS.** Illustration by Lois Axeman from *Gregory Gray and the Brave Beast* by Mary Collins Dunne. Copyright © 1972 by Regensteiner Publishing Enterprises, Inc. Reprinted by permission of Childrens Press. ■ **THOMAS Y. CROWELL CO.** Illustration by Phoebe Erickson from *Sea Shells* by Ruth H. Dudley. Copyright 1953 by Ruth H. Dudley./ Illustration by Albert Alden from *Blow Ye Winds Westerly* by Elizabeth Gemming. Copyright © 1971 by Elizabeth Gemming. Both reprinted by permission of Thomas Y. Crowell Co. ■ **JOHN DAY CO.** Illustration by Vivien Cohen from *Facts About Sex* by Sol Gordon. Copyright © 1969, 1970, 1973 by The John Day Co., Inc. ■ **DELACORTE PRESS.** Illustration from *Shawnee Lance* by Leroy Allen. Copyright © 1970 by LeRoy Allen./ Illustration by Jan Balet from *The Fence* by Jan Balet. Copyright © 1969 Otto Maier Verlag, Ravensburg. English translation copyright © 1969 Macdonald & Co. Both reprinted by permission of Delacorte Press. ■ **T.S. DENISON & CO.** Illustration by A.B. Graham from *Lucky Cloverleaf of the 4-H* by George Crout. © 1971 by T.S. Denison and Co. Reprinted by permission of T.S. Denison and Co. ■ **J.M. DENT & SONS, LTD.** Illustration by Erik Blegvad from *The Gammage Cup* by Carol Kendall. © 1959 by Carol Kendall./ Illustration by Hans Baumhauer from *Hans Andersen's Fairy Tales* translated by Reginald Spink. © J.M. Dent & Sons, Ltd., 1958. Both reprinted by permission of J.M. Dent & Sons, Ltd. ■ **THE DIAL PRESS.** Illustration by Martha Alexander from *Blackboard Bear* by Martha Alexander. Copyright © 1969 by Martha Alexander./ Illustration by Richard Egielski from *The Letter, The Watch, and the Ring* by John Bellairs. Copyright 1976 by John Bellairs. Pictures copyright

PHOTOGRAPH CREDITS

Joy Adamson: Harcourt; Leroy Allen: Peter Gresham; Edna W. Chandler: *Mountain Democrat* Photo; Alice M. Coats: Lisel Haas; Guy Daniels: Congrat-Butlar; Paule Cloutier Daveluy: Mia et Klaus; Lew Dietz: Holt; Kenneth M. Dodson: *Friday Harbor Journal;* Frances Eager: Hamish Hamilton, Inc.; Sara D. Gilbert: Ian R. Gilbert; Milton Glaser: Armen Kachaturian; Jean R. Gould: Joan Bingham; Ada Graham: Susie Fitzhugh; Frank Graham, Jr.: Susie Fitzhugh; Margaret Bloy Graham: David Akiba; Constance C. Greene: *Lewiston Sun-Journal;* William F. Hallstead: Max Araujo; Roy Hoopes: Spencer Hoopes; Francis R. Horwich: NBC Television; John Fitzgerald Kennedy: Chief R. L. Knudson; Monika Laimgruber: Ingrid Parge [Zurich]; Harper Lee: G.D. Hackett; Joan Levine: E.P. Dutton; Richard Llewellyn Lloyd: Mark Gerson; Michael Lydon: Ellen Mandel; Arthur S. Maxwell: Studio D'Art, Los Altos; Leon McClinton: Toburen Photography; Beverly Brodsky McDermott: Gerald McDermott; Kenton McFarland: The Ralph M. Parsons Co.; Alfred G. Milotte: Gary McCutcheon; Janet Nickelsburg: Wayland Lee; Chester G. Osborne: Lincoln; Ethelyn M. Parkinson: Lefebvre Photos; Alan Paton: Crown Studios, reprinted by permission of Charles Scribner's Sons; Frank H. Renlie: Barrel Wood; Franklin Russell: Paul Matthews; Gordon Shirreffs: Danick Studio; Rosemary Anne Sisson: Walt Disney Productions; Vian Smith: H.R. Rivers; Julia Montgomery Street: Bernadette Hoyle; Philip Turner: Oxford University Press; Gerald Weales: Jules Schick Photography; David Webster: Educational Development Center; Betty West: David Campbell, Photographer; Barbara Williams: Frank R. Porschatis.

SOMETHING ABOUT THE AUTHOR

ADAMSON, Joy (Friederike Victoria) 1910-

PERSONAL: Born January 20, 1910, in Troppau, Silesia; daughter of Victor and Traute Gessner; married Victor von Klarwill, 1935, Peter Bally, 1938, George Adamson, 1943. *Education:* Attended Staatspruefung Piano, Vienna, 1927; Kunstgewerbe Schule, Vienna, 1931-32; diploma in dressmaking, 1928, sculpting, 1929-30; graduate course to study medicine, 1933-35. *Home:* Elsamere, P.O. Box 254, Naivasha, Kenya.

CAREER: Painter, 1938—; researcher on wild animals, 1956—; writer, 1958—. Head of Elsa Wild Animal Appeal, United Kingdom, 1961, United States, 1969, Canada, 1971. *Exhibitions:* National Museum, Nairobi; State House, Nairobi; London Tea Center, 1970; Tryon Gallery, Nairobi, 1972; Edinburgh, 1976. *Member:* Nanyuki, Nairobi. *Awards, honors:* Royal Horticulture Society, Gold Grenfall Medal, 1947; Award for merit (silver medal), Czechoslovakia, 1970; Humane Society, Joseph Wood-Krutsch Medal, 1971.

WRITINGS: Born Free: A Lioness of Two Worlds, Pantheon, 1960; *Elsa: The True Story of a Lioness,* Pantheon, 1961; *Living Free: The Story of Elsa and Her Cubs,* Harcourt, 1961; *Forever Free: Elsa's Pride,* Collins, 1962, published in America under the title *Forever Free,* Harcourt, 1963; *Elsa and Her Cubs,* Harcourt, 1965; *The Story of Elsa,* Pantheon, 1966; *The Peoples of Kenya,* Harcourt,

JOY ADAMSON, with Pippa

As the lions became increasingly aware of their strength, they tested it on everything they could find.
■ (From the movie "Born Free," starring Bill Travers and Virginia McKenna. Copyright © 1966, by Columbia Pictures.)

1967; *The Spotted Sphinx,* Harcourt, 1969; *Pippa the Cheetah and Her Cubs,* Harcourt, 1970; *Joy Adamson's Africa,* Harcourt, 1972; *Pippa's Challenge,* Harcourt, 1972. Articles have appeared in *Journal of Royal Geographical Society, Field, Country Life, Blackwood Magazine, Geographical Journal, German Anthropological Journal, East African Annuals, British Geographical Magazine* and in several other popular magazines in England, United States and Austria.

SIDELIGHTS: Elsa and Her Cubs filmed by George Adamson, 1960; *Born Free,* filmed by Columbia Pictures, 1966, and as a TV series, 1975; *Pippa and Her Cubs,* filmed by London Weekend International, 1970; *Living Free,* filmed by Columbia Pictures, 1971.

HOBBIES AND OTHER INTERESTS: Riding, skiing, tennis, mountaineering, swimming, photography, sketching and painting.

FOR MORE INFORMATION SEE: Horn Book, December, 1969; *People,* October 4, 1976.

ADELSON, Leone 1908-

PERSONAL: Born June 13, 1908, in New York, N.Y. *Education:* New York University, M.S., 1947; graduate, New York University's Radio-TV workshop. *Politics:* "Reformed Democrat." *Residence:* New York, N.Y.

CAREER: Elementary school teacher in Brooklyn Public Schools, 1932-45; teacher of deaf children, New York, N.Y.; Ford Foundation Experimental Closed Circuit TV Program, 1946-60; N.Y. Board of Education, writer-producer of educational television, 1962-66. Volunteer guide for Friends of the Zoo (Bronx) and Wakehill Environmental Education Center; member of New York Board of Education's chancellor's hearing committee. *Member:* English Speaking Union, Association of Retired Supervisors.

WRITINGS—Juveniles: *Who Blew That Whistle?,* William Scott, 1946; *The Blowaway Hat,* Reynal-Hitchcock, 1946; *House with Red Sails,* McKay, 1948; *All Ready for Winter,* McKay, 1952; (with Lilian Moore) *Old Rosie,* Random House, 1952; (with Moore) *The Terrible Mr. Twitmeyer,* Random House, 1952; *Red Sails on the James,* McKay, 1953; (with Benjamin Gruenberg) *Your Breakfast,* Doubleday, 1954; *All Ready for Summer,* McKay, 1955; *All Ready for School,* McKay, 1957; *Please Pass the Grass,* McKay, 1960; *Flyaway at the Air Circus,* Grosset, 1962; (with Moore) *Mr. Twitmeyer and the Poodle,* Random House, 1963; *Dandelions Don't Bite,* Pantheon, 1972. Author of two children's records for Young People's Records.

SIDELIGHTS: "Mountains fascinate me and I can well understand how the passion of climbers blinds them to danger. I'll never forget my first trip to Europe and my first sight of the Jungfrau, all pink in the morning sun. I am deeply moved by such people as John Muir and his rugged pioneer mountaineering and deeply grateful for his early efforts to hold back the miners, ranchers and loggers. Alas, I am no mountaineer!"

FOR MORE INFORMATION SEE: Washington Post Children's Book World, November 5, 1972.

The little lion's tooth plant became the *dent-de-lion* (tooth-of-the-lion). Then it took on an English accent and became *dandelion.* As you can see, *dent* means tooth. ■ (From *Dandelions Don't Bite* by Leone Adelson. Illustrated by Lou Myers.)

AGNEW, Edith J(osephine) 1897-
(Marcelino)

PERSONAL: Born October 13, 1897, in Denver, Colo.; daughter of Charles Clinton and Ella (Dunlap) Agnew. *Education:* Park College, Parkville, Mo., A.B., 1921; graduate study at New Mexico Highlands University and Western State College of Colorado. *Politics:* Republican. *Religion:* Presbyterian. *Home:* 109 Camino Santiago, Santa Fe, New Mexico 87501.

CAREER: Teacher at high school in Delta, Colo., 1921-24, and Logan Academy, Logan, Utah, 1924-28; New York (N.Y.) Public Library, assistant in children's department, 1928-29; Agua Negra Mission School, Holman, N.M., kindergarten and primary teacher, 1929-39; Ganado Mission, Ganado, Ariz., teacher of English and librarian, 1940-44; Presbyterian Board of National Missions, New York, N.Y., writing assistant, 1945-50; Presbyterian Board of Christian Education, Philadelphia, Pa., editor of *Opening Doors,* 1950-57; Delta High School, Delta, Colo., part-time teacher of English, speech and Latin, 1957-62. *Member:* Shakespeare Study Club, P.E.O. Sisterhood, Delta Kappa Gamma, Sigma Tau Delta.

EDITH J. AGNEW

WRITINGS—All published by Friendship, except as indicated: *The Songs of Marcelino* (poetry), privately printed, 1936, Board of National Missions, Presbyterian Church in the U.S.A., 1953; *The House of Christmas* (play), Eldridge Publishing House, c.1940; *My Alaska Picture Story Book,* 1948; *Sandy and Mr. Jalopy,* 1949; *The Three Henrys and Mrs. Hornicle,* 1950; *The Gray Eyes Family,* 1952; (with Gabino Rendon) *Hand on My Shoulder,* Board of National Missions, Presbyterian Church in the U.S.A., 1953; *Beyond Good Friday* (play), 1953; *Nezbah's Lamb,* 1954; *Leo of Alaska,* 1958; *The Rain Will Stop* (play), 1958; *People of the Way,* Board of Christian Education, United Presbyterian Church in the U.S.A., 1959; (with Margaret Jump) *Edge of the Village* (play), 1959; *Larry,* 1960; *Treasures for Tomas,*

Mr. Brinkman scratched behind one ear. "Can't rightly say I do," he answered slowly. "I got lots of junk from lots of places, and my memory ain't what it used to be." ■ (From *Treasures for Tomás* by Edith J. Agnew. Illustrated by Brinton Turkle.)

1964. Contributor of poems, articles, and stories to periodicals, including *Horn Book, Opening Doors, Discovery, Presbyterian Life, Stories,* and *New Mexico Magazine.*

WORK IN PROGRESS: A book on Old Testament characters for World Books.

SIDELIGHTS: "It was fortunate for me and my child audiences that finding stories took me on so many interesting travels, or enabled me to use stories I already knew from my teaching assignments. The Navaho Indian country and Spanish New Mexico and Colorado are practically home to me. Special treks took me to Alaska, West Virginia, Oklahoma, and a Florida migrant camp. In all these places I found children basically alike as well as individually different.

"It is a joy now in retirement when one of my 'children' finds me here in Santa Fe and we renew old experiences.

"I retired early in order to keep house for my father, then already in his nineties. In 1968 I came to Santa Fe to share a house and yard with a friend of early teaching days. Only now and then do I do a bit of writing."

ALEXANDER, Martha 1920-

PERSONAL: Born May 25, 1920 in Augusta, Georgia; divorced; children: a son and a daughter. *Education:* Cincinnati Academy of Fine Arts. *Home:* Sag Harbor, New York.

AWARDS, HONORS: Nobody Asked Me if I Wanted a Baby Sister was a Children's Book Showcase title in 1972; Christopher Award, 1973, for *I'll Protect You from the Jungle Beasts.*

WRITINGS—All self-illustrated: *Maybe a Monster,* 1968, *Out! Out! Out!,* 1968, *Blackboard Bear,* 1969, *The Story Grandmother Told,* 1969, *We Never Get to do Anything,* 1970, *Bobo's Dream,* 1970, *Sabrina,* 1971, *Nobody Asked Me if I Wanted a Baby Sister,* 1971, *And My Mean Old Mother Will Be Sorry, Blackboard Bear,* 1972, *No Ducks in our Bathtub,* 1973, *I'll Protect You from the Jungle Beasts,* 1973, *I'll Be the Horse If You'll Play with Me,* 1975, *I Sure Am Glad to See You, Blackboard Bear,* 1976 (all published by Dial).

Illustrator: Charlotte Zolotow, *Big Sister and Little Sister,* Harper, 1966; Janice Udry, *Mary Ann's Mud Day,* Harper,

I have to go feed my bear now. I'll see you. ■ (From *Blackboard Bear* by Martha Alexander. Illustrated by the author.)

1967; Lois Wyse, *Grandmothers Are to Love,* Parents', 1967; Lois Wyse, *Grandfathers are to Love,* Parents', 1967; La Verne Johnson, *Night Noises,* Parents', 1968; Lois Hobart, *What is a Whispery Secret?,* Parents', 1968; Doris Orgel, *Whose Turtle?,* World, 1968; Lillie D. Chaffin, *I Have a Tree,* White, 1969; Louis Untermeyer, *You,* Golden, 1969; Liesel Moak Skorpen, *Elizabeth,* Harper, 1970; Liesel Moak Skorpen, *Charles,* Harper, 1971; Dorothea Frances Fisher, *Understood Betsy,* Holt, 1972; Joan M. Lexau, *Emily and the Klunky Baby and the Next-Door Dog,* Dial, 1972; Carol K. Scism, *The Wizard of Walnut Street,* Dial, 1973; *Poems and Prayers for the Very Young,* Random, 1973; Jean Van Leeuwen, *Too Hot for Ice Cream,* Dial, 1974; Liesel M. Skorpen, *Mandy's Grandmother,* Dial, 1975.

SIDELIGHTS: "In a way life began at forty-five for me as it was then I was given my first children's book to illustrate—the beginning of a career I really love. I also had one grandchild at that time who, incidentally, has inspired some of my stories.

"My education had been four years of fine arts school. I was then married and moved to Hawaii. Being married to a serious painter who, I believed, felt a certain disdain for anything other than 'fine arts,' I found it hard to find my way to a world of my own. During the following fifteen years I did many things related to my training. I taught children's and adult art classes and did murals and paintings for children, as well as decorative collages and mosaics for architects and decorators. I then dropped everything to do ceramics for two years. Still I never found the avenue of artistic expression that seemed uniquely my own.

"Then everything changed. After a divorce I moved to New York with two teen-age children and struggled to survive, mostly by freelancing for magazines. Though I enjoyed this work, it was financially extremely difficult and there was always a feeling of being behind the crest of a wave—feeling that there must be something else out there just for me. When I was given my first book to illustrate, it was still financially difficult, but for the first time I felt that here it *was*—the other side of the wave! It was as though I had searched all my life to find me—or home.

"After getting into children's books as an illustrator, I soon began having ideas for stories and made many efforts to write. It seemed quite hopeless, though, as they sounded good in my head but not on paper. Then I discovered that making a dummy rather than trying to tell the story only in words, opened a new door. The first book I had accepted for publication was a wordless book, *Out! Out! Out!* I felt then that with my inability to write I could only do wordless books. But soon I found that as I worked on a dummy, words and pictures began to come together as one, and I was hardly aware of the difference between them.

"Now I often am unaware until I see the galleys how many—or how *few*—words there are in my books. For example, when I did *Blackboard Bear* I was quite unaware until later that there are about fifteen pages with no words. The other day someone asked me to tell her the story I am working on presently, and I fumbled and fumbled and realized that so much of the story is in the gestures and expressions that I couldn't tell my own story in words. I just handed her the dummy.

MARTHA ALEXANDER

"I have now written thirteen books and I feel the source of the material for almost all follows a similar pattern. Usually I am touched by an incident or situation that triggers an idea for a story, generally relating to a child I know or one of my grandchildren. Then of course it almost always taps into a childhood feeling of my own. When a story is 'coming on,' it often feels as though a switch has been thrown that puts something in motion. The development of my stories seems to take one of two courses.

"One group has an entirely different feeling from the others and seems to develop almost in *spite* of me rather than *because* of me. This group includes *Blackboard Bear; And My Mean Old Mother Will Be Sorry, Blackboard Bear;* and *I'll Protect You from the Jungle Beasts.* Now each of these stories is about a teddy bear or an imaginary bear. I haven't the faintest idea why these stories seem to have developed differently from the others, but I'll try to describe the way they have happened.

"*Blackboard Bear* came about this way: I was visiting a four-year-old nephew I had never seen before. I was utterly fascinated by this child. He lived in the country and had never had any children to play with. He had a fantasy world that was unbelievable. I watched him race around playing cops and robbers, cowboys and Indians, elephants, lions, and other games. Whatever he was playing, he became that part. He told me wild tales of how he once fell into a huge pit and how his brave father rescued him. It was endless. Once he handed me a dozen baby kangaroos to keep for him. All of this was done with great drama and sincerity.

"After three days of visiting, I returned home and couldn't get this child out of my mind. The following night I couldn't sleep and got up and tried to write about it, but it didn't work. Then I made a dummy and the story began to unfold, word after word, picture after picture. They just seemed to appear on the paper without my help. I hadn't the foggiest idea of what was to come. *It* just happned to *me*. The next day I finished it and was quite skeptical about showing it to my editor—afraid she might find the end of the story shocking. I was wrong. Phyllis Fogelman, my editor at Dial, loved it. And that was the birth of *Blackboard Bear*.

"The whole process seemed to be going on in me, without much conscious control or effort. Something in my head was going round and round, moving from my head down my arm and through my pencil. It was like working on something with a blindfold on and taking it off to find I had done a book. It's very exciting when this happens. My subconscious seems to take over, without control or censoring from me.

"*Nobody Asked Me If I Wanted a Baby Sister* is an example of the second group of books, carefully planned to convey a feeling or idea I wish to develop. One day my daughter's two year old said to her, "Mommy, Leslie wants to go live with Grandma." Leslie was her six-month-old sister. I was struck by the fact that a two year old would already know or feel that it was unacceptable to say she wanted to get rid of that new baby sister. I thought a great deal about this and realized how many children are programmed to 'love the new baby.' How seldom have I ever heard pure resentment and jealousy expressed toward the baby by an older child. Yet how often have I heard of an older child biting or hitting or doing horrible things to the new baby. I feel quite strongly that if a child is allowed to express his negative feelings toward the baby that these attacks on the baby would be minimized, and the guilt that the older child often carries for his resentment and jealousy would be avoided.

"I told Phyllis Fogelman the story of my grandchild's remark about the new baby, and Phyllis told me of an experience of hers about a relative's new baby. The older child stood there patting the baby while the mother cooed: 'See how she likes her baby brother.' 'Little did she know,' Phyllis told me, 'that the older child was practically rubbing the skin off the baby's arm.'

"After exchanging several stories of this kind with Phyllis, I suddenly had a zany idea: Suppose I wrote a story about an older child giving the baby away? It would certainly tap into a powerful childhood feeling. But what would my editor think? Was it too far out? Here is where a good editor can make all the difference. Phyllis said, 'Why not? If you can make it work.' I might have dropped the idea then and there if she had not left the door open.

"Now I was really dying to have that baby 'given away' by its older brother. I had a real passion for this idea and worked on the story for quite a while. The first part came together easily, but the last half just didn't seem to work. At that point after Oliver gave the baby away, the family to whom he gave it brought it back because it wouldn't stop screaming. This outcome seemed unsatisfactory. Finally I realized that somehow Oliver had to resolve his feelings toward the baby and accept it as desirable, as in a real situation. This was the whole point of his open expression of negative feelings toward the baby to begin with. Oliver knew he wanted to get rid of the baby and set out to do so. As the story evolved, the events that followed changed his feelings toward the baby so that he wanted to bring her back home as she seemed now to be a desirable asset.

"When I had reworked the story to this more satisfying conclusion, I realized something. When I was eighteen months old a baby sister had been presented to me. I'm sure I never expressed my own feelings of resentment and jealousy toward my baby sister and this probably had a great deal to do with my strong desire to write a book about it. I hope any child with similar feelings who reads this book will find his own feelings becoming more acceptable through Oliver's resolution of the problem.

"If it sounds as though every effort I ever made to write a book has been successful, it is far from true. I have a whole drawer of beginnings, endings, and middles, but they don't go together. There are times when a book I'm working on seems to say *what* I want but not the *way* I want. Invariably I feel that if I could stand on my head and see it from a different angle, I'd find the solution.

"My editor has been an integral part of my books. Several have been born during conversations with her and in relation to her family—her husband, Shelly, and son, David. For me, Phyllis acts as a fine catalyst, unique and rare in my experience. My gratitude is infinite."

FOR MORE INFORMATION SEE: Horn Book, August, 1969, December, 1969, August, 1970, June, 1971, December, 1971, April, 1973; *Top of the News,* April, 1973; *Publishers Weekly,* February 3, 1975.

LEROY ALLEN

ALLEN, Leroy 1912-

PERSONAL: Born July 13, 1912, in McLeansboro, Ill.; son of Arden W. (a carpenter) and Eliza (Pierce) Allen; married Rita Kole (an artist), on April 7, 1961. *Education:* "Higher education by self-study. Have earned some college credits by attending night classes and taking correspondence courses." *Politics:* Republican (but not "hardshell"). *Religion:* Protestant. *Home:* 1207 Bryson Avenue, Simi Valley, Calif. 93065. *Agent:* Marie Wilkerson, Park Avenue Literary Agency, New York, N.Y. 10017.

CAREER: U.S. Navy, chief yeoman, 1931-75; "first joined Navy in 1931, left after four years, worked ensuing six years as warehouseman in Los Angeles. Went back in Navy in World War II, served from February, 1942-September, 1945, saw action in Pacific Theater. Returned to Los Angeles and worked at several jobs until 1951, when I rejoined the Navy, served until retired this year. First ship was battleship, *USS West Virginia,* but served thereafter mostly on destroyers. Have sailed every ocean and been 'on liberty' in every continent." *Member:* American Legion, Veterans of Foreign Wars, Fleet Reserve Association, Toastmasters International. *Awards, honors:* Three Freedoms Foundation Awards for essays.

WRITINGS: Desires of the Heart, Zondervan, 1951; *Across the Seas,* Zondervan, 1952; *Shawnee Lance,* Dell, 1970. Has also written "Barabbas" (booklet) and *Across the Seas* has been reprinted in magazines and read over radio in Chicago.

WORK IN PROGRESS: The Lonely Time (manuscript now with agent); a book with Civil War background, "featuring a white boy and a young Negro slave who are on their own together in Arkansas backwoods."

SIDELIGHTS: "My motivation is the belief that even a minor talent should not be left unexpressed. My major areas of interest for writing purposes are the Navy, Indian life at any time frame/any geographical area, and adventure in general.

"I have moderate fluency in French and Spanish (enough to get along in those countries). I am deeply interested in history, am a sports enthusiast (spectator mostly), and am probably the most happily married man you'll ever meet."

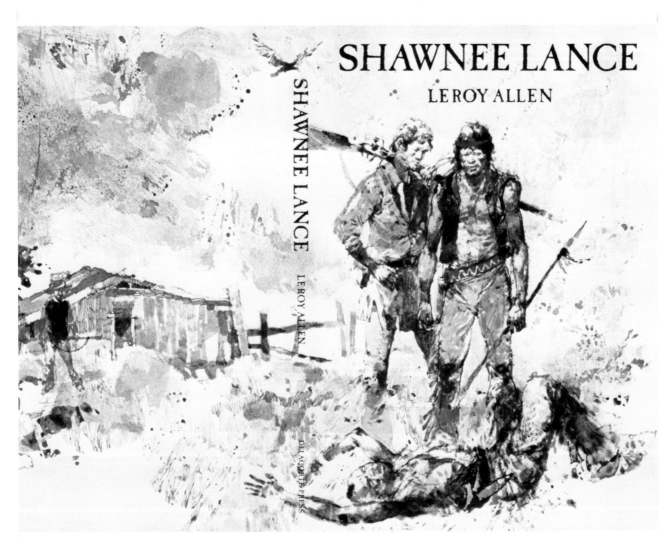

And at that moment a rifle cracked from the forest, and a Shawnee warrior fell, groaning, to the ground. ■ (From *Shawnee Lance* by Leroy Allen.)

When Grandmother Kate was a girl, her fair skin was sprinkled with nutmeg freckles. Her blond hair was so long that she could sit on it. ■ (From *When Grandmother Was Young* by Maxine Kumin. Illustrated by Don Almquist.)

ALMQUIST, Don   1929-

PERSONAL: Born July 21, 1929, in Hartford, Conn.; son of Nils Herbert (an electrician) and Jeannette (Perrow; a secretary) Almquist; married Kerstin R. Jesslen (a display manager), May 21, 1955; children: Kristina R., Jan Christian. *Education:* Rhode Island School of Design, B.F.A., 1951. *Politics:* Socialist. *Religion:* Episcopal. *Home and office:* 166 Grovers Avenue, Bridgeport, Conn. 06605. *Agent:* American Artists Representative, Inc., 60 West 45th Street, New York, N.Y. 10036.

CAREER: Free-lance illustrator; graphic artist. *Esquire Magazine,* New York, N.Y., assistant to the art director, 1951; Albert Bonnier Publishers, Stockholm, Sweden, creative director, 1964-1966. *Exhibitions:* Art Directors Club of New York, 1956-57; Society of Illustrators National Exhibition, 1960, 1962, 1965, 1972-74. *Military service:* U.S. Army, sergeant, two years. *Member:* Society of Illustrators, Illustrators Guild of New York, Society of Swedish Poster Artists and Designers, Nordiska Tecknares. *Awards, honors:* Philadelphia Art Directors Club, silver medal, 1956; Society of Illustrators, citation and certificates of merit, 1960, 1962, 1965, 1972-74.

ILLUSTRATOR: Ed Sullivan, *Christmas With Ed Sullivan,* McGraw, 1960; William Smith, *What Did I See?,* Crowell, 1961; Hodding Carter, *Doomed Road of Empire,* McGraw, 1962; Richard Wilbur, *Loudmouse,* Crowell, 1962, new edition, 1967; Jean Craig, *Spring is Like the*

Morning, Putnam, 1965; Don Almquist, *Don Fortrellade Ladan,* Bonnier, 1966; Florence P. Heide, *It Never is Dark,* Follett, 1967; Jean Craig, *Summer is a Very Busy Day,* Putnam, 1967; Patricia M. Martin, *Dolls From Cheyenne,* Putnam, 1967; Edward Lindemann, *Some Animals are Very Small,* Crowell, 1968; Maxine Kumin, *When Grandmother Was Young,* Putnam, 1969; Sylvia Van Clief and Catherine Woolley, *Cathy Uncovers a Secret,* Morrow, 1969.

DON ALMQUIST

Maxine Kumin, *When Mother was Young*, Putnam, 1970; Maxine Kumin, *When Great Grandmother was Young*, Putnam, 1971; William B. Fink, *Getting to Know New York State*, Coward, 1971; Catherine Woolley, *Ginnie and the Mystery Light*, Morrow, 1973; Catherine Woolley, *Libby Shadows a Lady*, Morrow, 1974. Illustrations have appeared in *Life*, *Reader's Digest*, *Woman's Day*, *McCall's*, *Saturday Evening Post*, *Cosmopolitan*, *Boy's Life*, *Esquire*, *Family Circle* and *Coronet*.

FOR MORE INFORMATION SEE: American Artist Magazine, May, 1959.

AMES, Gerald   1906-

PERSONAL: Born October 17, 1906, in Rochester, N.Y.; married Rose Wyler (a writer); children: Eva Lee Baird (first marriage), Joseph (stepson), Karl (stepson). *Education:* University of Rochester, B.A. *Home:* New York, New York.

CAREER: Writer. *Member:* Authors Guild.

WRITINGS: (All with wife, Rose Wyler) *Life on the Earth*, Schuman, 1953; *Restless Earth*, Abelard, 1954, 1956; *The Golden Book of Astronomy*, Simon & Schuster, 1955, revised edition titled *The New Golden Book of Astronomy*, Golden, 1959; *The Story of the Ice Age*, Harper, 1956; *The Earth's Story*, Creative Educational Society, 1957, 1967; *First Days of the World*, Harper, 1958; *The First People in the World*, Harper, 1958; *What Makes It Go?*, Whittlesey, 1958; *The Giant Golden Book of Biology: An Introduction to the Science of Life*, Golden, 1961, revised edition, *The*

GERALD AMES

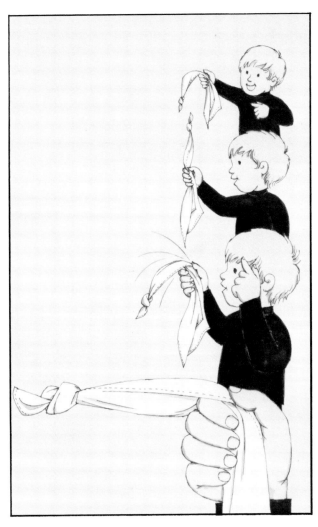

**Show a handkerchief
with a knot in one corner**
■ (From *Spooky Tricks* by Rose Wyler and Gerald Ames. Illustrated by Talivaldis Stubis.)

Golden Book of Biology: An Introduction to the Wonders of Life, Golden, 1967; *Proove It!*, Harper, 1963, Scholastic, 1965; *Planet Earth*, Golden, 1963; *Food and Life*, Creative Educational Society, 1966; *Magic Secrets*, Harper, 1967; *Spooky Tricks*, Harper, 1968; *Secrets in Stones*, Four Winds, 1970; *Funny Magic*, Parents', 1972.

FOR MORE INFORMATION SEE: Lee Bennett Hopkins, *Books Are by People*, Citation Press, 1969; *Third Book of Junior Authors*, edited by de Montreville and Hill, H. W. Wilson, 1972; *Junior Literary Guild*, September, 1972.

ANDERSON, C(larence) W(illiam)   1891-
1971

PERSONAL: Born April 12, 1891, in Wahoo, Neb.; married Madeline Paltenghi (a poet). *Education:* Attended Art Institute of Chicago, three years. *Home:* Mason, New Hampshire.

CAREER: Author and illustrator of books about horses. Worked his way through art school as a school teacher for

Tommy's father and mother and uncles and aunts had never had to ask what he wanted for his birthday or for Christmas. They knew. ▪ (From *Blaze and the Gray Spotted Pony* by C. W. Anderson. Illustrated by the author.)

two years; moved to New York, 1925, became a free-lance artist, developing an interest in horses; later qualified as a judge of hunters and jumpers by the American Horse Shows Association. His works have been displayed in galleries and museums throughout the United States. *Member:* American Society of Etchers, Society of American Graphic Artists.

WRITINGS—"Billy and Blaze" series, all self-illustrated and published by Macmillan, except as noted: *Billy and Blaze,* 1936, reissued, 1969; *Blaze and the Gypsies,* 1937, reissued, 1962; *Blaze and the Forest Fire,* 1938, reissued, Collier Books, 1972; *Blaze Finds the Trail,* 1950; *Blaze and Thunderbolt,* 1955; *Blaze and the Mountain Lion,* 1959; *Blaze and the Indian Cave,* 1964; *Blaze and the Lost Quarry,* 1966; *Blaze and the Gray Spotted Pony,* 1968; *Blaze Shows the Way,* 1969; *Blaze Finds Forgotten Roads,* 1970.

Fiction; all self-illustrated and published by Macmillan, except as noted: *And So to Bed,* Loring & Mussey, 1935; *Salute,* 1940, reissued, 1966; *High Courage,* 1941; *Bobcat,* 1949; *A Pony for Linda,* 1951; *Linda and the Indians,* 1952; *The Crooked Colt,* 1954; *The Horse of Hurricane Hill,* 1956; *Afraid to Ride,* 1957; *Pony for Three,* 1958; *A Filly for Joan,* 1960; *Lonesome Little Colt,* 1961; *Great Heart,* 1962; *Twenty Gallant Horses,* 1965; *Another Man o' War,* 1966; *C. W. Anderson's Favorite Horse Stories,* 1967; *The Outlaw,* 1967; *Phantom: Son of the Gray Ghost,* 1969; *The Blind Connemara,* 1971; *The Rumble Seat Pony,* 1971.

Nonfiction; all self-illustrated: *Black Bay and Chestnut: Profiles of Twenty Favorite Horses,* Macmillan, 1939; *Deep through the Heart: Profiles of Twenty Valiant Horses,* Macmillan, 1940, reissued, 1961; *Thoroughbreds,* Macmillan, 1942; *Big Red,* Macmillan, 1943; *Heads Up, Heels Down: A Handbook of Horsemanship and Riding,* Macmillan, 1944, reissued, 1961; *A Touch of Greatness,* Macmillan, 1945; *Tomorrow's Champion,* Macmillan, 1946; *Sketchbook,* Macmillan, 1948; *All Thoroughbreds,* Harper, 1948; *Post Parade,* Harper, 1949; *Horses Are Folks,* Harper, 1950; *Horse Show,* Harper, 1951; *Turf and Bluegrass,* Harper, 1952; *The Smashers,* Harper, 1954; *Grey, Bay, and Chestnut,* Harper, 1955.

Colts and Champions, Harper, 1956; *Accent on Youth,* Harper, 1958; *Bred to Run,* Harper, 1960; *Complete Book of Horses and Horsemanship,* Macmillan, 1963; *The Look of a Thoroughbred,* Harper, 1963; *The World of Horses,* Harper, 1965; *Before the Bugle,* Macmillan, 1968; *Horse of the Century: Man o' War,* Macmillan, 1970; *The Miracle of Greek Sculpture,* Dutton, 1970.

SIDELIGHTS: "I have always loved horses and like to draw them. The first horse I had was a big chestnut thoroughbred called Bobcat. He was a wonderful horse, the most intelligent horse I have ever known. He was not a young horse when I got him and cold winters and New England stabling had stiffened him so that his legs were not what they had been. But he went with spirit as far as he could and as well as he could. When he was no longer able to carry me, I retired him and got a big gray horse called Joker. He was a hunter and he loved hunting, but hacking bored him. When he wanted to he went wonderfully, but he had his moods. Bobcat would come at a wild gallop at a whistle or call even though he knew it meant work, but you had to go after Joker and have a piece of sugar or a carrot handy or you might not catch him.

CLARENCE WILLIAM ANDERSON

"In 1938 I built a stone studio of native granite on a hillside in a little New England village called Mason, New Hampshire. My friends used to call it The House That Blaze Built, because it was the earnings from the first Blaze books that enabled me to build it. Here I have worked over the years, but in the last few years I have had a studio apartment in Boston for the winter months. Over the years I kept horses and rode almost every day through the wood roads and over the hills. All the landscapes in my books, except for the western ones, are drawn from the country around Mason.

"Many of my readers like to draw horses and often write and ask for advice. Drawing horses is something that you have to work out for yourself, but here are a few suggestions. I've found it a good practice to always keep a sketch pad handy around the stable, and sketch from a horse whenever possible. He may not stand still very long, but try to do individual parts, like a hoof, a pastern, a hock, a shoulder, and you can move as he moves.

"Also study the bone structure as the horse moves or when you groom him. Feel his joints and know how they fit together. If there is no bone inside your drawing it will be weak and unconvincing.

"For action you may have to rely on a photograph, for the eye is not quick enough to see all the action at once, but try always to use the lines that give movement and don't just copy blindly. Some lines are static, some drive forward. Always accentuate the ones that give a feeling of movement. Even in drawing a standing horse, if you accentuate the right lines and forms he will seem ready to move. This is what you should strive for.

"I try to write about horses and people and children I know—the plot may be made-up but the characters are nearly always based on someone real. My first horse, Bobcat, was so much a person that I've used him over and over, changed a little, but with the same qualities. I feel that if you use things you know and have experienced they are more real to your readers.

"THE BLIND CONNEMARA is based almost entirely on fact. Everything but a few details of the plot is true. It concerns a young girl in a neighboring town who was given a blind white Connemara pony and got it to trust her so completely that in a show a judge, not realizing the pony was blind, said to the girl, The only fault I find with·your pony is that he's too bold. Anybody who has ever seen a blind horse going along uncertainly must realize what a compliment that was."

FOR MORE INFORMATION SEE: Illustrators of Children's Books: 1744-1945, Horn Book, 1947; *Junior Book of Authors,* edited by Kunitz and Haycraft, H. W. Wilson, 2nd edition, 1951; *Illustrators of Children's Books: 1946-1956,* Horn Book, 1958; Diana Klemin, *The Art of Art for Children's Books,* Clarkson Potter, 1966; *Illustrators of Children's Books: 1957-1966,* Horn Book, 1968; *Books Are by People* by Lee Bennett Hopkins, Citation Press, 1969; *Publishers Weekly,* April 26, 1971; *Antiquarian Bookman,* May 17, 1971; *Third Book of Junior Authors,* edited by de Montreville and Hill, H. W. Wilson, 1972.

ARCHER, Marion Fuller 1917-

PERSONAL: Born February 9, 1917, in Eugene, Ore.; daughter of O. LeRoy (a farmer) and Erma (Padden) Fuller; married Leonard B. Archer, Jr. (now director of Oshkosh, Wis., Public Library), February 14, 1945; children: Marian Fuller, Ruth Fleming, Jane Erma, Benjamin LeRoy. *Education:* University of Oregon, B.A. (honors), 1938; Columbia University, M.S. in L.S., 1941. *Politics:* Independent. *Religion:* Society of Friends. *Home:* 520 Mount Vernon St., Oshkosh, Wis. 54901. *Office:* Forrest R. Polk Library, Wisconsin State University, Oshkosh, Wis.

CAREER: Pocatello Public Library, Pocatello, Idaho, catalog librarian, 1941-43; Oregon College of Education, Monmouth, catalog librarian, 1943-44; Eugene Public Library, Eugene, Ore., children's librarian, 1944-45; Detroit Public Library, Detroit, Mich., catalog librarian, 1945-46; Wisconsin State College (now University), Oshkosh, assistant cataloger, 1963-71; Polk Library Educational Materials Center, assistant librarian, 1971-74; University of Wisconsin extension, Rhinelander School of Arts, teacher of workshop, 1971-74; University of Wisconsin, Oshkosh, instructor of literature for children, library science department, 1972-73; Polk Library, head cataloger, 1974—; co-founder, Polk Library Educational Materials Center Golden Archer Award for the favorite author of the year, chosen by the children of Wisconsin, 1974—.

MEMBER: National Federation of Press Women, National League of American Pen Women, Society of Children's Book Writers, Wisconsin Press Women, Wisconsin Regional Writer's Association, Association of Wisconsin State University Faculties, Wisconsin Library Association, Council for Wisconsin Writers (third vice-president; Chicago Children's Reading Round Table creative writing projects for children of Wisconsin, 1975-76), Friends of the University of Oregon Library, Friends of the Oshkosh Public

MARION FULLER ARCHER

Library, Phi Beta Kappa, Pi Lambda Theta, Pi Delta Phi, Sigma Pi Epsilon.

AWARDS, HONORS: Friends of American Writers, Chicago, honorable mention for *There Is a Happy Land,* 1964; Jade Ring Contest of Wisconsin Regional Writer's Association, 2nd prize for juvenile short story, 1965; Council for Wisconsin Writers Award for outstanding juvenile of the year by Wisconsin author, 1969, and State Historical Society of Wisconsin, award of merit, 1969, both for *Nine Lives of Moses on the Oregon Trail;* Council for Wisconsin Writers Award for outstanding juvenile of the year by a Wisconsin author, 1972, first place, juvenile book category, Wisconsin Press Women, 1973, first place, juvenile book category, National Federation of Press Women, 1973, all for *Sarah Jane;* second place, National League of American Pen Women Mid-Administration Creative Writing Contest, for lecture, "Walking With the Rainbow Round my Shoulder: Confessions of a Juvenile Author," April, 1975.

WRITINGS: There Is a Happy Land, Whitman, 1963; *Keys for Signe,* Whitman, 1965; (contributor) *Here Boy!*

"This is the key to the door at the foot of the stairway, the key to home. And this little one is the key to the tailor shop downstairs. Now you are free to come and go as you need to, going to school or running errands for me or going off to parties with new friends. You won't have to wait for your papa or me. You see, you are a real lady now." ■ (From *Keys for Signe* by Marion Fuller Archer. Illustrated by David Cunningham.)

(short story, "Markus and Barkus"), Whitman, 1966; *Nine Lives of Moses on the Oregon Trail*, A. Whitman, 1968; *Sarah Jane*, A. Whitman, 1972. Contributor of book review column to *Pocatello Tribune*, 1941-43.

WORK IN PROGRESS: Historical novel of Oshkosh, Wisconsin, 1875-76, for readers of upper elementary and junior high school; contemporary stories, "blossoming from the adventures of my son and his friends."

SIDELIGHTS: "I come from a family of story-tellers. One or another was always off on a gorgeous story at the drop of a hat—or without it. I have been a chronic scribbler since I was five, and hopelessly hooked on the writing habit since my first story was published in the *Oregon Farmer* children's page when I was seven.

"From that time on, I collected rejection slips in every shape, size, and color, until finally I set out to find the answer to the question: 'Ma, why is Oshkosh *so* different from Rutland?', asked by my four homesick children, loyal Vermonters all. I discovered that people, colorful, brave people, made that difference between our old home town and the new. People of twenty-four national groups settled in Oshkosh in the period of the Great Atlantic Migration. The more I read old diaries, old letters, and old newspapers, the more brave, fascinating people I discover, and the more fictional people spring to life in my mind, demanding to be let out of my head onto paper.

"Each of my books has begun with a girl with a problem, and the research to find the logical solution to her problem gave me the factual background for my fictional people—the created story was 'embroidered' on the canvas of reality. Children all over are fascinated to learn about the brave people who strived and suffered and achieved to build the fine hometown they now have. They invite me to talk to them about my books and how they came to be written.

"Since my first book, *There Is a Happy Land*, was published, I have talked to over 10,000 Wisconsin school children. I tell them that an author's mind is like the alchemist's crucible, with scraps of experiences, bits of research, wisps of dreams, and hints of suggestions from the children themselves, all brewed together, and finally poured out onto the pages of the book.

"I am a slow worker. I capture the first fire of inspiration in longhand. Then I rewrite and revise, until the words feel just right when I play them back to myself on the little tape recorder. My book children are as demanding as my flesh-and-blood children. Words are as frustrating and as thrilling to work with as the paints of the artist or the stone of the sculptor. Writing is hard work, but pure delight, and the greatest joy in life is when a child says to me, 'Mrs. Archer, I love your book. When are you going to write another one about the very same people?''

FOR MORE INFORMATION SEE: Post-Crescent, Appleton, Wisconsin, May 19, 1963; *Oshkosh Daily Northwestern*, May 30, 1963; *Badger History*, Wisconsin State Historical Society, January, 1964, Spring, 1973; *Milwaukee Journal*, October 9, 1964; *Wisconsin Library Bulletin*, September/October, 1966; *The Paper for Central Wisconsin*, May 10, 1968; *Biographies of Prominent People of the Fox River Valley*, volume 2, 1970.

RICHARD ARMSTRONG

ARMSTRONG, Richard   1903-

PERSONAL: Born June 18, 1903, in Northumberland, England; married (wife's name, Edith), in 1926; children: John.

CAREER: Writer. *Military service:* Merchant Navy. *Awards, honors: Sea Change*, Library Association Carnegie Medal, 1949; *Cold Hazard, Herald Tribune* Festival of Books, first prize, 1956; *Ship Afire!, The Big Sea, The Mutineers*, Literary Guild selections.

WRITINGS: The Winstone Drift, Dent, 1951; *Passage Home*, Dent, 1952; *Danger Rock*, Dent, 1955, published in America under the title *Cold Hazard*, Houghton, 1956; *The Lost Ship: A Caribbean Adventure*, Dent, 1956, Day, 1958; *Sea Change*, Dent, 1957; *No Time for Tankers*, Dent, 1958, Day, 1959; *The Lame Duck*, Dent, 1959; *Sailor's Luck*, Dent, 1959; *Ship Afire!*, Day, 1961, Hale, 1965; *Horseshoe Reef*, Dent, 1960, Duell, 1961; *Out of the Shallows*, Dent, 1961; *Sabotage at the Forge*, Dent, 1962; *Trial Trip*, Dent, 1962, Criterion, 1963; *Island Odyssey*, Dent, 1963; *Fight for Freedom: An Adventure of World War II*, McKay, 1966; *The Big Sea*, McKay, 1965; *This is Your Day*, Christophers, 1965; *Grace Darling, Maid and Myth*, Dent, 1965; *The Secret Sea*, McKay, 1966; *The Early Mariners*, Benn, 1967, Praeger, 1968; *A History of Seafaring*, Benn, 1967, Praeger, 1968; *The Mutineers*, McKay, 1968; *The Discoverers*, Benn, 1968, Praeger, 1969; (compiler) *Treasure and Treasure Hunters*, White, 1969; *The Merchantmen*, Praeger, 1969; *The Albatross*, McKay, 1970; *Add Meaning to Your Life*, Christophers, 1971; *Themselves Alone: The Story of Men in Empty Places*, Houghton, 1972.

"I suggest you all bed down and leave me to keep watch and tend the fire. A good night's sleep will make everything look different." ■ (From *Cold Hazard* by Richard Armstrong. Illustrated by C. Walter Hodges.)

SIDELIGHTS: "I was born in a coalfield town, where I grew up among miners and steelworkers and was educated with their sons in the village school. At age thirteen I went to work in the steel plant; the rest of my education was picked up along the way. I worked there for four years and progressed from coal shoveler to crane driver.

"After this I joined the Merchant Navy and travelled all over the world serving on tramp steamers, liners and oil tankers, for seventeen years. In the years that followed, I was able to draw on my background in the mills and at sea for my writing. In 1936, I settled in London doing various jobs including working on a small newspaper.

"Writing was just something that happened, I learned it while asea, but did not submit a manuscript until 1941; it was immediately accepted. After that I wrote for years in my spare time and in 1949 was awarded the Library Association Carnegie Medal for *Sea Change.*

"Life in London became such a strain that my wife and I found a cottage in the summer of 1954 and moved in that autumn. I unloaded my work commitments and since that time have worked full time as a professional writer. The cottage is over three-hundred years old and stands five-hundred feet up in the hills, a half-mile from the sea. From my window the horizon is thirty miles away and in clear weather I can watch the ships heading in from the Atlantic."

FOR MORE INFORMATION SEE: Roger Lancelyn Green, *Tellers of Tales,* Franklin Watts, 1965; Brian Doyle, *The Who's Who of Children's Literature,* Schocken Books, 1968; *Horn Book,* August, 1970; *Third Book of Junior Authors,* edited by de Montreville and Hill, H. W. Wilson, 1972.

AUSTIN, Margot

PERSONAL: Born in Portland, Ore.; daughter of Peter and Maude (Campbell) Helser; married Darrell R. Austin (an artist), 1933; children: Darrell D. *Education:* Attended St. Mary's Academy, Portland, Ore., National Academy of Design, New York, N.Y., and Grand Central School of Art, New York, N.Y. *Home address:* R.F.D. 3, Saw Mill Rd., New Fairfield, Conn. 06810.

CAREER: Writer and illustrator of children's books. Chairman of board, New Fairfield Free Public Library.

WRITINGS—Self-illustrated: ̦*Moxie and Hanty and Bunty,* Scribner, 1939; *Once Upon a Springtime,* Scribner, 1940; *Tumble Bear,* Scribner, 1940; *Barney's Adventure,* Dutton, 1941; *Peter Churchmouse,* Dutton, 1941; *Willamette Way,* Scribner, 1941; *Effelli,* Dutton, 1942; *Gabriel Churchkitten,* Dutton, 1942; *Trumpet,* Dutton, 1943; *Manuel's Kite String, and Other Stories,* Scribner, 1943; *Lutie,* Dutton, 1944; *Gabriel Churchkitten and the Moths,* Dutton, 1948; *Poppet,* Dutton, 1949; *Look Baby,* Platt, 1949.

The Three Silly Kittens, Dutton, 1950; *Growl Bear,* Dutton, 1951; *First Prize for Danny,* Dutton, 1952; *William's Shadow,* Dutton, 1954; *Brave John Henry,* Dutton, 1955; *Churchmouse Stories: A Collection of Peter Churchmouse, and Other Children's Favorites,* Dutton, 1956; *Archie Angel,* Dutton, 1957; *Cousin's Treasure,* Dutton, 1960.

Illustrator: *Mother Goose Rhymes,* Platt, 1938; Elizabeth Briggs Squires, *David's Silver Dollar,* Platt, 1940; *The Very Young Mother Goose,* Platt, 1963.

FOR MORE INFORMATION SEE: More Junior Authors, edited by Muriel Fuller, H. W. Wilson, 1963.

So Barney and his dog saw the circus after all! ▪ (From *Barney's Adventure* by Margot
Austin. Illustrated by the author.)

It was another two weeks before she was wrapped in a blanket and set in a rocking chair by the open window. She looked out to the beautiful spring world. The apple trees down in the orchard were in bloom, a drift of delicate pink. ■ (From *Voices in the Night* by Rhoda W. Bacmeister. Illustrated by Ann Grifalconi.)

BACMEISTER, Rhoda W(arner) 1893-

PERSONAL: Surname is pronounced *Bac*-my-ster; born February 28, 1893, in Northampton, Mass.; daughter of Charles Forbes (an editor) and Mary (Dawes) Warner; married Otto Bacmeister, November 7, 1917 (deceased); children: Margaret (Mrs. F. R. Gruger, Jr.), Lucretia (Mrs. Paul F. Harrison), Theodore Warner. *Education:* Vassar College, A.B. (honors), 1914; University of Chicago, A.M., 1915; additional study at University of Iowa, Columbia University, National College of Education, Bank Street College of Education, and University of Minnesota. *Agent:* McIntosh & Otis, Inc., 18 East 41st St., New York, N.Y. 10017.

CAREER: High school teacher in Toulon, Ill., 1915-16, 1923-27; Flower Hill Nursery School, Plandome, N.Y., teacher-director, 1928-30; Manhasset Bay School, Port Washington, N.Y., teacher, co-director, 1930-37; Works Progress Administration, Indiana state director of Adult Education for Family Living, 1938-41; high school teacher, Annandale, Minn., 1942-43; Lanham Act Centers, super-

visor in Philadelphia, Pa., 1943-45; free-lance writer and lecturer, 1945-50; Manhattanville Nursery, New York, N.Y., director, 1950-59; free-lance writer, lecturer, and conductor of conferences and short courses for teachers, 1959—. Instructor in early childhood education at Brooklyn College (now Brooklyn College of the City University of New York), 1947-48, and City College (now City College of the City University of New York), 1959-60; also teacher at other colleges and universities. *Awards, honors:* Parents' Institute award, 1947, for *Growing Together.*

WRITINGS: Caring for the Runabout Child, Dutton, 1937; *Jet* (story for children), Dutton, 1938; *Stories to Begin On,* Dutton, 1940; *Growing Together* (for parents), Appleton, 1940; *Sing About It* (songs for the very young), Schirmer, 1949; *Your Child and Other People,* Little, Brown, 1950; *All in the Family,* Appleton, 1951; *The People Downstairs,* Coward, 1964; *Voices in the Night,* Bobbs-Merrill, 1965. Contributor of nearly two hundred articles, stories, and poems to professional journals, magazines, and anthologies.

BAILEY, Ralph Edgar 1893-

PERSONAL: Born September 24, 1893, in East Greenwich, R.I.; son of George E. (a businessman) and Luella (Haley) Bailey; married Margaret Helen Suba, April 1, 1917; children: Brewster Burrows. *Education:* Attended East Greenwich Academy, East Greenwich, R.I., 1909-13. *Politics:* Independent. *Religion:* Protestant Episcopal. *Home and office:* 229 Schoolhouse Rd., Old Saybrook, Ct. 06475.

CAREER: Newspaperman in New England for forty-five years, holding most of the jobs from reporter to managing editor on daily papers in Providence, R.I., and Boston, Mass., prior to 1962; full-time author of junior books, 1962—. Editorial posts with *Providence News* and its suc-

RALPH EDGAR BAILEY

18   **Something about the Author**

Without the sturdily built prairie schooners, with their oxbow-shaped coverings of canvas, the West could not have been populated and become a part of the United States. ■ (From *Wagons Westward!* by Ralph Edgar Bailey. Jacket illustration by Richard Cuffari.)

cessors, *Providence News-Tribune,* and *Providence Star-Tribune,* 1914-37, included city editor, editor, and managing editor; did public relations for Republican State Central Committee of Rhode Island, Providence, 1938-40; variously rewriteman, chief of copy desk, and telegraph editor for *Boston Traveler,* 1941-62. *Military service:* National Guard, with Rhode Island Cavalry on Mexican border, 1916. *Member:* Boston Authors Club (board of directors, 1948-52).

WRITINGS: Argosies of Empire, Dutton, 1947; *Sea Hawks of Empire,* Dutton, 1948; *Tim's Fight for the Valley,* Dutton, 1951; *Tony Sees It Through,* Dutton, 1953; *Indian Fighter: The Story of Nelson A. Miles,* Morrow, 1965; *Fighting Sailor: The Story of Nathanael Fanning,* Morrow, 1967; *Guns Over the Carolinas,* Morrow, 1967; *Fight for Royal Gorge,* Morrow, 1968; *Wagons Westward: The Story of Alexander Majors,* Morrow, 1969.

WORK IN PROGRESS: A junior book about the adventures of an early American merchant sailor.

SIDELIGHTS: "Of my published books, *Argosies* and *Sea Hawks* are a romanticized history of international trade, from the Phoenicians down to the Portuguese, Dutch and English, and are required reference reading in their fields in many high school libraries."

FOR MORE INFORMATION SEE: Mildred B. Flagg, *Notable Boston Authors,* Dresser, 1965.

BALDWIN, Clara

PERSONAL: Born in Ironton, Mo.; daughter of John Taylor, Jr. (a lumberman) and Clara Ellen (Delano) Baldwin. *Education:* Attended Northwestern University; received private music instruction. *Residence:* Bethlehem, Pa.

CAREER: Secretary to her father, John T. Baldwin, Jr. (a lumberman), Chicago, Ill., 1932-44; lumber broker from 1944-47, Chicago. Simultaneously, in 1945, began a freelance career as writer and correspondent for such business publications as *Department Store Economist* (New York City), *Display World* (now *Visual Merchandising*—Cincinnati), *The Insurance Field* (Louisville), *Eastern Underwriter* (New York City); was Chicago correspondent for the insurance section of *The New York Journal of Commerce* (New York City); was Chicago correspondent for *Display World,* 1945-47, then special correspondent, 1947—. Writer around the world, 1947-48 for publications including *Manufacturing Confectioner, The Canner, American Boxmaker, Wood Magazine* (all of Chicago). For six months in 1949-50, executive editor for *The Insurance Buyer* and *The Insurance Broker* (Budlong Publications—New York City).

Other publications for which she has been correspondent, editor, or feature writer include *Candy Industry, Haire Publications, Sew Business, Housewares, Toys, Body Fashions, Stores,* all of New York City. *Member:* Nature Conservancy, State Historical Society of Missouri.

WRITINGS—Juveniles: *Cotton for Jim,* Abingdon, 1954; *Timber from Terry Forks,* Abingdon, 1956; *The Hermit of Crab Island,* Abingdon, 1958; *Little Tuck,* Doubleday, 1959. Work has been anthologized in *Grandma Moses' Storybook,* compiled and illustrated by Grandma Moses, Random House, 1961.

Author of script for film strip "Beginning with God," Lutheran Church in America, 1965. Contributor to children's magazines and other publications.

SIDELIGHTS: "Usually an author never knows the course of a book once it comes off the press. It was only by a strange fluke that I learned of one episode involving *Cotton for Jim.* It was presumably for 8-12 year olds. However, it inspired one high school boy in Pennsylvania to select that book as subject for his senior thesis. The young woman who told me was one of his classmates, and was startled when she realized I was the author of *Cotton for Jim.* 'It's amazing,' she told me, 'how much he found in the book.'

"Why did I write *Cotton for Jim*? I don't truly know. As a child of a lumberman who for many years operated a planing mill in Laurel, Mississippi, and who visited sawmills and stands of timber, often taking the family along for the ride—machines and industrial operations are a part of life ever since I was old enough to remember. I am still fascinated by how the wheels go round—machine wheels, or the mental wheels—what makes things in general tick. Industry reporting has built on that background. Perhaps that was the

CLARA BALDWIN

Frightened and startled, the turkeys let out great squawks, and the whole wild flock soared up. The two turkeys Little Tuck was holding rose up along with the others, carrying him between them. ▪ (From *Little Tuck* by Clara Baldwin. Illustrated by Paul Galdone.)

why of the cotton story. Possibly too it was seeing those fields of cotton in the south as we drove to sawmills and forests. Then there were the wagon loads of raw cotton waiting for a turn at the gin mills, or bales of processed cotton on loading platforms. It all seeped in as background. On top of that came the long research.

"*Timber From Terry Forks* was a must with a lumber background. Not only was my father and at least one of his brothers lumbermen, but so were their father and uncles, and their father's father. My great grandfather owned timber in southeast Missouri. And the family started there. At least on my mother's side we are Mayflower descendants, but on both sides pioneers in Missouri.

"*The Hermit of Crab Island* has a background that could well fill a book. The old hermit was for real. I met him—the winter after I came back from overseas and went to live on the Gulf Coast—hopefully to concentrate on creative work after an exhausting journey for the trades. I didn't completely succeed. I made a report for one newspaper on the oyster situation and a seasonal prospect on the shrimp fishing. That gave me an inside track for the background. Beyond that was tremendous research—including the biology of oysters, the oyster fishing and packing industry, and finally the in-depth ecology of the Gulf Coast. But the story began as a child, when we lived in Laurel where I took all my public schooling and graduated as valedictorian of the Laurel High School. Often on long weekends Dad would take the family to the Gulf Coast. To swim he would rent a motor launch or a sailboat (plus captain) and take us out to the offside of the islands, where the water was clean and salty and the bottom smooth sand. Same sort of experience that Larry and his friends have on Uncle Kurt's party.

"*Little Tuck* is more or less a tall tale of pioneer experience.

The result of in-depth research I was doing into Missouri history. As a native-born Missourian of pioneer families there had to be a Missouri book.

"And there is something else. As a child, no matter where my family lived, I was taken back for many years to spend a long, long summer on my Grandfather Delano's place in a small town in the Ozark Mountains. I am the oldest of four girls, but those summers I was the lone child. Almost every major piece of fiction I write for children has something of that Delano place in it. The woodshed and barn in *Cotton for Jim* is taken from Grandpa's place. The barn in *The Hermit of Crab Island* comes from there. No one except myself is aware probably but I know—from deep inside.

"My father was a lumberman and he and I were the office force. He operated under his own name. And I was even writing then. My first short story was published in 1934. I began work as a free-lance trade correspondent while serving as a lumber broker. It was still war time, kiln dried lumber was very scarce. I was generally involved with multiple assignments at one and the same time. For example as a lumber broker after my father died, one morning I had to go out to inspect a carload of lumber on team track. The customer had a complaint. I raced back to the office, put in a long distance call to the mill that had shipped the lumber to say we were rejecting the shipment. Immediately after that I changed shoes, hat, gloves (I had brought the spares to the office with me in the morning) and headed out to have lunch with a fashion editor. It was that kind of life."

BALET, Jan (Bernard) 1913-

PERSONAL: Born July 20, 1913, in Bremen, Germany; children: Peter. *Education:* Attended Arts and Crafts

JAN B. BALET

One day the father of the rich family got very angry when he saw the children of the poor family standing by the fence and sniffing.
"Go away you gang of thieves!" he yelled at them. ■ (From *The Fence* by Jan Balet. Illustrated by the author.)

School, Munich, Germany and Academy of Fine Arts, Munich, Germany. *Home:* La Landelle, 60990 Le Coudray St., St. Germer, France.

CAREER: Writer; illustrator; painter. *Mademoiselle* magazine, New York, N.Y., art director; *Seventeen* magazine, New York, N.Y., art director. Did advertisements for New York department stores and for many national firms. *Exhibitions:* Art Directors Club. *Awards, honors:* Art Directors Club, two gold medals, fifteen awards of merit.

WRITINGS—All self-illustrated: *Amos and the Moon*, Oxford, 1948, Walck, 1959; *Ned and Ed and the Lion*, Oxford, 1949; *What Makes an Orchestra*, Walck, 1951, Scholastic, 1965; *The Five Rollatinis*, Lippincott, 1959; *The Gift: A Portuguese Christmas Tale*, Delacorte, 1967; *Joanjo: A Portuguese Tale*, Delacorte, 1967; *The King and the Broom Maker*, Delacorte, 1968; *The Fence: A Mexican Tale*, Delacorte, 1969; *Ladismouse; or, The Advantages of Higher Education*, Walck, 1971.

Illustrator: Dorothea Zack Hanle, *The Golden Ladle*, Ziff-Davis, 1945; Pedro Antonio de Alarcon, *Tales from the Spanish*, Story Classics, 1948; Helen Wing, *Rosalinde*, Container Corp., 1952; Patricia Jones (adaption from Grimms' Fairy Tales), *Rumpelstiltskin*, Container Corp., 1955; Patricia Jones (adapted), *Fair, Brown and Trembling: An Irish Fairy Tale*, Container Corp., 1957; Martha Bennett King, *Birthday Angel*, Container Corp., 1959; Martha Bennett King (retold from Hans Christian Andersen), *The Snow Queen*, Container Corp., 1961; *The Princess and the Pea*, Parents' Magazine Press, 1962; *The Magic Fishbone*, Parents' Magazine Press, 1963; George Selden, *The Mice, the Monks and the Christmas Tree*, Macmillan, 1963; Aileen Brothers and Cora Holsclaw, *Just One Me*, Follett, 1967; James Krüss, *Ein-, Eich- & Mondhorn*, Betz, 1968. Contributor of illustrations to a number of magazines.

FOR MORE INFORMATION SEE: American Artist, November, 1946, January, 1951; *Graphis No. 51*, 1954; *Illustrators of Children's Books: 1946-56*, Horn Book, 1958; *Vogue*, August 1, 1959; *Third Book of Junior Authors*, edited by de Montreville and Hill, H. W. Wilson, 1972.

BARKER, Melvern 1907-

PERSONAL: Born November 24, 1907, in Providence, R.I.; son of Joseph Edward (a salesman) and Martha (Anslow) Barker; married Dorothy Wight (a public school art supervisor), June 29, 1935; children: Judith Mayhew (Mrs. Barry Burns Lutender), Karen Ann (Mrs. Richard M. Duffy). *Education*: Rhode Island School of Design, graduate, 1931; studied at Provincetown School of Painting, 1931, Art Students League, New York, N.Y., 1933. *Religion*: Protestant. *Residence*: Chilmark, Mass. *Agent*: Florence Crowther, 350 West 57th St., New York, N.Y. 10019.

CAREER: In 1930's worked as art director of advertising agency in Hartford, Conn., advertising artist for the Macy chain of newspapers, Yonkers, N.Y., taught private classes in painting and drawing, adult education classes in illustration and graphic arts; settled on Martha's Vineyard, off Massachusetts coast, 1941, and went to sea with fishing fleet for almost ten years; resumed teaching as instructor at Vesper George Art School, Boston, Mass., 1949-50, in Saugerties Public Schools, Saugerties, N.Y., 1959-60, at Monroe-Woodbury High School, Monroe, N.Y., 1962-63; Vesper George School of Art, teacher, 1968-74. Portrait artist with United Service Organization camp shows during World War II.

WRITINGS: *Southeast of Noman's: A Trip Dragging Aboard the Southern Cross* (adult fishing story with lithographs), John Day, 1948.

Children's picture books, all self-illustrated: *Little Sea Legs*, Oxford University Press, 1951; *Six O'Clock Rooster*, Ox-

MELVERN BARKER

ford University Press, 1953; *Little Island Star*, Oxford University Press, 1954; *Country Fair*, Oxford University Press, 1955; *How Little Boats Grew*, Lippincott, 1955; *The Different Twins*, Lippincott, 1957; *Shipshape Boy*, Scribner, 1961.

WORK IN PROGRESS: Two children's books; adult book on swordfishing.

HOBBIES AND OTHER INTERESTS: Swimming, boating, golf, and walking the beaches.

FOR MORE INFORMATION SEE: *Illustrators of Children's Books, 1946-1956*, Horn Book, 1958.

BECKER, Beril 1901-

PERSONAL: Born August 24, 1901, in Slonim, Russia; son of Jeremiah and Yetta (Rabinowitz) Becker; married Ruth Ellis. *Education*: Columbia University, B.A., 1926. *Home*: Apdo. Postal 752, Cuernavaca, Morelos, Mex.

CAREER: U.S. Merchant Marine, radio operator, 1923-25; Batten, Barton, Durstine & Osborne, New York, N.Y., script writer, 1936; owner-manager of art gallery, New York, N.Y., 1947-51; Consolidated Appraisal Co., New York, N.Y., art appraiser, 1950-51; Yale and Towne Manufacturing Co., New York, N.Y., field researcher, 1952-56; Interstate Industrial Reporting Service, New York, N.Y., industrial reporter, 1957-58; Lewis Gittler Associates, New York, N.Y., public relations work, 1958-63; now full-time writer. *Wartime service*: U.S. Merchant Marine, 1942-45; chief radio operator.

WRITINGS: *Paul Gauguin: The Calm Madman*, A. & C. Boni, 1931; *Whirlwind in Petticoats* (biography of Victoria Woodhull), Doubleday, 1947, reissued as *The Spitfires*, Pyramid, 1955, 2nd revised edition, 1971; *Mechanical Man*, Putnam, 1959; *Captain Edward L. Beach: Around the World Under Water*, Encyclopaedia Britannica, 1961; *Jules Verne*, Putnam, 1966; *Dreams and Realities of the Conquest of the Skies* (Junior Literary Guild selection), Atheneum, 1967. Contributor to *Reader's Digest* and *Pageant*.

WORK IN PROGRESS: *Dreams and Realities of the Conquest of Space*, two volumes, to be published by Atheneum.

SIDELIGHTS: "My writing career was cut off abruptly when my wife became the victim of a crime in which she had to give up all our life savings at the point of a gun. I can write about it calmly today because I have learned to let bygones be bygones and I am resuming my writing with a new sense of enthusiasm that is both a surprise and a delight to me.

"You can imagine the traumatic impact of being the victim of a crime wave that left us penniless. What might have been a disaster turned out to be a major challenge to rearrange my life. I read the handwriting on the wall . . . mene, mene, tekel upharsin, not so much for me but, as I felt at that time, for an arrogance-ridden American Empire. As it happened, a friend, a doctor with a very large practice, had the same sense of doom for a crime-ridden New York City. He persuaded me and my sick wife to join him in emigrating to Mexico, where our social security, at least, could keep us alive. We became part of the large American colony in Cuernavaca.

"I had contracted to write two volumes on the *Dreams and Realities of the Conquest of Space* for Atheneum. I had already completed the first volume in 1971. Both the editor and I agreed it needed extensive revisions. I discovered that revisions demanded a new perspective. Then I learned that the interest in space had declined suddenly after the landing on the moon. The entire project needed that new perspective. Thus began my agonizing reappraisal, a long research on man, history and the universe. Finally, a new pattern of cultural evolution emerged. I made the discovery that every major advance in the history of civilization had its origin in man's preoccupation with the movements of stars.

"I came to see that the space projects were more than a passing fancy. They are an imperative in the expanding history of civilization. I came to understand that the sky (and not visiting spacemen) were the true teachers of mankind. Man came out of the material world of stars and will return to the stars out of which he evolved. The human brain has been and will be the god-like manipulator of matter. When the brain of the caveman incised a line every night on his stone weapon (34,000 B.C.), he began the process that would give him the mastery of the universe. The lunar calendar of the Ice Age and the sowing of the mutated grains in the following thaw were milestones in man's struggle to secure a firmer grip on survival. Astronomy became the mother of all the sciences, bringing language and numbers as tools of civilization.

BERIL BECKER

"The Greeks replaced the willful gods of the ancient civilizations with their mathematical model of natural laws. The Chinese compass launched the exploration of the globe. The mathematics from Copernicus to Newton made it clear that the atmosphere had weight and that space was a vacuum, the clue for inventors to search for an atmospheric engine to pump out the underground waters in coal mines. The invention of the perfected steam engine led to the industrial revolution that gave us the steamship and the railroad. The energy of lightning was trapped within power houses. The compacted underground jungles of the age of the dinosaurs and the liquid form of the oxygen in the atmosphere were sparked to send a metal dinosaur to the moon. The heat of the sun and the below zero cold of space will fashion the matter of the earth and the moon into the power houses, automatic factories and habitats of our first space city.

"Of such is the road to the kingdom of heaven, the way out of man's predicament today, the transformation of our war civilization into the coming cybernetic peace civilization. The children of today will live to see the vast exodus of our billions into space. The 2,000 pages of notes that I have accumulated in my years of research in Cuernavaca are destined for a series of books that will prepare the minds of children to become citizens of the world. The first to be completed will be *The View From 1990,* a non-fiction account of how we will make the switch from a war civilization to a peaceful one. It will be followed by my history of space to include the occupancy of space. Following these, equally outlined in great detail, will be a narrative of man and the universe from a cosmic point of view. God willing, I trust they will be completed and read before the coming menace of the Crunch (ecological, nuclear or the Dark Ages) becomes irreversible."

Mechanical Man has been translated into 17 different languages, and is used as a textbook in Japan.

BEISER, Germaine   1931-

PERSONAL: Born March 2, 1931, in Massachusetts; daughter of Arthur (an electronics engineer) and Germaine (Paradis) Bousquet; married Arthur Beiser (a physicist; writer); children: Nadia Louise, Alexa Susan, Isabel Victoria. *Education:* Massachusetts Institute of Technology, B.S., 1952; New York University, M.S., 1954. *Home:* Iles des Embiez, 83140, LeBruse, France. *Office:* Simpson Thacher and Bartlett, 1 Battery Park Plaza, New York, N.Y. 10004.

CAREER: Physicist. *Member:* Ocean Cruising Club.

WRITINGS—All with husband, Arthur Beiser: *Physics for Everybody,* Dutton, 1956; *The Story of Cosmic Rays,* Dutton, 1962; *The Story of the Earth's Magnetic Field,* Dutton, 1964; *The Story of Gravity,* Dutton, 1968. Has also written with her husband, study guide for *The Mainstream of Physics,* 1962 and study guide for *Basic Concepts of Physics,* 1962.

SIDELIGHTS: "I lived in the United States until 1963. Traveled by cruising sailboat up and down the Atlantic coast until at last I sailed across to Scotland. Have since lived in Denmark, England, France and Spain, arriving in each case under sail."

Another reason that the problem of cosmic-ray origin has attracted so many able minds is the improbability of ever finding the answers by purely experimental means. ■ (From *The Story of Cosmic Rays* by Germaine and Arthur Beiser. Illustrated by Joseph M. Sedacca.)

BELL, Norman (Edward)   1899-

PERSONAL: Born July 26, 1899, in Winnemucca, Nev.; son of William John (a mine owner) and Freelie (Choate) Bell; married Ysabel Mary Mannix, September 9, 1939; children: Lucinda Cecile. *Education:* University of Nevada, B.A., 1927. *Home:* 17370 Buena Vista Ave., Sonoma, Calif. 95476.

CAREER: Ranch hand in Nevada, delivery truck driver in San Francisco, and Standard Oil Co. clerk in Nev. and Calif., 1920-27; *Reno Evening Gazette,* Reno, Nev., reporter, 1927; *Nevada State Journal,* Reno, reporter, 1928-32; Associated Press, reporter, editor, feature writer in San Francisco, Fresno, and Sacramento; war correspondent in Pacific areas of World War II from South Pacific to Aleutians; correspondent in San Diego, 1932-64; free-lance writer, 1964—. *Military service:* U.S. Army, 1917-19.

WRITINGS—Juveniles: *Linda's Air Mail Letter,* Follett, 1964; *The Weightless Mother,* Follett, 1967.

WORK IN PROGRESS: Stories for children, including one about a boy who ran himself into a streak of greased lightning, and one about a boy with a tooth in his ear.

SIDELIGHTS: Bell writes that it was the success of his children's feature story on the Russian Sputnik I satellite that "inspired me to try writing for children after retirement from AP."

HOBBIES AND OTHER INTERESTS: Handyman improvements to his home.

BENDICK, Robert L(ouis)   1917-

PERSONAL: Born February 8, 1917, in New York, N.Y.; son of Louis G. (a businessman) and Ruth (Feis) Bendick; married Jeanne Garfunkel (a writer and illustrator), November 24, 1940; children: Robert L., Jr., Karen Ann (Mrs. Michael Watson). *Education:* Attended New York University, 1936-37, and C. H. White School of Photography, 1938-39. *Politics:* Democrat. *Religion:* Jewish. *Home and office:* 360 Grace Church St., Rye, N.Y. 10580.

CAREER: Columbia Broadcasting System (CBS) Television, New York, N.Y., cameraman, 1940-42, director of news, special events, and sports, and executive producer or director of several individual programs, 1945-52; Cinerama Corp., New York, N.Y., co-producer and director of "This Is Cinerama" and director of "Cinerama Holiday," 1952-53; National Broadcasting Corp. (NBC) Television, New York, N.Y., producer of "Today Show," 1953-55, 1958-60, "Wide, Wide World," 1956, "Twenty-Five Years of Life," 1961, "U.S. Steel Opening of the 1964 World's Fair," 1964, "The First Look" (children's series), 1966-67; producer-director of "Merrily We Roll Along," 1962, "Bell Telephone Science Trilogy," 1961-62, "America's Cup Races," 1962, and segments of "The American Sportsman," 1964, 1969. Producer for C. V. Whitney Productions and Merian C. Cooper, both 1956-57. Producer of All Latin-American Network 1968 Olympics, National Educational Television's "The Great American Dream Machine" pilot programs, 1970-72; executive producer of Children's Television Workshop's "Feeling Good," 1975. President of Bendick Asso-

ROBERT BENDICK

Most people buy clothes for fun. Or to make themselves feel good. You hardly ever *need* something to wear to keep warm or decent. ■ (From *The Consumer's Catalog of Economy and Ecology* by Jeanne and Robert Bendick. Illustrated by Karen Watson.)

ciates (educational audio-visual company), 1966—. Lecturer at New York University and University of Oklahoma. *Military service:* U.S. Army Air Forces, filmed combat documentaries, 1943-45; served in China-Burma-India theater; received Air Medal with two oak leaf clusters.

MEMBER: National Academy of Television Arts and Sciences (member of board of governors; chairman of New York Emmy Awards Commission; member of International Emmy Awards Committee), Directors Guild of America, Urban League of Westchester County (member of board of directors). *Awards, honors:* Peabody Award from school of journalism, University of Georgia, 1948, for "United Nations in Action"; Emmy nomination from Academy of Television Arts and Sciences, 1955, for "The American West"; Albert Lasker Award from the Albert and Mary Lasker Foundation (for medical journalism), 1958, for "Today Show"; Christopher Award, 1955, for "This Is Cinerama"; Swiss Government directorial award, 1955, for "Cinerama Holiday"; Ohio State Science Award, 1966, for "The First Look"; shared in Emmy awards, 1970-71 and 1971-72, for "The Great American Dream Machine."

WRITINGS—All with wife, Jeanne Bendick: *Television Works Like This* (juvenile), McGraw, 1965; *Filming Works Like This* (juvenile), McGraw, 1970; *The Consumer's Catalog of Economy and Ecology,* McGraw, 1975; *Finding Out About Jobs: Television Reporting,* 1976; *Energy from Wind and Tide,* Garrard, 1977.

Photographer: Jeanne Bendick, *Exploring the Ocean Tide Pool,* Garrard, 1975.

SIDELIGHTS: "A vital subject to me is the impact of television on society—the failure of television to understand or respond to its incredible responsibility." He has worked on films in Europe, Asia, Alaska, Southeast Asia, New Zealand, and Australia. Bendick Associates has produced films for McGraw-Hill and N.B.C. and film strips for many companies including: "The Seasons," "Starting Points in Science," "Reading Adventures in Everyday Science," and, with Jeanne Bendick, "Monsters and Other Science Mysteries."

HOBBIES AND OTHER INTERESTS: Photography, sailing, fishing, oceanography.

FOR MORE INFORMATION SEE: More Junior Authors, edited by Muriel Fuller, H. W. Wilson, 1963.

BENEDICT, Dorothy Potter   1889-

PERSONAL: Born April 15, 1889, in Chicago, Ill.; daughter of Edward C. (a composer) and Emma (McKinley) Potter; married Charles C. Benedict (a pilot, U.S. Air Service), December 27, 1919 (killed in plane crash, 1925); children: Charles C., Jr. (deceased), Patricia (Mrs. Harrison Lobdell, Jr.), Calvert P. *Education:* Took special courses in playwriting at University of Chicago and in languages at Berlitz Schools in United States, France, and Switzerland. *Home and office:* 6200 Oregon Ave., Washington, D.C. 20015. *Agent:* McIntosh & Otis, Inc., 18 East 41st St., New York, N.Y. 10017.

CAREER: American Red Cross canteen worker in France, World War I; secretary in Headquarters, U.S. Air Service, Washington, D.C., following the war, and translator from the French of a book on air strategy; during World War II worked in Plans Division, Air Staff, Washington, D.C., and later as a consultant to the Air Force (speech writer).

WRITINGS: Pagan the Black, Pantheon, 1960; *Fabulous,* Pantheon, 1961; *Bandoleer,* Pantheon, 1963. Contributor of short stories to *Ladies' Home Journal, Seventeen,* and other magazines.

WORK IN PROGRESS: Three books.

BETHANCOURT, T. Ernesto 1932-
(Tom Paisley)

PERSONAL: Name originally Thomas E. Passailaigue; born October 2, 1932, in Brooklyn, N.Y.; son of Aubrey Ernesto (a truck driver) and Dorothy (Charest) Passailaigue; married Nancy Yasue Soyeshima (a ceramics designer), May 9, 1970; children: Kimi, Thea. *Education:* Studied pre-law evenings at City College of the City University of New York. *Politics:* Registered Democrat. *Religion:* Roman Catholic. *Home:* 141 Norfolk St., Brooklyn, N.Y. 11235.

CAREER: Singer, guitarist, composer, full-time, 1958-72; writer of RCA Record Club magazine, *Medley,* 1972; resumed full-time performing and writing, 1973—. Has held numerous odd jobs including a stint during the 1950's as an undercover claims investigator for Lloyd's of London's New York office. *Military service:* U.S. Navy, 1950-53. *Member:* American Federation of Musicians, American Society of Composers, Authors, and Publishers. *Awards, honors:* Popular Division Awards from American Society of Composers, Authors, and Publishers, 1969-70.

WRITINGS—Juvenile novels: (Under pseudonym T. Ernesto Bethancourt) *New York City Too Far from Tampa Blues,* Holiday House, 1975; *Mutt!* (fantasy), Holiday House, 1976.

Began writing his own songs, as well as comedy material for others, during mid-1960's; wrote social satire in music, "I Want to Be the Token Negro at the Party," performed in New York, N.Y., at Upstairs at the Downstairs, 1967, and additional material performed there, 1967-71; staff lyricist with Cy Coleman, 1970-71, writing libretto and lyrics for "Cities," as yet unproduced, and other works; four songs have been published in Silver Burdett's textbook series, "Music," 1973, 1974, 1975. Also author of two unproduced television pilot programs. Contributing editor, *High Fidelity,* 1967-68.

WORK IN PROGRESS: A novel.

SIDELIGHTS: 'While investigating a claim [for Lloyd's of London] in Mt. Vernon, N.Y., which is close by a race track, I found a place that would pay me more money to play and sing than I could make in the claims business. I never looked back. Had more fun playing and singing for horsey types than filing reports. Ended up in Greenwich Village during the folk music boom of the early 60's, playing in coffee houses with such now well known people as Bill Cosby, Bob Dylan, Peter, Paul and Mary, et al.

T.E. BETHANCOURT

"When folk music became a national craze, I toured the country playing colleges, auditoriums, and night clubs. Appeared on national TV at the time on a show called 'Hootenanny'. For a brief time I had the good fortune to know the late Josh White. . . . I had a chance to learn such blues guitar as I play from Josh, who was a profound influence on my work.

"When the Beatles hit and folk music sank below the waters of the Mersey, I went into a number of small clubs and lounges. It was at this time that I began to write for acts other than myself." Paisley's effort "to go straight" by writing for *Medley* magazine in 1972 was "the most stultifying twelve months in my life. While in the process of re-establishing myself as a performer, I was encouraged to finish the four chapters of a novel I had begun earlier and abandoned in the interest of making a living. The book was published as *New York City Too Far from Tampa Blues.*

"I live with my family in a little five room house in the Manhattan Beach section of Brooklyn. It's quiet and tree lined; only a short walk from the beach or Sheepshead Bay. During the off season, you can walk on the beach and see nothing but the ocean and sand; think your own thoughts without being bugged by the outside world.

"I guess that's it for T. E. Bethancourt/Tom Paisley, neither of which is my true name, by the way. I changed my name to Paisley when I began to perform full time. (If you put *Passailaigue* up in lights, you'd die of the heat.) Bethancourt is one of my father's family names.

"I am the son of an hispanic father who drove a truck for all his working life and never went past third grade in grammar school. My mother is a New York born housewife who qualifies as the parental intellectual. She graduated from grammar school and she actually reads books. My father's reading and writing in either English or Spanish is limited at best. My three sisters attended the same high school as I did, but I am the only member of my family who got to college, if only for three years at night. All three of my sisters were secretaries for a brief time before they married and began raising an alarming number of children apiece. (We're catholics.) I'm the family oddball.''

HOBBIES AND OTHER INTERESTS: ''I'm a classic car nut and movie buff.''

BLAINE, Margery Kay 1937-
(Marge Blaine)

PERSONAL: Born December 20, 1937, in New York, N.Y.; daughter of Louis (a pharmacist) and Rosalind (a teacher; maiden name, Klein) Bendis; married Edward Blaine (a high school assistant principal), December 22, 1957; children: Jonathan William, Jennifer Petra. *Education:* Brooklyn College (now of the City University of New York), B.A., 1958; graduate study at University of Colorado, New School for Social Research, Cornell University, and Brooklyn Museum Art School. *Politics:* Liberal Democrat. *Home and office:* 352 Marlborough Rd., Brooklyn, N.Y. 11226.

CAREER: Kindergarten teacher in Brooklyn, N.Y., 1958-62, 1964-67.

WRITINGS: (Under name Marge Blaine) *The Terrible Thing That Happened at Our House,* Parents' Magazine Press, 1975. Stories in several reading series. Contributor to magazines and newspapers; regular contributor to *Village Voice* ''Kids'' column.

WORK IN PROGRESS: A series of children's books with contemporary settings and themes.

My mother used to be a real mother. ■ (From *The Terrible Thing That Happened at Our House* by Marge Blaine. Illustrated by John C. Wallner.)

MARGERY KAY BLAINE

SIDELIGHTS: "In my own writing for children I hope to broaden horizons, to encourage growth and understanding, and to entertain as well as educate. Writing has been a great joy and satisfaction to me. I especially enjoy reading my own stories to children in schools or libraries and getting a direct response.

"In addition to my writing, I am involved in weaving, photography, and hiking. I read a great deal (children's books to modern fiction) . . . and am presently discovering the 19th-century English novelists."

FOR MORE INFORMATION SEE: Kirkus Reviews, March 1, 1975; *New York Times Book Review,* May 4, 1975.

BRADBURY, Ray (Douglas) 1920-

PERSONAL: Born August 22, 1920, in Waukegan, Ill.; son of Leonard Spaulding and Esther (Moberg) Bradbury; married Marguerite Susan McClure, September 27, 1947; children: Susan, Ramona, Bettina, Alexandra. *Education:* Attended schools in Waukegan, Ill., and Los Angeles, Calif. *Politics:* Independent. *Religion:* Unitarian Universalist. *Agent:* Don Congdon, Harold Matson Co., 22 East 40th St., New York, N.Y. 10016.

CAREER: From high school, where he founded and edited a mimeographed quarterly, *Futuria Fantasia,* and where he also received the only formal training in the short story that he has ever had, Bradbury went into a little theater group in Los Angeles, sponsored by Laraine Day. Dropped out after a year and became a newsboy in downtown Los Angeles, 1940-43, to finance his writing. Started his literary career with short stories, writing on a rigid daily schedule, and sold his first story in 1941; full-time writer, 1943—, breaking into the slick magazines under a pseudonym after selling several dozen stories to the pulps by 1945. *Member:* Writers Guild of America, West (board, 1957-61). *Awards, honors:* Benjamin Franklin Award for best story of 1953-54 in an American magazine, "Sun and Shadow" in *Reporter;* Commonwealth Club of California gold medal, 1954, for *Fahrenheit 451;* $1,000 award from National Institute of Arts and Letters, 1954, for contribution to American literature; Boys' Clubs of America Junior Book Award, 1956, for *Switch on the Night;* short film, "Icarus Montgolfier Wright," was nominated for Academy Award, 1963; joint winner (with Philip Dunne) of the Valentine Davies Award, March 26, 1974.

WRITINGS: Dark Carnival (short stories), Arkham, 1947; *The Martian Chronicles* (short stories), Doubleday, 1950, new edition, 1973; *The Illustrated Man* (short stories), Doubleday, 1951; (editor and contributor) *Timeless Stories for Today and Tomorrow,* Bantam, 1952; *The Golden Apples of the Sun* (short stories), Doubleday, 1953; *Fahrenheit 451* (novel), Ballantine, 1953; *The October Country* (short stories), Ballantine, 1955; *Switch on the Night* (juvenile), Pantheon, 1955; (editor and contributor) *The Circus of Dr. Lao* (short stories), Bantam, 1956; *Dandelion Wine* (short stories), Doubleday, 1957, new edition, 1975; *A Medicine for Melancholy* (short stories), Doubleday, 1959; *The Day it Rained Forever* (short stories), Hart-Davis, 1959; *Something Wicked This Way Comes* (novel), Simon and Schuster, 1962; *R is for Rocket* (anthology for young adults), Doubleday, 1962; *The Anthem Sprinters and Other Antics* (five one-act plays), Dial, 1963; *The Machineries of Joy* (short stories), Simon and Schuster, 1964; *The Autumn People,* Ballantine, 1965; *The Vintage Bradbury* (selections of Bradbury stories), Vintage Books, 1966; *S Is for Space* (stories for young people), Doubleday, 1966; *The Day It Rained Forever* [and] *The Pedestrian* (two plays), Samuel French, 1966; *Twice Twenty-Two* (contains "Golden Apple of the Sun" and "A Medicine for Melancholy"), Doubleday, 1966; *Tomorrow Midnight,* Ballantine, 1966; *I Sing the Body Electric,* Knopf, 1969; *Madrigals for the Space Age* (for mixed chorus and narrator, with piano accompaniment), Associated Music Publishers, 1972; *The Halloween Tree* (juvenile), Knopf, 1972; *The Wonderful Ice Cream Suit* (play), 1972; *When Elephants Last in the Dooryard Bloomed,* Knopf, 1973; *Zen and the Art of Writing,* Capra Press, 1973; *Long After Midnight,* Knopf, 1976.

Film plays: (Adapter) "It Came from Outer Space," Universal, 1953; (screen story) "The Beast from 20,000 Fathoms," Warner Bros., 1953; (with John Huston) "Moby Dick," Warner Bros., 1956; (wrote screenplay with George C. Johnson) "Icarus Montgolfier Wright," Format Films, 1962 (nominated for Academy Award as best animated short subject of the year); "An American Journey" 1964 (commissioned by the U.S. Government Pavilion at the New York World's Fair); (wrote screenplay with Edwin Boyd under pseudonym Douglas Spaulding) "Picasso Summer," Warners/Seven Arts, 1972.

Television plays: Four shows for "Suspense"; "The Jail" for "Alcoa Premiere" and eight shows for "Alfred Hitchcock Presents."

RAY BRADBURY

Stage plays: "The World of Ray Bradbury" (three one-acts), premiere in Los Angeles, 1964; "The Wonderful Ice Cream Suit" (three one-acts), premiere in Los Angeles, 1965; "Dandelion Wine," produced off-Broadway at the Phoenix Side Show, February, 1974; "The Anthem Sprinters." Harry Belafonte optioned "The Man in the Ice Cream Suit" for a possible Broadway musical, 1976. A one-hour radio drama, "Leviathan '99," was produced by British Broadcasting Co., 1966.

Bradbury estimates that he has published well over 400 stories, mostly in the fantasy field, with earlier publication in pulps, later in national magazines, including *New Yorker, Harper's, Mademoiselle, Saturday Evening Post, Charm,* and in literary quarterlies. He is represented in more than 700 anthologies. "The World of Ray Bradbury" opened in New York in 1965.

SIDELIGHTS: Bradbury fell in love with Hollywood when he moved there at thirteen: "I stayed on for endless performances of Blackstone the Magician, forcing my father to come drag me whining from the theater, for I had just discovered how he made a horse disappear centerstage. I walked or skated ten miles a day every day, all summer long when I was fourteen, to hang around the cinema studios and see famous people. I rummaged trash cans behind the CBS radio studios to filch out and save (to this day) scripts broadcast a few hours before by Burns and Allen. . . ."

In a speech to Science Fiction writers, Bradbury said: "I started at eight collecting Buck Rogers comic strips. A big influence in my life was Edgar Rice Burroughs' *John Carter: Warlord of Mars.* I collected Flash Gordon when I was thirteen or fourteen. I began reading science fiction, when I was eight or nine.

"Everything confronting us in the next thirty years will be science fictional, that is, impossible a few years ago. The things you are doing right now, if you had told anyone you'd be doing them when you were children, they would have laughed you out of school. I'm sure you all went through the same experience. I was the only person at Los Angeles High School who knew the Space Age was coming. Totally alone among 4,000 students, I insisted we were going to get the goddamn rocket off the ground, and that made me the class kook, of course. I said, 'Well, we're going to do it anyway.'

"I've been tremendously influenced by the mass media. We've all been told not to pay any attention to the mass media, and now, very late in the day, we discover that many excellent things occur in these fields and out of the mediocre, excellence grows. We *can* learn from these fields.

"I'm influenced by radio. I'm influenced by motion pictures. I've seen every film ever made. I've seen most of the stage plays of our time. I have the words of all the popular songs put away in here, I'll never use them for anything; they're just there, but I flunked algebra—OK.

"I believe that the most important intellectual magazine and most responsible intellectual magazine in the United States today is *Mad* magazine. Why do I say this continually in colleges and high schools and get a wonderful response? Because *Mad* is responding to the major problems of our time which are machines and the effect of the mass media on all of us.

"Most of the intellectual magazines are ignoring this, are so damn serious about it that you reject what they say immediately. But *Mad* magazine by making great fun of these things, making fun of the Republican and the Democratic party at the same moment, of poking fun at television, television advertising, of the bad motion picture, of the corruption of the art galleries in America by gallery owners who don't know a good painting from a hot rock. Corruption in every level is being attacked by *Mad* magazine in the best way, not with super-intellectuality, but by super-creative aesthetic emotion—looking right at the thing and saying, 'The king is naked.'

"The important work, strangely enough, quite often is being carried out in the field of the comic strip—of criticizing our time, pulling the skin off, revealing the bone. I'm interested in all of these things. If you're not, then you are a snob, and if you're a snob, then you will never grow and you won't be able to take back into your own field things you need from all these various fields. The field of poetry, the field of painting, the field of drama, of the motion picture, of the newspaper, of the book, of the novel, of the short story—and what have you. I have been astounded to see that while we are science fiction people living in a science fictional time, quite often our arts neglect this.

"Consider: we are being destroyed by *one* device right now! The automobile. It stands over our culture, dominates our real-estate, influences our money, creates the total atmosphere of the whole country. The greatest issue facing us was *not* Vietnam, strangely enough, but the automobile which devours our cities, poisons the atmosphere, and has now killed two million people. A *huge* science fictional problem that we've taken fifty years to *begin* to pay attention to! A man like Ralph Nader comes along, points at the things

■ (From the movie "Fahrenheit 451," starring Oskar Werner and Julie Christie.   Copyright © 1967 by Universal Pictures.)

and we say, 'Hey, ya, it exists.' What are we going to do about it? Well, it's going to take another ten, fifteen or twenty years to do a job of redesigning, and rethinking who's in charge of the asylum.

"I'm fascinated then, as a moralist to come along with my fables. I'm a moral fablest, a teller of cautionary tales, someone who looks at the machines we have now and says if this is true, ten years from now that will be true, and thirty years from now the other thing will be true. I've had a lot of fun growing up in this age. I'm a real child of my time.

"I was very fortunate a few years ago to write the screen play *Moby Dick* for John Huston. But, it took me about eight months of reading and rereading the novel *Moby Dick* before I finally woke one morning in London and cried, '*I am Herman Melville.*' Nobody believed me, but I believed it and then my creative work really began. In one day I rewrote the last forty pages of the screen play and all came right. It was suddenly a creative enterprise.

"When I went to work for John Huston, he didn't understand my way of creating, and we came to a certain problem writing the screen play. We were pushing too hard; we spent days going over this problem with friends, calling them in, saying, 'How do we solve the problem of doing this scene?' One night with Huston and a friend, I protested, 'Look, we're *pushing,* we can't *think* our way through to answers this way!'

"You really can't think beyond a certain point. You collect data and then when you're brim full, you have to be wise enough to walk away, and relax, and forget it. When you have forgotten it, then is when this wonderful 'thinking' occurs that solves the problem for you. I don't know how it works, but it works.

"Huston made fun of me. I said, 'I'll tell you what, we'll all quit work now, we've been talking for twelve hours straight, we're driving each other mad, right up the walls. I'm going back to Dublin and go to bed. I'm going to put a pad and pencil by my bed. You do the same, Huston, and you, Peter Viertal (another friend), put a pad and pencil by your bed. One of the three of us will wake in the morning with the answer to the problem.'

"Well, they threw back their heads and laughed at me. I said, 'No, no, this is the way it's going to work.' I went back to Dublin; I went to bed. At seven in the morning the phone rang. It was Huston on the phone: 'Ray, I've got it!' And he *did* have it. And from then on he gave me no nonsense about creativity. It works in mysterious ways.

"I found that my best thinking is emotional thinking. You get heated up on a thing and you drive on through with your emotion which means you are really collecting many facts at a secret level, or you have already collected them. Intuition is finding out what you know that you don't know that you know. It's there but it hasn't been tapped yet.

"Quite often I give myself word-association tests to see what's collected in here. I haven't the faintest idea when I start a short story where in hell the thing is going. But it writes itself out; it has a need to come into the open. I'll put down a word like 'nursery' for instance. I say to myself. 'What kind of nursery am I talking about? The past? No, the present? No. What about the future? What will 'nurseries' be like in the future?

"What about television on every wall, every one of the walls, so that you surround yourself with an environment? And you stand in the middle of that environment, and you say to the walls of that room, 'South America, some part of Brazil,' and suddenly this environment surrounds you. What if you say to the room, 'Give me Paris at the blue hour of twilight, the Arc de Triomphe, the Champs Elysee, the River Seine, flowing through Paris?' What if I say, 'Egypt? Give me the sphinx and the pyramids,' and the room will create these things for me?

"I wrote this story; 'The Veldt,' out of word associating on paper about this nursery, and suddenly, there on paper, I found myself with a family who discovers that the room has become parental authority. The room is paying attention to the children, the children paying attention to the room. When the parents come along and try to shut the room off, the children cry, 'Oh don't kill it, don't kill it!' We know then the room is a living thing to the children. It is full of their heroes and of people and places that they know. At the end of the story, which became a play of mine, the parents very foolishly disrupt the room too abruptly, kill it. The children tamper with the room, call the parents down during the middle of the night, run into this room, the door slams and locks, they find themselves in the middle of an African veldt. They look around. There is a blazing sun in the sky and, running across the veldt towards them is this pride of fantastic lions, which run and run and run and come out of the walls of the room and eat them up. End of story.

"Now, what am I doing? I am writing large metaphors about my time, but not self-consciously—emotionally. I take in from my time, I digest it, and then I put it back out on paper in the form of a technological fairy tale of the near future. These are automatically symbols that we are handling right now, trying to make do with as parents, or as people responding to television. I think I can teach by telling suspense stories. Science fiction is a wonderful shorthand way of telling us the truth about the thing that is right in front of us.

"Our problem is that we're solving thirty year old problems, or ten year old problems, or five year old problems. We always misapply ourselves, don't we? We never plan far enough ahead so we're solving today's problems today.

Which means you have got to look ahead thirty years in order to stay up with what's happening in front of you at this very moment. I think we can guess what's going to happen with our freeways. We're refusing to recognize the fact that it's going to happen, but it will. There are many things we know, and we refuse knowledge on. I'm interested then in continuing to write stories in these fields.

"This is quite a remarkable time, because up until the last 100 years, ideas were not on the loose among us. This is an astonishing age in the fact that during the last 100-150 years, we finally began to build three dimensional ideas. During the 2,000 year period before that, about all we have to point to is three dimensional architecture, ideas built in various shapes; painting, which represents certain kinds of ideas, and sculpture which you can touch and walk around. The wheel, comparatively speaking, was used for very little until just a few years ago.

"Suddenly, though, the ideas of man are being extruded forth in plastic and all kinds of metal forms, and are going out on their own. They're dynamic; they move of themselves. Sometimes we get the feeling that they are independent of ourselves. The umbilical cord seems cut and part of my job is to reattach the umbilical cord and make sure the food keeps passing back and forth between these ideas on the move, these machines, and the men who created them.

"To give you another example of the way I respond to my society—I've often walked, a strange thing to do, in Los Angeles. I don't drive, I've never learned. As a result of walking, policemen stop me and say, 'What are you doing?' I fly into a fury and say, 'I'm putting one foot in front of the other.' That's the wrong answer.

"You see it's kind of a super quiz they hold on the spot. You watch the policemen's brows add furrows, one wrinkle after another. The more answers you give, the more puzzled they become, because you're obviously a criminal of some type. I try to explain the logic of the criminal in a technological time is to participate in the technology. Therefore, you don't walk to work as a criminal for Christ's sake. You drive up in your Rolls Royce; and you go in and burgle the joint, come out and drive away. Everything is on wheels. You arrive pretending to be a house mover; you move a house. (Someone stole a house in L.A. recently. It wasn't easy, but it was so outrageous they did it in front of everyone!)

"The more I try to explain this, the more trouble I get into with the police, until finally I remember one night I became so irritated with them that I took a small package of soda crackers out of my pocket, put them in my mouth as I talked to the policeman and sprayed him with crumbs. He couldn't quite decide if I was being hostile. He tried to feel if the flakes were hurting, and whether he was bleeding anywhere, then contented himself with brushing them off and letting me go.

"What did I do? Paranoid that I am, I went home and wrote a story called 'The Pedestrian,' in which a man in the future is stopped for walking and finally taken away for psychiatrical examination for regressive tendencies.

"We are seeing a lot of this now because the streets of L.A. are empty in most places; the sidewalks are so empty that when you meet another pedestrian you practically fall into

Something about the Author

each other's arms and embrace because you haven't seen another of your kind, a walker in the night, in a long while. These changes in our society fascinate me. A society of ideas in three dimensional form on the move fascinates me.

"I used to twit intellectuals by asking, 'Who is the greatest avant-garde thinker in America today?' And then this long pause, and I said, 'Walt Disney,' and then I'd wait. And, of course, there was chaos usually because they didn't want to think of Walt Disney as a creative person. Those of you who have seen out at Disneyland his humanoid robot of Abraham Lincoln know something of what I am beginning to indicate here. I see in the creation of Abraham Lincoln the beginning of a series of robots we can build and computerize through the years ahead in museums of robot history for ourselves. So that you can go into these museums and believe in your own past.

"Now one of the great problems we have and why we are often doomed to repeat our errors from the past is we don't have adequate teachers to tell us of it, and we don't really believe that man has spent two billion years on this planet, growing from a mere chemistry into a fish form of some sort, and then out on the land, and finally, the anthropoidal creature who decided to become human. It's very hard for us to encompass this just from a book. The aesthetic relationship is all wrong. It's like seeing King Kong on television. You hold King Kong in your lap and he should be holding you in his. Too often, you're holding history in your lap. That's all wrong. It should be holding you so you really believe in it.

"So now the Disney studio is experimenting with humanoid robots so that some of you here today will be part of the activity of building the robot museums of the future, so we can do what? Go through all of history and really believe that we made the huge effort of survival up until now. Which means you can walk into that museum, walk down an aisle, go across a Grecian plain, and there under a laurel tree, find Plato and Aristotle. You sit, and you break bread with these humanoid robots, and you turn to Plato and say, 'How goes it with the Republic?' And he tells you. And you turn to Aristotle, and you say 'That point about the poetics now; would you clarify it for me,' and Aristotle speaks his poetics through the afternoon.

"So it appears we are at the beginning of the primitive stage of computerizing men's souls. When you tell some intellectuals this, they pull back as if they might yell, 'Baron Frankenstein, don't pull that switch. You are messing with things better left to God.' Well, damn it all, I want to pull that switch. I am the great blasphemer.

"One of the great problems is having enough teachers in the world to help us become human. While a man like Bertrand Russell was alive, you could have flown to London and made a cast of his entire body, create a robot in his size, shape, and color (which is very easy to do nowadays), put electrodes on his body, computerize his movements so that the robot then duplicated every action of the living Bertrand Russell, so that ten thousand afternoons Bertrand Russell could still have lived for us, sat at a table with us. And then put all of his best speeches, his best philosophy, his best thoughts, on tape so that he would speak them in his own tongue to us thirty centuries from now.

"We can lock truths and ideas into this kind of machinery. We can build history museums so we can go there to visit Aristophanes or Euripedes, watch Julius Caesar go off to Britain and come back and be killed in the Roman forum. Let's watch Hitler at Nuremberg because this was the greatest theatrical man in the history of the world. He knew how to put on fantastic pageants. He knew how to use this new empathy device, motion pictures, with The Triumph of the Will, and Lenie Reifenstahl to convince us the way of the future was with Germany and was irreversible and was great. When you came out of seeing that film, you wanted to sign up with the Bund immediately.

"We have to be able to study evil as well as good in order to grow. Any man who says, 'I am all good; I know it all,' is immediately evil. He can't grow; he's a fanatic. He will not bend; he will only break, and you have to break him. Hitler denied that he was evil, and therefore, became evil.

"We, then, as creative people, have to make a study of what he did and borrow some of his theatricality for our empathy machines to be used for good purposes. The machines are amoral. We can choose to use them morally or immorally, and we must opt to use them morally more often than not. Let us then begin the work of trapping the glorious truths and thoughts of the living men around us—the teachers who can really help us in the coming years."

Bradbury puts forth his theme in the following excerpt from *I'll Sing the Body Electric*.

"Grandma took his regard, and ours, and held them simply in her now empty hands, as gifts, and just as gently replied:

"'I am given things which I then give to you. I don't *know* that I give, but the giving goes on. You ask what I am? Why, a machine. But even in that answer we know, don't we, more than a machine. I am all the people who thought of me and planned me and built me and set me running. So I am people. I am all the things they wanted to be and perhaps could not be, so they built a great child, a wonderous toy to represent those things.'

"'Strange,' said Father. 'When I was growing up, there was a huge outcry at machines. Machines were bad, evil, they might dehumanize—'

"'Some machines do. It's all in the way they are built. It's all in the way they are used. A bear trap is a simple machine that catches and holds and tears. A rifle is a machine that wounds and kills. Well I am no bear trap. I am no rifle. I am a grandmother machine, which means more than a machine.'

"'How can you be more than what you seem?'

"'No man is as big as his own idea. It follows, then, that any machine that embodies an idea is larger than the man that made it. And what's so wrong with that?'

"'I got lost back there about a mile,' said Timothy. 'Come again?'

"'Oh, dear,' said Grandma, 'How I do hate philosophical discussions and excursions into esthetics. Let me put it this way. Men throw huge shadows on the lawn, don't they? Then, all their lives, they try to run to fit the shadows. But the shadows are always longer. Only at noon can a man fit his own shoes, his own best suit, for a few brief minutes. But now we're in a new age where we can think up a Big Idea and run it around in a machine. That makes the machine more than a machine, doesn't it?'

" 'So far so good,' said Tim. 'I guess.'

" 'Well isn't a motion-picture camera and projector more than a machine? It's a thing that dreams, isn't it? Sometimes fine happy dreams, sometimes nightmares. But to call it a machine and dismiss it is ridiculous.'

" 'I see *that*!' said Tim, and laughed at seeing.

" 'You must have been invented then,' said Father, 'by someone who loved machines and hated people who *said* all machines were bad or evil.'

" 'Exactly,' said Grandma. 'Guido Fantoccini, that was his real name, grew up among machines. And he couldn't stand the clichés any more.'

" 'Cliches?'

" 'Those lies, yes, that people tell and pretend they are truths absolute. Man will never fly. That was a cliche truth for a thousand thousand years which turned out to be a lie only a few years ago. The earth is flat, you'll fall off the rim, dragons will dine on you; the great lie told as fact, and Columbus plowed it under. Well, now, how many times have you heard how inhuman machines are, in your life? How many bright fine people have you heard spouting the same tired truths which are in reality lies; all machines destroy, all machines are cold, thoughtless, awful.

" 'There's a seed of truth there. But only a seed. Guido Fantoccini knew that. And knowing it, like most men of his kind, made him mad. And he could have stayed mad and gone mad forever, but instead did what he had to do; he began to invent machines to give the lie to the ancient lying truth.

" 'He knew that most machines are amoral, neither bad nor good. But by the way you built and shaped them you in turn shaped men, women, and children to be bad or good. A car, for instance, dead brute, unthinking, an unprogrammed bulk, is the greatest destroyer of souls in history. It makes boy-men greedy for power, destruction, and more destruction. It was never *intended* to do that. But that's how it turned out.

"Grandma circled the table, refilling our glasses with clear cold mineral spring water from the tappet in her left forefinger. 'Meanwhile, you must use other compensating machines. Machines that throw shadows on the earth that beckon you to run out and fit that wondrous casting-forth. Machines that trim your soul in silhouette like a vast pair of beautiful shears, snipping away the rude brambles, the dire horns and hooves to leave a finer profile. And for that you need examples.'

" 'Examples?' I asked.

" 'Other people who behave well, and you imitate them. And if you act well enough all the hair drops off and you're no longer a wicked ape.'

"Grandma sat again.

" 'So, for thousands of years, you humans have needed

kings, priests, philosophers, fine examples to look up to and say, "They are good, I wish I could be like them. They set the grand good style." But, being human, the finest priests, the tenderest philosophers make mistakes, fall from grace, and mankind is disillusioned and adopts indifferent skepticism or, worse, motionless cynicism and the good world grinds to a halt while evil moves on with huge strides.'

" 'And you, why, you never make mistakes, you're perfect, you're better than anyone *ever*!'

"It was a voice from the hall between kitchen and dining room where Agatha, we all knew, stood against the wall listening and now burst forth.

"Grandma didn't even turn in the direction of the voice, but went on calmly addressing her remarks to the family at the table.

" 'Not perfect, no, for what is perfection? But this I do know: being mechanical, I cannot sin, cannot be bribed, cannot be greedy or jealous or mean or small. I do not relish power for power's sake. Speed does not pull me to madness. Sex does not run me rampant through the world. I have time and more than time to collect the information I need around and about an ideal to keep it clean and whole and intact.

Name the value you wish, tell me the Ideal you want and I can see and collect and remember the good that will benefit you all. Tell me how you would like to be: kind, loving, considerate, well-balanced, humane . . . and let me run ahead on the path to explore those ways to be just that. In the darkness ahead, turn me as a lamp in all directions. I *can* guide your feet.'

" 'So,' said Father, putting the napkin to his mouth, 'on the days when all of us are busy making lies—'

" 'I'll tell the truth.'

" 'On the days when we hate—'

" 'I'll go on giving love, which means attention, which means knowing all about you, all, all, all about you, and you knowing that I know but that most of it I will never tell to anyone, it will stay a warm secret between us, so you will never fear my complete knowledge.' "

Fahrenheit 451, was filmed by Universal, 1966; "The Illustrated Man" was filmed by Warner Bros. and contained three interwoven short stories: "The Veldt," "The Long Rain," and "The Last Night of the World," 1969; "The Screaming Woman", was produced as a ninety minute TV-movie, 1972; the short story "Murderer" was adapted for Boston's WGBH-TV, 1976. "Madrigals for the Space Age" was performed at the Dorothy Chandler Pavilion, January, 1976.

Recordings: *Fahrenheit 451* (Bradbury talks about the creation of his book and reads key episodes), Listening Library, 1976; "Bradbury Reads Bradbury," Listening Library, 1976.

HOBBIES AND OTHER INTERESTS: Painting in oil and watercolor; collecting Mexican tribal dance masks.

The house beckoned with its towers, invited with its gummed-shut doors. Pirate ships are a tonic. Ancient forts are a boon. But a house, a *haunted* house, on All Hallows' Eve? Eight small hearts beat up an absolute storm of glory and approbation. ■ (From *The Halloween Tree* by Ray Bradbury. Illustrated by Joseph Mugnaini.)

FOR MORE INFORMATION SEE: "Talk with Mr. Bradbury," *New York Times Book Review,* August 5, 1951; "The Case Against Bradbury," by Edward Wood, *Journal of SF,* Fall Issue, 1951; *The Ray Bradbury Review,* 1952, edited and published by William F. Nolan; *Magazine of Fantasy and Science Fiction,* May, 1963, includes special section on Bradbury, with article and updated bibliography by Nolan; "Interview with a Genius," *Show Magazine,* December, 1964; *Psychology Today,* April, 1968; *New York Times Book Review,* October 29, 1972; *Contemporary Literary Criticism,* edited by Carolyn Riley, Gale Research Co., volume 1, 1973, volume 3, 1975; William F. Nolan, *The Ray Bradbury Companion,* Gale Research Co., 1974; *The Writer,* February, 1974; *Genesis,* May, 1974; *Writers Digest,* December, 1974, February, 1976; *Time,* March 24, 1975; *Los Angeles Times,* April 27, 1975; *True,* September, 1975; *Literary Cavalcade,* October, 1975; *Performing Arts,* October, 1975; *Free Press,* November 28-December 4, 1975.

Film: "Story of a Writer" (30 min., b/w), Sterling.

BRANFIELD, John (Charles) 1931-

PERSONAL: Born January 19, 1931, in Burrow Bridge, Somerset, England; son of Allan Frederick (a civil servant) and Bessie (Storey) Branfield; married Kathleen Elizabeth Peplow, 1955; children: Susan, Frances, Stephen, Peter. *Education:* Queens' College, Cambridge, M.A., 1956; University of Exeter, M.Ed., 1972. *Home address:* Mingoose Villa, Mingoose, Mount Hawke, near Truro, Cornwall, England. *Agent:* A. P. Watt & Son, 26/28 Bedford Row, London WC1R4HL, England.

CAREER: Camborne Grammar School, Cornwall, England, English teacher and head of department, 1961—.

WRITINGS: A Flag in the Map, Eyre & Spottiswoode, 1960; *Look the Other Way,* Eyre & Spottiswoode, 1963; *In the Country,* Eyre & Spottiswoode, 1966; *The Poison Factory* (juvenile), Harper, 1972 (published in England as *Nancekuke,* Gollancz, 1972); *Why Me?* (juvenile), Harper, 1973 (published in England as *Sugar Mouse,* Gollancz, 1973); *The Scillies Trip,* Gollancz, 1975.

Television film: *The Day I Shot My Dad,* BBC film, 1975.

SIDELIGHTS: "One evening I was marking exercise books when Susan, who was fourteen, said, 'You ought to write a children's book, Dad!' 'I'm not very good at making up stories,' I replied. 'It's quite easy,' she said, 'All you need is a search, and somewhere for it to happen.'

"We decided that the story would have to happen in Cornwall, because that's where we live and the place we know best, and then we discussed what sort of search it could be. We dismissed hidden treasure and smuggled goods as too obvious, and then suddenly we thought of the factory on the cliffs where gas is made for chemical warfare.

"Susan had heard of some men who had worked there and who had become ill and even died. Suppose one of them had a daughter, and this daughter felt that she had to find out whether her father had died because of his work. . . .

"And so the story of *The Poison Factory* began. I didn't think I'd ever write it, but Susan insisted. One Easter holiday I spent every day writing, and in the evening Susan read what I had written and criticised it. We had to stop when the term started, but I finished the story in the summer holidays.

"Since then there have been stories for Frances and a film for Stephen. I'm wondering now what Peter's story will be."

HOBBIES AND OTHER INTERESTS: Walking, sailing.

FOR MORE INFORMATION SEE: Children's Literature in Education/12, APS Publications, Inc., 1973.

BREINBURG, Petronella 1927- (Bella Ashey, Mary Totham)

PERSONAL: Born April 16, 1927, in Paramaribo, Suriname, South America; daughter of Charles and Emma (Telg) Van Rhemen; married Emiel Charles Breinburg (an engineer), December 12, 1945; children: Lloyd Kenneth, Aubrey Deryck. *Education:* City of London College, diploma in English, 1965; attended Avery Mill Teachers College, 1969-72, and Goldsmith College, London, 1972-74. *Politics and religion:* None. *Home:* 7 Tuam Rd., Plumstead, London SE182CX, England. *Office:* Hurstmere Secondary School for Boys, Sidcup, Kent, England.

CAREER: School teacher in Paramaribo, Suriname, 1945-61; has worked variously in a factory, as a post office clerk, nurses assistant, and teacher in London, England, 1961-74; full-time writer, 1974—. Has done volunteer work for the Red Cross and Girls' Life Brigade in Suriname, South America, 1942-61; lecturer in creative writing and outdoor storyteller at various libraries in London, 1972-74; part time teacher in English and creative writing, Hurstmere Secondary School for Boys, 1974—. *Member:* Royal Society of Health, Greenwich Playwright Circle, Greenwich Poetry Society. *Awards, honors:* Royal Society of Health award, 1962; Suriname Linguistic Bureau "honorary place" award, 1972, for *Legend of Surinam;* Library Association of London Kate Greenaway Medal "runner-up," 1974, for *My Brother Sean.*

WRITINGS—Children's books: *Legend of Surinam,* Panther House, 1971; *My Brother Sean,* Bodley Head, 1973; *Shawn Goes to School,* Crowell, 1973; *Doctor Shawn,* Crowell, 1974 (published in England as *Doctor Sean,* Bodley Head, 1974); *Tiger, Tinker and Me,* Macmillan, 1974; *Sean's Red Bike,* Bodley Head, 1975; *Sally-Ann,* Bodley Head, 1975; *What Happened at Rita's Party,* Longman, in press.

Plays: "A Streak of Gold" (for children; one-act), first produced in London, England, 1972; "Some Creation" (for older children; one-act), first produced in London, 1972; "Requiem" (adult play; one-act), first produced in London at Greenwich Youth Theatre, 1973; "Velvet Curtains" (adult play; three-act), first produced at Greenwich Youth Theatre, 1974.

Work represented in anthologies, including *Tell Me a Story* and *Tell Me Another Story,* edited by Dorothy Edwards, Methuen, 1974; (under pseudonym Bella Ashey) *Plum in Common,* edited by Dulan Barber, David Poynter, 1974;

The Haunted and the Haunter, edited by Kathleen Lines, Bodley Head, 1975; *Collected Stories,* edited by Veronica Harvey, Evans, in press. Contributor of poems, short stories, and articles, sometimes under pseudonym Bella Ashey, to British publications.

WORK IN PROGRESS: Us Boys of Westcroft, a novel for young adults; collections of ghost stories set in Suriname; *Teaching in London.*

SIDELIGHTS: "I was born in Paramaribo, the capital of Suriname in South America. At the age of seven I went to live in Beekhuize with my parents and my aunt with her husband Jules. We were among the number of people who were buying house-plots in Beekhuize which, until then was a large plantation belonging to one man.

"Beekhuize, where I was to spend most of my childhood, soon became very unique. It was just outside the city of Paramaribo, so was neither city nor village. For example, whereas in the village people did farming, we were only allowed to grow flowers and small items such as tomatoes and peppers. When my brother Jaques and I wanted to catch fish or crabs we had to walk for at least one hour or grab Uncle Jules' old bike, (we grabbed it when he was not looking because he hated lending it to us) and ride for a long time. We took turns pedalling but I preferred to be the one pedalling with Jaques sitting on the back.

"I went to school in the city, first to St. Rosa elementary, then to St. Margreta convent high. In each case my school was a long way from home and I had to travel backwards and forwards on a train, or walk. I often spent my train fare on sweets and things, so walked which took just over an hour brisk trotting. Since school began at eight sharp it meant that I had to leave home by at least seven, no later. At school we all spoke Dutch which was the main language, but once outside we spoke Sranang-tongo which at that time was only a dialect, but can now be learnt from books. Many of my friends spoke Hindustani which was the language of their foreparents. Others spoke Javanese, Chinese or Lebanese, depending on where their foreparents came from. As a child I myself spoke fluent Hindustani learnt from my pals and neighbours. At high school we learnt foreign languages with German being at the top of the list. English too was popular, then came French and Spanish. I have forgotten my Spanish now, but managed to keep my English going very well.

"I never thought of myself becoming a writer. I was told lots of stories by my Aunt Petronella who was Nenne-dofy, meaning storyteller and high priestess. I always wanted to travel though, and I did. I lived in most of the countries around Suriname, namely Guyana, French Guyana, Venezuela. I have visited Brazil briefly.

"I'd say that my writing career began in England. It started with my writing long letters home telling them of the *real* London and how different it was to the London and England given to us in books. I was terribly disillusioned. I first saw London as a big sugar estate with chimneys pouring out black smoke. Hard working people pouring out of dark basements. The interior of the houses was the biggest shock. Nothing like what we were told in books. Many of the houses were old and shaky, many had no baths and the toilets were outside, just like on sugar plantations, only in London it can be freezing cold! Imagine having to visit the

PETRONELLA BREINBURG

toilet in the back garden during a snow storm and in the middle of the night—hence my first spooky spine-chilling story set in London. That ghost story set in London was read on the radio in Suriname. I then began to write about London, fiction and non-fiction, to send to Suriname.

"As I started to work with children in London, I began to have to tell stories about my homeland, also folk-tales told to me by my aunt. I had a big surprise then. The children to whom I told the stories set in Suriname and other South American countries, were given as different a picture of those countries as I was given of England. They thought that everyone in those countries lived in mud huts, had tigers peering at them, and snakes running between their legs. They could not believe that I actually rode a bike to go and catch crabs, or that I ever wore shoes, or ate anything else but bowls of rice.

"My first book written in English was *Legend of Surinam.* It was inspired by children I had been telling Suriname tales to. They wanted to read these tales for themselves but they were not available in books. The only tales from my part of the world they had heard of were a couple of 'Nancy stories', they never heard stories about Libas (witches), Bakroes (leprechauns) or No-mere-mans (giants). The actual writing of the book was done under the watchful eyes of my youngest son who at that time was about twelve years old. He told me how to write the book to suit that age group and kept checking the chapters as I went on. That book has since won a literary award in South America.

"I write many 'true-to-life' stories inspired by single incidents, or by people I have met. The first one *My Brother*

"We've got lots of nice kids," said the teacher to Shawn.

(From *Shawn Goes to School* by Petronella Breinburg. Illustrated by Errol Lloyd.)

Sean was inspired by a little boy I knew. He badly wanted to go to school but his mother never took him. Not until he was nearly six and ready for infant school. That boy often came to my flat and I told him stories, mainly to keep him out of mischief. I also gave him crayons to draw the people in my story. Hence the idea of a picture book about a little boy who badly wanted to go to school. That book was highly acclaimed and also won a literary prize, and is now available in four languages.

"At first I found it very difficult to get my stories with Negroes as the main characters published in England. In those days, publishers did not publish books with Negroes as the leading characters except political books dealing with political ideas, therefore it took me many years—I wrote *My Brother Sean* in about 1969 but did not get it published until late 1973.

"I now have little, if any, trouble, to get my work accepted and write full-time. My two sons are now grown up but I'm kept company by my cat Claudius II. There was a Claudius I, but he got lost when I was away for a long time. He ran off, I suppose to find me, then got himself lost.

"None of my ambitions have been fulfilled, perhaps because I keep changing them. My latest desire is to climb over the walls of Buckingham Palace, and run around the Queen's garden shouting: 'Come get me if you can.' Maybe it's a stupid desire, I don't know, but there it is!"

BROWN, George Earl   1883-1964

PERSONAL: Born February 12, 1883, in Toronto, Kan.; son of George Washington and Mary Janet (Watkins) Brown; married Hazel Marie Harris (a teacher); children: Mary Lou (Mrs. Keith Blakely), Robert W. *Education:* Kansas State Teachers College, State Life Certificate, 1907; Indiana University, student, one year; Colorado State Teachers College, A.B., 1913; Columbia University, A.M., 1926; City University of New York, graduate courses. *Religion:* Methodist. *Home:* 310 East Church St., Carlsbad, N.M.

CAREER: Taught school for fifty-five years, thirty-nine years as superintendent of schools at LeRoya and Garden City, Kan., Palouse and Wenatchee, Wash., Greeley, Colo., and Ocean City, N.J. Sunday School teacher for more than fifty years. *Member:* Colorado State Education Association (president), Masons, Rotary Club (governor of District 50, 1936-37).

WRITINGS: Our Living Bible for Young People, Naylor, 1962.

FOR MORE INFORMATION SEE: Current Argus, Carlsbad, N.Y., October 5, 1962.

(Died October 28, 1964)

BRYANT, Bernice (Morgan)   1908-

PERSONAL: Born April 6, 1908, in St. Louis, Mo.; daughter of Swiney and Augusta (Kuster) Morgan; married Louis Henry Bryant, June 16, 1928 (deceased); children: Bernice. *Education:* Illinois State Teacher's College, summer student, 1924, 1925; University of Illinois, student,

BERNICE BRYANT

1926-27; Chicago Academy of Fine Arts, summer student, 1934. *Home:* Brymor, Strasburg, Va.

CAREER: Penn Hall Preparatory School and Junior College, Chambersburg, Pa., social dean until retirement in 1968. Author of books for children. *Member:* Authors League of America, Midland Authors, Professional Writer's Club, Children's Reading Round Table. *Awards, honors:* Illinois Women's Press Club Award for *Trudy Terrill, Eighth Grader.*

WRITINGS: Yammy Buys a Bicycle, Albert Whitman, 1941; *Pedie and the Twins: A Read-it-Yourself Story,* Albert Whitman, 1942; *Future Perfect: A Guide to Personality and Popularity for the Junior Miss,* Bobbs-Merrill, 1944, revised edition, 1957; *Trudy Terrill, Eighth Grader,* Bobbs-Merrill, 1946; *Everybody Likes Butch,* Childrens Press, 1947, revised edition published as *Let's Be Friends,* Childrens Press, 1954; *God's Wonder World: A Book of Devotional Readings for Children,* Bethany, 1944; *Trudy Terrill, High School Freshman,* Bobbs-Merrill, 1948; *Fancy Free,* Bobbs-Merrill, 1949; *Follow the Leader,* Houghton, 1950; *Miss Behavior: Popularity, Poise and Personality for the Teenage Girl,* Bobbs-Merrill, 1948, revised edition, 1960; *Dan Morgan, Boy of the Wilderness,* Bobbs-Merrill, 1952, revised edition published as *Dan Morgan, Wilderness Boy,* 1962; *P's and Q's for Boys and Girls: A Book About Manners,* Bobbs-Merrill, 1953, revised edition, 1963; *Party ABC's: A Guide to Party Planning and Behavior for Beginning Hosts and Hostesses—10 to 14 Years Old,* Bobbs-Merrill, 1954; *George Gershwin: Young Composer,* Bobbs-Merrill, 1965.

WORK IN PROGRESS: Another book for Bobbs-Merrill's "Childhood of Famous Americans" series.

SIDELIGHTS: "Authors of books for children usually go back to their own childhood for the deep down feelings and

Molly placed the musket in his arms. He couldn't take his eyes off it. His gun! His very own! Now he wouldn't have to use Pa's musket when he went hunting. ■ (From *Dan Morgan Wilderness Boy* by Bernice Bryant. Illustrated by Nathan Goldstein.)

reactions to circumstances. I do. In many of my books I have a 'now' background and a 'now' child that a child of today can identify with. Most always the child has been patterned after my own little girl. As I wrote I found that my own little girl had the same reactions to the new that I had had. There are many, many firsts in the life of a child. It made me know that children of every age, nation, race and religion have feelings in common. Don't we all?

"When I was four years old my parents moved from St. Louis to a small town in southern Illinois. My mother's relatives thought my father was taking her into the wilderness. We three children thought we were in heaven.

"At the edge of town we had an immense yard bordering a far-as-the-eye-could-see, waving wheatfield on one side and a thick and dark green woods on another. But we were not permitted out of our fenced-in yard except when we were with an adult. Our imaginations told us why. There were bears and wolves in the woods. My older brother's nine-year imagination made for hair-raising stories and dramas that we acted in the back yard. Our parents and St. Louis relatives were an appreciative audience.

"My mother, with an over-protected upbringing, was slow in giving us the freedom of the wide expanses of prairie land. It was several years before we were permitted to pick the wild blackberries that grew along the dusty country roads or chase through the woods just for the fun of chasing. She did learn to enjoy picnic lunches beside Silver Creek that meandered throughout the countryside. Neither did my father become a true nature lover, except for the love of knowing the heavens. On summer evenings, he would flop on the lawn with us and point out the Big Dipper, Orion's Belt, the Pleiades and tell us the stories of all.

"Mama insisted that we not forget the big city and its ways. Being the only children in the entire family (there had come a fourth) we had doting aunts and uncles who actually vied with each other to have us spend holidays with them. Forest Park Highlands and the tapestried beds of flowers were like a fairyland. The Veiled Prophet's Parade was like the pictures in books. I loved it all, the lights, the shows, the museums, even the trolleys and the songs of the fruit peddlars and icemen.

"Home again, I wrote poems about the sights and sounds of the city. I became more aware of the beauty of the country, too. I was inspired to write about what I knew. They all were young-mind poems.

"My first big writing project was in collaboration with my best friend, Doe. She was a passive child of nine, with soft brown eyes and long, velvet brown hair. Just the opposite of me with my short yellow curls. I had been forced into passivity by a siege of diptheria followed by a weakened heart.

"It was summer and Doe and I sat under a mulberry tree in her back yard, where we could look across the railroad tracks to the home of Walter. We both loved Walter, with a nine-year-old's love. Of course, we did not mention this to each other or to Walter.

"I don't remember who thought of the project of writing a novel. Doe wrote the first chapter. A shining, white knight, who looked like Walter, fell deeply in love with a dark haired princess.

"As I read that, my forced passivity burst out of confinement. I couldn't wait to write the next chapter. In chapter two, the shining white knight fell in love with a beautiful golden haired princess.

"Poor knight. He zigged-zagged from one to the other for a number of weeks. One day, I gave up, took my composition book home and finished the story. No need to tell who his true love was.

"My childhood was good and warm with love, security and discipline. I was never bored. How could I be? Busy people, young or old, are not bored. I was happy. Perhaps not always. But I don't ever remember my parents being concerned whether I was or not. We had our chores, time for ourselves, time to study, books to read and family excursions. We all grew up loving each other.

"I stress good family living in my books."

BURTON, William H(enry) 1890-1964

PERSONAL: Born October 9, 1890, in Fort Worth, Tex.; son of George Charles and Agnes Ann (Selbie) Burton; married Virginia Lee Nottingham, 1920. *Education:* University of Oregon, B.A., 1915; Columbia University, Ed.M., 1917; University of Chicago, Ph.D., 1924. *Politics:* Democrat. *Religion:* Episcopalian. *Home and office:* 3434 Willamette Ave., Corvallis, Ore.

CAREER: Taught in rural, elementary, and secondary schools in Oregon, intermittently, 1914-18, at Oregon College of Education, Monmouth, 1918; Washington State College, Pullman, assistant professor, 1919-21; Minnesota State Teachers College, Winona, director of student teaching and principal training, 1921-23; University of Cincinnati, Cincinnati, Ohio, director of student teaching, 1924-26; University of Chicago, professor of education, 1926-31; University of Southern California, Los Angeles, professor of education, 1932-38; Harvard University, Cambridge, Mass., director of student teaching, 1938-54, retired 1954. Also adviser to Oregon State Department of Education, visiting professor of education at Oregon College of Education, chairman of Educational Committee at Pacific University.

MEMBER: Association for Curriculum Development (president, 1927), National Society for Study of Education (yearbook commission, 1950), International Reading Association, John Dewey Society, Association for Student Teaching, National Society of Teachers of Education, Phi Delta Kappa. *Awards, honors:* Pacific University, Litt.D., 1955.

WRITINGS: Supervision and the Improvement of Teaching, Appleton, 1922; (with A. S. Barr) *The Supervision of Instruction,* Appleton, 1926; *The Nature and Direction of Learning,* Appleton, 1929; (contributor) *The Supervision of Elementary Subjects,* 1929; *An Introduction to Education,* Appleton, 1934; (with Barr and L. J. Brueckner) *Supervision: A Social Process,* Appleton, 1938, 3rd edition (with Brueckner), 1955; *Guidance of Learning Activities,* Appleton, 1944, 3rd edition, 1962; (with Blair) *Growth and Development of the Preadolescent,* Appleton, 1951; (with Grace K. Kemp and Clara Belle Baker) *Reading in Child Development,* Bobbs, 1956; (with R. B. Kimball and R. L. Wing) *Education for Effective Thinking,* Appleton, 1960; *The Profession of Education,* Appleton, 1967.

Something about the Author

Elementary school primers and readers, with teachers' manuals and work books, all written with others: *Get Ready to Read, Don and Peggy, Come and See, Here We Play, Days of Fun, Our Happy Ways, Meet Our Friends, Our Good Neighbors* (all in "Reading for Living" series, published by Bobbs, 1950). *Up and Away, Animal Parade, Picnic Basket, Blazing New Trails, Flying High, Shooting Stars* (all "Developmental Reading Text-Workbooks," published by Bobbs in 1961).

Monographs: (With others) *Children's Civic Information, 1924-35,* University of Southern California Press, 1936; (with Mary O'Rourke) *Workshops for Teachers,* Appleton, 1957. More than fifty articles in periodicals.

HOBBIES AND OTHER INTERESTS: Local history, golf, and gardening.

(Died April 3, 1964)

CAMPBELL, Ann R. 1925-

PERSONAL: Born January 30, 1925, in Boston, Mass.; daughter of Jonathan Stone (a banker) and Pauline (Pollard) Raymond; first married to Gordon P. Baird, then to Peter A. Campbell; married third husband, Peter Paul Luce (a management consultant), October 28, 1967; children: (first marriage) Jonathan Raymond Baird, Gordan Prentiss Baird. *Education:* Vassar College, A.B., 1946; graduate study at American University, 1954; University of Colorado, M.A., 1975. *Religion:* Presbyterian. *Address:* P.O. Box 1882, Boulder, Colo. 80302.

CAREER: Miss Fine's School, Princeton, N.J., teacher, 1955-57; Brooklyn Friends School, Brooklyn, N.Y., teacher, 1957-59; H. M. Snyder & Co., New York, N.Y., promotion manager, 1960-63; Franklin Watts, Inc., New

York, N.Y., advertising and promotion manager, 1963-67; free-lance editor, writer, and book illustrator, 1967—. *Member:* Publisher's Advertising Club (New York; past vice-president), Artists Equity Association.

WRITINGS: Let's Find Out about Color, Watts, 1966, reissued with new illustrations, 1975; *Let's Find Out about Boats,* Watts, 1967; *Let's Find Out about Farms,* Watts, 1968; (self-illustrated) *Start to Draw,* Watts, 1968; (self-illustrated) *Let's Find Out About a Ball,* Watts, 1969; *Picture Life of Richard M. Nixon,* Watts, 1969; (photographs & diagrams by author) *Painting: How to Look at Great Art,* Watts, 1970.

SIDELIGHTS: "Currently am a pilot with 650 hours. Took solo trip to Mexico and Central America to do research on masters thesis at University of Colorado. Landed at remote ruin sites in the jungle. It was a fascinating trip."

CARPENTER, Patricia (Healy Evans) 1920- (Patricia Healy Evans)

PERSONAL: Born May 22, 1920, in Milwaukee, Wis.; daughter of Harry Thomas and Ann (Barney) Healy; married Kenneth J. Carpenter (assistant director, University of Nevada Library); children: Judith Sherry (Mrs. Gershon Legman). *Home:* 1454 Exeter Way, Reno, Nev. 89503. *Education:* Attended San Francisco City College, San Francisco State College, University of Arizona, and University of Nevada.

PATRICIA CARPENTER

It is fun to sail in a sailboat.
The wind blows on the sails and you
    WHIZ along.
■ (From *Let's Find Out About Boats* by Ann Campbell. Illustrated by the author.)

1 2 3 O'Lary
My first name is Mary.
Don't you think that I look cute,
In my papa's bathing suit?
■ (From *Rimbles* by Patricia Evans. Illustrated by Gioia Fiammenghi.)

CAREER: Writer and illustrator of children's books. *Member:* California Folklore Society (former regional vice-president).

WRITINGS—Under name Patricia Healy Evans; all but two books self-illustrated: *The Mycophagists' Book* (adult), Peregrine Press (San Francisco), 1951; *An Alphabet Book,* Peregrine Press, 1953; (compiler) *Jump Rope Rhymes,* Porpoise Bookshop (San Francisco), 1954; *Hopscotch,* Por-

poise Bookshop, 1955; *Who's It?,* Porpoise Bookshop, 1956; *Jacks,* Porpoise Bookshop, 1956; (compiler) *Sticks and Stones,* Porpoise Bookshop, 1960; (compiler) *Rimbles* (collection of children's games, rhymes, songs, and sayings), Doubleday, 1961; *A Modern Herbal* (adult), Porpoise Bookshop, 1961.

Illustrator: Ernest Peninou and Sidney Greenleaf, *Winemaking in California* (two volumes, adult), Porpoise Bookshop, 1954; Henry H. Evans, *First Duet,* Peregrine Press, 1956; Henry H. Evans, *Small New Poems,* Porpoise Bookshop, 1957.

SIDELIGHTS: "I never planned to be an 'author' but was intensely interested in folklore. All of the children's books were really written, unconsciously, by children. I only filled in the spaces in between. The cookbooks of course are my own tested recipes. Alas, all are out of print and even I don't have copies. I was once introduced at a California Folklore Society meeting, as 'the only one among us who works from original sources.' I have stuck to that.

"Although I have an immense amount of collected material from children, I do not know whether or not another book will result. I think it must, in spite of arthritis which has clipped my wings."

CARTNER, William Carruthers 1910-

PERSONAL: Born January 22, 1910, in South Shields, England; son of Edward (a policeman) and Margaret (Graham) Cartner; married Lillian Armstrong, August 4, 1941; children: Elizabeth Anne. *Education:* School of Art, art teaching diploma, 1930. *Home:* 2 Ryelands Park, Easington, Saltburn, Cleveland, England.

CAREER: Middlesbrough College of Art, Middlesbrough, Yorkshire, England, lecturer in graphics and typography, 1949-70. *Military service:* Royal Air Force, flying officer, 1941-46. *Member:* Printing Historical Society, Society for Italic Handwriting.

WRITINGS—For children: *Fun with Architecture,* Kaye & Ward, 1969; *The Young Calligrapher,* Warne, 1969; *Fun with Palaeontology,* Kaye & Ward, 1971, published in the United States as *What Happened on Earth Before Man Arrived,* Sterling, 1972; *Fun with Geology,* Kaye & Ward, 1972; *Fun with Botany,* Kaye & Ward, 1973.

𝔚rought ironwork was made specially to harmonize with existing antiquities 𝔄𝔅ℭ𝔉𝔊𝔍𝔎ℜ𝔒𝔔ℜ𝔖𝔗𝔘𝔙𝔛𝔜𝔷

The gothic style was a product of northern Europe, and prevailed well into the sixteenth century, in print as in writing. Pen decoration was used in the capitols, with knots and flourishes in great variety. . . . ■ (From *The Young Calligrapher* by William C. Cartner.)

Illustrator: G. Watson, *Fun with Ecology*, Kaye & Ward, 1968.

WORK IN PROGRESS: Fossils of the Yorkshire Lias: Jurassic.

SIDELIGHTS: "To counter the social problems of city life, children should be encouraged by all possible means to follow an interest in crafts and hobbies and outdoor activities and nature study."

HOBBIES AND OTHER INTERESTS: Outdoor pursuits in natural sciences, preservation of wildlife.

CHANDLER, Edna Walker   1908-

PERSONAL: Born November 16, 1908, near Macksville, Kan.; daughter of Clarence Sheldon (a farmer) and Mamie (Johnson) Walker; married Joseph Ortman Chandler (a school principal), June 8, 1930 (died, 1971); children: Ted, Don, Ruby, Robert, Nancy. *Education:* Friends University, student, 1925-27; Sacramento State College, B.E., 1958. *Religion:* Christian.

CAREER: Worked way through high school and two years of college. Began teaching in Kansas elementary school at eighteen, intending to return to college later. Taught three years, was married, and resumption of education was delayed by five children. In the meantime her husband had joined the Indian Service, and the family lived in South Dakota, in Alaska, 1939-42, Montana, and New Mexico before finally settling in California. There she taught for seven years, mainly in schools near Sacramento, studied for her delayed degree, and started writing her own stories for use in the classroom. Full-time writer, except for occasional substitute teaching, 1959-63. American Field Service Foreign Student Exchange program, chairman of home selection in Carmichael area; active in church work. Speaker on topics related to books. *Member:* Delta Kappa Gamma, California Writers, Authors League, American Association of University Women, Authors Guild, Suburban Writers. *Awards, honors:* National League of American Pen Women, first prize for unpublished novel, 1955.

WRITINGS—"Cowboy Sam" series: *Cowboy Sam and Big Bill, Cowboy Sam and Freckles, Cowboy Sam and Dandy, Cowboy Sam and Miss Lily, Cowboy Sam and Porky, Cowboy Sam, Cowboy Sam and Flop, Cowboy Sam and Shorty, Cowboy Sam and Freddy, Cowboy Sam and Sally, Cowboy Sam and the Fair, Cowboy Sam and the Rodeo, Cowboy Sam and the Airplane, Cowboy Sam and the Indians, Cowboy Sam and the Rustlers* (all published by Benefic), 1951-62, new editions of complete series, 1970-74.

"American Indians" series: *Buffalo Boy, Little Wolf and the Thunder Stick, Young Hawk, Juanito Makes a Drum, Tall Boy and the Coyote, Little Cedar's Tooth, Taka and His Dog, Kala's Pet* (all published by Benefic), 1956-63.

"Tom Logan" series: *Pony Rider, Cattle Drive, Secret Tunnel, Gold Nugget, Stagecoach Driver, Talking Wire, Track Boss, Gold Train, Cattle Cars, Circus Train* (all published by Benefic).

"Tony Story Books"—All illustrated by author's son, Don Chandler: *Who's Boss in Tony's Family*, 1962, *Tony and the*

EDNA WALKER CHANDLER

Little Blue Car, 1962, *Tony and the Tree House*, 1963, *Tony and His Friend Jeff*, 1963 (all published by Duell, Sloan & Pearce).

Other books: *The Missing Mitt*, Ginn, 1955; (with Barrett Willoughby) *Pioneer of Alaska Skies* (biography), Ginn, 1959; *Water Crazy*, Duell, Sloan & Pearce, 1962; *Charley Brave*, Whitman, 1962; *The New Red Jacket*, Whitman, 1962; *The Boy Who Made Faces*, Whitman, 1964; *Crystal Pie*, Duell, Sloan & Pearce, 1965; *Chaff in the Wind*, Pageant, 1965; *Will You Carry Me?*, Whitman, 1965; *Five-Cent, Five-Cent*, Whitman, 1967; *With Books on Her Head*, Meredith, 1967; *Popcorn Patch*, Whitman, 1969; *Almost Brothers*, Whitman, 1971; *Women in Prison*, Bobbs, 1973; *Indian Paint Brush*, Whitman, 1975. Contributor to newspapers and magazines, 1934—, including fillers for *Denver Post*, articles in *American Boy, Woman's World, American Forest, Chevron U.S.A., Highlights for Children, This Week, Alaska Sportsman, Sea, Christian Home*.

WORK IN PROGRESS: An autobiography, *Beds I Have Slept In.*

SIDELIGHTS: "One of the questions I am asked most often is 'Where do you get your ideas for the stories, books, and articles you write?'

"The answer seems to me so simple . . . ideas are everywhere! You only have to be equipped with a built-in radar to receive and a mental sponge to hold those ideas. Then if they are to be shared with others, you need a certain kind of stubbornness which we call self-discipline, and of course, a love of words and good command of whatever language you use.

"I grew up on a farm in Central Kansas, the oldest of ten children. Farm and ranch pleasures and problems were ev-

Kolu sat down and cried. She had worked so hard. Now everything was gone. ■ (From *Five Cent, Five Cent* by Edna Walker Chandler. Illustrated by Betty Stull.)

eryday life to me. Because I was the oldest I was quite regularly given the job of looking after the younger children while our Mamma worked in the garden, helped with milking during harvest time, cooked soap in the back yard or did other things which did not require the presence of younger children. As my brothers and sisters got older I had to find a way to manage them which was not physical! I learned that I could keep them quiet and happy for a long time with story telling of familiar stories to which I added my own personal literary embroidery. I used these same techniques later when I became a teacher. Nothing like a rousing cowboy tale to control stormy day jitters! While using the same methods to teach reluctant readers in the late 1940's I began the *Cowboy Sam* series.

"The magic of a pencil hit me when I first started to school. My beloved stories could be changed a bit by different words here and there. I could make my own stories by putting together in certain ways these strange hen scratches called the ABC's. What fun!

"When I was eleven years old I got my first monetary reward for writing . . . an essay on *Why My Father Should Insure His Life.* A very perceptive teacher had seen this flair for words and she often threw challenges such as this at me, partly to keep me busy and out of the way, I'm sure. But this was the beginning of my training as a writer . . . author, if you please, once I had cashed that first check for $2.50.

"Because of my husband's work as an educator with the U.S. Indian Service we lived on several reservations while our own five children were growing up. Here was a wealth of background material for stories. Still later came five years in Liberia, West Africa when my husband was with AID (Agency for International Development) and out of that three books came into being. After we had been there for a few months, the office discovered my writing background and I was asked to work as a textbook specialist under the AID program. My work was twofold—writing textbooks listed by the government of Liberia as most needed, and training Liberian teachers to do the same.

"An author's only limitations are time and energy. The wonderful world and all its people are still with us, reaching out to be understood.

"Sometimes people who hadn't seen me for a long time would ask my husband, 'Well, how's Edna? Is she still writing?' His answer would often be 'Why don't you ask if she's still breathing?'

"And that's what being an author means to me . . . especially when I'm writing for young people. It's my own special reason for being."

The original manuscript and art work from *Five-Cent, Five-Cent* are included in the Kerlan Collection of Children's literature and art in the University of Minnesota.

CHENEY, Theodore Albert 1928-
(Ted Cheney)

PERSONAL: Born January 1, 1928, in Milton, Mass.; son of Ralph Albert and Ruth (Rees) Cheney; married Dorothy Catherine Bates, September 3, 1949; children: Glenn Alan, Ralph Hunter, Bonnie Bates, Burke Adams. *Education:* Boston University, A.B., 1951, M.A. (geography), 1952; Fairfield University, M.A. (communication), 1973. *Politics:* "Progressive conservative." *Religion:* Protestant. *Home:* 399 Round Hill Rd., Fairfield, Conn. 06430. *Office:* Graduate School of Corporate and Political Communication, Fairfield University, Fairfield, Conn. 06430.

CAREER: Park Aerial Surveys, Inc., photogrammetrist, 1952-54; Cornell University, Ithaca, N.Y., assistant professor of photogrammetry, 1954-58; Geotechnics & Resources, Inc., White Plains, N.Y., vice-president, 1958-64; Dunlap & Associates (a "think tank"), Darien, Conn., senior scientist, 1964-69; Fairfield University, Fairfield, Conn., lecturer in communication and administration coor-

THEODORE ALBERT CHENEY

A modern icebreaker smashes its way by ramming at the edge of the pack until the ship's curved bow slides right up on the ice. After enough of the heavy ship is on top of the ice, the ice fails and breaks. ▪ (From *Land of the Hibernating Rivers* by T. A. Cheney. Photos by T. A. Cheney.)

dinator, 1969—. *Military service:* U.S. Navy, 1945-47. *Member:* Authors Guild of America, Authors League of America.

WRITINGS: (Editor) *Burma: Landforms, Forestry, Geology,* Cornell University Press, 1956; *Fort Churchill, Manitoba, Canada: An Environmental Analysis,* Cornell University Press, 1957; *Land of the Hibernating Rivers* (juvenile), Harcourt, 1968; *Camping by Backpack and Canoe,* Funk, 1970.

WORK IN PROGRESS: A novel set in Hudson Bay, *Below Harding's Fjord;* editing *Performance Appraisal,* by Howard Smith and Paul Brourer; research for a book about creativity and problem solving, *Soft Logic.*

SIDELIGHTS: "I volunteered to go to Little America, Antarctica, at age seventeen while in the U.S. Navy which led to a life-long interest in polar matters—out of which came my first book.... Camping and canoeing as Boy Scout leader over the years led to the second book."

CHU, Daniel 1933-

PERSONAL: Born June 11, 1933, in Nanking, China; son of Shih-ming and Grace (Zia) Chu. *Education:* Brown University, A.B., 1955; Northwestern University, graduate study, 1956. *Politics:* Democrat ("most of the time"). *Home:* 186 Riverside Dr., New York, N.Y. 10024. *Office:* Newsweek, Inc., 444 Madison Ave., New York, N.Y. 10022.

CAREER: Pawtucket Times, Pawtucket, R.I., reporter, 1956-59; Scholastic Magazines, Inc., New York, N.Y., senior associate editor, 1959-71; Newsweek Inc., New York, N.Y., associate editor, 1971-73, general editor, international editions, 1974—. *Military service:* U.S. Army Reserve, 1958-64, active duty, 1958, 1961-62. *Member:* American Newspaper Guild, Sigma Delta Chi, Brown University Club (New York).

WRITINGS: (With Elliott Skinner) *A Glorious Age in Africa,* Doubleday, 1965; (with Samuel Chu) *Passage to the Golden Gate: A History of the Chinese in America to 1910,* Doubleday, 1967; (editor) *America's Hall of Fame,* Scholastic Book Service, 1969; *China,* Scholastic Book Services, 1973. Scholastic Magazines, Inc., auto editor, 1965-67.

SIDELIGHTS: "[I] traveled extensively in childhood.... Have retained a minimal knowledge of spoken Chinese. Actually, I don't find myself especially interesting. And if sometimes opinionated, I do my best not to foist my personal viewpoints on others—vital issues or not."

HOBBIES AND OTHER INTERESTS: Reading, music, sailing (as a participant), most other sports (as a spectator), and automobiles.

The wonder of it all was that so many managed, somehow, to arrive at the end of their journey with their hopes and health intact. ▪ (From *Passage to the Golden Gate* by Daniel and Samuel Chu. Illustrated by Earl Thollander.)

E. RICHARD CHURCHILL

CHURCHILL, E. Richard 1937-

PERSONAL: Born May 25, 1937, in Greeley, Colo.; son of Emery Roy and Olive (Whitteker) Churchill; married Linda Ruler (now a junior high school teacher), August 18, 1961; children: Eric Richard, Robert Sean. *Education:* Colorado State College, A.B., 1959, M.A., 1962. *Home:* Rt. 1, Box 329B, Kersey, Colo. 80644.

CAREER: Part-time and sometime full-time public library employee in Greeley, Colo., for total of seventeen years; Park Elementary School, Greeley, Colo., fifth grade teacher, 1959-74; Maplewood Middle School, Greeley, Colo., resource teacher, 1974—. *Military service:* Colorado Air National Guard, 1961-1967.

WRITINGS: (With Edward H. Blair) *Games and Puzzles for Family Leisure,* Abingdon, 1965; *Everybody Came to Leadville,* Timberline, 1971; *The McCartys: They Rode with Butch Cassidy,* Timberline, 1972; *Colorado Quiz Bag,* Timberline, 1973; *Doc Holliday, Bat Masterson, and Wyatt Earp: Their Colorado Careers,* Timberline, 1974; *Math Duplicator Masters for Basic Math,* Walch, 1974; *The Six Million Dollar Cucumber,* Watts, 1976.

All with wife, Linda Churchill: (with Edward H. Blair) *Fun with American History,* Abingdon, 1966; *Puzzle It Out,* Scholastic, 1971; *Short Lessons in World History,* Walch, 1971; *How Our Nation Became Great,* Walch, 1971; *Community Civics Case Book,* Walch, 1973; *Enriched Social Studies Teaching,* Fearon, 1973; *Puzzles and Quizzes,* Scholastic, 1973; *American History Activity Reader,* Walch, 1974; *World History Activity Reader,* Walch, 1975; *Case-*

book on Marriage and the Family, Walch, 1975; *Hidden Word Puzzles,* Scholastic, 1975; *Puzzles and Games for Concepts and Inquiry* (kits), Allyn & Bacon, 1975; *You and the Law,* Walch, 1976; *Twentieth-Century Europe Activity Reader,* Walch, 1976.

WORK IN PROGRESS: Sets of duplicator masters for middle school and upper age children in math, geography, history, and home economics, for Walch; *Holiday Jokes and Riddles,* for Watts; *Casebook on Family Health Care,* for Walch; *Ancient History Activity Reader,* for Walch; *The Middle Ages Activity Reader,* for Walch; *101 Shaggy Dog Jokes,* for Scholastic.

SIDELIGHTS: "When I made my first sale of cartoon ideas to cartoonist, Morrie Turner, while I was still in college, I was hooked on the idea of writing.

"Since then, my writing interests have included jokes and riddles, puzzles, recreational ideas, and Western history. Many of our geography and history publications have included puzzles for the students as a part of the work. It has been my feeling that learning can combine a bit of fun without detracting from the intent of the lesson.

"Whenever possible, we travel as a family. Such travel not only gives the family a time of togetherness but broadens our outlook. We have made rather extensive family outings to England and Scotland, to Canada, New England, the Southwest, and the Rocky Mountain region.

"My two sons, Eric and Sean, have grown up with the idea that when Dad is at the typewriter they need to be somewhere else. Then when proofs come, it is a time for children to be neither seen nor heard. Their constant exposure to our writing has convinced both boys they, too, wish to write. It was with their help that *The Six Million Dollar Cucumber* was put together. *Holiday Jokes and Riddles* not only provided the boys with an opportunity to join forces in collecting and revising but will be their first time to share credit lines with me. Perhaps a second generation of Churchill writers has already begun publication."

CLARK, Patricia (Finrow) 1929-

PERSONAL: Born January 3, 1929, in Walla Walla, Wash.; daughter of Vernon Hyatt (a salesman) and Alys (Olson) Finrow; married William Emmer Clark, July 27, 1957; children: William E., Jr., Michelle, Christopher, Pamela Monica. *Education:* Prairie Bible Institute, Alberta, Canada, diploma, 1950; Aoyama Gakuin, Tokyo, Japan, student, 1954-55; University of Washington, Seattle Pacific College, B.A. in Ed., 1958. *Religion:* Interdenominational. *Home:* 7329 12th N.E., Seattle, Wash. 98115.

CAREER: Evangelical Alliance Mission, Chicago, Ill., missionary to Japan, 1951-64; Island Lake Bible Camp, Seattle, Washington, camp director, 1964-70; Worldwide Dental Health Service, missionary to Liberia, 1972-76; American Cooperative school, Monrovia, Liberia, secondary English teacher, 1973—.

WRITINGS: Jan Ken Pon (true stories about Japanese children), Moody, 1961; (with husband, William E. Clark) *Children of the Sun,* Tuttle, 1965; *Bobby in Japan,* New Life Press, 1967; *An African Flower,* E.L.W.A. Press, 1973.

PATRICIA CLARK

WORK IN PROGRESS: Child of the Spring, a biography of a Japanese nurse, and Fly, Liberia, Fly.

SIDELIGHTS: "When I was about ten we moved to a small rented house in Sumner, Washington. My daddy was sick and mother was having a hard time providing for us. For recreation that summer my two brothers, two sisters and I went to all of the free things—Red Cross swimming lessons, company picnics, and the public library which was just an antique house, dark and musty, but it was cool in there and I spent many hours reading and dreaming about other lands.

"My mother had beautiful handwriting. She collected poems and sayings in a tattered scrap book and loved to sing and talk to us in verses and rhymes. I wanted to be like her.

"When I was in third grade I was given a part in a college play and received drama lessons. We made a theater in our garage where we entertained our neighbors with plays my sister, Eleanor, wrote. As I continued to take part in various stage plays and perform monologues for clubs and meetings I began to understand and feel for people. Perhaps that helped me to put feelings and descriptions down on paper. In the eighth grade my favorite teacher was Miss Wilda Ingels. She had a lovely speaking voice and I loved to hear her read. She suggested many books to me and helped to develop my creative abilities.

"My father died when I was fifteen and it was just about that time that I became acquainted with the Bible. Reading it changed my life. When I committed my life to the Lord Jesus I felt that He was asking me to share this faith with others. When I was twenty-two years old I sailed on a ship called 'The Flying Dragon.' I wrote my first published story about standing on the deck looking down into that magic land of Japan.

"While living in Japan I attended a Japanese university, started churches in isolated places, and had many strange and exciting experiences. Often I met people or heard stories that I wanted to share with my family and friends back home, so I began to record short stories about them. I think I should also mention that typing is of utmost importance if you want to write. Thoughts come so swiftly and if you have to write them by hand it is very wearisome.

"Now we are living in Africa and again I feel compelled to share stories about my African friends with others. Recently there was a storm here in Liberia, a dear little girl I know was struck by lightning and instantly killed. Her name was Mary and she was the only half-black, half-German, girl in the jungle, where I live. I wish you could have known Mary. You would have loved her. Before it started to rain she left the mission to get some cassava . . . you see, there I go again."

COATES, Ruth Allison 1915-

PERSONAL: Born May 18, 1915, in Mt. Carmel, Ill.; daughter of Earl L. (an editor) and Esther (Ross) Allison; married Robert E. Coates (a lawyer), December 24, 1939; children: Margaret Ann (Mrs. Richard Polese), Nancy Lynn Coates Loker, David Allison, Steven Wendell. Education: Bethel College, Hopkinsville, Ky., A.A., 1936; Indiana University, A.B., 1938. Home and office: 4340 Knollton Rd., Indianapolis, Ind. 46208. Agent: Ruth Cantor, 156 Fifth Ave., Room 1005, New York, N.Y. 10010.

CAREER: Commercial artist in department stores in Indianapolis, Ind., 1938-41, and in San Antonio, Tex., 1942. Former portrait artist, now working in silk screen and collage; work has been shown in exhibits and in a one-man show in Indianapolis. Member: Graphics Society, Authors Guild, Hoosier Salon, Spiritual Frontiers, Astara. Awards, honors: Robert Martin Award from New York Poetry Forum contest, 1970, for poem, "The Loaf."

WRITINGS: Great American Naturalists (juvenile), Lerner, 1974. Short story listed in Best American Short Stories of 1971, edited by Martha Foley, Houghton, 1971 and The Real Book of First Stories, Rand McNally, 1973. Contributor of short stories, poems, and articles to Teen, Minnesota Review, Parents' Magazine, Phylon, Guideposts, and other periodicals.

SIDELIGHTS: "I have been writing for as long as I can remember: high school plays that were performed, editing and illustrating a college yearbook, gag lines for syndicated cartoons, greeting card verses, a brief stint as a newspaper reporter, stories and articles in religious publications, poetry for adults and children. These are 'practice scales' of the writer.

"Finally, one arrives at a field that interests him the most. Doing biography is my delight, especially doing those people who should be known, but aren't. . . . I am a great believer in people's lives crossing because there's a plan unfolding, a plan often beyond the grasp of our limited intuition. Hence all word-building is an awesome responsibility to me. . . . The spirit world, the historical world, the world not yet discovered—all these have more solidity to me than the apparent, touchable world. Doing biographies involves research into history and other lands. Another delight. But writing short stories is not far behind. To create characters who live and breathe and tug at the heartstrings of the reader—this is a joy all writers understand.

"I am a writer dealing in and forever investigating clues, or keys, to the meaning of the constantly shifting illusion that lies about us. It's a spirited adventure—my mother is Swedish. She has seen angels and auras—which must account for my fascination with the mystical.

"Though primarily a writer, I still 'dabble' in art. I trained many years under a fine portrait artist. I am currently doing silk screen prints. I have had my work in numerous juried shows over the years.

"I owe much to my gentle father who was a small-town editor and short story writer and to my mother who at eighty-seven is alert and still finds God in every sunrise and bird song. Both my parents were one-room school teachers, the

So many myths and tall tales have been told about Johnny Appleseed that many people think he *is* a myth. But Johnny Appleseed was a real person, a naturalist who lived during America's early pioneer days. ■ (From *Great American Naturalists* by Ruth Allison Coates.)

dedicated sort. They taught me to find goodness and honesty, kindness and virtue . . . faith, in just about everything and everybody. I hope these qualities emerge in my writing."

HOBBIES AND OTHER INTERESTS: World religions, reading, travel.

COATS, Alice M(argaret)   1905-

PERSONAL: Born June 15, 1905, in Birmingham, England; daughter of Robert Hay (a Baptist minister) and Margaret (MacConnachie) Coats. *Education:* Attended Birmingham College of Art, 1922-27, Slade School of Art, University of London, 1927-28, and Academie Andre Lhote, Paris, 1932. *Home:* 9, Upper Lansdowne Mews, Bath BA1 5HG, England.

CAREER: Landscape artist and designer. *Wartime service:* Women's Land Army, 1939-45. *Member:* Royal Horticultural Society, Garden History Society, Hardy Plant Society.

RUTH ALLISON COATES

ALICE M. COATS

someday? Why not *now*?' So I set to work with no training and no very great expectations; but by the time the book was ready to be submitted to my first publisher (who accepted it) I found it was regarded as 'a work of scholarship.' Since then I have just gone on writing books about flowers, and the people associated with them, and have abandoned painting altogether. I am happy in having found my true vocation.''

COCHRAN, Bobbye A.   1949-

PERSONAL: Born November 4, 1949, in New Albany, Ind.; daughter of John Robert (an engineer) and Sara Marie (Bobo; a secretary) Cochran. *Education:* Indiana University, 1967-69; Washington University, St. Louis, Mo., B.F.A., 1973. *Home:* 1750 North Clark St., Suite 1307, Chicago, Ill. 60614. *Agent:* John Ball and Associates, Chicago, Ill. *Office:* 625 N. Michigan Ave., Chicago, Ill. 60611.

CAREER: Frank James Productions, St. Louis, Mo., 1972-73; Stan Gellman Graphic Design, St. Louis, Mo., 1973; Creative Source Design Studio, Chicago, Ill., 1973-75. Presently a free-lance illustrator. *Exhibitions:* American Institute of Graphic Arts Traveling Exhibit, New York, N.Y., 1973; Washington University Steinberg Hall, St. Louis, Mo., 1973; Society of Illustrators (Illustrators 16), New York, N.Y., 1974; Artists' Guild of Chicago, Chicago, Ill., 1974. *Awards, honors:* American Institute of Graphic Arts award, 1973; Society of Illustrators (Illustrators 16) certificate of excellence, 1974; Artists Guild of Chicago, two awards of merit and excellence and two cash awards, 1974; Graphis Annual, 1975/76, recognition award.

ILLUSTRATOR: Howard Beek, *Concept and Statement* (chapter 7), Scott-Foresman, 1974; Beverly Bedell, *The Magic Little Ones,* Follett, 1975; *The Wonder Storybooks: Brave and Bold,* Harper, 1976; *The Tales They Tell,* Harper, 1976. Has designed book jackets for leading publishers

BOBBYE COCHRAN

WRITING: The Story of Horace (juvenile), Faber, 1938; *The Travels of Maurice* (juvenile), Faber, 1939; *Flowers and Their Histories,* Hulton, 1956, 2nd edition, McGraw, 1968; *Garden Shrubs and Their Histories,* Vista Books, 1963; *The Quest for Plants,* McGraw, 1969; *The Book of Flowers,* McGraw, 1973; *The Treasury of Flowers,* McGraw, 1975; *Lord Bute,* Shire, 1975. Contributor to gardening and horticulture journals, including *Journal of the Royal Horticultural Society, Gardener's Chronicle, Popular Gardening,* and *Garden History.*

SIDELIGHTS: ''I was given my first little garden plot when I was four years old; and ever afterwards I was an enthusiastic gardener. So when the war broke out I volunteered for the Women's Land Army, because making things grow was the only really useful thing that I knew how to do. I had already illustrated two children's books, but almost all the copies of *The Travels of Maurice* were destroyed at the binders in one of the big London blazes. So it is now very rare.

''After the war I found it difficult to get back to painting and designing. I seemed to have lost whatever talents I once possessed. One day I remarked to my mother that I would like someday to write a history of garden plants (there being, then, no books on the subject) and she replied, 'Why

and has been a frequent contributor of illustrations to *Playboy* and *Oui* Magazines.

SIDELIGHTS: "I am presently working as a free-lance illustrator in the Chicago area. I enjoy working in the advertising field, as well as publishing, for many agencies. Basic mediums I use are dyes, watercolor, pen and ink, as well as designers gouache.

"Travel experiences include a wide sampling of the United States with a forthcoming trip to Europe planned."

HOBBIES AND OTHER INTERESTS: Photography, ceramics, tennis, swimming and music.

Who made these things?
They are very good.
We will find out.
■ (From *The Magic Little Ones* by Beverly Bedell. Illustrated by Bobbye Cochran.)

ETHEL M. COMINS

COMINS, Ethel M(ae)

PERSONAL: Born May 16, in Clayton, N.Y.; daughter of Hayes and Alice (Burnham) Comins. *Education:* Attended Plattsburgh State Normal School (now State University of New York College at Plattsburgh), 1919; Syracuse University, B.S., 1930; New York University, M.S., 1936; additional study at Institute de Allende, San Miguel de Allende, Mexico. *Home:* R.F.D. 1, Steele's Point, Clayton, N.Y. 13624.

CAREER: High school teacher in Margaretville, N.Y., 1919-20, Carthage, N.Y., 1920-22, Syracuse, N.Y., 1922-30, and Queens, N.Y., 1930-61; author, artist. Evening school instructor in secretarial studies, Queens College (now of the City University of New York), 1955-61. Member of the board, and art director, Thousand Islands Museum. *Member:* National League of American Pen Women (Queens branch president, 1956-58; New York State president, 1960-62; national contest chairman, 1962-64; Sarasota branch, recording secretary, 1976-78), North Country Artists Guild, Jefferson County Historical Society, Art League of Manatee County, Thousand Islands Museum Artists (president, 1970-72), Delta Kappa Gamma.

AWARDS, HONORS—For writing: Awards from National League of American Pen Women, 1956, for play "Disqualified," 1957, for play "A Quiet Evening," and 1968, for novel *A Cloak of Pride;* Deep South Writers Conference first prizes, 1964, for play "Outdoor Art Show," 1967, for feature article, 1970, for column "Addie Barton Explores Art,"

and honorable mention, 1968, for *Cloak of Pride;* award from British Amateur Press Association, 1970, for short story. For artistic work: Awards from Tupper Lake, Jefferson County Fair, and Cranberry Lake, all 1973, Old Forge (N.Y.), 1973, 1975, and North Country Artists Guild, 1974, 1975.

WRITINGS—Young adult novels; all published by Bouregy: *The Magic School House,* 1964; *Cloth of Dreams,* 1967; *Island Castle,* 1968; *Beyond the Night,* 1969; *Her Father's Daughter,* 1970; *The Black Jade Filly,* 1971; *Mystery Island,* 1973; *Moon Goddess,* 1974.

Plays: "Disqualified" (one-act), Iowa Publishing Co.; "A Quiet Evening" (one-act), Iowa Publishing Co. Author of coloring book, "Jeffrey Donaldson's Visit to Watertown," City of Watertown (N.Y.), 1969. Also author of novel, *Cloak of Pride* as yet unpublished. Contributor of articles to *York State Tradition, Thousand Island Sun,* and *Jefferson County Historical Bulletin.*

SIDELIGHTS: "My childhood was spent on a farm on the banks of the Saint Lawrence River. I was allowed to ride horseback when I was only four years old and still recall my beloved little horse, Fanny, with affection. We owned a rowboat in which I learned to row and enjoy fishing. Swimming was another pleasure from an early age.

"My love for the Saint Lawrence River has always been a part of my life. After I left the farm to begin my career as a teacher, I always returned to the river for summer vacations. . . . I now own a home on the Saint Lawrence where I can watch the big boats move slowly by on the Seaway. A fiberglass boat equipped with a 40 h.p. motor is tied to my dock and I still enjoy fishing and swimming."

HOBBIES AND OTHER INTERESTS: International travel.

■ (From *The Black Jade Filly* by Ethel M. Comins. Illustrated by Edrien.)

He went fishing every day. ■ (From *The Little Fish That Got Away* by Bernadine Cook. Illustrated by Crockett Johnson.)

COOK, Bernadine 1924-

PERSONAL: Born September 6, 1924, in Saginaw, Mich.; daughter of Luke C. (a salesman) and Evelyn (Rand) Smith; married George Cook, Jr., October 24, 1942 (died March 22, 1964); children: George Daniel, Joan Louise (Mrs. James Hylton), Marcie Ann (Mrs. Ronald Blair), Lise Dawn (Mrs. Allen Pettyjohn), Brian Lee. *Education:* Graduate of high school in Bay City, Mich. *Religion:* Protestant. *Home:* 10625 East Garrison Rd., Durand, Mich. 48429.

CAREER: Worked at various jobs for a total of about three years prior to 1972; Saginaw County Mental Health Services, Saginaw, Mich., public information officer, 1973—.

WRITINGS: The Little Fish That Got Away, W. R. Scott, 1956; *Curious Little Kitten,* W. R. Scott, 1956; *Looking for Susie,* W. R. Scott, 1959; *If,* Little People's Press, in press.

SIDELIGHTS: "I love to travel, to meet new people, to see new places, experience new surroundings. British Columbia is a favorite spot, although I have only been there three times. Yellowstone Park both fascinates and terrifies me. At the pyramids near Mexico City I felt as though I were very close to the secret of creation. New York City was exciting. I fell in love with the friendly little chameleons in Florida. The Black Hills of Dakota were both serene and magnificent. Wyoming found a special place in my heart—the openness—the grandeur. But the Canadian Rockies, the Frasier Canyon, the Kottinay Mountains and the Shuswap River, the virgin forest of the Big Ben Highway, they all spell to me the handwork of a creator too magnificent to comprehend. And here at home, in Michigan, I find the same sense of awe just sitting on my steps on a moonlit night, smelling the woods and fields across the road, and marveling at all the stars in the universe.

"Sometimes I feel very lost and alone—and other times I feel as though I were one with all creation—the woods and field and earth and people around me.

"As to motivation for writing? I suppose an insistence to express, to release, what I hold inside."

BERNARDINE COOK

KAY COOPER

COOPER, Kay 1941-

PERSONAL: Born July 26, 1941, in Cleveland, Ohio; daughter of Jack Edwin (an engineer) and Margaret (Stevens) Cooper; married John James Watt III (a pharmacist), June 20, 1964; children: Ann Michelle, Susan Kathleen. *Education:* University of Michigan, B.A., 1963. *Politics:* Independent. *Religion:* Protestant. *Home:* 222 East Hazel Dell Lane, Springfield, Ill. 62707.

CAREER: Reporter on *Indianapolis News,* Indianapolis, Ind., 1960, *Freeport Journal-Standard,* Freeport, Ill., 1963-64, and *Springfield Sun,* Springfield, Ill., 1966-67. Lincoln Memorial Garden and Nature Center, trail guide, 1966-69, 1972—. *Member:* P.E.O., Springfield Children's Reading Round Table (president, 1976), Springfield Audubon Society, Kappa Delta.

WRITINGS: A Chipmunk's Inside-Outside World, Messner, 1973; *All About Rabbits as Pets,* Messner, 1974; *All About Goldfish as Pets,* Messner, 1976. Contributor of articles and reviews to *Journal of the Illinois State Historical Society.* Contributor of natural science articles to children and adult magazines.

WORK IN PROGRESS: Deer of the Sangamon; That Valuable Bird: The Blue Jay.

SIDELIGHTS: "Much of my appreciation for the out of doors came from living in the state of Georgia. It was here that I came to know nature. I spent many hours walking beneath the ever-changing pines. My favorite place to study was on a large rock in the middle of a quiet stream which

Now there came to the little animal a feeling of warmth from his mother's body. He snuggled against her, burying his pink, hairless body in her fur. In that moment, he squeaked softly.
■ (From *A Chipmunk's Inside-Outside World* by Kay Cooper. Illustrated by Alvin E. Staffan.)

weaved its way back and forth across the pine forest. It was on this rock that I first began to write.

"Newspaper writing was fascinating for me. I loved to write under pressure, and make deadlines. When I wrote for the *Indianapolis News* I believed that the greatest writer in the world was a particular rewrite man on the *News* staff. He could take a story over the telephone, pound it out on his typewriter, and produce a short story without any revisions!

"When I married, I became more interested in the natural world through the interests of my husband. He prompted me to write about nature. (He also is a very good proof reader!)

"When our daughters were born, I knew that I didn't want to miss watching them grow up. I gave up my newspaper job, and started to write at home. At first, I sold magazine articles. Then, one day, a magazine article became too long. I sold that script as a book.

"Since that time, I have written several books and sold most of them. When writing, I try to never take time away from my family. Therefore, most of my writing is done while the children are in school. I usually write in our study from which I can see the lake and surrounding woodland.

"My greatest joy in writing is to explain a complicated scientific concept so clearly that an elementary child can easily understand it. I compose quickly, but with a lot of revision."

HOBBIES AND OTHER INTERESTS: Sailing, swimming, rug hooking, and needlework.

CORMACK, M(argaret) Grant 1913-

PERSONAL: Born September 8, 1913, in Belfast, Ireland; daughter of William Sutherland (civil engineer) and Christina (Sinclair) Cormack. *Education:* Methodist College, student, 1927-31; Queen's University, B.A. (honors in English), 1935; University of Rennes, diplome superieur, 1937; additional study at Alliance Francaise, Paris, University of Zurich. *Politics:* Alliance Party of Northern Ireland. *Religion:* Methodist. *Home:* 13 Maryville Park, Belfast BT9 6LN, Northern Ireland. *Office:* Carolan Grammar School, Carolan Rd., Belfast BT7 3HF, Northern Ireland.

CAREER: Taught at Larne (Northern Ireland) Technical School, 1936-42, Belfast High School, Belfast, 1943-49, Methodist College, Belfast, 1949-58; Carolan Grammar School, Belfast, head of English department, 1958—. *Member:* Irish P.E.N. (secretary, 1954-59, vice-chairman, 1959-60, chairman, 1960-61, 1970-72, secretary, 1975, Belfast Centre), Ulster Society for Teachers of English (president, 1966-68), National Trust, various animal welfare societies. *Awards, honors:* James Orr Memorial challenge cup for poetry, 1939; won Drama Critic Competition, Association of Ulster Amateur Dramatic Societies, 1945; Festival of Britain Poetry Prize, awarded by city of Armagh, 1951; East Belfast Festival poetry award, 1974.

WRITINGS: Animal Tales from Ireland, Harrap, 1954, Day, 1955; *When Ireland Went to Spain,* Harrap, 1959; *How the Rabbit Took a Ride,* Meredith Press, 1962. Contributor of book reviews and literary articles to newspapers and magazines in Ireland.

M. GRANT CORMACK

CORNELL, Jeffrey 1945-
(J. Cornell)

PERSONAL: Born September 22, 1945, in Bridgeport, Conn.; son of Arthur William and Maryjo (Madaloni; a real estate broker) Cornell; married Janice C. Builter, December 31, 1966; children: Todd Jeffrey, Kelly Patterson. *Education:* Paier School of Art (majored in fine art and illustration), 1968-1972. *Home:* 114 Hillcrest Rd., Fairfield, Conn. 06430. *Agent:* Lillian Studer, J. J. DuBane, 347 Madison Ave., New York, N.Y. 10017. *Office:* 18 Reef Rd., Fairfield, Conn. 06430.

CAREER: Free-lance illustrator. Fairfield Sidewalk Art Show Committee. *Exhibitions:* Society of Illustrators, New York, N.Y., 1974, 1975. *Military service:* U.S. Air Force, sergeant, 1964-1968. *Member:* Westport Artist Association.

ILLUSTRATOR: Richard Peck, *Through a Brief Darkness,* Viking, 1973; Elizabeth Witheridge, *Just One Indian Boy,* Atheneum, 1974; *May I Cross Your Golden Bridge?,* Atheneum, 1975; Steven Rayson, *The Crows of War,* Atheneum, 1975; *Deltoid Pumpkin Seed,* Ballantine, 1975; *Tell About Someone You Love,* Macmillan, 1975; *The Way of the Tamarisk,* Dell, 1975; John P. Marquand, *The Late George Apley,* Franklin Library, 1976.

SIDELIGHTS: "I eat, sleep, and drink art. I love illustrating, it has all the elements I need to keep busy doing something all the time, so even if I don't have a job there are still hundreds of things to do relating to my illustrating. The fast pace concept and problem solving, research and pressure are what keep me happy.

"The illustrations and paintings I do for myself are done the same way, to me there is no difference. The only difference

SIDELIGHTS: "I am afraid the works are rather scanty. For almost fifteen years (from 1959), I was looking after ill and elderly parents, as well as doing my job. Most of the time I was too overtaxed and dispirited to write. Our terrible Irish troubles of the last five years also tend to make one too depressed for creative work—although I did write a regular column for the *Alliance* monthly newspaper in the early years of the Party (1970-73). Perhaps I'll get my 'second wind' yet—one never knows!

"I really cannot think of anything very interesting to say about my motivation or methods of writing. I just love Ireland and love animals, and I suppose that somewhere along the way the two coalesced! Imagination, sympathy and humor seem to me the important factors—and good style."

M. Grant Cormack speaks French and German. Her short stories, talks, and poems have been broadcast in England as well as Ireland.

HOBBIES AND OTHER INTERESTS: Literature, all things Irish (especially history, legend, folklore, Irish drama and Irish writing), animals, birds, the countryside, gardening, education, politics, art and architecture, and travel.

JEFF CORNELL

■ (From *The Crows of War* by Steven Rayson. Illustrated by Jeff Cornell.)

between illustrators and so called 'easel painters' is that illustrators find a buyer and then paint a painting while the easel painter does the painting then finds a buyer.

"My paintings are done in mixed mediums. I find it more fun. I have to constantly solve new problems and I think people enjoy looking at them more. It makes people think—ask questions—'What's that? How did he do that?' I love this.

"I try to take any job on to solve the concept and research problems. Asking questions and going to the library are really enjoyable—of course I also enjoy the painting. Taking all the elements and putting them together in a good design—that's terrific!

"My wife, my two children and myself don't travel too much. Every summer, my wife and I drive to Chatham on Cape Cod for a week and during the winter to Vermont for a few quiet weekends. We have an interesting house and spend most of our time at home with friends.

"Someday I'd like to teach illustration, perhaps one day a week. I find the younger kids so interesting—I think I would get more out of the students than the students would out of me. It would be great if I could just pull their thoughts and feelings out and help them put it on paper. I love to try and motivate people. The few times I have taught, I know I have done just that.

"When I was a third-year student I had the pleasure of meeting three of the great illustrators: Bernie Fuchs, Mark English and Bob Heindel. These three helped me so much; they motivated and encouraged me and treated me as an equal. I owe them tremendous thanks and I hope that I can do the same for some youngster who is trying to get into illustration."

CRANE, Caroline   1930-

PERSONAL: Born October 30, 1930, in Chicago, Ill.; daughter of Roger Alan (a foundation executive) and Jessie Louise (a social worker; maiden name, Taft) Crane; married Yoshio Kiyabu (now a travel agent), July 11, 1959; children: Crane Ryo, Laurel Rei. *Education:* Bennington College, A.B., 1952; Columbia University, graduate study at Russian Institute, 1952-53. *Home:* 317 West 93rd St., New York, N.Y. 10025. *Agent:* Muriel Fuller, P.O. Box 193, Grand Central Station, New York, N.Y. 10017.

CAREER: U.S. Committee for United Nations Children's Fund, New York, N.Y., writer, 1957-60; author of books for young people. *Member:* Authors Guild of Authors League of America.

WRITINGS: Pink Sky at Night, Doubleday, 1963; *Lights Down the River,* Doubleday, 1964; *A Girl Like Tracy,* McKay, 1966; *Wedding Song,* McKay, 1967; *Don't Look at Me that Way,* Random House, 1970; *Stranger on the Road,* Random House, 1971.

WORK IN PROGRESS: Young adult novel *The Silver Prison;* an adult novel and two adult mysteries; adult nonfiction, *The Palestinian Experience,* based on taped interviews with a minimum of commentary.

CAROLINE CRANE

SIDELIGHTS: "From the age of ten, it was my burning ambition to be an actress. This, indirectly—and fortunately—led me into writing. As a child, the only way I could act, outside of school plays, was by organizing my friends into a drama group. The only way I could find parts I really liked was to write the plays myself. This group was active for several years during World War II. We were non-profit, of course, taking in contributions to cover our expenses and donating the rest to the Red Cross, Bundles for Britain, and other wartime causes. When the war ended, our group 'adopted' a French orphan and supported her with the proceeds from our performances.

"All that time I had no thought of writing, except as it furthered my acting ambitions. At age thirteen, when the war was still in progress, I wrote a novel about the Nazi occupation of Norway. I expected to sell it to Hollywood and play the lead in the film version. As it happened, Hollywood never saw it, nor did anyone else, except my parents and my English teacher. The latter described it as 'a little far-fetched.'

"Still stagestruck, I entered college and majored in drama, with a minor in Russian language and literature. After three years of touring with the college group and acting in summer stock, I decided I was really not meant for show business, and finished college with an emphasis on Russian studies. However, my interest and background in the theater provided the material for my first two books, *Pink Sky at Night* and *Lights Down the River.* With these somewhat autobiographical novels out of the way, I launched into 'problem' stories. My third book, *A Girl Like Tracy,* was sparked by a true family situation described to me by my mother, who was then a social caseworker. A scene in that book gave me the idea for my fourth novel, *Wedding Song.* My fifth book was inspired by the neighborhood in which I live, and my sixth by a dream I once had.

"This is the stuff on which stories are made: one tiny idea that takes hold and grows into a whole world, an enchanted landscape. It is these other worlds and their people which, in turn, catch hold of me, and I can't do anything but write. For that same reason, I have never cared much for writing short stories. If I am interested enough in a set of characters or a situation to write about them at all, I want to do a novel, and stay with them for a good long time."

HOBBIES AND OTHER INTERESTS: The ancient history and archaeology of Asia and Africa; dogs, animal welfare.

CRONBACH, Abraham   1882-1965

PERSONAL: Born February 16, 1882, in Indianapolis, Ind.; married Rose Hentel, 1917; children: Marion Davis. *Education:* University of Cincinnati, B.A., 1902; Hebrew Union College, rabbi, 1906; University of Cambridge, student, 1911-12; University of Berlin, student, 1912; Lehramstalt, student, 1912. *Home:* 3098 Riddle View Lane, Cincinnati, Ohio.

CAREER: Temple Beth-El, South Bend, Ind., rabbi, 1906-15; Free Synagogue, New York, N.Y., assistant rabbi, 1915-17; Temple Israel, Akron, Ohio, rabbi, 1917-19; Chicago Federation of Synagogues, Chicago, Ill., chaplain, 1919-22; Hebrew Union College, Cincinnati, Ohio, professor, 1922-50. *Hebrew Union College Annual,* Cincinnati, Ohio, secretary, 1939-65. Frequent lecturer. *Member:* American Association of Social Workers, Central Conference of American Rabbis, American Sociological Society, Alpha Kappa Delta, Phi Beta Kappa, Social Workers Club, Jewish Peace Fellowship, American Council for Judaism, Cosmic Club. *Awards, honors:* Social Justice Award, Religion and Labor Foundation.

WRITINGS: Prayers of the Jewish Advance, Block, 1924; *Jewish Peace Book,* Union of American Hebrew Congregations, 1932; *Religion and Its Social Setting,* Sinai Press, 1933; *The Quest for Peace,* Sinai Press, 1934, J. S. Ozer, 1972; *The Bible and Our Social Outlook,* Social Press, 1941; *Judaism for Today,* Bookman Associates, 1954; *The Prophets: Our Concurrence and Our Dissent,* Hebrew Union College Press, 1956; *Realities of Religion,* Bookman Associates, 1957; *Autobiography,* Hebrew Union College Archives, 1959; *Stories Made of Bible Stories,* Bookman Associates, 1961; *Reform Movements in Judaism,* Bookman Associates, 1963; *Unmeant Meanings of Scripture,* Hebrew Union College Press, 1965. Numerous articles for pamphlets, periodicals and collections.

(Died April 2, 1965)

CROUT, George C(lement)   1917-

PERSONAL: Born February 10, 1917, in Middletown, Ohio; son of Ebert (a policeman) and Myrtle M. (a teacher; maiden name, Williamson) Crout. *Education:* Miami University, Oxford, Ohio, B.S., 1938, M.A., 1941, M.E., 1948, Specialist in Ed., 1955; further graduate study at Bowling Green University, 1962, Appalachian State University, 1963, University of Michigan, 1964, and George Peabody College for Teachers, 1965. *Politics:* Independent. *Religion:* Methodist. *Home:* 48-A Miami Dr., Monroe, Ohio 45050.

CAREER: Middletown (Ohio) public schools, teacher, 1938-42, 1946-48, principal of elementary schools, 1948-75; presently newspaper columnist, author and lecturer. Miami University, Oxford, Ohio, instructor in Evening College, 1946-47. *Military service:* U.S. Army Air Forces, 1942-45; served in Pacific theater; became staff sergeant; received six battle stars. *Member:* National Education Association, National Association of Elementary School Principals, Ohio Education Association, Ohio Department of Elementary School Principals, Ohio Historical Society, Canal Society of Ohio, Butler County Historical Society, Middletown Historical Society (trustee), Phi Beta Kappa, American Legion. *Awards, honors:* American Educators Medal of Freedoms Foundation.

WRITINGS—Children's books, except as noted: (With illustrator Herbert W. Fall) *Stories of Our School Community,* Perry Printing Co., 1960, 4th edition, 1970; Wilfred D. Vorhis, editor, *Middletown U.S.A.: All American City* (adult), Perry Printing Co., 1960; (with Edith McCall) *Where the Ohio Flows,* Benefic, 1960; *Ohio Caravan* (poems), Perry Printing Co., 1961; *Seven Lives of Johnny B. Free,* Denison, 1961; *Middletown Diary* (adult), privately

GEORGE C. CROUT

"The kitchen in the old farmhouse—the scene of many a romp, marble game, nutcracking and taffy making, and tricks on dogs and cats." ■ (From *Lucky Cloverleaf of the 4-H* by George Crout. Illustrated by A. B. Graham.)

printed, 1965; *Lincoln's Littlest Soldier,* Denison, 1969; *Lucky Cloverleaf of the 4-H,* Denison, 1971; (with McCall) *You and Ohio,* Benefic, 1971; *Middletown Landmarks,* Perry Printing Co., 1974; *You and Dayton,* News Publishing Co., 1976.

Plays for children: *Do It Yourself Christmas Plays,* Eldridge Publishing Co., 1960; *Little Star Lost,* Eldridge Publishing Co., 1960; *The Tinsel Fairy,* Eldridge Publishing Co., 1964; *Santa's Christmas Satellite,* Eldridge Publishing Co., 1970. Contributor to journals and newspapers.

WORK IN PROGRESS: Miami Valley Vignettes; Ohio: Its People and Cultures.

SIDELIGHTS: "One rainy afternoon, when a very young boy visiting my grandparents, I sneaked up the dusty winding staircase that led to a large half-lighted attic. After listening to the rain on the slate roof above and exploring the attic from end to end, I noted in one corner a large, wooden chest.

"It was close to a small window. Carefully I opened it, and discovered a series of compartments, which were, in fact, filled with family keepsakes. There were two old Bibles with family records, deeds to the family homestead dating back to 1816, numerous picture albums, including many tintypes and various other relics such as great-grandfather's powder horn. Other chests were filled with home-made quilts, outdated clothes, and various pieces of furniture from past generations. When I went back downstairs covered with the telltale black dust of the attic, grandmother told me that the big chest had been brought by her forefathers all the way from England. Once having discovered the attic, I made many more trips up those steps.

"Then to add to my interest in the past, my own birth had taken place at the old homestead, my grandparents having built a new house leaving the old home to my parents. It had originally been a log house, with many additions and new weather boarding, but I could say that I was born in a log cabin.

"My other grandparents (I was fortunate enough to have known all four), lived in a rambling old farmhouse surrounded by barns and sheds. These, too, were filled with reminders of pioneer times—discarded hand-made furniture, wooden tools, and antiquated farm implements.

"These early experiences turned my interests to history. In the textbooks on my state, I try to bring the past back for young people to enjoy. Other books with Midwest backgrounds recall stories and events of other times.

"Each book is written with some purpose in mind. It is planned so as to give the reader some ideas in handling a problem which he might face. Each book or play is based upon some personal experience of some part of my life. In the case of *Lincoln's Littlest Soldier* we explore attitudes toward war—most boys have had to face up to this problem through the years. Being a soldier in World War II gave me background for this story. *Lucky Cloverleaf* contains material based upon the years spent on an Ohio farm.

"Since I have spent my life as a schoolmaster, children read and comment on the manuscripts before publication."

HOBBIES AND OTHER INTERESTS: Gardening, lecturing, collecting historical items.

CRUMP, Fred H., Jr. 1931-

PERSONAL: Born June 7, 1931, in Houston, Tex.; son of Fred H. and Carol Crump. *Education:* Sam Houston State Teachers College, B.S., 1953, M.S., 1961. *Home:* 94 Santa Anita, Rancho Mirage, Calif. 92270.

CAREER: Formerly junior high school art teacher in Orange, Tex., in Palm Springs, Calif., 1960—. Illustrator of children's books.

WRITINGS—Self-illustrated: *Marigold and the Dragon,* Steck, 1964; *The Teeny Weeny Genie,* Steck, 1966. Contributor to *Playmate* magazine.

Illustrator, all written by Garry and Vesta Smith and published by Steck, unless otherwise noted: *Creepy Caterpillar,* 1961, *Flagon the Dragon,* 1962, *Mitzi,* 1963, *Jumping Julius,* 1964, *Leander Lion,* 1966, *Florabelle,* 1968, *Clickety Cricket,* 1969, *Poco,* Blaine-Ethridge, 1975.

WORK IN PROGRESS: Presently working on a bi-lingual book set in Mexico.

SIDELIGHTS: "I'm still teaching junior high art in Palm Springs, California, and still spending the summers doing work for children's publications. An ideal arrangement. And between bouts of 'loafing' and reading and taking long rides and going to movies, I get some drawing and writing done."

FRED H. CRUMP, JR.

. . .chubby fairies do not float too well without magic.
■ (From *Marigold and the Dragon* by Fred H. Crump. Illustrated by the author.)

CUNLIFFE, John Arthur 1933-

PERSONAL: Born June 16, 1933, in Colne, England; married Sylvia Thompson (a musician); children: Julian Edward. *Education:* North-Western Polytechnic, fellow of library association, 1957; Charlotte Mason College, teaching qualification, 1975. *Home:* 32 Greenside, Kendal, Cumbria LA9 4LD, England. *Agent:* A. P. Watt & Son, 26-28 Bedford Row, London WC1R 4HL, England. *Office:* Castle Park School, Kendal, Cumbria LA9 4LD, England.

CAREER: Castle Park School, Kendal, England, librarian and teacher. *Member:* Society of Authors, National Union of Teachers.

WRITINGS—For children: *Farmer Barnes Buys a Pig,* Deutsch, 1964, Lion Press, 1969; *Farmer Barnes and Bluebell,* Deutsch, 1966; *Farmer Barnes at the County Show,* Deutsch, 1966, published in the United States as *Farmer Barnes at the County Fair,* Lion Press, 1970; *The Adventures of Lord Pip,* Deutsch, 1970; *Farmer Barnes and the Goats,* Deutsch, 1971; *The Giant Who Stole the World,* Deutsch, 1971; *Riddles and Rhymes and Rigmaroles,* Deutsch, 1971; *The Giant Who Swallowed the Wind,* Deutsch, 1972; *Farmer Barnes Goes Fishing,* Deutsch, 1972; *The Story of Giant Kippernose,* Deutsch, 1972; *The Great Dragon Competition,* Deutsch, 1973; *The King's Birthday Cake,* Deutsch, 1973; *Small Monkey Tales,* Deutsch, 1974; *Farmer Barnes and the Snow Picnic,* Deutsch, 1974; *The Farmer, the Rooks, and the Cherry Tree,* Deutsch, 1975; *Giant Brog and the Motorway,* Deutsch, 1975; *Farmer Barnes Fells a Tree,* Deutsch, in press. Contributor to *Children's Book Review.*

SIDELIGHTS: "It's a great privilege to write for children—the most avid, attentive, and enthusiastic audience anywhere in the world. Only the best writing is good enough for them."

FOR MORE INFORMATION SEE: Library Journal, May 15, 1969; *Times Literary Supplement,* December 6, 1974.

JOHN ARTHUR CUNLIFFE

CUNNINGHAM, Dale S(peers) 1932-

PERSONAL: Born May 27, 1932, in Elmira, N.Y.; son of Arthur G. and Aletha (Speers) Cunningham. *Education:* Hamilton College, A.B., 1954; graduate study at Sorbonne, University of Paris, 1954, and Johann Wolfgang Goethe-Universitat, 1954-55; Columbia University, A.M., 1959; graduate study at Bryn Mawr College, 1962-65, and at Princeton University. *Address:* Box 401, Main Office, Camden, N.J. 08101.

CAREER: Renssalaer Polytechnic Institute, Troy, N.Y., instructor in English and German, 1960-61; Rutgers University, Camden Campus, Camden, N.J., instructor in German, 1961-65; Smith, Kline & French Laboratories, Philadelphia, Pa., medical writer, 1965; Uniworld Languages, Philadelphia, Pa., translations director, 1965-73, president, 1973—. Editor, translator, and translations consultant. *Member:* Modern Language Association of America, American Translators Association (secretary, 1963-64; director, 1965-69; president, 1969-71), American Association of University Professors, Delaware Valley Translators Association (vice-chairman, 1962-63; chairman, 1963-64), P.E.N., Bund Deutscher Uebersetzer, Verband Deutscher Uebersetzer (honorary), Chambre Belge des Traducteurs (honorary). *Awards, honors:* Fulbright assistantship in Germany, 1954-55.

WRITINGS: Pioneers in Science, Sterling, 1962; *Picture Book of Music and Its Makers,* Sterling, 1963.

Translator and adapter: (With Margrete Cunningham) Walter Sperling, *How to Make Things out of Paper,* Sterling, 1961; (with Margrete Cunningham) Gerhard Gollwitzer, *The Joy of Drawing,* Sterling, 1961; Bruno Knobel, *Camping-Out Ideas and Activities,* Sterling, 1961; Gerhard Gollwitzer, *Abstract Art,* Sterling, 1962; Harald Doering, *A Bee is Born,* Sterling, 1962; (with Marianne Das) Dieter Krauter, *Experimenting with the Microscope,* Sterling, 1963; (with Ida H. Washington) Rudolf Dittrich, *Juggling,* Sterling, 1963; Rudolf Dittrich, *Tricks and Games for Children,* Sterling, 1964.

Contributor of articles, translations, and notes to learned journals, including *Meta.* Former contributing editor, *Babel.*

WORK IN PROGRESS: Die Welt von heute, an intermediate German reader, for Houghton; several translations; research in the history and theory of translation.

SIDELIGHTS: "*Pioneers in Science* is the result of my teaching experience at a technical institute at the time C. P. Snow's little book on *The Two Cultures* was published. My publisher wanted a book on scientists for a series he was doing; and the idea appealed very much to me.

"Several hundred hours went into the research, and if the book has a moral, it is that there was no great split between the scientists and humanists (at least until early in the nineteenth century) and that the leaders in science through the time of Einstein were men with broad ranges of interest not concerned with very narrow specialization in a particular branch of science or the humanities.

This swarm landed on my garden swing, probably because the old queen found flight too difficult and had to land on the first available spot. ■ (From *A Bee Is Born* by Harald Doering. Translated and adapted by Dale S. Cunningham.)

"*Pioneers in Science* is written so that it can be understood by people in their early teens. Of course, this meant that many complicated scientific ideas had to be oversimplified.

"A second book written for the same series, *Music and its Makers,* was also intended to be a first book for young people who wish to know something about music from the beginnings up to the twentieth century. Like *Pioneers in Science,* this book attempts to present a clear factual idea about what the individuals achieved in their work as well as glimpses of them as people.

"Both these books are profusely illustrated, and hunting down pictures that were not usual in this sort of book was an interesting by-product of the writing. The effort was particularly successful in *Pioneers in Science,* which contains authentic reproductions from scientist's books printed centuries ago as well as previously unpublished photographs of Einstein and Max Planck."

DANIELS, Guy 1919-

PERSONAL: Born May 11, 1919, in Gilmore City, Iowa; son of Guy Emmett (a gentleman farmer) and Gretchen (Van Alstine) Daniels; married Margaret Holbrook (now a teacher), November 14, 1943; married second wife, Anne McCrea, January 13, 1963; married third wife, Vernell Groom, December 2, 1967; children: (first marriage) Brooke (Mrs. Donald Hinrichsen); (second marriage) Matthew; (third marriage) Guy III. *Education:* University of Iowa, B.A., 1941, graduate student, 1941-42. *Home and office:* 416 East 65th St., New York, N.Y. 10021. *Agent:* Gunther Stuhlmann, 65 Irving Pl., New York, N.Y. 10003.

CAREER: Trans-World Airlines, International Division, chief language instructor at Training School, Reading, Pa., and Newark, Del., 1946-47; U.S. Government, Washington, D.C., "petty bureaucrat," 1947-52; full-time writer and translator, 1952—. *Military service:* U.S. Navy, 1942-45; became lieutenant junior grade; received combat star. *Member:* Authors Guild, P.E.N., Phi Beta Kappa.

WRITINGS: Poems and Translations, Inferno Press, 1959; *Progress, U.S.A.* (novel), Macmillan, 1968.

Translations: Erich Auerbach, *An Introduction to Romance Languages and Literature,* Putnam, 1961; Stendhal, *Racine and Shakespeare,* Crowell-Collier, 1962; *A Lermontov Reader,* Macmillan, 1965; *Fifteen Fables of Krylov* (juvenile), Macmillan, 1965; *Ivan the Fool, and Other Tales of Leo Tolstoy* (juvenile), Macmillan, 1966; *The Tsar's Riddles* (juvenile), McGraw, 1967; Nikolai Leskov, *The Wild Beast* (juvenile), Funk, 1968; *The Complete Plays of Vladimir Mayakovsky,* Washington Square, 1968; Mikhalkov, *Let's Fight, and Other Russian Fables* (juvenile), Pantheon, 1968; *The Falcon under the Hat: Favorite Russian Merry Tales and Fairy Tales* (juvenile), Funk, 1969.

Russian Comic Fiction, New American Library, 1970; Ivan Bunin, *Velga* (juvenile), S. G. Phillips, 1970; Mayakovsky, *Timothy's Horse* (juvenile), Pantheon, 1970; *Foma the Terrible* (juvenile), Delacorte, 1970; Andre Castelot, *Napoleon,* Harper, 1971; Yevgeny Riabchikov, *Russians in Space,* Doubleday, 1971; Chekhov, *The Wolf and the Mutt* (juve-

nile), McGraw-Hill, 1971; *The Peasant's Pea Patch* (juvenile), Delacorte, 1971; Colette Portal, *The Beauty of Birth* (juvenile), Pantheon, 1971; Pierre Louys, *Mimes des Courtisanes,* Cercle des Editions Privées, 1973; Honoré de Balzac, *The Unknown Masterpiece,* Cercle des Editions Privées, 1973; Henry de Montherlant, *Pasiphae,* Cercle des Editions Privées, 1973; Valery Chalidze, *To Defend These Rights,* Random House, 1974; Andrei Sakharov, *My Country and the World,* Knopf, 1975; Roy Medvedev, *A History of the Civil War on the Don,* Knopf, in press; Sergei Prokofiev, *The Autobiography of Sergei Prokofiev,* Doubleday, in press; André Bazin, *The Cinema of Cruelty,* The Third Press, in press; (in collaboration with the composer, Joseph Roff) *Three Russian Folk Songs,* Carl Fischer, Inc., in press; S. M. Shtemenko, *Army in the Last 100 Days of World War II,* Doubleday, in press; A. Demidov, *The Russian Ballet,* Doubleday, in press.

Contributor of original poetry, fiction, and articles to anthologies and periodicals, including *New Republic, Nations, New Directions, Kenyon Review,* and *Beloit Poetry Journal;* translations of poetry, fiction, and essays have also appeared in anthologies, *New Republic, Playboy, Vogue,* and elsewhere. Associate editor, *Trace* (magazine), 1956-58; member of advisory board, *Soviet Studies in Literature.*

WORK IN PROGRESS: Translation of Valentin Rasputin's *Live and Remember,* for Macmillan.

SIDELIGHTS: "Rather deeply involved in 'classical' (i.e., largely nineteenth-century) Russian authors, especially the poets. Am getting mired down in this vast bog to the detriment of my poetry (abandoned) and fiction (lately resumed with a vengeance)." In addition to translating ability in Russian and French, Guy Daniels has some competence in Spanish and Italian.

GUY DANIELS

They started flapping their wings, and the whole flock rose into the air. Up, up they flew, high into the sky, with the peasant, the cart, and the horse trailing along behind them. ■ (From *The Peasant's Pea Patch* translated by Guy Daniels. Illustrated by Robert Quackenbush.)

DAVELUY, Paule Cloutier 1919-

PERSONAL: Born April 6, 1919, in Ville-Marie, Temiscamingue, Quebec, Canada; daughter of Philippe and Gabrielle (Guay) Cloutier; married Andre Daveluy (a writer), June 26, 1944; children: Danielle, Sylviane, Pierre, Brigitte, Marie-Claude, Andre, Jr. *Education:* Studied at Pensionnat Mont-Royal, Bon Conseil Institute, and University of Montreal. *Politics:* "French-Canadian, so: a touch of nationalism." *Religion:* Roman Catholic. *Home:* 12062 Saint-Germain Blvd., Montreal H4J 2A5, Quebec, Canada.

CAREER: Secretary to Andre Daveluy before marriage, and still his secretary at home. Member of board of directors, Editions Jeunesse (publishers). *Member:* La Societe des Ecrivains Canadiens, Communications-jeunesse (president, 1970-73, member of board of directors, 1973—), Federation des Unions de Familles. *Awards, honors: L'Ete Enchante* received Prix du roman of the Canadian Association of Educators in the French Language, medal of Canadian Library Association as best children's book of the year, and the English translation, *Summer in Ville-Marie* was included on the *New York Times* list of the hundred best books for children, 1962; *Drole d'Automne* received the Prix du Salon du Livre and medal of Canadian Library Association, 1962; *Cet Liver-la* received the Quebec Literary award, 1968; La Societe des Ecrivains Canadiens prize for the whole of her writings for young people.

WRITINGS: Les Guinois, L'Atelier, 1957; *Cherie Martin* (novel), L'Atelier, 1957; *L'Ete enchante* (novel for teen-agers), L'Atelier, 1958 (translation by Monroe Stearns published in America as *Summer in Ville-Marie,* Holt, 1962); *Drole d'Automne* (novel for teen-agers), Le Pelican, 1962; *Sylvette et les adultes* (novel for teen-agers), Editions Jeunesse, 1962; *Sylvette sous la tente bleue,* Editions Jeunesse, 1964; *Cinq Filles Compliques,* Editions Jeunesse, 1965; *Cet Liver-la,* Editions Jeunesse, 1967; (translator into French with husband) *Complete Do-It-Yourself Manual,* Reader's Digest, 1974; (translator) *Guide de la Conture Bratique et creative,* Reader's Digest, 1975; (translator into French) Elizabeth Yates, *Pipe Paddle and Song,* Editions Heritage, 1976. Contributor to French-Canadian newspapers, magazines, radio, and television.

SIDELIGHTS: "In September 1970 together with librarians, authors, illustrators, etc. I founded, an association dedicated to the interests of French Canadian literature for children: *Communication-Jeunesse.* I was president of this association for two-and-one-half years and am now, by choice, a member of the board of directors. This association has published, up to now, two brochures of biography and bibliography of French-Canadian authors for young people and a book (*Creation culturelle pour la jeunesse*) and is actually very active in its field organizing conferences, colloquies, exhibits, etc. It fills a void in French Quebec, children have been used to reading books published in France and Belgium. Now they are encouraged to read books intended

PAULE CLOUTIER DAVELUY

especially for them. Although *Communication-Jeunesse* has met with difficulties, it still alerts people to the particular problems of this field of publication."

Paule Daveluy is one of the few authors writing for French-Canadian teenagers. The lack of books for this category of youth, she feels "makes patriotism and the search of an identity a difficult affair for young people quartered between two countries."

FOR MORE INFORMATION SEE: Montreal Gazette, November 22, 1962; *La Presse,* November 22, 1962; *Profiles,* Canadian Library Association, 1975; Louise Lemieux, *Plein's feux sur la litterature de jeunesse au Canada francais,* Lemeac, 1972.

DAWSON, Mary 1919-

PERSONAL: Born September 13, 1919, in Kent, England; daughter of William Harbutt (an author) and Else (Munsterberg) Dawson; married John Blackett Jeffries (a psychiatrist), August 22, 1944 (died January, 1963); children: Pamela Orr, Timothy, Dougal, Rosalind. *Education:* Attended Headington School, Oxford, England, 1927-36; trained as state registered nurse, Oxford, England, 1940-44. *Religion:* Church of England. *Home:* Lothlorien, 1, Woodshears Drive, Malvern, Worcestershire, England.

CAREER: Author and free-lance writer. Justice of the Peace since 1971. *Member:* Malvern Writers' Circle (chairman, twice), Malvern Musical Society, Magistrates' Association.

WRITINGS: Tecwyn, the Last of the Welsh Dragons, Parents' Magazine Press, 1967; *How Do You Do* (textbook), Schoningh [West Germany], 1972; *Tinker Tales,* Parents' Magazine Press, 1973. Contributor to *Humpty Dumpty, Jack and Jill, Christian Science Monitor, American Nursing Journal, Denver Post* and other magazines. Several poems set to music, published by Banks, Thames Publishing. Also published in *Punch, Homes and Gardens, The Lady,* medical journals and others.

WORK IN PROGRESS: Sequel to *Tecwyn;* anthology of poems for juveniles; an autobiography.

SIDELIGHTS: "I have written and told stories for as long as I can remember; and read my first broadcast story in 1959. When my husband died I decided to give myself six months to try to make this my job. Fortunately I began to sell my work, and although I did not manage to keep my family by my writing alone, I felt I could make this my work. Each year the work has extended, and this year some poems of mine, set to music as a song-cycle, were performed at our Three Choirs Festival in Worcester. Also some songs and carols have been set and published. Scripts for *Woman's Hour* are currently at the British Broadcasting Company—written after a memorable visit of six weeks to California this summer. During that time I made a special visit to Grand Canyon for some atmosphere for the sequel to *Tecwyn,* now underway.

"I have eight grandchildren, and frequent visitors of all ages. A 'grasshopper' mind, like mine, can be a nuisance, as I am frequently interrupted by new ideas; but it serves me well, and keeps me busy. Another of my interests is work in the

MARY DAWSON

"Whatever is it?" shrieked Mrs. Morgan stepping backwards into the laundry basket. ■ (From *Tecwyn: The Last of the Welsh Dragons* by Mary Dawson. Illustrated by Ingrid Fetz.)

juvenile area of our Court; and I sit on both the adult and juvenile Bench with my colleague magistrates. Fortunately my writing thrives under pressure, and there is plenty of it at all times. Recently I have written a new guide to our fine Malvern Priory—a new type of writing for me.

"As to what I write? I write for myself and then find out where this fits in in the realm of publishing. My poems arrive—often at most inconvenient times—and have to be written down. If I sell them that is an added bonus; better still if a composer wishes to set them to music. Writing is a hard job, make no mistake; but there is nothing I would rather do."

de BANKE, Cecile   1889-1965

PERSONAL: Born August 12, 1889, in London, England. *Education:* Educated in England. *Home:* 25 Cottage St., Wellesley, Mass. 02181. *Agent:* Laurence Pollinger Ltd., 18 Maddox St., Mayfair, London W. 1, England.

CAREER: Left England in 1915 to join a repertory company in South Africa, where she later had her own school of speech and drama and directed the Cape Town Repertory Theatre; came to United States in 1930 and taught at Wellesley College, Wellesley, Mass., 1932-55, became associate professor of speech and drama. Lecturer and writer; speech therapist at various times at Cushing Veterans Administration Hospital, Framingham, Mass., at Neurological Clinic, Massachusetts General Hospital, Boston, and Bellevue Rehabilitation Center, New York, N.Y. *Member:* English-Speaking Union.

WRITINGS: The Art of Choral Speaking, Baker Co., 1937; *The A.B.C. of Speech Sounds,* Baker Co., 1942; *Shakespearean Stage Production: Then and Now,* McGraw, 1953; *Hand over Hand: An Autobiography* (years in England), Hutchinson, 1957; *Bright Weft* (autobiography; years in South Africa), Hutchinson, 1958; *Tabby Magic* (juvenile), Hutchinson, 1959; *American Plaid* (autobiography; years in America), Hutchinson, 1961; *More Tabby Magic* (juvenile), Hutchinson, 1961. Author of four booklets on choral

speaking published by Baker Co., 1942-47. Contributor to *Shakespeare Quarterly, Queen's Quarterly,* and other literary journals.

FOR MORE INFORMATION SEE: Cecil de Banke, *Hand over Hand,* Hutchinson, 1957, *Bright Weft,* Hutchinson, 1958, *American Plaid,* Hutchinson, 1961.

(Died January 2, 1965)

DE LAGE, Ida   1918-

PERSONAL: Born July 16, 1918, in New York, N.Y.; daughter of Joseph Patrick (a teacher) and Mary Catherine (Sheridan) McCourt; married Maurice Francois De Lage (a papermaker), June 9, 1946; children: Patrick Joseph, Marie Louise. *Education:* Attended New York State Teachers College (now State University of New York College at New Paltz). *Home:* 253 Edison St., Clifton, N.Y. 07013.

CAREER: Writer for children.

WRITINGS—Juvenile; all published by Garrard: *The Farmer and the Witch,* 1966; *Weeny Witch,* 1968; *The Witchy Broom,* 1969; *The Old Witch Goes to the Ball,* 1969; *The Old Witch and the Snores,* 1970; *What Does a Witch Need?,* 1971; *Hello, Come In,* 1971; *Beware! Beware! A Witch Won't Share,* 1972; *Pink, Pink,* 1973; *The Old Witch and the Wizard,* 1974; *Good Morning Lady,* 1974; *A Bunny Ride,* 1975; *The Witches Party,* 1976.

SIDELIGHTS: "It was Halloween night, 1928. For children growing up in the valleys of the Taconic foothills of the Berkshires, rich in folklore, this was a night of wonderful, scary fun. Even the most timid child was allowed out after supper to brave the dark on this magical night. Shaky courage was bolstered with a winking jack-o-lantern. Behind each bush and tree a witch or a ghost might be lurking. At any moment the old witch who lived up on the hill (hadn't we seen her cave and the remnants of her fire?) might come swooping down from the sky on her broom, shrieking and cackling and liberally casting her terrible spells from her jug of magic brew.

"Oh, Mother Bunny!
Please give us a ride."
"No, no, no, little bunnies.
Baby bunnies hop.
They do not ride.
■ (From *A Bunny Ride* by Ida DeLage. Illustrated by Tracy McVay.)

"That old witch lives on for today's children in some of my Halloween stories. She is perpetually busy with her tricks and problems and is always cooking up her magical brew to scatter her devastating spells, just for witchy fun. Occasionally the old witch herself calls on classrooms at Halloween time, with her cackles and basket of rubber snakes and lizards and big, wiggly spiders.

"Some of my stories are characterized by the small woodland animals so beloved by children. The great pleasure of all my writing for children is in providing invitational supplementary reading for primary grades. How gratifying to READ a book all by yourself, as those newly learned magical letters fall into place with meaning! An appetite for reading is established immediately with the introduction of the written word. If the experience is attainable and joyful in primary grades, the pattern follows on through a lifetime. For books don't end with school. Books are a pleasure forever."

de PAOLA, Thomas Anthony 1934-(Tomie de Paola)

PERSONAL: Born September 15, 1934, in Meriden, Conn.; son of Joseph N. (a union official) and Florence (Downey) de Paola. *Education:* Pratt Institute, B.F.A., 1956; California College of Arts and Crafts, M.F.A., 1969; Lone Mountain College, doctoral equivalency, 1970. *Residence:* Wilmot Flat, N.H. *Agent:* Florence Alexander, 50 East 42nd St., New York, N.Y. 10017.

CAREER: Professional artist and designer, 1956—; teacher of art; writer and illustrator of juvenile books. Newton Col-

IDA DE LAGE

"Why will Nana Upstairs fall out?" Tommy asked.
"Because she is ninety-four years old," Nana Downstairs said.
"I'm four years old." Tommy said.
"Tie me in a chair too!"
■ (From *Nana Upstairs and Nana Downstairs* by Tomie de Paola. Illustrated by the author.)

lege of the Sacred Heart, Newton, Mass., instructor, 1962-63, assistant professor of art, 1963-66; San Francisco College for Women (now Lone Mountain College), San Francisco, Calif., assistant professor of art, 1967-70; Chamberlayne Junior College, Boston, Mass., instructor in art, 1972-73; Colby–Sawyer College, New London, N.H., associate professor, designer, and technical director in theater department, 1973-76; New England College, Henniker, N.H., associate professor, 1976—. Painter and muralist, with many of his works done for Catholic churches and monastaries in

New England; designer of theater and nightclub sets; work exhibited in eight one-man shows since 1961 and in group shows.

AWARDS, HONORS: Awards for typography and illustration, Boston Art Directors' Club, 1968; Silver Award of Franklin Typographers (New York), 1969; two books included in American Institute of Graphic Arts exhibit of outstanding children's books, *The Journey of the Kiss*, 1970, and *Who Needs Holes?*, 1973; *Andy, That's My Name* was

THOMAS de PAOLA

included in *School Library Journal*'s list of best picture books of 1973 and *Charlie Needs a Cloak*, 1974; *Charlie Needs a Cloak* also was a Children's Book Showcase title, 1975. Friends of American Writers Award as best illustrator of a children's book, 1973, and Children's Book Showcase title, 1973, for *Authorized Autumn Charts of the Upper Red Canoe River Country; Strega Nona* was a Caldecott Honor Book, 1976.

WRITINGS—All under name Tomie de Paola; all self-illustrated: *The Wonderful Dragon of Timlin*, Bobbs-Merrill, 1966; *Fight the Night*, Lippincott, 1968; *Joe and the Snow*, Hawthorn, 1968; *Parker Pig, Esquire*, Hawthorn, 1969; *The Journey of the Kiss*, Hawthorn, 1970; *The Monsters' Ball*, Hawthorn, 1970; *The Wind and the Sun*, Ginn, 1972; *Nana Upstairs, Nana Downstairs*, Putnam, 1973; *Andy, That's My Name*, Prentice-Hall, 1973; *Charlie Needs a Cloak* (Junior Literary Guild selection; ALA notable book), Prentice-Hall, 1973; *The Unicorn and the Moon*, Ginn, 1973; *Watch Out for the Chicken Feet in Your Soup* (Junior Literary Guild selection), Prentice-Hall, 1974; *The Cloud Book*, Holiday House, 1975; *Michael Bird-Boy*, Prentice-Hall, 1975; *Strega Nona*, Prentice-Hall, 1975; *When Everyone Was Fast Asleep*, Holiday House, 1976.

Illustrator, under name Tomie de Paola: Pura Belpre, *The Tiger and the Rabbit and Other Tales*, Lippincott, 1965; Lisa Miller, *Sound*, Coward, 1965; Miller, *Wheels*, Coward, 1965; Jeanne B. Hardendorff, editor, *Trickey Peik and Other Picture Tales*, Lippincott, 1967; Joan M. Lexau, *Finders Keepers, Losers Weepers*, Lippincott, 1967; Melvin L. Alexenberg, *Sound Science*, Prentice-Hall, 1968; James A. Eichner, *The Cabinet of the President of the United States*, F. Watts, 1968; Leland Blair Jacobs, compiler, *Poetry for*

Chuckles and Grins, Garrard, 1968; Melvin L. Alexenberg, *Light and Sight*, Prentice-Hall, 1969; Samuel and Beryl Epstein, *Take This Hammer*, Hawthorn, 1969; Mary C. Jane, *The Rocking-Chair Ghost*, Lippincott, 1969; Nina Schneider, *Hercules, the Gentle Giant*, Hawthorn, 1969.

Eleanor Boylan, *How to Be a Puppeteer*, McCall Publishing, 1970; Samuel and Beryl Epstein, *Who Needs Holes?*, Hawthorn, 1970; Barbara Rinkoff, *Rutherford T. Finds 21 B*, Putnam, 1970; Philip Ballestrino, *Hot as an Ice Cube*, Crowell, 1971; Samuel and Beryl Epstein, *Pick It Up*, Holiday House, 1971; John Fisher, *John Fisher's Magic Book*, Prentice-Hall, 1971; William Wise, *Monsters of the Middle Ages*, Putnam, 1971; Peter Zachary Cohen, *Authorized Autumn Charts of the Upper Red Canoe River Country*, Atheneum, 1972; Sibyl Hancock, *Mario's Mystery Machine*, Putnam, 1972; Rubie Saunders, *The Franklin Watts Concise Guide to Babysitting*, F. Watts, 1972; Samuel and Beryl Epstein, *Hold Everything*, Holiday House, 1973; Valerie Pitt, *Let's Find Out About Communications*, Watts, 1973; Katheryn F. Ernst, *Danny and His Thumb*, Prentice-Hall, 1973; Samuel and Beryl Epstein, *Look in the Mirror*, Holiday House, 1973; Alice Low, *David's Windows*, Putnam, 1974; Charles Keller and Richard Baker, *The Star-Spangled Banana*, Prentice-Hall, 1974; Martha and Charles Sharp, *Lets Find Out about Houses*, F. Watts, 1975; Mary Calhoun, *Old Man Whickutt's Donkey*, Parents' Magazine Press, 1975; Norma Farber, *This Is the Ambulance Leaving the Zoo*, Dutton, 1975; Lee B. Hopkins, *Good Morning to You, Valentine*, HarBrace, 1976; John Graham, *I Love You, Mouse*, HarBrace, 1976; Bernice Cohn Hunt, *The Whatchamacallit Book*, Putnam, 1976.

Conceived, designed, and directed puppet ballet, "A Rainbow Christmas," at Botolph in Cambridge, Mass., 1971.

WORK IN PROGRESS: *The Quicksand Book*, for Holiday House; *Helga's Dowry*, a troll love story, for HarBrace.

SIDELIGHTS: "Growing up before television, I had what I can only consider the good fortune to be exposed to radio and I never missed that wonderful Saturday morning show, 'Let's Pretend.' I have always felt that that particular program, plus the fact that my mother was in love with books and spent many long hours reading aloud to my brother and me, were the prime factors that caused me to announce to my first grade teacher that when I grew up I was going to make books with pictures.

"Because a love of books was always encouraged at home, naturally I was introduced to the library as soon as I could print my name. In the children's wing I was immediately in love with two things other than the wonderful books. There was a beautiful ceiling-high mural of knights and princesses all around the room, and a large framed map of fairyland.

"When my two sisters began to grow up I suddenly had a built-in audience for my homemade puppet shows and games of make-believe. In fact, I made my first book for my sister Maureen's seventh or eighth birthday. It was called *Glimmera, the Story of a Mermaid*. It provides a lot of family chuckles now and especially for Maureen's four children.

"The idea for *Charlie Needs a Cloak* just appeared one day. I myself learned to spin wool and weave when I lived in Vermont so the story flowed very simply and naturally. I feel that if I don't actually get involved personally with my characters, whether they be human or animal, and find some personal characteristics either of myself or friends in them, they are not 'real.' And that is of prime importance to me—that fantasy be 'real,' from the child-in-all-of-us point of view.

"My Italian grandmother was the model for the heroine of *Watch Out for the Chicken Feet in Your Soup.* Like Joey's grandmother in the story she pinched my cheeks, talked 'funny,' and made Easter bread dolls that were a highlight of my young life. There's a lot of me in the character of Joey, and Joey's friend Eugene is a combination of all my friends through the years who were entranced by my grandmother —her house, accent, and cooking, not to mention the chicken feet.

"She always put chicken feet in the chicken soup, and I was fascinated. It certainly was something to brag about. You know: 'My Daddy does this'; 'Well, my Daddy does that'; 'My Mommy, etc.' And finally, I could mow down my opponents with 'My Grandma puts chicken feet in the soup!' Da dah! Stardom! I also remember a wonderful moment when my aunts fought over who was going to get the foot floating in the soup.

"My grandmother absolutely believed that everyone was hungry and that everyone must put away tons of food to keep their strength up. More than once I was paralyzed by a plate of spaghetti that rivaled the print of Mt. Vesuvius on the wall in height."

Tomie de Paola's works are included in the Kerlan collection at the University of Minnesota.

FOR MORE INFORMATION SEE: Illustrators of Children's Books: 1957-1966, Horn Book, 1968; *Saturday Review/World,* April 4, 1973; *Junior Literary Guild,* September, 1974; *The Horn Book,* April, 1974, August, 1975, October, 1975; *Top of the News,* April, 1976; *Publishers' Weekly,* July 19, 1976.

DERMAN, Sarah Audrey 1915-

PERSONAL: Born August 28, 1915, in Rock Island, Ill.; daughter of Jacob and Bessie (Meyer) Derman. *Education:* Attended Milwaukee State Teachers College, 1932-36; additional courses at University of Wisconsin, Marquette University. *Home:* 1653 North Prospect Ave., Apt. 111, Milwaukee, Wis. 53202.

CAREER: Teacher of primary grades at Victory School, Town of Lake, Milwaukee, Wis., 1936-50, West Allis, Wis., 1950-51, Oak Creek, Wis., 1951-54, East Granville, Wis., 1954-58, South Milwaukee, Wis., 1958-70; Indian Community School, Milwaukee, Wis. *Member:* International Platform Association, Association of Reading Clinicians, Wisconsin Pen Women, Wisconsin Teachers Association, National Teachers Association, Allied Authors (Milwaukee), Theta Sigma Phi.

WRITINGS—Juveniles: Plush, Follett, 1952; *The Snowman Who Wanted to Stay,* Whitman, 1956; *Pretty Bird,* Beckley-Cardy, 1957; *Pony Ring,* Beckley-Cardy, 1957; *Monkey Island,* Beckley-Cardy, 1958; *Big Top,* Beckley-Cardy, 1958; *Surprise Egg,* Beckley-Cardy, 1958;

SARAH AUDREY DERMAN

Poker-Dog, Beckley-Cardy, 1960; *A Party in the Pantry,* Republic, 1963. Poetry included in *Milwaukee Star Times, Milwaukee Journal,* and magazines.

SIDELIGHTS: "My early childhood was spent on the banks of the Mississippi River, first living in grandfather's house in Rock Island, Illinois, later moving to Davenport, Iowa.

"A vivid memory comes to mind of the charming, illuminated paddle-wheeled ferry boat spanking through the water of the Mississippi River, bridging one state with another for a very small toll fee.

"I never cease to wonder at the changing river scene. When the river spilled over the banks, children would rush down to the very edge, picking up clam shells to sell to the Pearl Button Factory at 10¢ a bag. Excited voices could be heard at times calling, 'I think I found a pearl!'

"After a severe winter, inundation was inevitable. Then neighbors and families would get together, helping each other. Furniture, household belongings, etc. were moved from floor one to floor two. I came early to learn a bit of philosophy in regard to nature. Nature is awesome, to be utilized and admired but never to be ignored.

"Rock Island, Illinois was a quiet town with a distinctive rural landscape—mud roads, tall grasses, and fireflies. I began to form early images of my surroundings. Once, while observing a flowering crab tree, I visualized the tree as a graceful ballet dancer, with long trunk limbs, gnarled toes arabesquing in the wind—then in a split second changing into

But what was this? Round red berries, so bitter they made his eyes water and his lips pucker, and squirming ANTS, tickling and prickling under his tongue. ■ (From *Plush* by Sarah Derman. Illustrated by William Gschwind.)

a bride with pink petals, piled high, swirled on a green carpet in solemn ceremony. Trees, clouds, stars, birds and flowers never failed to enchant and amaze me.

"Our family then moved to Madison, Wisconsin where I attended Longfellow Grade School and Madison Central High School.

"Mother was quite a philosophical poet, always singing old folk songs or reciting Tennyson, Whitman or Longfellow.

"As children we were told to sing, compose or recite while doing household chores. Scrubbing the floor was two poems and one song, while doing the dishes was perhaps one original recitation.

"If we ever felt sad or unhappy and asked Mother just why we felt that way, she would answer, 'Do something worthwhile and you will feel better; for happiness is like a butterfly—chase it and it will elude you—but if you turn your thoughts to other pursuits, it will softly light on your shoulder and caress your cheek.'

"I then graduated from Milwaukee State Teachers' College and became a teacher at Victory School in Town of Lake, Wisconsin. School supplies were scarce and the children could not afford to buy more than one book—so, I began creating my own material using the hectograph machine for printing and making facsimiles of books. This almost naturally brought me to the Milwaukee County Zoo where I spent many hours studying the habitat and habits of animals.

"When I wrote *Monkey Island,* I knew Big Joe, King of the Island, so well that I almost believe that he ran up the hill to ring the bell announcing my arrival.

"*Plush,* the polar bear, was written with a scientific thread running through it—bringing out the theme of acclimatization. Mr. William Gschwind, a Swiss woodcarver, was the illustrator.

"Along with the supplementary library books and textbooks, I managed to invent an instrument which I called a 'Phonoboard.' It resembles a piano keyboard—the initial sound, phonograms and inflectional endings are played like clusters of sounds. It has been used for the teaching of reading in building word power.

Something about the Author

"As for my avocation, I would say that I delight in learning foreign languages. German was studied at high school; French, Spanish at the University. Greek was taught to me in the Greek Orthodox Church along with the children. I was tutored in Russian by a friend who originated from Siberia. Later, I even managed to get in a bit of Sanskrit.

"I am a collector of rare books and am the proud possessor of approximately 1,000 books which I read constantly.

"At present, poetry has found a place in my life. If an event happens at our zoo in Milwaukee, such as: Samson, the gorilla, takes unto himself a bride, called Terra; this delights me and my creative powers are put into use.

Poetry is:
   Silver bobbin
     wound tightly
       unbroken threads
        life's thoughts
          back-stitched
           feathered
             cross-stitched
              honeycombed
             lazy dazily
               embroidered on
                rich velvet
                  exquisite pillow
                   of my forget-me-knots"

DEVLIN, Harry 1918-

PERSONAL: Born March 22, 1918, in Jersey City, N.J.; son of Harry George (general manager of Savarin Co.) and Amelia (Crawford) Devlin; married Dorothy Wende (an artist and writer), August 30, 1941; children: Harry Noel, Wende Elizabeth (Mrs. Geoffrey Gates), Jeffrey Anthony,

HARRY DEVLIN

■ (From the film "Winter of the Witch," starring Hermione Gingold. Produced by Learning Corporation of America.)

Alexandra Gail (Mrs. James Eldridge), Brion Phillip, Nicholas Kirk, David Matthew. *Education:* Syracuse University, B.F.A., 1939. *Religion:* Congregationalist. *Home:* 443 Hillside Ave., Mountainside, N.J. 07092.

CAREER: Artist, 1939—. Lecturer at Union College (Cranford, N.J.), 1966, chairman of Tomasulo Art Gallery; member of New Jersey State Council on the Arts, 1970— (chairman, grants committee, 1976—); member of Rutgers University's advisory council on children's literature; president of board of trustees of Mountainside Library, 1968-70. *Military service:* U.S. Naval Reserve, artist for Office of Naval Intelligence, active duty, 1942-46; became lieutenant.

MEMBER: Society of Illustrators, National Cartoonists Society (past president; honorary president), Artists' Equity Association (New Jersey), Authors Guild of Authors League of America, Dutch Treat Club. *Awards, honors:* New Jersey Teachers of English award, 1970, for *How Fletcher Was Hatched!;* award of excellence from Chicago Book Fair, 1974, for *Old Witch Rescues Halloween;* New Jersey Institute of Technology award for *Tales of Thunder and Lightning,* 1976.

WRITINGS—Self-illustrated books for children: *To Grandfather's House We Go,* Parents' Magazine Press, 1967; *The Walloping Window Blind,* Van Nostrand, 1968; *What Kind of House Is That?,* Parents' Magazine Press, 1969; *Tales of Thunder and Lightning,* Parents' Magazine Press, 1975.

Self-illustrated children's books, with wife, Wende Devlin: *Old Black Witch,* Encyclopaedia Britannica Press, 1963; *The Knobby Boys to the Rescue,* Parents' Magazine Press, 1965; *Aunt Agatha, There's a Lion Under the Couch,* Van Nostrand, 1968; *How Fletcher Was Hatched!,* Parents'

The zoo keepers gently led the old lion away to his home in the zoo. ■ (From *Aunt Agatha There's a Lion Under the Couch* by Wende and Harry Devlin. Illustrated by Harry Devlin.)

Magazine Press, 1969; *A Kiss for a Warthog,* Van Nostrand, 1970; *Old Witch and the Polka Dot Ribbon,* Parents' Magazine Press, 1970; *Cranberry Thanksgiving,* Parents' Magazine Press, 1971; *Old Witch Rescues Halloween,* Parents' Magazine Press, 1973.

Films: Author and host of "Fare You Well Old House" and "Houses of the Hackensack," both for New Jersey Public Broadcasting, 1976.

WORK IN PROGRESS: A book of American domestic architecture, 1776-1876, *Made in America;* illustrating *Cranberry Christmas,* by wife, Wende Devlin.

SIDELIGHTS: "Our first book sold over a million copies, which beguiled us into the belief that we could write. Wende writes more and better than I can. I write only about those things that I think may fascinate and pay no heed to trends or styles."

Old Black Witch was adapted by Gerald Herman as the film, "The Winter of the Witch," Parents' Magazine Films, 1972.

FOR MORE INFORMATION SEE: New York Times Book Review, May 9, 1965, January 4, 1970; *Library Journal,* May 15, 1969, May 15, 1970.

DEVLIN, (Dorothy) Wende 1918-

PERSONAL: Born April 27, 1918, in Buffalo, N.Y.; daughter of Bernhardt Philip (a veterinarian) and Elizabeth (Buffington) Wende; married Harry Devlin (an artist and writer), August 30, 1941; children: Harry Noel, Wende Elizabeth (Mrs. Geoffrey Gates), Jeffrey Anthony, Alexandra Gail (Mrs. James Eldridge), Brion Phillip, Nicholas Kirk, David Matthew. *Education:* Syracuse University, B.F.A., 1940. *Politics:* Independent. *Religion:* Congregationalist. *Home and office:* 443 Hillside Ave., Mountainside, N.J. 07092. *Agent:* Dorothy Markinko, McIntosh & Otis, Inc., 18 East 41st St., New York, N.Y. 10017.

CAREER: Free-lance portrait painter and writer. Member of Rutgers University's advisory council on children's literature. *Member:* Authors Guild of Authors League of Amer-

Something about the Author

WENDE DEVLIN

ica, Woman Pays Club (New York City). *Awards, honors:* New Jersey Teachers of English award, 1970, for *How Fletcher Was Hatched!;* award of excellence from Chicago Book Fair, 1974, for *Old Witch Rescues Halloween.*

WRITINGS—All books for children, with husband, Harry Devlin; all illustrated by Harry Devlin: *Old Black Witch,* Encyclopaedia Britannica Press, 1963; *The Knobby Boys to the Rescue,* Parents' Magazine Press, 1965; *Aunt Agatha, There's a Lion Under the Couch,* Van Nostrand, 1968; *How Fletcher Was Hatched!,* Parents' Magazine Press, 1969; *A Kiss for a Warthog,* Van Nostrand, 1970; *Old Witch and the Polka Dot Ribbon,* Parents' Magazine Press, 1970; *Cranberry Thanksgiving,* Parents' Magazine Press, 1971; *Old Witch Rescues Halloween,* Parents' Magazine Press, 1973; *Cranberry Christmas,* Parents' Magazine Press, 1976. Wrote poem feature page, "Beat Poems for a Beat Mother," *Good Housekeeping,* 1963-71.

SIDELIGHTS: "My husband and I became children's book oriented when we had seven of our own. We had a built in sounding board for ideas and I can't think of more worthwhile work than pleasing and developing a child's mind and imagination."

An adaptation by Gerald Herman of *Old Black Witch* was filmed as "The Winter of the Witch," with Hermione Gingold as the witch, 1972.

FOR MORE INFORMATION SEE: New York Times Book Review, May 9, 1965, January 4, 1970; *Library Journal,* May 15, 1969, May 15, 1970.

DIETZ, Lew 1907-

PERSONAL: Born May 22, 1907, in Pittsburgh, Pa., son of Louis Andrew (an engineer) and Bertha (Staiger) Dietz; married Denny Winters (a painter). *Education:* New York University, student, 1927-30. *Politics:* Democrat. *Home and office:* Rockport, Me. *Agent:* Curtis Brown, 575 Madison Ave., New York, N.Y.

CAREER: Crowell Publishing Co., New York, N.Y., copywriter, 1930-33; *Camden Herald,* Camden, Me., editor, 1948-49; *Maine Coast Fisherman,* assistant editor, 1959-61; *Outdoor Maine,* assistant editor, 1961-62.

WRITINGS: Jeff White: Young Woodsman, 1949, *Jeff White: Young Trapper,* 1950, *Jeff White: Young Guide,* 1952, *Jeff White: Young Lumberjack,* 1954, *Jeff White: Forest Fire Fighter,* 1956, *Pines for the King's Navy,* 1958, *Full Fathom Five,* 1959, *Wilderness River,* 1961, *Savage Summer,* 1964, *The Allagash,* Holt, 1968, *Touch of Wildness,* Holt, 1970, *The Year of the Big Cat,* 1970, (with Harry Goodridge) *A Seal Called Andre,* Praeger, 1975 (all published by Little, Brown, unless otherwise noted). Contributor of short stories to *Collier's, Saturday Evening Post,* and of articles to *Field and Stream, Sports Illustrated, Ford Times.*

SIDELIGHTS: "I have lived in Maine and written about Maine for over forty years. My writing has been a projection of my pleasure of being in the woods and observing the creatures of the wild. I live with my painter wife, Denny Winters, close to the sea and we draw our creative sustenance

LEW DIETZ

[Sue] vowed when she was twelve that she'd forsake marriage and become an old maid veterinarian, a vow she kept only until she met. . .a fellow student at the University of Maine. ■ (From *A Seal Called Andre* by Harry Goodridge and Lew Dietz. Photos by Stan Waterman.)

from the same ambience. I found Maine as a home when I was a young man and I'm satisfied that I will never have another home. I write for both adults and young people and there is little difference in my approach. Young people respond to good writing and know good writing from bad. Whatever my audience it behooves me to write the best I can, for first of all what I must do is satisfy myself."

The Year of the Big Cat, 1970, was filmed by Disney under the title, "The Return of the Big Cat."

HOBBIES AND OTHER INTERESTS: Hunting, fishing, natural history, and marine biology.

DINSDALE, Tim 1924-

PERSONAL: Born September 27, 1924, in Aberyswyth, Wales; son of Felix and Dorys (Smith) Dinsdale; married, 1951; children: Simon, Alexandra, Dawn, Angus. *Education:* Attended Kings School, Worcester; De Havilland Aeronautical Technical School, graduate, 1943. *Home:* 17 Blewbury Drive, Tilehurst, Reading, Berkshire, England.

CAREER: An aeronautical engineer, he trained and worked in the aircraft industry for twenty years, five years of that period in Toronto and Montreal, Canada. His work has been connected principally with the development and flight testing

of jet engines. *Military service:* Royal Air Force, 1944-47; pilot. *Member:* Royal Aeronautical Society, Royal Photographic Society of Great Britain.

WRITINGS: Loch Ness Monster, Routledge and Kegan Paul, 1961, Chilton, 1962; *The Leviathans,* Routledge & Kegan Paul, 1966, Futura Books, 1976; *Monster Hunt,* Acropolis, 1972; *The Story of the Loch Ness Monster,* Target Books, 1973; *Project Water Horse,* Routledge and Kegan Paul, 1975.

WORK IN PROGRESS: A children's book, *Introducing the Tumtwiggles and Their Very Strange Adventures,* the first in the series, "The Dingleberry Books."

SIDELIGHTS: Dinsdale, whose crafts include photography, has made many expeditions to Loch Ness and his film of the "phenomenon" has been shown on television in Great Britain and the United States.

"I am of the opinion that in this era of scientific development and knowledge we still know very little about ourselves as human beings. There are areas of ignorance which are studiously avoided, despite much material evidence to establish this ignorance. It is, and will be, my purpose to explore these areas—and present the facts concerning them in a series of non-technical books for the layman; and for young people in particular: in whom I find an openness of mind, and a degree of intelligence which fits the space age in which we live."

TIM DINSDALE

This obviously genuine photograph. . . , outlines the Okanagan Lake Monster in every detail. Head, neck, humps and tail are clearly in evidence. Note also refinement in feeding posture. . . . ∎ (From *The Leviathans* by Tim Dinsdale. Photos by Owen Templeton.)

These birch bark canoes were so light a man could carry one on his back. At the same time they were so strong a single canoe held many men. ∎ (From *O Canada* by Isabel Barclay. Illustrated by Cécile Gagnon.)

DOBELL, I(sabel) M(arian) B(arclay)   1909- (Isabel Barclay)

PERSONAL: Born July 17, 1909, in Montreal, Quebec, Canada; divorced. *Education:* McGill University, B.A., 1930; Radcliffe Institute of Historical and Archival Management, certificate, 1956. *Agent:* Mrs. Deryck Waring, 25 West 43rd St., New York, N.Y.

CAREER: McGill University, McCord Museum, Montreal, Quebec, archivist of Canadian history, 1956-68, chief curator, 1968-70, director, 1970—.

WRITINGS—Children's books, under name Isabel Barclay: *Worlds Without End,* Doubleday, 1956; *O Canada,* (Notable Canadian Children's Book), Doubleday, 1964; *Art of the Canadian Indians and Eskimos,* Queen's Printer (Ottawa), 1969.

WORK IN PROGRESS: Native Land, an ethnography commissioned by the National Museum of Man in Ottawa.

DODSON, Kenneth M(acKenzie)   1907-

PERSONAL: Born October 11, 1907, in Luanda, Angola, Africa; son of William Patterson (a missionary) and Catherine (MacKenzie) Dodson; married Oletha McCorkle, March 9, 1935; children: Richard Kenneth, Jeanie Nadine. *Education:* Taylor's Nautical Academy, completed nautical science course, 1930; Seattle Technical Institute, master mariner, 1938; University of Washington, Seattle, creative writing courses, 1948-52. *Religion:* Baptist. *Home and office:* 1342 Rosario Rd., Anacortes, Wash. 98221.

CAREER: U.S. Merchant Marine, largely American Mail Line, from seaman to master, 1925-42; free-lance writer,

Traveling together, Wim and Hector explored many places. They visited Yokohoma and Singapore, and all the ports between. ■ (From *Hector the Stowaway Dog* by Kenneth Dodson. Illustration by Peter Spier.)

1950—. *Military service:* U.S. Navy, Pacific Fleet Amphibious Forces, 1942-47; now lieutenant commander, U.S. Navy (retired); received nine battle stars, Philippine Island Presidential Unit Citation, and Japan Occupation, Philippine Island Reoccupation medal with two stars, American Defense and Asiatic-Pacific medals, Merchant Marine Combat Medal, and other medals. *Member:* Puget Sound Maritime Historical Society, Disabled Officers Association, Retired Officers Association, U.S. Naval Institute, Pacific Northwest International Writers Conference (vice-president, 1958; trustee, 1957-59). *Awards, honors:* First award in fiction, Washington State Press Club, 1954; Governor's Invitational Writers' Day, certificate of recognition, 1966, for contributions to cultural life of State of Washington; Diploma for distinguished achievement, 1973, Cambridge, England.

WRITINGS: Away All Boats, Little, 1954; *Stranger to the Shore,* Little, 1956; *Hector the Stowaway Dog,* Little, 1958; *The China Pirates,* Little, 1960; (contributor) *American Men at Arms,* edited by F. van Wyck Mason, Little, 1964; (contributor) *Animals You Will Never Forget,* Reader's Digest Association, 1969; *From Make-Believe to Reality,* Fleming H. Revell, 1973. Contributor of source material to Carl Sandburg's *Remembrance Rock,* 1947, and contributor of articles to national magazines.

WORK IN PROGRESS: Kunane, a story of a Hawaiian boy from his viewpoint for boys and girls; *Carl Sandburg: A Friendship; The Forgotten General: The Life of General John Gibbon, 1827-96.*

SIDELIGHTS: "My two boyhood ambitions were to go to sea and learn how to command a ship and to write books about the sea. Both wishes have come true for me. I consider myself primarily as a professional seaman who writes, rather than a writer who has been to sea. However, I now regard writing as a serious, full-time job. I'm glad that most of my stuff sells well and is read abroad, but every new page is a challenge to write better prose. I want to understand people better and discover what is significant about them. The longer I work on a sentence, the simpler it becomes. I have a positive religious faith and philosophy, and believe that there is a market for realistic but clean books. No sick stuff for me.

"Now that we have six grandchildren, I find boys and girls more interesting than ever. Kids are such fun because, if adults will allow, they are just themselves: natural human beings who aren't hiding behind those protective masks most of us adults assume.

"I enjoy old ladies and men with their riches of life experience, especially if they have that wonderful sense of humor that laughs in the face of time. Of course, I love my wonderful family—but also the deer which eat our roses, the raccoon family that comes for a daily visit and handout. I love the blue water and the green islands of this Puget Sound country and the great variety of birds to be studied during the various seasons. I still love fishing and beachcombing, and whenever we get back to our favorite Hawaiian Island, Kauai, to dive around the reefs for coral and shells and to watch how fish behave in their natural element. I have been blessed with a full and happy life."

■ (From the television movie "The Ballad of Hector the Stowaway Dog," starring Guy Stockwell. Copyright © 1963 by Walt Disney Productions.)

KENNETH M. DODSON

Kenneth Dodson reports that he still is puzzled because *Stranger to the Shore* sold more copies in Australia than in the United States. All of his books have been published in at least three countries abroad, and *Away All Boats,* which was filmed by Universal-International with the active co-operation of the U.S. Navy, was translated into six languages and published in ten countries. *Hector the Stowaway Dog* was filmed by Walt Disney, 1964.

HOBBIES AND OTHER INTERESTS: Hiking, beachcombing, and swimming, he would "rather fish than eat."

DOWDEY, Landon Gerald   1923-

PERSONAL: Born August 2, 1923, in Washington, D.C.; son of Landon Ashton and Dorothy (Fogarty) Dowdey; married Mary Shinners, June 6, 1947; children: Patrick Francis, Martin Joseph, Kathleen. *Education:* Wharton School of Finance, University of Pennsylvania, B.S., 1946; Georgetown University, J.D., 1948. *Home:* 3731 Warren St., N.W., Washington, D.C. 20016. *Office:* 1629 K St., N.W., Washington, D.C. 20006.

CAREER: Lawyer; writer. Private practice in association with the late Levi David and Emmett Leo Sheehan, 1948-59; now heads own firm: Dowdey & Bartow (with Norman H. Bartow), 1960-67; Dowdey, Levy & Cohen (with S. David Levy and Neil J. Cohen), 1968-73; Dowdey & Urbina (with Richardo Urbina), 1973—. *Member:* American Bar Association, National Lawyers Guild, American Civil Liberties Union, Bar Association of the District of Columbia.

WRITINGS: Religion Against Poverty, Citizens for Educational Freedom, 1964; *Journey to Freedom* (ALA Notable book), Swallow, 1969; (with Julius Hobson) *The Damned Information,* Washington Institute for Quality Education, 1970; (with Ramsey Clark, Harry Kalvin, Jr. and editors of Swallow Press) *Contempt,* Swallow, 1970.

SIDELIGHTS: "My practice brings me before federal courts and tribunals all over the country, and before Congressional Committees ranging from Ways and Means to Un-American Activities. I have served as trial counsel in numerous criminal cases against public personalities then described as 'militants' but now recognized as responsible community leaders.

"I have been counsel to many socially significant national and local organizations. And have been instrumental in the organization of Washington's earliest low-income housing efforts and social action projects throughout the country.

HOBBIES AND OTHER INTERESTS: Dowdey is an accomplished painter, poet and musician.

LANDON GERALD DOWDEY

**The windows of our house are butter yellow,
inside are different people
who do different things in different ways
and think different things.**
■ (From *When Light Turns Into Night* by Crescent Dragonwagon. Illustrated by Robert Andrew Parker.)

DRAGONWAGON, Crescent 1952-

PERSONAL: Born November 25, 1952, in New York, N.Y.; daughter of Maurice (a biographer) and Charlotte (a children's book writer; maiden name, Shapiro) Zolotow; married Crispin Dragonwagon (an archaeologist), March 20, 1970 (divorced August 10, 1975). *Education:* Educated in Hastings-on-Hudson, N.Y., and Stockbridge, Mass. *Religion:* Buddhist. *Home address:* Dairy Hollow, Eureka Springs, Ark. 72632.

CAREER: Cook and writer. *Member:* Authors Guild of Authors League of America, Association of Journalists and Authors.

WRITINGS: Rainy Day Together (juvenile), Harper, 1970; *The Commune Cookbook,* Simon & Schuster, 1971; *The Bean Book,* Workman Publishing, 1973; *Putting Up Stuff for the Cold Time,* Workman Publishing, 1973; *Strawberry Dress Escape* (juvenile), Scribner, 1975; *When Light Turns into Night* (juvenile), Harper, 1975; *Wind Rose,* Harper, 1976. Contributor to popular magazines, including *Cosmopolitan, Seventeen, Organic Gardening, New Ingenue,* and *Aphra.*

WORK IN PROGRESS: Your Owl Friend, for Harper; poems, drawings, keeping a journal.

SIDELIGHTS: "My personal favorite of the books I've done would have to be *When Light Turns into Night.* To me, the big dilemma in life has to do with balancing the need to be with other people with the need to be alone, which is what *Light* is about. It seems to me that one without the other goes nowhere.

"I think there are many 'different' children—kids who seem out of step with their contemporaries, kids who are often lonely, kids who are asking questions of themselves that most people don't ask until later on in life. . . . I wish someone had told me that if you change yourself, the world changes. This is very important, and many people never get it. To change the world, change yourself. . . ."

HOBBIES AND OTHER INTERESTS: Practicing yoga and meditation, drawing, gardening, reading.

CRESCENT DRAGONWAGON

DUDLEY, Ruth H(ubbell) 1905-

PERSONAL: Born May 14, 1905, in Champlain, N.Y.; daughter of Edward M. and Maude (Hubbell) Dudley. *Education:* Northwestern University, B.S., 1928; Columbia University, graduate study, 1928-29. *Home:* 13560 St. Andrews Dr., #3L, Seal Beach, Calif. 90740.

CAREER: Oak Park Pictorial News, Oak Park, Ill., society editor, 1929-30; employed in sales promotion with Sears, Roebuck & Co., Chicago, Ill., 1930-32, Montgomery Ward & Co., Chicago, 1932-34, Calpro Sales Co., Beverly Hills, Calif., 1934-38, Perfection Bakery, Santa Monica, Calif., 1938-40, and Douglas Aircraft, Santa Monica, 1941-45; real estate agent, 1945-50; free-lance writer and photographer, 1950—.

MEMBER: National Audubon Society, Save the Redwoods League, National Wildlife Federation, Wilderness Society, Save the Children Federation, Sierra Club, National Writers Club, Leisure Whirlers Square Dance Club, Whirler Girls Exhibition Group, Zeta Tau Alpha, Delta Kappa Gamma.

WRITINGS—For children, unless otherwise noted: *Hank and the Kitten,* Morrow, 1947; *Sea Shells,* Crowell, 1953; *Good Citizens, Good Neighbors,* Melmont, 1953; *At the Museum,* Melmont, 1956; *My Hobby is Collecting Seashells and Coral* (young adult), Childrens Press, 1955; *Our American Trees,* Crowell, 1956; *Tip Top Wish,* Crowell, 1958; *Favorite Trees of Desert, Mountain, and Plain* (young adult), Funk, 1963; *Partners in Nature* (young adult), Funk, 1965. Contributor of articles and photographs to popular

magazines, including nature and sport magazines, and *Child Life.*

SIDELIGHTS: "I was born and raised in the beautiful region of Lake Champlain, N.Y. and the Adirondacks. My mother, especially, was a great nature lover and I guess it rubbed off on me. We spent many summers camping on Lake Champlain, fishing, boating, swimming and enjoying nature. During several winters in Florida I enjoyed studying the interesting variety (at that time) of sea shells along the coast, and later in California along the southern coast there. Hence my first nature book, *Sea Shells.*

"I am an ardent conservationist; love trees, wildlife, wilderness areas, belong to a good many clubs and organizations along this line and do what little I can to protect our wildlife and preserve our natural beauties. I hoped, in writing my various books and articles on nature, to inspire a greater understanding and appreciation of nature in our small fry, teenagers, and young adults—the leaders of tomorrow, so they will conserve and enjoy, not destroy."

HOBBIES AND OTHER INTERESTS: Hiking, bicycling, camping, shelling, ceramics, flora and fauna of desert, mountains and seashore, birds, cats, photography, square dancing, "my nieces and nephews," travel (to southern Europe, Alaska, and the Caribbean).

RUTH H. DUDLEY

The sea urchin is completely covered with spines sticking out in all directions. . .If you ever have tried to handle one of these bristling creatures you know why they often are called sea porcupines. ■ (From *Sea Shells* by Ruth H. Dudley. Illustrated by Phoebe Erickson.)

DUNNE, Mary Collins 1914-
(Regina Moore)

PERSONAL: Born January 15, 1914, in County Down, Ireland; daughter of George William (a calker) and Brigid (Byrne) Collins; married Stephen John Dunne (a teamster), January 11, 1937; children: Nancy (Mrs. Thomas Roberts), Mary Anne (Mrs. Jon Ploof), Bernadette, Christine. *Education:* Studied creative writing at University of San Francisco, University of California, San Francisco City College, and California State University at San Francisco. *Politics:* Democrat. *Religion:* Roman Catholic. *Home:* 266 Jules Ave., San Francisco, Calif. 94112. *Agent:* John K. Payne, Lenniger Literary Agency, Inc., 437 Fifth Ave., New York, N.Y. 10016.

CAREER: Writer. *Member:* California Writers' Club.

WRITINGS: Alaskan Summer (juvenile), Abelard-Schuman, 1968; *Reach Out, Ricardo* (juvenile), Abelard-Schuman, 1970; *Gregory Gray and the Brave Beast* (juvenile), Childrens Press, 1972; *Nurse of the Midnight Sun,* Bouregy, 1973; *Standby Nurse,* Bouregy, 1974; *Cruise of the Coral Queen,* Bouregy, 1975; *Nurse of the Vineyards,* Bouregy, 1975; *The Secret of Captains' Cave* (juvenile), Putnam, 1976. Contributor of articles and short stories (some under pseudonym Regina Moore) to numerous magazines.

WORK IN PROGRESS: Return to Timberlake, a Gothic novel; and several children's stories.

SIDELIGHTS: "A few months before I was born in Ireland, my father had to go to America seeking work. My mother was to follow with me soon after my birth. Various circumstances interfered, and my father and I never saw each other until I was six years old.

"We lived briefly near Philadelphia, Pennsylvania and in Salt Lake City, Utah, then in and near San Francisco, California, where I have lived ever since. In twelve years of schooling I attended ten different schools. Economically haphazard, we were secure in our faith and family love. Until age twelve I was an only child (then I acquired my brother, later my sister). Being alone a lot I read everything in sight. I wrote verses and melodramatic stories which I printed in tiny books of folded tablet paper. At school I liked English courses, dreaded math. In high school I was on paper and yearbook staffs.

"I graduated in hard times when one had to scratch and struggle for a job. Did office work and cashiering in a large department store. Married Steve, who'd been my boyfriend since high school, and in time we had four daughters. I was a good storyteller to them but for years the only writing I did was grocery lists and letters to out-of-state relatives. The six of us spent vacations camping and took one cross-country train trip. (In recent years my husband and I have traveled a good deal, by auto, plane, ship.)

"As the girls grew up I left such activities as PTA and Girl Scout leadership to attend creative writing courses at nearby colleges. My short stories began to sell to juvenile and

MARY COLLINS DUNNE

83

Lionel held up his prize. ■ (From *Gregory Gray and the Brave Beast* by Mary Collins Dunne. Illustrated by Lois Axeman.)

teenage magazines. One teacher had a strong influence on my writing career, the late Howard Pease, author of many books for young people, a splendid teacher and good friend. He encouraged me to go on to books. In 1968 my first book appeared. I learned that my habit of writing only when I was inspired or in the mood would never produce a finished book, so the discipline of regular working hours evolved. I found that research on backgrounds, historical data and the like, was hard work but very enriching.

"I get plot ideas from anywhere, newspapers, observation, experience, or a mixture of these. My starting point is always a character and what he might do in a certain situation. I search Vital Statistics for names and get pets' names from Lost and Found ads. I like the freedom of creating fictional towns in authentic locales, checking zip code lists so I won't use similar names. I draw maps of areas and floor plans of houses. I write short biographies of all important characters. Most of this never gets into the book but makes me know my people better.

"Writing is gratifying but not easy. You can leave the typewriter as exhausted as though you'd just dug up your entire garden. But it's never drudgery. The difficult, grinding days are more than balanced by exhilarating times when the writing flows. I think it's good now and then to write poetry or prose, not for print, but to feed the soul.

"Since writing I have gained respect for fine authors, reverence for the masters, and awe for such as Tolstoy with his *War and Peace*."

HOBBIES AND OTHER INTERESTS: Gardening, swimming, spectator baseball, travel.

EAGAR, Frances 1940-

PERSONAL: Born March 26, 1940, in London, England; daughter of Ronald (a surgeon) and Elinor (an archaeologist) Reid; married Michael Eagar (a teacher), September 6, 1963; children: Charlotte Elisabeth, Sophia Helen. *Education:* Studied at New Hall, Convent of the Holy Sepulchre, 1951-59, London College of Secretarial Studies, 1959-60, and Sorbonne, University of Paris, 1961-63. *Politics:* Left wing-liberal. *Religion:* Roman Catholic. *Home:* Ingram's Hall, Shrewsbury School, Shrewsbury, Shropshire, England.

CAREER: Teacher at Eton College Choir School, Eton, England, 1963-64, and Faulkner House School, London, England, 1964-65.

WRITINGS: The Little Sparrow, Hamish Hamilton, 1972; *The Donkey Upstairs,* Hamish Hamilton, 1972; *The Tin Mine,* Hamish Hamilton, 1973; *The Dolphin of the Two Seas,* Hamish Hamilton, 1973; *Midnight Patrol,* Hamish Hamilton, 1974; *Cuckoo Clock Island,* Hamish Hamilton, 1974; *Timetangle,* Hamish Hamilton, 1976.

WORK IN PROGRESS: A novel set in Devon; a history of the Incas for Cambridge University Press "Topic" series.

SIDELIGHTS: "I was born during the war, and evacuated to Scotland as Essex was in danger of being invaded. After the war (which I do not recall except the excitement of air raids in the middle of the night), we returned to Essex where I lived with my five brothers and sisters in a rambling old

FRANCES EAGAR

farm house that was mentioned in the *Domesday Book*. It was believed to be haunted, but if this was so, the spirits felt very friendly to me. We had ponies, donkies, snakes, dormice, ducks, etc., in the house, and had a very free and independent childhood.

"My twin sister and I attended a convent boarding school where the nuns were great fun, and we thoroughly enjoyed being there. My mother was eccentric on our holidays, she used to take us searching Cornwall or Wales for the Excalibur; we greatly enjoyed these expeditions, regardless of the fruitlessness.

"After school I went to the Sorbonne where I lazed away the time, and on reflection found the hours spent sitting in sidewalk cafes to have been some of the most important times of my life. I married when the rain came through the soles of my best shoes, and have been happily married ever since.

"My husband taught at Eton College, and now at Shrewsbury. We have two little girls. My greatest relaxation is to watch waves, mill streams, waterfalls, or listen to jazz. I enjoy beachcombing, polishing pebbles, and watching catamarans we have made out of flotsam and jetsam, sail away out of sight.

"For me childhood is a time of particular clarity and I still enjoy observing things with the innocent eye of a child. Escapism? Nostalgia? In short, I write because I want to write."

FOR MORE INFORMATION SEE: Growing Point, March, 1975.

EAGLE, Mike 1942-

PERSONAL: Born April 26, 1942, in Yonkers, N.Y.; son of Gene (a housepainter) and Irene Eagle; married Mary Grace DeRita (a teacher), August 21, 1965; children: Michael Christopher. *Education:* University of Hartford Art School, Hartford, Conn., certificate in painting, 1964, B.F.A. (cum laude), 1965. *Home and Office:* 7 Captain's Lane, Old Saybrook, Conn. 04675. *Agent:* Dick Morrill Associates, 210 East 47th St., New York, N.Y. 10017.

CAREER: Aetna Life & Casualty Co., Hartford, Ct., illustrator, 1965-66. Now free-lance illustrator. *Exhibitions:* Society of Illustrators national exhibitions, New York, N.Y., 1971-74; Sofi, New York, N.Y., 1971, 1973; Connecticut Academy of Fine Arts, 1973; group shows. *Military service:* U.S. Army, 1966-1969, became first lieutenant. *Member:* Society of Illustrators, Graphic Artists Guild, Connecticut Academy of Fine Arts, Connecticut Art Directors' Club.

ILLUSTRATOR: E. T. Hoppmann, *The Child From Far Away,* Addisonian, 1970; Herbert H. Wong and Matthew F. Vessel, *Plant Communities: Where Can Cattails Grow?,* Addisonian, 1970; Beryl Netherclifts, *Mystery of Castle Steep* (jacket), Knopf, 1970; Alan M. Fletcher, *Fishes That Travel,* Addisonian, 1971; Frances Mossiker, *More Than a Queen,* Knopf, 1971; *Lord of the Chained* (jacket), Morrow, 1971; Barbara Brenner, *Is It Bigger Than a Sparrow?,* Knopf, 1972; *Susie Did It!,* Magic Circle/Houghton, 1972; *Touch Chauncy* (jacket), Morrow, 1973; *Curse of Laguna Grande* (jacket), Morrow, 1973; *The Phantom Cyclist* (jacket), Follett, 1974; *Full Forty Fathoms,* Morrow, 1975; *Julia and the Third Bad Thing,* Follett, 1975. Various stories in *Bank Street Reader* for Houghton, Field Enterprises, Open Court, Cricket.

SIDELIGHTS: "My interest in art stems from my childhood as it has with most artists, I'm sure. My first ambition was to be an animator for the Disney Studios. When I was in sixth grade, I wrote to them asking what was required of me in order to become one of their artists. They responded with some sound advice which holds true for anyone wishing to pursue any kind of artistic endeavor: draw! Draw the figure! Draw hands, faces, and feet. Draw cows, ducks, barns, boats, trees, flowers, everything! But DRAW! So I'm glad to say I got that basic message early in life.

**The next day we peeked over the garden wall.
We wanted to see who had moved in.
We saw her.**
■ (From *Is It Bigger Than a Sparrow?* by Barbara Brenner. Illustrated by Mike Eagle.)

"I entered art school still fully intent upon becoming a Disney animator, but five years of drawing, design, painting and art history introduced me to other kinds of pursuits available. By my fourth and fifth years I wanted to be an illustrator/painter.

"One of the great experiences of my life was having been selected during my fourth year of school to be an assistant to Austin Purves, muralist, of Litchfield, Connecticut. Mr. Purves had been commissioned to execute working drawings (cartoons) for a mosaic mural depicting Saint Joseph, the patron saint of working people and the family, for the east apse of the National Shrine of the Immaculate Conception in Washington, D.C. During 1964-65, I worked on the project with Mr. Purves, reproducing at full-scale his working drawings, first in charcoal and then oil on heavy drawing paper. His craft and professionalism had and continues to have a great influence on me and my work.

"I had a rather late start as a free-lance artist/illustrator. Although I graduated from school in 1965, I didn't have my

first assignment until 1969, after my military service and after a great deal of fruitless experimentation and soul-searching.

"Let me digress a moment and tell all aspiring artists that there are two distinct ways to approach the art of illustration; as an imitator or as an innovator. The field of illustration is filled with many who imitate, or at least follow closely, the successful formulas of other artists. Those 'other artists,' as you may have guessed, are the innovators. Let me add that there is nothing wrong with being an imitator if you are so inclined and equipped. As a matter of fact, it is a sound way to develop a personal form. But it can be quite disadvantageous if one fails to recognize the pitfalls of imitation; being overly concerned with producing the 'look' or 'surface' in the fashion of another artist's style and, therefore, never quite making contact with the subject matter on a personal plan. Ultimately the artist suffers for want of a personal identity. His is a dual presence; Joe Jones who works like John Jackson. Appreciating another artist's work is commendable, but it can never be your own. To appreciate another's work, to learn from it and at some point evolve your own work from it is the thing to do.

"I bring attention to all this for various reasons. Many students of illustration look at the work of major illustrators and assume that they have to do the same thing in order to be an illustrator, much less a successful one. This is true for many working professionals as well. Some one does something new and interesting and immediately everyone else jumps on their bandwagon thereby creating the 'trend.'

"I made the same assumptions when I began to free-lance in 1969. I would say, 'Oh, look at what so-and-so is doing, it's great! And it must be selling! I'll do the same thing!' So I

MIKE EAGLE

would work in acrylics like this artist and in opaque color like that guy, and something else like the other so-and-so. I began to drive myself nuts. Worst of all, I was going absolutely nowhere. Then it finally occurred to me; I wasn't having any fun, the pictures I had been making were mere ghosts of what they should have been. They couldn't begin to compete with the kind of work that had supposedly inspired them. In my haste to develop a 'slick,' good-looking surface I completely disregarded the fundamental idea in picture making; creating imagery.

"Then one day I decided to have fun drawing my way. And right then and there I realized what I had been doing wrong. What I should have been doing all along was to follow my own instincts; to design, draw and paint a picture in accordance with my own needs and feelings. In short, to interpret a subject my way. I've been trying to do things in my own fashion ever since.

"My work is primarily ink and watercolor. I use very little photography, preferring to draw from the model and/or subject as much as is practically possible. My most practical and trustworthy model is myself. I have mirrors set up around my drawing table so that I may draw ears, mouths, profiles, exaggerated facial expressions and so forth. Best of all, I'm available twenty-four hours a day and very inexpensive.

"Finally for relaxation I enjoy professional football, golf, swimming, golf, family travel, golf, boating, golf, working in our garden and, oh yes, golf."

EBEL, Alex 1927-

PERSONAL: Surname sounds like "Pebble"; born November 14, 1927, in Mexico City, Mexico; son of Wilhelm and Maria (Lezano) Ebel; married Bertha Carreras, February 8, 1945; children: Xenia, Roldk, Eldryk. *Education:* Mexico Academy of Fine Arts, four years, teacher degree. *Politics:* "Disappointed Republican. Hopeful Democrat (at present)." *Religion:* Roman Catholic. *Home and office:* 30 Newport Rd., Yonkers, N.Y. 10710.

CAREER: Free-lance illustrator; Commercial Studios, Inc., New York, N.Y., art director. *Exhibitions:* One-man show, Field Museum, Chicago, Ill., 1965; Carbide Building, New York, N.Y., 1971; Society of Illustrators, New York, N.Y., 1973-75. *Awards, honors:* Society of Illustrators, citation for merit, 1971, 1974; Society of Publication Designers, certificate of merit, 1972, 1973, 1974; Chicago Society of Communicating Arts, certificate of excellence, 1973, 1974; American Institute of Graphic Arts, certificate of excellence, 1974.

ILLUSTRATOR: Isaac Asimov, *The Moon,* 1966, Philip B. Carona, *The Planet Earth,* 1967, Philip B. Carona, *Earth Through the Ages,* 1968, (co-illustrator) Isaac Asimov, *Galaxies,* 1968, Julian May, *Climate,* 1969, Isaac Asimov, *The Sun,* 1972 (all published by Follett). Also illustrated *Yearbook,* 1965, *Childcraft Annual,* 1971-72, 1973, and *Science Year,* 1971, 1976, for Field Enterprise.

SIDELIGHTS: "I was brought up in a cultured atmosphere, learned to love books, science, music and art in my childhood.

ALEX EBEL

And toward the end of the Mesozoic Era, a great time of mountain-building took place. The Rocky Mountains were formed. All over the Earth, there were many volcanoes and earthquakes. ■ (From *Earth Through the Ages* by Philip B. Carona. Illustrated by Alex Ebel.)

"I am deeply impressed by Teilhard de Chardin's ideas about consciousness evolution, also feel that mankind will reach its summit mostly through love for science and art!

"Bulk of artistic production consists of magazine illustrations through which I am better known. Media is watercolors, dyes and air brush.

"I am very interested in astronomy and space travel. A recent trip around the world was made by freighter with stopovers in Tahiti and Society Islands, living among the natives for several months. I speak Spanish, and some French and Italian, and have built my own house."

HOBBIES AND OTHER INTERESTS: Skin diving, mountain climbing, sky diving and home movies.

EGIELSKI, Richard 1952-

PERSONAL: Born July 16, 1952, in New York, N.Y.; son of Joseph Frank (a police lieutenant) and Caroline (Rzepny; an executive secretary) Egielski. *Education:* Studied at Pratt Institute, 1970-71; graduate of Parsons School of Design, 1971-74. *Home and office:* 7 West 14th St., New York, N.Y. 10011.

CAREER: Illustrator. *Exhibitions:* "Illustrators 16" annual national exhibit held at Society of Illustrators, New York, N.Y., 1974, "Illustrators 18," 1976.

RICHARD EGIELSKI

A board creaked behind her. Suddenly the curtain was whipped aside, and Rose Rita turned to find Gert Bigger standing over her. ■ (From *The Letter, the Witch, and the Ring* by John Bellairs. Illustrated by Richard Egielski.)

ILLUSTRATOR: Moonguitars, Houghton, 1974; *The Porcelain Pagoda,* Viking, 1976; *The Letter, the Witch and the Ring,* Dial, 1976.

SIDELIGHTS: "I work strictly with watercolors, most work done in black and white. In my pictures I strive to give a sense of common life and humanity to the characters I paint."

EMRICH, Duncan (Black Macdonald) 1908-
(Blackie Macdonald)

PERSONAL: Born April 11, 1908, in Mardin, Turkey; son of Richard Stanley Merrill (a missionary) and Jeannette (a missionary; maiden name, Wallace) Emrich; married Sally Richardson Selden, November 20, 1955. *Education:* Brown University, A.B., 1932; Columbia University, M.A., 1933; University of Madrid, Doctor en Letras, 1934; Harvard University, Ph.D., 1937; additional study at Sorbonne, University of Paris, University of Aix-en-Provence, University of Cologne, and Escuela de Estudios Arabes. *Home:* 2029 Connecticut Ave. N.W., Washington, D.C. 20008. *Agent:* John Cushman Associates, 25 West 43rd St., New York, N.Y. 10036. *Office:* Department of Literature, American University, Washington, D.C. 20016.

CAREER: Columbia University, New York, N.Y., instructor in English literature, 1937-40; University of Denver, Denver, Colo., assistant professor of English, 1940-42; Library of Congress, Washington, D.C., chief of archives of American folksong, 1945-46, chief of folklore section, 1946-55; U.S. Department of State, cultural attaché at American embassy in Athens, Greece, 1955-58, cultural affairs officer and consul at American Consulate General in Calcutta, India, 1959-62, public affairs officer at American embassy in Lome, Togo, West Africa, 1963-66; U.S. Information Agency, Washington, D.C., desk officer for former French West African countries, 1966-69; American University, Washington, D.C., professor of folklore, 1969—. Fulbright lecturer on American civilization at Universities of Rome, Naples, Messina, and Palermo, 1948-49. U.S. representative, International Folk Music Council, London, and International Folklore Conference, Paris, both 1948. Weekly radio broadcaster on folklore, on National Broadcasting Co. program "Weekend," 1953-55. *Military service:* U.S. Army, 1942-45; served with Military Intelligence in Washington, D.C., also served in England, France, and Germany; named American historian to General Eisenhower; became major; received Croix de Guerre. *Member:* Various American folklore societies, Helenic-American Union (founder), Indo-American Society (founder), Parnassos Society (Athens; honorary member), National Council on Reli-

What are five things small boys are never without?
a pea shooter
a water pistol
baseball cards
a hole in their pants
a runny nose.
■ (From *The Whim-Wham Book* collected by Duncan Emrich. Illustrated by Ib Ohlsson.)

DUNCAN EMRICH

printed, 1940; *Casey Jones, and Other Ballads of the Mining West,* W. H. Kistler Stationery Co. (Denver), 1942; *It's an Old Wild West Custom,* Vanguard, 1949; *Comstock Bonanza: Western Americana of J. Ross Browne, Mark Twain, Sam Davis, Bret Harte, James W. Gally, Dan de Quille, Joseph T. Goodman* [and] *Fred Hart,* Vanguard, 1950; (editor with Charles Clegg) *The Lucius Beebe Reader,* Doubleday, 1967; *The Folklore of Love and Courtship: The Charms and Divinations, Superstitions and Beliefs, Signs and Prospects of Love, Sweet Love,* American Heritage Press, 1970; *The Folklore of Weddings and Marriage: The Traditional Beliefs, Customs, Superstitions, Charms, and Omens of Marriage and Marriage Ceremonies,* American Heritage Press, 1970; (author) *Folklore on the American Land,* Little, Brown, 1972; *American Folk Poetry: An Anthology,* Little, Brown, 1974.

Contributor to folklore journals, and to *Saturday Review, Reader's Digest, Library of Congress Quarterly, Holiday, Moslem World, American Heritage,* and other periodicals; contributor of articles, under pseudonym Blackie Macdonald, to *Police Gazette.*

SIDELIGHTS: "I like people, I like folklore, I like to collect, I like to write. The English language is a wonderful thing—from the polished purity of the 18th century to the superb mangling of the present day Bronx. A phrase can make a day—from Montana: 'Well, there goes a ten-dollar Stetson on a five-cent head.' Worth living to read or hear that."

FOR MORE INFORMATION SEE: Horn Book, October, 1970, August, 1971, February, 1972, April, 1973; "The Calendar," Children's Book Council, January 1972-April 1972; *Christian Science Monitor,* April 27, 1972; *New York Times Book Review,* December 19, 1972; *Choice,* December, 1974.

gion in Higher Education. *Awards, honors:* Hicks Prize in English and Preston Gurney Literary Prize, both from Brown University, 1932; Shattuck Scholar, 1935-36, and Edward Austin fellow, 1936-37, both at Harvard University; Guggenheim fellow, 1949; *The Nonsense Book* was named Children's Book of Library of Congress, 1970, Best Book of the Year of *School Library Journal,* 1970, American Library Association Notable Book, 1970, Top Honor Book of Chicago Book Clinic, 1971, Children's Book of the Year by Child Study Association of America, and received the Lewis Carroll Shelf Award, 1971; *The Hodgepodge Book* was named Outstanding Children's Book of *New York Times Book Review,* 1972.

WRITINGS—Children's books: *The Cowboy's Own Brand Book,* Crowell, 1954; (compiler) *The Nonsense Book of Riddles, Rhymes, Tongue Twisters, Puzzles and Jokes from American Folklore* (ALA Notable Book), Four Winds Press, 1970; (compiler) *The Book of Wishes and Wishmaking,* American Heritage Press, 1971; (compiler) *The Hodgepodge Book: An Almanac of American Folklore, Containing All Manner of Curious, Interesting, and Out-of-the-Way Information Drawn from American Folklore, and Not to Be Found Anywhere Else in the World; As Well as Jokes, Conundrums, Riddles, Puzzles, and Other Matter Designed to Amuse and Entertain—All of It Most Instructive and Delightful,* Four Winds Press, 1972; *The Whim-Wham Book,* Four Winds Press, 1975.

Adult books; compiler, except as noted: *Who Shot Maggie in the Freckle and Other Ballads of Virginia City,* privately

FADIMAN, Clifton (Paul) 1904-

PERSONAL: Born May 15, 1904, in Brooklyn, N.Y.; son of Isidore Michael (a pharmacist) and Grace Elizabeth (a nurse) Fadiman; married Pauline Elizabeth Rush (an editor), 1927 (divorced, 1949); married Annalee Whitmore Jacoby (a writer), 1950; children: Jonathan, Kim, Anne. *Education:* Columbia University, A.B., 1925. *Home:* 4668 Via Roblada, Santa Barbara, Calif. 93110.

CAREER: Ethical Culture (now Fieldston) High School, New York, N.Y., teacher of English, 1925-27; People's Institute, New York, N.Y., lecturer, 1925-33; Simon & Schuster (publishers), New York, N.Y., assistant editor, 1927-29, general editor, 1929-35; *New Yorker* magazine, New York, N.Y., book editor, 1933-43; master of ceremonies or host of radio and television programs, including: "Information, Please!," 1938-48, "Conversation," 1954-57, as well as "Mathematics," "What's in a Word?," "This is Show Business," "Quiz Kids," and "Alumni Fun"; free-lance writer and lecturer, 1957—; Encyclopaedia Britannica Educational Corp., consultant in humanities, writer and general editor, "Humanities Film Series," 1963—. Teacher of great books classes in New York, Chicago and San Francisco; Regents Lecturer, University of California at Los Angeles, 1967; instructor, Santa Barbara Writers Conference, 1973, 1974; Woodrow Wilson Foundation Lecturer,

**There's never *been* a DRAGON, wild *or* tame,
But they were scared of dragons all the same,
Scared of his pointed tail, his dreadful claws,
His batlike wings, and fire-breathing jaws.**
■ (From *Cricket's Choice* edited by Clifton Fadiman and Marianne Carus. Illustrated by Wallace Tripp.)

Pomona College, 1974; member of board of judges, Book-of-the-Month Club, 1944—, and National Book Award for Children's Books, 1974; member of board of directors, Council for Basic Education; member of advisory board, California Center Films for Children; consultant to Fund for the Advancement of Education, Academy for Educational Development, National Advisory Council for the National Humanities Series, and Center for the Study of Democratic Institutions. *Member:* California Citizens for Better Libraries, Phi Beta Kappa. *Awards, honors: Saturday Review of Literature* award for distinguished service to American Literature, 1940, for radio program "Information, Please!"; American Library Association, Clarence Day Award, 1969.

WRITINGS: Party of One: The Selected Writings of Clifton Fadiman, World Publishing, 1955; *Any Number Can Play* (essays and criticism), World Publishing, 1957; *The Voyages of Ulysses* (juvenile), Random House, 1959; *The Adventures of Hercules* (juvenile), Random House, 1960; *The Lifetime Reading Plan* (essays and criticism), World Publishing, 1960; *The Story of Young King Arthur* (juvenile), Random House, 1961; *Appreciations: Essays,* Hodder & Stoughton, 1962; *Enter, Conversing* (essays), World Publishing, 1962; *Wally the Word Worm* (juvenile), Macmillan, 1964; *The Literature of Childhood* (lecture), University of Denver Graduate School of Librarianship, 1971; (with Sam Aaron) *The Joys of Wine,* Abrams, 1975.

Translator: Friedrich Nietzsche, *Ecce Homo* [and] *The Birth of Tragedy*, Modern Library, 1926; (with William A. Drake) Franz Werfel, *The Man Who Conquered Death*, Simon & Schuster, 1927; Desider Kostolanyi, *The Bloody Poet: A Novel about Nero*, Macy-Masius, 1927.

Editor: *Living Philosophies*, Simon & Schuster, 1931; *The Voice of the City and Other Stories by O. Henry*, Limited Editions Club, 1935; (and author of introduction and biographical notes) W. H. Auden and others, *I Believe: The Personal Philosophies of Certain Eminent Men and Women of Our Time*, Simon & Schuster, 1939 (published in England as *I Believe—The Personal Philosophies of 23 Eminent Men and Women of Our Time*, Allen & Unwin, 1940, revised edition, 1962); (and author of prologue and commentary) *Reading I've Liked: A Personal Selection from Two Decades of Reading and Reviewing*, Simon & Schuster, 1941; *The Three Readers: An Omnibus of Novels, Stories, Essays and Poems*, Press of the Readers Club, 1943; (and author of introduction) Henry James, *The Short Stories of Henry James*, Random House, 1945; (and author of introduction) Charles Dickens, *The Posthumous Papers of the Pickwick Club*, Simon & Schuster, 1949; (with Charles Van Doren) *The American Treasury, 1945-1955*, Harper, 1955; *Fantasia Mathematica; being a Set of Stories, Together with a Group of Oddments and Diversions, All Drawn from the Universe of Mathematics*, Simon & Schuster, 1958.

CLIFTON FADIMAN

Clifton Fadiman's Fireside Reader, Simon & Schuster, 1961; (and author of introduction) *Dionysus: A Case of Vintage Tales about Wine*, McGraw, 1962; *The Mathematical Magpie; being More Stories, Mainly Transcendental, plus Subsets of Essays, Rhymes, Music, Anecdotes, Epigrams, and Other Prime Oddments and Diversions, Rational and Irrational, All Derived from the Infinite Domain of Mathematics*, Simon & Schuster, 1962; (and author of introduction) *Party of Twenty: Informal Essays from Holiday Magazine*, Simon & Schuster, 1963; (with Allan A. Glatthorn and Edmund Fuller) *Five American Adventures*, Harcourt, 1963; (and author of introduction) *Fifty Years; being a Retrospective Collection of Novels, Novellas, Tales, Drama, Poetry, and Reportage, and Essays*, Knopf, 1965; (and compiler with Jean White) *Ecocide—and Thoughts Toward Survival*, Center for the Study of Democratic Institutions, 1971; (with Marianne Carus) *Cricket's Choice*, Open Court, 1974.

Author of introductions to more than thirty books, including works by Edith Wharton, Leo Tolstoy, Herman Melville, Sinclair Lewis, John P. Marquand, Stendhal, Joseph Conrad and others, 1931—. Regular contributor to *Holiday* magazine, 1951-65, and to *This Week*, 1950's—. Member of board of editors, *Transatlantic*, 1943-45, *Encyclopaedia Britannica*, 1955—, and Open Court Publishing Co.; associate editor, *Gateway to the Great Books*, 1950's—; senior editor, *Cricket: The Magazine for Children*, 1972—.

WORK IN PROGRESS: A large-scale critical history of world children's literature.

SIDELIGHTS: "When I was young, I decided I would never be first-rate at anything. So I said to myself: Clifton, you are going to be second, third, and tenth-rate at as many things as possible. It was a conscious decision.

"When you get older, you get along with children better and that's a wonderful thing. Remember, the Grimm brothers got their tales from old people. This is a platitude, but there is a child in each one of us. The question is how long he's around. Some people as they age find the child in them growing.

"If children were read verse from the very earliest age, without being told solemnly that it is verse, in fact without being told what it is at all, they might feel that poetry is just as 'natural' as prose. We make such a fuss about the sanctity of verse, as if it were a kind of holy writ. Thus a good many children begin to be prejudiced against it."

HOBBIES AND OTHER INTERESTS: Wine and "the avoidance of exercise."

FOR MORE INFORMATION SEE: Time, December 10, 1973; *Children's Literature in Education/17*, APS, Summer, 1975; *Publishers' Weekly*, October 27, 1975.

FARJEON, (Eve) Annabel 1919-
(Sarah Jefferson)

PERSONAL: Born March 19, 1919, in Berkshire, England; daughter of Herbert (an author) and Joan (an artist; maiden name, Thornycroft) Farjeon; married Hugh Adams, May 30, 1945 (deceased); married Igor Anrep (a cardiologist), July 9, 1949; children: (first marriage) Olivia; (second marriage) Benjamin. *Education:* Privately tutored by governess

ANNABEL FARJEON

and father. *Home:* 42 Southwood Lane, London N.6, England. *Agent:* A. M. Heath & Co. Ltd., 40 William IV St., London W.C.2, England.

CAREER: Sadlers Wells Ballet Co., London, England, ballet dancer, 1934-42; *Time & Tide,* London, assistant literary editor, 1946-48; *New Statesman,* London, ballet critic, 1949-64; *Evening Standard,* London, ballet critic, 1959-73; writer.

WRITINGS—Books for children: *The Alphabet,* J. Cape, 1941; *Maria Lupin,* Abelard, 1967; *The Siege of Trapp's Mill,* Dent, 1972, Atheneum, 1974; *Poems,* privately printed, 1973; *The Poetry of Cats,* Batsford, 1974. Contributor to BBC broadcasts, and to *Life & Letters, New Writing, New Statesman, Evening Standard* (under pseudonym Sarah Jefferson), *Daily Telegraph, Guardian,* and *Observer.*

WORK IN PROGRESS: A children's book, *The Unicorn Drum,* for Kaye & Ward; an adult novel, *The Ivy Memorial;* an autobiography.

SIDELIGHTS: "My spelling always was bad, but if a teacher complained my father would say that what I wrote was the important thing, so long as it could be understood—after all, Shakespear spelt his name different ways. Mostly I was educated at home and wrote a lot of poetry, my ambition to become a poet battling with my ambition to become a ballerina.

"At eleven I began ballet lessons and joined Sadler's Wells Ballet Company at the age of sixteen. However, I was more suited to writing than dancing, though six years on the stage in company with great stars like Margot Fonteyn were some of the most exciting in my life.

"Certainly writing stories, whether for grown-ups or children, is what I like to do best, and though family life may interfere and hold me up, even for years, I have never really stopped. My children's stories' have, so far, been about the everyday world, but I have an increasing urge to write fairy tales."

FASSLER, Joan (Grace) 1931-

PERSONAL: Born September 23, 1931, in New York, N.Y.; daughter of Jacob V. and Rose (Sandrowitz) Greenberg; married Leonard J. Fassler (an attorney), July 26, 1953; children: David Gary, Ellen Beth. *Education:* College of the City of New York (now City College of the City University of New York), B.B.A., 1953; Columbia University, M.A., 1965, Ph.D., 1969. *Home:* 80 Hickory Hill Dr., Dobbs Ferry, N.Y. 10522. *Office:* Child Study Center, Yale University, 333 Cedar St., New Haven, Conn. 06510.

CAREER: Seventeen-at-School (magazine), New York, N.Y., editorial assistant, 1954-55; *Seventeen* (magazine), New York, N.Y., reader mail editor, 1955-56; Columbia University, Teachers College, New York, N.Y., research assistant at Research and Demonstration Center for Education of Handicapped Children, 1966-67, project associate, 1967-69, research associate, 1969-70, research consultant, 1970-71; Yale University, Child Study Center, New Haven, Conn., research associate in child development and children's literature, 1972—. Visiting lecturer at University of New Hampshire, 1970-71; moderator of "Conversations with the Very Young," on WNYC-Radio, 1970.

MEMBER: Authors League of America, Association for Childhood Education International, American Orthopsychiatric Association (program committee), American Psychological Association, Council for Exceptional Children, National Association for the Education of Young Children, Psi Chi.

WRITINGS—Juveniles: *The Man of the House,* Behavioral Publications, 1969; *All Alone with Daddy,* Behavioral Publications, 1969; *One Little Girl,* Behavioral Publications, 1969; *Don't Worry, Dear,* Behavioral Publications, 1971; *My Grandpa Died Today,* Behavioral Publications, 1971; *The Boy with a Problem,* Behavioral Publications, 1971; *Howie Helps Himself,* Whitman, 1975.

Contributor of research articles to education and psychology journals.

Videotapes: *The Man of the House, All Alone with Daddy, One Little Girl, Don't Worry Dear, My Grandpa Died Today, The Boy with a Problem,* were shown on the Pete and Willy Show, WHCT-TV, Hartford, Conn., summer, 1972. Video cassettes were produced in 1971 by Videorecord Corporation, Westport, Conn.

WORK IN PROGRESS: Research on child development and children's literature, especially concerned with the use of books and stories to help children grow.

"Oh yes," said David's mother. "You will be the first one I will call if any dragons come in to bother me." ∎ (From *The Man of the House* by Joan Fassler. Illustrated by Peter Landa.)

SIDELIGHTS: "As a research psychologist working with normal and handicapped children, I saw a great need for more books for young children dealing with selected topics of importance in early child development. For example, as an outgrowth of my work with handicapped children, I wrote *One Little Girl* (the story of a 'slow' child) and *Howie Helps Himself* (the story of a boy confined to a wheelchair). I have attempted to write books for children whenever my own experiences with young children suggest that an important theme merits further storybook portrayal, and whenever my own feelings assure me that there is indeed a story to be told."

FOR MORE INFORMATION SEE: The Reading Teacher, volume 26, October, 1972; *Growing Up with Books,* 1972; *The Instructor,* May, 1975; *Young Children,* January, 1976.

FOSTER, F. Blanche   1919-

PERSONAL: Born January 6, 1919, in Centerville, Tenn.; daughter of L. George (a clergyman) and Blanche (a teacher; maiden name, Nunnelly) Foster; married Francis L. Robinson (divorced). *Education:* Tennessee State University, B.S., 1940; Atlanta University, B.L.S., 1947; University of Michigan, A.M.L.S., 1952; further graduate study at Wayne State University, Sophia University, and University of Ghana. *Religion:* Presbyterian. *Home:* 2239 Spruce St., Terre Haute, Ind. 47807. *Office:* South High School, 3737 South Seventh St., Terre Haute, Ind. 47802.

CAREER: Teacher of English at Darwin High School, Cookville, Tenn., 1940-43; Camp Breckenridge, Ky., librarian, 1944-45; U.S. Navy Department, processor, 1945-46; Huston-Tillotson College, Austin, Tex., librarian, 1947-49; Anderson High School, Austin, Tex., librarian, 1949-51; li-brarian for public schools in Detroit, Mich., 1951-71, assistant director of "Focus on Afro-American Culture" program, 1968; University of Ibadan, Ibadan, Nigeria, lecturer in library science, 1971-73; South High School, Terre Haute, Ind., librarian, 1974—. *Member:* Women's International League for Peace and Freedom, American Library Association, American Federation of Teachers, American Association for the Advancement of Colored People, Young Women's Christian Association, Alpha Kappa Alpha. *Awards, honors:* Recognition award from Indiana Black Caucus, 1975.

F. BLANCHE FOSTER

In dancing, the Dahomeyan uses his arms in thrusts to express certain emotions. His leaps and turns may express his frivolity or set purpose. ■ (From *Dahomey* by F. Blanche Foster. Illustrated by M. Rouille.)

WRITINGS: Kenya, F. Watts, 1969; *People to Know Better,* Good Reading Communications, 1971; *Dahomey,* F. Watts, 1971; *The West Indies: A Conceptual View,* Carlton, in press. Contributor to *Michigan Challenge.*

SIDELIGHTS: "The stories my grandmother related greatly influences my feelings about Africa. She told us of her trip to America on a slave ship with her brothers when she was a very little girl. She told us of the beauties of her land by the waters. And she told us about slavery. . . . What would I be doing if I had been born a black girl in Africa and where would I be? . . . As an adult I have tried to see as many places in the world as I can. Everywhere I go I seem to be attracted to the children who differ in shades of skin color or dress. We get along well together and it is with them and my students that I enjoy some of my best moments of happiness."

HOBBIES AND OTHER INTERESTS: Collecting maps.

FOX, Lorraine

PERSONAL: Born in Brooklyn, N.Y.; daughter of Theodore J. (an accountant) and Florence (Gatto) Fox; married Bernard L. Dandrea (an illustrator), December 28, 1950. *Education:* Attended Pratt Institute and Brooklyn Museum Art School. *Religion:* Lutheran. *Home and office:* 4 Kings Terrace Road, Kings Point, Long Island, N.Y. 11024. *Agent:* Frank and Jeff Lavaty, 45 East 51st St., New York, N.Y. 10022.

CAREER: Free-lance illustrator. Famous Artists School, Westport, Conn., instructor; Parsons School of Design, New York, N.Y., instructor. Has lectured in colleges and universities extensively. *Exhibitions:* Society of Illustrators, Nassau Community College, Marymount College, Pratt Institute, Parsons School of Design, Brooklyn Museum, Silvermine Gallery, Connecticut, City Center Gallery, numerous group shows. *Member:* Society of Illustrators. *Awards, honors:* Society of Illustrators, gold medal and awards of excellence; Philadelphia Art Directors Show, silver medal; numerous awards from city art directors shows and painting shows.

ILLUSTRATOR: Shirley Jackson, *9 Magic Wishes,* Crowell-Collier, 1963; Mark Van Doren, *Somebody Came,* Quist, 1966; *Options,* Girl Scouts of America. Also wrote *The Nursery Book* and *Language for Daily Use.* Has done numerous text books, book covers, cookbooks and Harlin Quist books.

LORRAINE FOX

SIDELIGHTS: "Working solely to fit the demands of editorial, advertising or book assignments can be confining to me. I find it a necessity to constantly try to expand inner vision. As life experiences unfold, the point of view of my inner world may change. Therefore, I try to spend as much time as I possibly can despite my busy schedule, drawing, painting (in oils) or doing watercolors from my imagination. To enrich this 'inner repertoire' I also draw from nature. A great many are entirely abstract or surreal. Medium or technique is not a main concern of mine. I believe one could spend a lifetime exploring a single medium and never exhaust its possibilities. What concerns me is to become more knowledgeable about my personal attitude toward drawing and painting. I could not have solved many of my commissioned works had I not gone through the more personal work I made reference to. This is probably one of the reasons for the longevity of my career in a business which is in a constant state of change.

"I try to convey these thoughts to the students I teach. I stress the search for 'self' among other ideas. I feel that a great part of 'self' lies within the unconscious and it is my attempt as a teacher to try to awaken a dormant imagination.

"Traveled in Europe for ten years—especially Italy where my husband and I painted. We both speak Italian. I studied voice and had hoped to have a concert career, but abandoned it to art.

"There were two teachers who had the most influence on my work: Will Burtin (a designer) and Reuben Tam (a painter)."

FOR MORE INFORMATION SEE: Idea Magazine, number 124, 1974-75.

FRANCIS, Pamela (Mary) 1926-

PERSONAL: Born September 4, 1926, in Ipswich, England; daughter ,of Jack Lincoln (a metallurgist) and Anna May (Hughes) Francis. *Education:* King's College, London, B.A. (honors), 1947. *Home:* 29 Turnberry Way, Crofton Place, Orpington, Kent, England.. *Office:* Imperial Chemical Industries Ltd., Millbank, London S.W.1, England.

CAREER: Imperial Chemical Industries Ltd., London, England, employed in secretarial position, 1948-55, 1971-74, editor of house magazine, 1969-71, officer of Americas zone, international coordination, 1975—. Lived in Argentina, 1955, Peru, 1955-57, and 1959-69, and was Lima correspondent for *Times* (London), 1959-69, and for *Statist,* 1965-67. *Awards, honors:* Prize awarded by Editorial Doncel (Madrid), 1964, for folktale in Spanish; Award of Merit from CRAV (Chile) in contest sponsored by UNESCO, 1968, also for folktale in Spanish.

WRITINGS—All for young people: *Spanish Conquest in America,* Wheaton & Co., 1964; *Life in Ancient Peru,* Wheaton & Co., 1965; *What Became of the Mayas?,* Wheaton & Co., 1969; *Ricardo Palma: Tradiciones peruanas* (text), Pergamon, 1969. Story included in *Cuentos peruanos,* Editorial Doncel, 1965.

SIDELIGHTS: "Writing and pre-history have been two of my chief interests since about the age of eight and the passion for things Spanish made its appearance not much later.

PAMELA FRANCIS

However, due to the Second World War and other circumstances I was only able to visit Spain for the first time in 1953, but that visit clinched it. My interest grew and spread to embrace Latin America where I spent many happy years between 1955 and 1969. Peru in particular is a fascinating country; its people are friendly, its scenery is magnificent and its history and literature repay anyone's study.

"I certainly hope that I shall be able to spend more time in Spanish America in the future and perhaps write about it again. In the meantime I am enjoying my annual holidays in Spain and having a look at the places which gave birth to those tough, courageous, greedy men who became the conquistadores."

FOR MORE INFORMATION SEE: Times Literary Supplement, October 16, 1969.

FREWER, Glyn   1931-

PERSONAL: Born September 4, 1931, in Oxford, England; son of Louis (superintendent of Rhodes House Library, Oxford) and Dorothy (Poulter) Frewer; married Lorna F. Townsend (a teacher of piano and violin), August 11, 1956; children: Neil, Sean, Claire. *Education:* St. Catherine's College, Oxford, B.A. (honors in English language and literature), 1955, M.A., 1959. *Home:* Wychwood, Stanstead Rd., Caterham, Surrey, England. *Agent:* Bolt & Watson Ltd., 8 Storey's Gate, London, England. *Office:* Masius, Wynne-Williams & D'Arcy-MacManus, 2 St. James's Sq., London S.W.1, England.

GLYN FREWER

CAREER: British Council, student officer in Oxford, England, 1955; advertising copywriter, various agencies, 1955-65; Masius, Wynne-Williams Ltd., London, creative manager, 1965-74; Masius, Wynne-Williams & D'Arcy-MacManus, London, associate director, 1974—; Freeman of City of Oxford, 1967. *Military service:* Royal Army Ordnance Corps, 1950-52. *Member:* Society of Authors.

WRITINGS—Juveniles: *Adventure in Forgotten Valley* (Junior Literary Guild selection), Faber, 1962, Putnam, 1964; *Adventure in the Barren Lands,* Faber, 1964, Putnam, 1966; *The Last of the Wispies,* Faber, 1965; *The Token of Elkin,* Heinemann, 1970; *Crossroad,* Heinemann, 1970; *The Square Peg,* Heinemann, 1972; *The Raid,* Heinemann, 1976. Teleplays—26 episodes of "Simon in the Land of Chalk Drawings," for ITV (United Kingdom), 1976. Radio play, "The Hitch-hikers," produced by British Broadcasting Corp., 1957.

SIDELIGHTS: "I spent the first eighteen years of my life in Oxford, England, and I cannot remember a time when I was not interested in natural history, particularly bird-watching. Scouting and camping gave me opportunities to further this interest which, in turn, led to a love of travel. A visit to Europe in 1947 introduced me to hitch-hiking and every possible vacation after that I went abroad, hitch-hiking, either alone or with a friend; trips I still look back on with the utmost pleasure. Everything we needed was on our backs and we went where the mood—or traffic—took us, often to countries we had not originally planned to visit. In all, I covered over 17,000 miles 'by thumb' through twelve European countries.

"At school, I was asked for accounts of these trips for the school magazine and I found I enjoyed writing them. I soon moved across to trying poems and short stories and I began to feel that very special kind of satisfaction which only writing can bring. I carried on writing stories long after I left school, just for the pleasure of it, and when I eventually won a short-story competition and saw my first story in print, I knew writing was for me.

"Once that was decided, I tried writing something that would give me a chance to bring in the other subject I enjoyed, natural history. I was no expert but I felt I could weave what I did know into an adventure story which is how I came to write my first book, *Adventure in Forgotten Valley.* Prehistory had always fascinated me and it was sheer pleasure to write about the monsters and bring them to life. And this brings me to a point I took a long time to learn; that the best kind of stories seem to come when writers write to please themselves. Writing to please other people usually has a *colder* feel to it, from the mind more than from the heart. As a professional advertising copywriter, I was well placed to feel the difference between the two kinds of writing. By day, I wrote what other people wanted—advertisements and commercials; evenings and weekends, I wrote to please myself. The fact other people liked the stories was a bonus brought about as much by luck as judgment.

"It was only after my first book was chosen by the Junior Literary Guild for school use that I realised authentic background facts not only help to make a story more convincing, but can actually help the reader to learn. From that moment on, I have made sure that all my background details—mostly dealing with wildlife and prehistory—are as accurate as possible. I see no reason why a story cannot be helpfully informative as well as entertaining.

"Apart from writing, I think I best enjoy the various activities that take me, with my family, out into the countryside where we live. My two sons are keen on fishing, my daughter fast becoming an expert on butterflies and flowers, my wife enjoys visiting the many historical houses and sites that England has to offer. I also walk a lot, long walks, often too far for the family and I particularly like the South Downs in the autumn when the birds are migrating in their thousands. Today, instead of netting and ringing them as I once did, I write occasional articles for bird magazines. All in all, I find there is never enough time to do all the things I want to do."

FOR MORE INFORMATION SEE: Caterham Weekly Press, March 13, 1964; *Caterham Times,* June 23, 1972.

FRIENDLICH, Richard J. 1909-
(Dick Friendlich)

PERSONAL: Surname is pronounced *Frend*-lick; born January 20, 1909, in San Francisco, Calif.; son of Samuel J. (a salesman) and Josephine (Schoenfeld) Friendlich; married Elisabeth Turner (a writer); children: Francia Ann. *Education:* Stanford University, A.B., 1932. *Politics:* Democrat. *Home:* 2465½ Onion St., San Francisco, Calif. *Agent:* Curtis Brown Ltd., 575 Madison Ave., New York, N.Y. 10022. *Office:* San Francisco Chronicle, San Francisco, Calif.

CAREER: Held a series of odd jobs that included work for a short-lived literary magazine, selling classified ads for *New*

RICHARD J. FRIENDLICH

York Times, and work as shipping clerk; *San Francisco Chronicle,* San Francisco, Calif., sports writer, 1935—. *Military service:* U.S. Army, Signal Corps, 1942-45; became master sergeant; received Bronze Star and three battle stars for Italian campaigns. *Member:* U.S. Basketball Writers Association (president, 1965-66), Baseball Writers of America, Authors Guild, Sigma Delta Chi.

WRITINGS—Youth books; under name Dick Friendlich; all published by Westminster except as indicated: *Pivot Man,* 1949, *Warrior Forward,* 1950, *Goal Line Stand,* 1951, *Line Smasher,* 1952, *Play Maker,* 1953, *Baron of the Bull Pen* (Junior Literary Guild selection), 1955, *Left End Scott,* 1956, *Clean Up Hitter,* 1957, *Gridiron Crusader,* 1958, *Backstop Ace,* 1959, *Lead Off Man,* 1960, *Full Court Press,* 1961, *All Pro Quarterback,* 1962, *Relief Pitcher,* 1964, *Pinch Hitter* (Junior Literary Guild selection), 1965, (editor) *An Anthology of Sports Stories,* Scholastic Book Services, 1965, *Touchdown Maker,* Doubleday, 1966, *Fullback from Nowhere,* 1967.

WORK IN PROGRESS: An untitled juvenile, for Westminster.

HOBBIES AND OTHER INTERESTS: Bridge.

FULLER, Lois Hamilton 1915-

PERSONAL: Born August 13, 1915, in Bayonne, N.J.; daughter of Emmett S. (a banker) and Mabel (Havens; a musician) Hamilton; married Donald L. Fuller (scientist), October 15, 1938; children: Margaret, John. *Education:* Smith College, A.B., 1937; University of California (Berkeley), graduate student, 1939; Churchman Business College, executive-secretarial course, 1945; University of Maryland, graduate student, 1960. *Politics:* Independent. *Religion:* Presbyterian. *Home:* 1310 Shoshone St., Boise, Idaho 83705.

CAREER: Briarcliff Junior College, Briarcliff Manor, N.Y., English teacher, 1937-38; Churchman Business College, Easton, Pa., English and shorthand teacher, 1945-46; public schools, Ridgewood, N.J., substitute teacher, 1957; elementary schools, Montgomery County, Md., substitute teacher, 1958—. *Member:* Authors Guild of the Authors League of America, Mystery Writers of America, Children's Book Guild (Washington, D.C.), Children's Reading Round Table.

WRITINGS: (With Mary Shiverick Fishler) *The Mystery of the Old Fisk House,* Abingdon, 1960; *Keo, The Cave Boy,* Abingdon, 1961; *The Jade Jaguar Mystery,* Abingdon, 1962; *Fire in the Sky: Story of a Boy of Pompeii,* Abingdon, 1965; *Swarup Returns,* Children's Book Trust, 1968; *Little Tiger, Big Tiger,* Children's Book Trust, 1970. Contributor of short stories and verse to children's magazines.

WORK IN PROGRESS: Easy-to-read books.

SIDELIGHTS: "I grew up in Queens Village, Long Island, New York in a suburban neighborhood that included people of different ethnic, religious, and occupational backgrounds. I was interested in my friends' beliefs—we were Protestants, Catholics, and Jews—and years later, when I took a course at Smith College in comparative religion, I learned for the first time, of Hinduism, Buddhism, and other Asian reli-

LOIS HAMILTON FULLER

gions. I took philosophy courses and was fascinated by the variety of ideas.

"Then in my senior year, a sociology course introduced me to Margaret Mead's studies of people of different cultures. I knew I wanted to travel and see first-hand what other people in the world were like. Fortunately my husband's interests were similar, even though his field was science.

"We have travelled all over the United States, in Canada, Mexico, Europe and Asia. He has always encouraged me in my work and helped me in every way. My children shared his attitude and were first editors of my Abingdon books. My books were for them and their friends, so I worked in a mystery whenever I could. They learned with me what editors and librarians would buy from a children's author and what material they didn't want.

"I have always loved to read mysteries and I love to write them, but educational material must be included, in most cases, if books are to be considered worth including in a library budget. I derive my material, usually, by steeping myself in the history of a country that interests me. Then I think about a main character and when he or she has become real to me, I think about plot.

"I have enjoyed making up stories since I was a child and told them to my friends. Writing, of course, is much harder work than story-telling, but it is thrilling for an author to re-

ceive letters from children she has never met but who have enjoyed her books and let her know it."

HOBBIES AND OTHER INTERESTS: Swimming, bridge, fishing.

FOR MORE INFORMATION SEE: Montgomery County Sentinel, Montgomery County, Md., June 30, 1960; *Washington Post Potomac Magazine,* September 10, 1961; *Ridgewood Sunday News,* Ridgewood, New Jersey, October 28, 1962; *Detroit Free Press,* November 19, 1962.

FUNKE, Lewis 1912-

PERSONAL: Born January 25, 1912, in New York, N.Y.; son of Joseph (in construction) and Rose (Keimowitz) Funke; married Blanche Bier (a teacher), July 5, 1938; children: Phyllis, Michael. *Education:* New York University, A.B., 1932. *Home:* 61 Alta Dr., Mt. Vernon, N.Y. 10552. *Agent:* Curtis Brown, Ltd., 60 East 56th St., New York, N.Y. 10022.

CAREER: New York Times, New York, N.Y., free-lance sportswriter, 1928-32, staff sportswriter, 1932-44, member of general news and movie staff, 1944, drama editor, 1945-73; Queens College of the City University of New York, lecturer, 1973-75. Visiting professor, Florida State University, 1974—; director, Theatre Oral History Program, Charles MacArthur Center for American Theatre, 1974—; public relations consultant, Eugene O'Neill Memorial Theatre Center, 1973—.

WRITINGS: (Editor with John E. Booth) *Actors Talk about Acting: Fourteen Interviews with Stars of the Theatre,* Random House, 1961 (published in England as *Actors Talk about Acting: Nine Interviews with Stars of the Theatre,* Thames & Hudson, 1962); (with Max Gordon) *Max Gordon Presents,* Geis, 1963; (with Helen Hayes) *A*

LEWIS FUNKE

Something about the Author

Ossie stood as if hypnotized. He almost didn't hear Ruby say, "Better get going." A situation like that sometimes happens to actors on an opening night.
■ (From *The Curtain Rises* by Lewis Funke. Illustrated by H. B. Vestal.)

Gift of Joy, M. Evans, 1965; *The Curtain Rises: The Story of Ossie Davis* (juvenile), Grosset, 1971; *Playwrights Talk about Writing,* Dramatic Publishing, 1974; (editor) *Actors Talk about Theatre,* Dramatic Publishing, 1976.

SIDELIGHTS: "As is true of so much in life, my writing career seems, in retrospect, to have turned on a chance remark made by a girl about a year or so my junior when I was about twelve years old and living in an apartment house in The Bronx, New York. It was a lower middle-class apartment house, with a candy store on the street floor, a great hangout which has all but disappeared from contemporary life as far as young people in the suburbs are concerned, and a great loss, indeed. I always seemed to have been pretty good at writing compositions, had done a lot of reading from the time I was introduced to the New York Public Library System, and knew a lot of words unfamiliar to many of my peers. So, one evening standing on the stoop of the house next to the candy store, this girl—her name, mind you was Minerva (and she had a sister, Daphne)—said to me that she thought I ought to be a newspaperman, a journalist because I could write and it was an exciting profession and I 'would meet such interesting people.' Somehow that made a connection and when I was in junior high school I became an editor of the semi-annual publication. In high school I joined the staff of the school paper and because of my interest in sports, eventually became the sports editor and columnist.

"Chance again came into my life one Monday morning when the managing editor of the paper, who was working weekends for the defunct *Brooklyn Eagle,* told me that Arthur Daley, then the schoolboy sports editor of *The New York Times* and later its columnist, needed someone to cover our school's home games. I got the job, receiving $1 a game. That got my foot in the door and later after I had been graduated from college, I made the staff of the paper. Curiously, I subsequently became the drama editor through no effort of mine. I had begun writing for various magazines on a variety of subjects and I guess I developed something of a reputation on the paper. I had left the sports department, had been on temporary assignment in the movie department and then in the general news department when I was asked whether I would like to become the drama editor. Of course, I grabbed it because, in addition to sports I'd always been interested in the theater and the arts. Being an inveterate moonlighter, not to mention the incentive of money, I continued to write for the different magazines.

"The first book I did came about as a result of a luncheon date with a friend. That was *Actors Talk About Acting* for which we went around with a tape recorder interviewing leading actors about their craft. Then I met Max Gordon, now the dean of American producers—the man who presented such hits as *Born Yesterday* and *The Solid Gold Cadillac* and he was anxious to have his autobiography written. I agreed to do it. My major success, however, was to come with a book I did with Helen Hayes called, *A Gift of Joy.* One of the nice things about that, aside from its becoming a best-seller, was that I had to spend two weeks with Miss Hayes at her house in Cuernavaca, Mexico.

"I am now sort of semi-retired. Between worrying about my tomatoes and the slugs in the flower beds and trying to improve my golf, I also teach and continue my tape recording with actors and playwrights. I also tape record the memories of important people in the theater for the Charles MacArthur Center for American Theatre, sponsored by Florida State University. Obviously, I'm not ready for complete retirement and I'm not sure that I ever will be provided my health holds up. Just vegetating, doing nothing except playing, seems a bit useless and self-indulgent."

Funke's writing assignments abroad have included England, France, Israel, Yugoslavia, Germany, Italy, and elsewhere.

HOBBIES AND OTHER INTERESTS: Golf, gardening.

The ship was a vision of hell, hissing and flaming on the surface of the mysterious ocean.

102

■ (From *Blow Ye Winds Westerly* by Elizabeth Gemming. Illustrated by Albert Alden.)

ELIZABETH GEMMING

GEMMING, Elizabeth 1932-

PERSONAL: Born December 27, 1932, in Glen Cove, N.Y.; daughter of Alexander Henry (a teacher and school principal) and Ruth (a secretary; maiden name, Smith) Prinz; married Klaus Gemming (a book designer), July 3, 1957; children: Marianne, Christina. Education: Wellesley College, B.A., 1954; University of Munich, graduate study, 1954-55. Home: 49 Autumn St., New Haven, Conn. 06511.

CAREER: Teacher of English in German secondary schools, Munich, 1954-55; Pantheon Books, Inc., assistant editor and member of promotion staff, 1955-57; free-lance writer, editor, and translator, 1957—. Member: Phi Beta Kappa. Awards, honors: Fulbright scholarship, University of Munich, 1954-55.

WRITINGS—Juveniles, except as indicated: Huckleberry Hill: Child Life in Old New England, Crowell, 1968; (with husband, Klaus Gemming) Learning through Stamps series, Barre-Westover, Volume I: The World of Art, 1968, Volume II: Around the World, 1968, Volume III: Portraits of Greatness, 1969; Blow Ye Winds Westerly: The Seaports and Sailing Ships of Old New England, Crowell, 1972; Getting to Know New England, Coward, 1970; Getting to Know the Connecticut River, Coward, 1974; Block Island Summer (adult book; photographs by Klaus Gemming), Chatham Press, 1972; Born in a Barn: Farm Animals and Their Young (photographs by Klaus Gemming), Coward, 1974; Maple Harvest: The Story of Maple Sugaring, Coward, 1976.

Translations from German—All juveniles: Renato Rascel, Piccoletto: The Story of the Little Chimney Sweep, Pantheon, 1958; Max Bolliger, Sandy at the Children's Zoo, Crowell, 1967; Alfons Weber, Elizabeth Gets Well, Crowell, 1970.

WORK IN PROGRESS: A juvenile, Squirrel Wood, with photographs; working with her husband, a photographer, book designer and book production consultant.

HOBBIES AND OTHER INTERESTS: Travel (Europe, especially France and Austria), American cultural history, medieval history and art, knitting (especially the Icelandic style), family history (is descended from Mayflower pilgrims), visiting old graveyards in rural New England.

FOR MORE INFORMATION SEE: New York Times Book Review, November 3, 1968; Children's Book World, November 3, 1968.

GEORGE, S(idney) C(harles) 1898-

PERSONAL: Born June 2, 1898, in Grimsby, England. Education: Educated in England. Home: 40 Nea Rd., Highcliffe, Christchurch, Dorset BH23 4NB, England.

CAREER: Served in the Royal Garrison Artillery of the British Army, 1917-20; career officer in Royal Air Force, 1924-53, serving in India, Palestine, Transjordan, Egypt, Sudan, Malaya, Australia, retiring as group captain. Novelist and children's writer. Member: Society of Authors, Institute of Chartered Accountants (fellow), Chartered Institute of Secretaries (fellow). Awards, honors: Officer of the Order of the British Empire, 1948; member of the Royal Victorian Order, 4th class, 1953.

WRITINGS: Cairo Card, R. Hale, 1937; Singapore Nights, Jarrolds, 1942; Wiles of Lim Quong, Jarrolds, 1943; Strange Courtship, Macdonald, 1946; Bright Moon in the Forest, Jarrolds, 1946; Girl in the Cabaret, Macdonald, 1947; Locust Years, Jarrolds, 1947; Devil's Delight, Macdonald, 1948; Bamboo Rod, Jarrolds, 1951; Planter's Wife, Jarrolds, 1951; Reluctant Infidel, Museum Press, 1954; Witch Doctor, Museum Press, 1955; Father Was a Horse, Museum Press, 1955, Soldier of the Line, Museum Press, 1956; Jutland to Junkyard (nonfiction), Patrick Stephens, 1973.

Children's books: Lost Empire, Warne, 1937; Blue Ray, Warne, 1938; Red Goddess, Warne, 1939; Secret Six, Blackie & Son, 1940; Eagle of the Desert, Warne, 1944; Escape from Singapore, Hollis & Carter, 1946; Pirates of the Lagoon, Warne, 1946; Burma Story, Warne, 1948; Two Spies, Warne, 1948; Midshipman's Luck, Warne, 1955; Daughters of Arabia, Warne, 1958; Amat's Elephant, Macmillan, 1959; Round the Map (nonfiction), six volumes, E. J. Arnold, 1963; Man Needs the Sun (nonfiction), Hamish Hamilton, 1963; The Happy Fisherman, Hamish Hamilton, 1965; The Long White March, Hamish Hamilton, 1965; The Shadow of the Guillotine, E. J. Arnold, 1965; Toko and the Bear, Hamish Hamilton, 1965; The Trouble Maker, E. J. Arnold, 1965; Fire in the Bracken, E. J. Arnold, 1966; Sound the Bugle, E. J. Arnold, 1966; Barge Boy, Oliver & Boyd, 1968; Chiho and Tong See: A Tale of Korea, Chatto & Windus, 1969; Mouse-Deer and the Swordfish, E. J. Arnold, 1970; Mouse-Deer's Race with Snail, E. J. Arnold,

S. C. GEORGE

Chinese who began life as a poor peasant in China and rose to eminence in Singapore, a diver who helped in the salvage of the scuttled German High Seas fleet from Scapa Flow in Scotland and many others whose lives had followed strange courses.

"In ancient temples along the River Nile, in Roman amphitheatres in the Near East and in Indian temples hewn from the living rock in a remote past my imagination has been stimulated, and the past has seemed to be not so long ago.

"Morning is my best time for writing when I expect to complete between 1,500 and 2,000 words. This work is revised several times and the complete story may be rewritten three or four times before being sent to a publisher. Research is usually necessary and this can occupy much more time than the writing of the actual story.

"I find it necessary to write regularly whether or not I feel like it, and like most writers I soon discovered that authorship depends more upon perspiration than inspiration.

"For me inspiration is the tiny spark from which the story catches fire. *Chiho and Tong See* grew out of voluntary work I was doing in connection with refugees, *Toko and the Bear* from a short paragraph in a newspaper, *The Shadow of the Guillotine* from an obscure verse on an old tomb in Christchurch (England) churchyard.

"I now write almost exclusively for young people because I feel that stories are more real and satisfying to them than they are to adults, and that through fiction they are helped to understand the harsh world they will soon be entering."

1970; *Sir Peace of the Forest,* E. J. Arnold, 1970; *Black Gold,* Chatto & Windus, 1970; *Hidden Treasure* (nonfiction), David & Charles, 1972; *The Vikings* (nonfiction), David & Charles, 1973.

SIDELIGHTS: "I cannot recall a time when I did not want to write, and at an early age I began what was to become a fat pile of rejection slips.

"I first saw myself in print in my school magazine, probably because I was responsible in part for its being founded. My first paid acceptance was a poem in an Indian review when I was serving with the British Army in India in 1918. Then with slowly increasing success I wrote articles and stories of all kinds for magazines and children's periodicals until I decided that to write books would be more satisfying.

"In between wars I worked for a time on a farm in the Australian bush before returning to accountancy to obtain professional qualifications.

"Two of my forebears fought at Waterloo, a fact which helped to develop my interest in the first half of the nineteenth century, an age when explorers, prospectors, pioneers, engineers, soldiers, writers and artists were busy in a world full of adventure. Several of my books have been set in this period.

"Countries I have visited have enabled me to provide convincing backgrounds for stories, and I talked with all kinds and conditions of people, including a Malayan witch doctor who claimed that he put a spell on his local team's football, a

GILBERT, Sara (Dulaney) 1943-

PERSONAL: Born October 5, 1943, in Washington, D.C.; daughter of Ben Bane (a journalist) and Jean (an editor; maiden name, Brownell) Dulaney; married Ian R. Gilbert (a lawyer), August 31, 1963 (separated); children: Sean Dulaney. *Education:* Attended Pembroke College, 1961-63; Barnard College, B.A. (with honors), 1966. *Residence:* New York, N.Y. *Agent:* Marilyn Marlowe, Curtis Brown Ltd., 575 Madison Ave., New York, N.Y. 10022.

CAREER: Cowles Communications, New York, N.Y., encyclopedia editor and writer, 1966-68. *Awards, honors:* Mr. Freedom Award from Religious Liberty Association, 1972, for articles.

WRITINGS: *Three Years to Grow: Guidance for Your Child's First Three Years,* Parents' Magazine Press, 1972; *What's a Father For?,* Parents' Magazine Press, 1975; *Fat Free,* Macmillan, 1975. Contributor to *Baby Care, Ms, Good Housekeeping, Travel, Campfire Girl, Negro Digest, Liberty, Metrolines,* and *National Businesswoman.*

WORK IN PROGRESS: A book on food for teenagers.

SIDELIGHTS: "I had always hoped to be able to write professionally and took it up with encouragement from my husband as a practical matter—to be able to have my own life and work while having time and freedom to care for a family. I tend, perhaps naturally, to write about topics that directly concern me, and find that I learn a lot from what I write, which is the point."

SARA GILBERT

HOBBIES AND OTHER INTERESTS: Gardening.

FOR MORE INFORMATION SEE: Kirkus Reviews, February 1, 1975; *Booklist,* March 1, 1975; *New York Times Book Review,* May 4, 1975; "The Calendar," Children's Book Council, September, 1975-February, 1976.

GLASER, Milton   1929-
(Max Catz)

PERSONAL: Born June 26, 1929, in New York, N.Y.; son of Eugene and Eleanor (Bergman) Glaser; married Shirley Girton (now an art gallery director), August 13, 1957. *Education:* Cooper Union, graduate, 1951; also studied at Academy of Fine Arts, Bologna, Italy. *Religion:* Hebrew. *Home:* 54 St. Mark's Pl., New York, N.Y. 10016. *Office:* 755 Second Ave., New York, N.Y. 10017.

CAREER: Artist and illustrator. Art and Design Studio, New York, N.Y., president, 1954—; Push Pin Studios, New York, N.Y., president, 1954-74. Director of four-year design program, School of Visual Arts; chairman of the board, *New York Magazine;* vice-president, *Village Voice,* 1974-75. *Member:* American Institute of Graphic Arts (vice-president), Alliance Graphique International. *Awards, honors:* Fulbright scholarship to Bologna, Italy; Gold Medal, Society of Illustrators; American Institute of Graphic Arts medalist one-man show at the Museum of Modern Art, 1975.

WRITINGS: (With wife, Shirley Glaser) *If Apples Had Teeth,* Knopf, 1960; (with Jerome Snyder) *The Underground Gourmet,* Simon & Schuster, 1965; *Milton Glaser Graphic Design,* Overlook Press, 1973; (with Jerome Snyder) *The Underground Gourmet Cookbook,* Simon & Schuster, 1975.

Illustrator: Alvin Tresselt, *The Smallest Elephant in the World,* Knopf, 1959; Conrad Aiken, *Cats and Bats and Things with Wings* (poetry), Atheneum, 1965; Mikhail Sholokhov, *Fierce and Gentle Warriors,* Doubleday, 1967; Gian-Carlo Menotti, *Help, Help, the Globolinks,* McGraw, 1970; George Mendoza, *Fish in the Sky,* Doubleday, 1971; *Asimov's Illustrated Don Juan,* Doubleday, 1972.

WORK IN PROGRESS: Mirror of Your Mind.

SIDELIGHTS: "There is a mystique about children's books as being a place for adventure and creativity, for taking risks, for extending the possibilities of defining what a children's book can be. But in fact the criteria are the usual: How similar is a new title to other successes, how significant is the author's name already, how closely does it cling to the established formulas.

"Statistically there are never a great number of good people doing anything at one time. But in some ways the level of achievement was once higher. A lot of the older books look better, and those of one-hundred years ago look better than those of twenty-five years ago, even over and above the value they have accrued with nostalgia. The old techniques

MILTON GLASER

To whit
to whoo
he stares
right through

■ (From *Cats and Bats and Things with Wings.* Poems by Conrad Aiken. Drawings by Milton Glaser.)

were more difficult to master and required a higher technical competence; they tended to weed out the mediocre and the dilettantes. Today's easy photomechanical processes provide less resistance.''

FOR MORE INFORMATION SEE: Graphis, Number 92, July, 1962; *Industrial Design,* July, 1962; *Idea,* October, 1964; Diana Klemin, *The Art of Art for Children's Books,* Clarkson Potter, 1966; *Illustrators of Children's Books: 1957-66,* Horn Book, 1968; Diana Klemin, *The Illustrated Book,* Clarkson Potter, 1970; *Graphis 155,* Volume 27, 1971/72; *New York Times Book Review,* May 6, 1973, November 26, 1973; *American Artist,* May, 1974.

GLYNNE-JONES, William   1907-

PERSONAL: Born December 19, 1907, in Llanelly, South Wales; son of Henry (a carpenter) and Matilda (Morgan) Jones; married Doris Passmore, July 30, 1932; children: Edgar Dennis Jones. *Education:* Attended grammar school

WILLIAM GLYNNE-JONES

in Llanelly. *Politics:* Socialist. *Religion:* Anglican. *Home:* 10 Ossian Rd., London N.4, England.

CAREER: Steel moulder in heavy steel foundry, 1923-43; released on medical grounds in 1943, and went to London to try free-lance writing; has worked as a reader for *Argosy,* Hutchinson's juvenile publications, Metro-Goldwyn-Mayer British Film Studios; was London film correspondent for South African press; British civil service, 1959-73, and part-time writer. *Awards, honors:* Atlantic Award for Literature of Rockefeller Foundation for uncompleted manuscript of novel, *Farewell Innocence,* 1946; Queen's bounty.

WRITINGS—Juveniles, unless otherwise noted: *He Who Had Eaten of the Eagle* (short stories), MacLellan, 1945; *Brecon Adventure,* Lutterworth, 1945; *The Runaway Train,* Lutterworth, 1946; *The Magic Forefinger, and Other Welsh Fairy Stories,* Broadman, 1946; *The Mouse and the Cuckoo,* Skilton, 1947; *Trail of Frozen Gold,* Harrap, 1948; *Dennis and Co.,* Warne, 1949; *Pennants on the Main,* Warne, 1950; *Farewell Innocence* (novel), Laurie, 1950; *Ride the White Stallion* (novel), Laurie, 1951; *Summer Long Ago* (novel), Nevill, 1954; *A Time to Seek* (autobiography), New Dawn, 1956; *Old Time Tales From Many Lands,* Mowbray, 1959; *The Childhood Land* (novel), Batsford, 1960; *Legends of the Welsh Hills,* Mowbray, 1960; *Holiday Adventure,* Spring Books, 1960; *Tales of Long Ago,* Mowbray, 1961; *The Fox's Cunning, and Other Stories,* Mowbray, 1962.

School readers: *If Pigs Had Wings, The Golden Boy, Yukon Gold,* and *The Buccaneers.* More than three hundred short stories published in *Pick of Today's Stories, Best Short Stories, New Short Stories, Welsh Short Stories, Strand, Lilli-*put, *Queen, International Review, Evening News, Evening Standard, Esquire, West Country, Tomorrow, New Masses, Adventure,* other popular and literary magazines; more than two hundred short stories contributed to radio and television in Great Britain, Australia, New Zealand, South Africa, Eire, and other countries.

WORK IN PROGRESS: Two Fair Ladies, a biographical study.

SIDELIGHTS: "I was born of working-class parents in Llanelly, South Wales—a town noted for its exports of tinplate and journalists! An industrial town of some 25,000 inhabitants, terraced streets of mean houses and almost perpetually wreathed by the smoke and steam of the tinplate works, steelworks, steel rolling mills, and foundries.

"We were a Welsh-speaking family; one of my ancestors sailed to South America and settled in Patagonia with the Welsh emigrants who made the hazardous journey in the nineteenth century. Another emigrated to the United States and made his home in Salt Lake City. A first cousin of mine, William John Hughes, went to London as a boy of sixteen to take up a stage career. Later he emigrated to America (1914) and appeared on Broadway, then became a star of the silent films in Hollywood. Towards the end of his life he renounced his career and became a minister of religion to the Paiute Indians at Fort McDermitt, Wadsworth, Nixon, Nevada. He was a man of three identities—born William John Hughes, acted under the name of Gareth Hughes, and ended his life as Brother David. He died at the Movie Actors' Country House and Hospital, Woodland Hills, California, in 1965. The *Reader's Digest* carried a feature on him entitled, 'Star in the Desert,' an extract from one of Fulton Oursler's books.

"Myself, I was born with a speech impediment and found great difficulty in being understood orally. However, I was compensated with an ability to express myself fluently in writing. As a boy in a local elementary school, my essays and compositions impressed the headmaster and they were read out to every class in the school. I gained a scholarship to the grammar school at the age of ten, and remained there until the age of fourteen, when economic pressures forced my parents to take me from school and set me to work in order to help support the family (I had three sisters younger than I). My first job was to boil tea for the manual workers in a chemical factory.

"I had loved my school and was loath to leave, for I had made excellent progress in all my exams, and had hoped to enter University. In my very early years I read voraciously, but although gregarious, I would often seek solitude in the topmost branches of trees or seat myself on a ledge half way up the steep face of an old stone quarry where I would immerse myself in my books. I well remember that I read all Baroness Orczy's novels, and many of Dumas's seated in the tree tops!

"At the age of nineteen I went to work in a heavy steel foundry, where I remained for twenty years, but the depression hit South Wales and the actual time I worked for the foundry was about twelve years . . . unemployment was rife.

"At the age of nineteen I was determined to write a novel. I had written 20,000 words and proudly showed it to my father. He completely disillusioned me by stating that I had not experienced life sufficiently to write a novel.

"I NEVER WROTE AGAIN until 1942. (I was then 35 years old, had been married ten years, and father to our little son.) During the first year that I resumed my writing in the front parlour in the evenings after work at the foundry, I was successful in placing six with the BBC. This initial success encouraged me, and I began to write in earnest and study the works of the famous short story writers.

"In 1943 my health deteriorated and I was discharged from the foundry. I could find no other employment, but an editor in London had noticed my short stories and advised me to come to London to fulfill my then strong ambition to become a writer.

"I took a chance, and went to London with the intention of finding a home there for my wife and son if I made good. I wrote short stories, read for *Argosy* magazine and Hutchinson's. I rented a small back room. The going was hard, for after remitting money to my wife and child I was left with approximately £1.10 to live on.

"I was under-nourished, nerve-wracked by the constant bombing of London, and suffered a great *'hiraeth,'* or longing for home which all Welshmen experience. Was hospitalised and underwent surgery for an internal abscess but didn't let my wife know for I realised she would ask me to come home. I was DETERMINED to establish myself as an author.

"A journalist friend counselled me to write a novel, but I was a short story writer and felt that a novel was beyond my capacity. However, my friend was persistent, so I wrote my first book for children, entitled, *Brecon Adventure,* which dealt with the mid-Wales town of Brecon nestling in the beautiful Vale of Usk. I knew the town intimately for I had often visited my married sister who lived there. I researched into the historical details of the old town, then created a plot and characters. The book was immediately accepted, and the same publisher took my next book for children, *The Runaway Train.*

"I now felt more confident and a series of children's books were accepted. But it was not easy—inspiration, yes! And perspiration, too! For I wrote in longhand, then revised as I typed with my one finger!

"Writing was now my profession. I became more observant than ever, jotting down notes on dialogue I overheard, various characters I met, scenes from city, town and village; cloud formations; ideas for plots; themes, etc., entering my notes into a notebook or if a notebook was not available, on scraps of paper, cigarette packets, newspaper margins—the notes to be collated later and typed for future reference. It is essential that a writer should take notes; it is useless relying on memory entirely. One recalls a dream when waking, but within a few minutes the details of the dream are lost.

"Although I persevered with my writing and was financially secure, ill-health dogged me, and in 1956—having had my first adult novels and more children's books published, I suffered a nervous breakdown which kept me totally inactive for two years.

"I now see the cause for my breakdown—I was over-worked. Reading for *Argosy,* Hutchinson's, Metro-Goldwyn-Mayer British Film Studios, London Film correspondent for South African film journals, writing everything in longhand, the typing, the business side (I never employed an agent, even up to the present day).

"I LOVE writing, and when doing so am completely immersed in it—giving no thought at all to the financial end. The joy of creating a story, a children's book, a novel, a play supercedes everything. But obviously, after the work is completed one has to consider the SALE!

"In 1959 I entered the civil service, but still continued to write and other books, stories, etc., were published. I retired from the service in 1973, but here I am, still consumed and delighted with the creative process.

"Being Welsh, I am naturally very proud of my country and my race, so my books and stories invariably have a Welsh background.

"Incidentally, a 'William Glynne-Jones Collection' of my books for children is housed in the Lena Y. de Grummond Library at the University of Southern Mississippi, and my original manuscripts were purchased by the National Library of Wales this year."

HOBBIES AND OTHER INTERESTS: Swimming, angling, reading, classical music; films, especially early silent classics; and oil painting.

GOLANN, Cecil Paige   1921-

PERSONAL: Surname is pronounced Go-*lann;* born January 20, 1921, in New York, N.Y.; daughter of Daniel Leonard (a physician) and Ethel (Block) Golann. *Education:*

CECIL PAIGE GOLANN

Just as Abraham was about to slay Isaac, the angel appeared. "Abraham!" he called out. "Stop at once! Do not raise your hand against the boy." ■ (From *Mission on a Mountain* by Cecil P. Golann. Illustrated by H. Hechtkopf.)

Barnard College, B.A. (summa cum laude), 1941; Columbia University, M.A., 1942, Ph.D., 1952. *Home:* 425 Riverside Dr., New York, N.Y. 10025. *Agent:* Patricia Lewis, 255 West 34th St., New York, N.Y. 10001.

CAREER: Hunter College, New York, N.Y., lecturer in English, 1953-55; Thomas Alva Edison Foundation, New York, N.Y., director of mass media awards, 1955-57; National Broadcasting Co. Television, New York, N.Y., program researcher, 1958-62; Crowell Collier & Macmillan, Inc., New York, N.Y., associate editor, 1962-67, senior editor, 1967-71. *Member:* American Philological Association, New York Classical Club, Phi Beta Kappa. *Awards, honors:* Fulbright fellowship to Italy, 1952-53; Ford Foundation Fund for the Advancement of Education grant to attend the Hunter College Ford Seminar in College Teaching, 1954-55.

WRITINGS: Our World: The Taming of Israel's Negev (juvenile), Messner, 1970.

WORK IN PROGRESS: Impact, a novel about Israel during the Six-Day War, completion expected in 1977; *Bronzebeard,* a novel about Nero and St. Paul, 1978.

SIDELIGHTS: "I wanted to be a writer ever since I can remember, but the need to earn a living forced me to devote my time first to teaching, then to miscellaneous jobs, and finally to editing manuscripts at Crowell-Collier.

"I am especially interested in the Humanities, have traveled considerably, especially in Europe and the Middle East, and know several foreign languages (Latin, Greek, French, German, Italian)."

GORDON, Sol   1923-

PERSONAL: Born June 12, 1923, in Brooklyn, N.Y.; married Judith Salzberger (a social worker); children: Josh. *Education:* University of Illinois, B.A. and M.A., both 1947; University of London, Ph.D., 1953. *Home:* 868 Ostrom Ave., Syracuse, N.Y. 13210. *Office:* Institute for Family Research and Education, 760 Ostrom Ave., Syracuse, N.Y. 13210.

CAREER: Clinical psychologist in Israel, 1948-51; Philadelphia Child Guidance Clinic, Philadelphia, Pa., chief psychologist, 1954-61; Middlesex County Mental Health Clinic, New Brunswick, N.J., chief psychologist, 1961-65; Yeshiva University, Ferkauf Graduate School of Humanities and Social Sciences, New York, N.Y., associate professor of psychology and education, and director of Project Beacon, 1965-69; high school teacher of psychology in Englewood, N.J., 1969-70; Syracuse University, Syracuse, N.Y., professor of child and family studies, and director of Institute for Family Research and Education, 1970—. Visiting lecturer at University of Pennsylvania, Newark State College, and New York University, 1961-69; visiting lecturer and consultant, Urban Studies Center and Upward Bound program, Rutgers University, 1961-69; consultant to Children's Hospital and Jewish Family Service, Philadelphia, Pa., and Headstart program in Mississippi, 1961-69. *Military service:* U.S. Army, 1942-45.

MEMBER: American Psychological Association (fellow), American Orthopsychiatric Association (fellow), American

SOL GORDON

Group Psychotherapy Association, National Council on Family Relations, American Association of Sex Educators and Counselors, Sex Information and Education Council of the United States, Society for the Scientific Study of Sex, American Association of Marriage and Family Counselors. *Awards, honors:* Award from Educational Foundation for Human Sexuality, 1974.

WRITINGS: (Editor) *Pressures That Disorganize in Secondary Schools,* New Jersey Secondary Schoolteachers Association, 1966; (editor with Risa Golob) *Recreation and Socialization for the Brain-Injured Child,* New Jersey Association for Brain-Injured Children, 1966; *Facts about Sex for Today's Youth,* John Day, 1970, revised edition, 1973; *Signs: A Non-Reading Approach to Reading,* New Readers Press, 1971; *Psychology for You,* Oxford Book, 1972, 2nd edition, 1974; *Facts about VD for Today's Youth,* John Day, 1973; *Family Planning Education for Adolescents,* U.S. Government Printing Office, 1973; *The Sexual Adolescent,* Duxbury, 1973; (editor with Gertrude Williams) *Clinical Child Psychology: Current Practices and Future Perspectives,* Behavioral Publications, 1975; *Girls Are Girls and Boys Are Boys: So What's the Difference* (juvenile), John Day, 1975; *Did the Sun Shine before You Were Born?* (juvenile), Third Press, 1975; (editor) *Sexuality Today and Beyond,* Duxbury, in press; *Let's Make Sex a Household Word,* John Day, 1975; *Living Fully, A Guide to Enhancing Self-Image,* John Day, 1975; *You,* Quadrangle, 1975; (with Mina Wollen) *Parenting: A Guide for Young People,* Oxford Book Co., 1975.

Pamphlets: *The Brain-Injured Adolescent,* New Jersey Association for Brain-Injured Children, 1964, revised edition, 1966; (with Winifred Kempton and Medora Bass) *Love, Sex, and Birth Control for the Mentally Retarded: A Guide for Parents,* Planned Parenthood Association of Southeastern Pennsylvania, 1971, revised edition, 1973; *On Being the Parent of a Handicapped Youth: A Guide to Enhance the Self-Image of Physically and Learning Disabled Adoles-*

Although you may not always agree with that person's opinions, if you are in love, the two of you will settle your differences without trying to hurt each other.
■ (From *Facts About Sex* by Sol Gordon. Illustrated by Vivien Cohen.)

cents and Young Adults, New York Association for Brain-Injured Children, 1973.

Contributor: Robert Dentler and other editors, *The Urban R's,* Praeger, 1967; Paul Graubard, editor, *Children against Schools,* Follett, 1969; *The Hidden Handicap,* California Association for Neurologically Handicapped Children, 1970; B. D. Starr, editor, *The Psychology of Adjustment,* Random House, 1970; Herbert Schulberg, Frank Baker, and Sheldon Roen, editors, *Developments in Human Services,* Behavioral Publications, 1973.

Comic books—all published by Ed-U Press: "Ten Heavy Facts about Sex," 1971; "Drug Youse: A Survivor's Handbook," 1971; "VD Claptrap," 1972; "Protect Yourself from Becoming an Unwanted Parent," 1973; "Gut News," 1974; "Juice Use," 1974.

Films: "Signs," four filmstrips, with teacher's guide, Educational Activities, 1973; "Getting It Together Is Life Itself," Educational Activities, 1973. Television: "This Program Is about Sex," a series of sixty-five programs for Canadian Global Network.

Contributor of about twenty articles to education and medical journals, including *Journal of School Health, PTA, Osteopathic Physician, Changing Education, Journal of Special Education,* and *Journal of Clinical Child Psychology.*

SIDELIGHTS: "I established Ed-U Press, a subsidiary of the Institute for Family Research and Education that I direct. It develops, publishes, and distributes a variety of educational materials for professionals, parents and youth. Ed-U Press is devoted to communicating with (not turning off) today's youth about love, morality, sex, drugs, smoking, alcohol and nutrition. It focuses on the proposition that adults often have worthwhile things to say."

GORSLINE, Douglas (Warner) 1913-

PERSONAL: Born May 24, 1913, in Rochester, N.Y.; son of Henry W. (a real estate broker) and Sarah (Warner) Gorsline; married Elisabeth Perkins, 1936 (divorced, 1959); children: John, Jerry. *Education:* Attended Yale University and Art Students League, New York. *Residence:* France. *Agent:* Ted Riley, 252 East 49th St., New York, N.Y. 10017.

CAREER: Artist; work in numerous private and public collections, including Butler Institute of American Art, Library of Congress, National Academy of Design, St. Paul Art Gallery, and Houghton Library, Harvard University; has had one-man shows in galleries and institutions nationwide, most recently at Schoelkopf Gallery, New York, Pearl Fox Gallery, Philadelphia, and Memorial Art Gallery, Rochester. Art instructor, Art School of the National Academy, 1960-62; free-lance illustrator. *Member:* National Academy of Design. *Awards, honors:* Purchase awards from American Academy of Arts and Letters, 1962, National Academy of Design, 1963, St. Paul Gallery, 1963, and Springfield Museum, 1965; Tiffany Foundation grant, 1963;

DOUGLAS GORSLINE

**When Pa and me had our picture taken by Matthew Brady, Brady gave us a big album to
look at, and Pa said he hoped folks wouldn't think he was making out like he was reading
me the Bible. ▪** (From *Me and Willie and Pa* by F. N. Monjo. Illustrated by Douglas Gorsline.)

and about a dozen other awards from groups and organizations, including American Watercolor Society, Audubon Artists, and National Arts Club.

WRITINGS: (Both self-illustrated) *Farm Boy,* Viking, 1950; *What People Wore: A Visual History of Dress from Ancient Times to Twentieth Century America,* Viking, 1952.

Illustrator: Marian King, *Young Mary Stuart, Queen of Scots,* Lippincott, 1954; Florence W. Rowland, *Jade Dragons,* Walck, 1954; Bernardine Kielty, *Marie Antoinette,* Random House, 1955; Anne Molloy, *Captain Waymouth's Indians,* Hastings, 1956; Louisa May Alcott, *Little Men,* Grosset, 1957; Fred Reinfeld, *Trappers of the West,* Crowell, 1957; Catherine O. Peare, *Charles Dickens: His Life,* Harper, 1959; Bernardine Kielty, *Jenny Lind Sang Here,* Houghton, 1959.

Louise D. Rich, *First Book of the Early Settlers,* Watts, 1960; Walter D. Edmonds, *They Had a Horse,* Dodd, 1962; Paul Horgan, *Citizen of New Salem,* Farrar, Straus, 1962; Jeanne L. Gardner, *Sky Pioneers: The Story of Wilbur and Orville Wright,* HarBrace, 1963; James P. Wood, *Hound, Bay Horse and Turtle Dove,* Simon & Schuster, 1963; Clyde R. Bulla, *Viking Adventure,* Crowell, 1963; James P. Wood, *Trust Thyself: A Life of Emerson for the Young Reader,* Pantheon, 1964; Nina B. Baker, *Nickels & Dimes: The Story of F. W. Woolworth,* HarBrace, 1966; John and Patricia Beatty, *At the Seven Stars,* Macmillan, 1967; Rosemary S. Nesbitt, *Great Rope,* Lothrop, 1968; Ruth Loomis, *Valley of the Hawk,* Dial, 1969.

Ferdinand Monjo, *Vicksburg Veteran,* Simon & Schuster, 1971; Ferdinand Monjo, *Me & Willie & Pa,* Simon & Schuster, 1973; Clement C. Moore, *The Night Before Christmas,* Random, 1975; Peggy Mann and Katisa Prusina, *A Present for Yanya,* Random House, 1975; Alida S. Malkus, *Story of Good Queen Bess,* Grosset.

WORK IN PROGRESS: Picture books for Random House.

SIDELIGHTS: Gorsline enjoys travel in Europe and has made a recent trip to the People's Republic of China.

FOR MORE INFORMATION SEE: Illustrators of Children's Books: 1946-1956, Horn Book, 1958; *Illustrators of Children's Books: 1957-1966,* Horn Book, 1968.

GOULD, Jean R(osalind)   1919-

PERSONAL: Born May 25, 1919, in Greenville, Ohio; daughter of Aaron J. and Elsie (Elgutter) Gould; divorced. *Education:* Attended University of Michigan for two years; University of Toledo, A.B., 1937. *Politics:* Reform Democrat.

CAREER: Amalgamated Clothing Workers Union, National Education Office, New York, N.Y., editorial and rewrite work, part-time, 1952—; National Opinion Research Center, Princeton, N.J., research and public opinion work. Democratic Party, county committeewoman. *Member:* Tilden Democratic Club (executive board), Authors Guild, Authors League, International P.E.N., United World Federalists. *Awards, honors:* Thomas A. Edison Award and prize for special excellence in contributing to character develop-

JEAN R. GOULD

ment of children, 1959, for *That Dunbar Boy;* fellowships at MacDowell Colony and Huntington Hartford Foundation, the latter in 1962 for work on Robert Frost book; fellowship at Yaddo, 1964, and Huntington Hartford Foundation, 1965, both for biographical studies of American playwrights; Ohiana Library Association-American Association of University Women award for "best biography of the year," 1969, for *The Poet and Her Book;* residence grants to Ossabow Island Project, 1967, 1976, and Wurlitzer Foundation, 1968, 1975.

WRITINGS—Youth books: *Fairy Tales,* Whitman, 1944; *Miss Emily* (biography of Emily Dickinson), Houghton, 1946; *Jane* (biography of Jane Austen), Houghton, 1947; *Young Thack* (biography of Thackeray), Houghton, 1949; *Sidney Hillman,* Houghton, 1952; *Fisherman's Luck,* Macmillan, 1954; *That Dunbar Boy* (biography of Paul Laurence Dunbar), Dodd, 1958.

Adult books: (Editor and contributor) *Homegrown Liberal,* Dodd, 1954; *Young Mariner Melville* (Literary Guild selection), Dodd, 1956; *A Good Fight: F.D.R.'s Conquest of Polio,* Dodd, 1960; *Winslow Homer: A Portrait,* Dodd, 1962; *Robert Frost: The Aim was Song,* Dodd, 1964; *Modern American Playwrights,* Dodd, 1966; *The Poet and Her Book: A Biography of Edna St. Vincent Millay,* Dodd, 1969; *Walter Reuther: Labor's Rugged Individualist,* Dodd, 1972; *Amy: The World of Amy Lowell and the Imagist*

Movement (excerpted in *Yankee Magazine,* October, 1975), Dodd, 1975.

WORK IN PROGRESS: A new multiple biography dealing with modern American women poets.

SIDELIGHTS: "I often say that I was born with printer's ink in my veins, as my parents were in the minor publishing business, and my aunt was a newspaperwoman from 1922 until her retirement three years ago at the age of eighty—a total of fifty years. My uncle was a top advertising man, who offered one of the first courses in copywriting ever taught at a University, University of Toledo. (Although I was born in the small town of Greenville, in southern Ohio, we moved to Toledo when I was six or seven, so most of my education and growing years took place there.)

"I learned about type-sizes and styles, picas, make-up, all the mechanics of publishing almost before I started to write. I say 'almost' because I did have the temerity to write, direct, and act in a play at the tender age of ten; it was a dramatization of a scene from 'Rebecca of Sunnybrook Farm,' I blush to say. And probably was inspired by the fact that among other things, my parents published theater programs.

"I acquired a love of the drama from every angle; my sister and I attended rehearsals, knew the leading players as well as character and bit players. One tangible result of this, of course, is my book on *Modern American Playwrights;* and I am now attempting to tell the story of those stagestruck days in our family. (Two of my brothers went into the theater, one remained there. The other, also a writer, switched to journalism.) I have written a good many one-act plays for children most of which were published in *Plays.*

"My mother, when she wasn't editing, or writing 'fillers' for theater programs, wrote poetry. Not very good poetry, but it tempted me to try. Mine was not much better than hers, so when I began writing professionally, I decided I would write *about* poets and poetry. Starting with my great love, Èmily Dickinson, I have so far produced biographies of six American poets, Amy Lowell being the sixth."

HOBBIES AND OTHER INTERESTS: Politics, gardening, watercolor painting, and cooking.

FOR MORE INFORMATION SEE: Villager, New York, N.Y., April 20, 1961, February 12, 1976.

David found himself next to a boy just his size, who welcomed him with a wink that said plainly, "We'll have some fun together." ■ (From *That Dunbar Boy* by Jean Gould. Illustrated by Charles Walker.)

ADA GRAHAM

GRAHAM, Ada 1931-

PERSONAL: Born August 22, 1931, in Dayton, Ohio; daughter of James D. and Jeannette (Steller) Cogan; married Frank Graham, Jr. (a writer), October 31, 1953. *Education:* Bowling Green State University, student, ·1949-52; Hunter College, A.B., 1957. *Residence:* Milbridge, Me. 04658.

CAREER: Teacher in public schools of New York, N.Y., 1957-58, 1964-65, at Baldwin School, New York, 1958-59, and in Sullivan, Me., 1965-67; Summer Head Start Program, Washington County, Me., teacher, 1967-70. Organizer and supervisor of summer nature program in Milbridge, Me., 1967-70; founder and director of Narraguagus Child Development Association, 1971. *Awards, honors:* Outstanding Science Books for Children awards from National Science Teachers Association and Children's Book Council, 1972, 1974, and 1975.

WRITINGS—Juveniles, with husband, Frank Graham, Jr.: *The Great American Shopping Cart,* Simon & Schuster, 1969; *Wildlife Rescue,* Cowles, 1970; *Puffin Island,* Cowles, 1971; *The Mystery of the Everglades,* Random House, 1972; *Dooryard Garden,* Four Winds, 1974; four volumes of Golden/Audubon Primers: *The Floor of the Forest, Birds in our World, The Winter Woods, Changes Everywhere,* Golden, 1974; *The Careless Animal,* Doubleday, 1975; *Milkweed and Its World of Animals,* Doubleday, 1976; *Foxtails, Ferns, and Fish Scales: A Handbook of Art and Nature,* Four Winds, 1976.

WORK IN PROGRESS: A series of four Audubon readers sponsored by the National Audubon Society, about whales, coyotes, falcons and beneficial insects, to be published by Dell.

SIDELIGHTS: "I was born and lived throughout my childhood in a rural setting. It was three miles to the nearest town and a mile to the nearest neighbors with children. Since my sister was three years younger than I and my brother an infant, I drew my companions from books and the radio.

"I was a devoted client of the local library. One summer when school closed I was told by my parents not to bring any books home from the library because our visits to town were so irregular that I would not be able to return them on time. But the thought of a long summer without books was too much for me. I smuggled some books home and hid them in a drawer of my bureau. When the overdue slips began to arrive it took a lot of invention to convince my parents that they were a mistake on the library's part. The books were at last discovered—to my relief. The punishment, which I cannot remember, must have been slight compared to the anguish of knowing that my secret would finally come out.

"For a long time afterward it did not occur to me that I would ever take part in writing a book. Books were magical, and even when I married a writer I chose to become a teacher. But while teaching I found myself creating my own materials, taking more timely, complex and relevant materials and reworking them for my students—not so much to impart facts as to keep them reading about anything that would interest them. My motivation in writing books today is the same—to make the topic interesting and keep people reading.

"Since my husband and I joined forces to write in 1969 we have published nearly a dozen books, and more are on the way. Ironically, while it was fiction that created my world as a child, the books I write now are about nature and conservation. That is, they are about *science,* which is the subject that gave me the most distress as a child student."

Ada Graham traveled and lived in Europe with her husband for two years (1959-61), living in Italy, Austria and France.

HOBBIES AND OTHER INTERESTS: Outdoor activities, gardening and music.

GRAHAM, Frank, Jr. 1925-

PERSONAL: Born March 31, 1925, in New York, N.Y.; son of Frank (a newspaperman) and Lillian (Whipp) Graham; married Ada Cogan, October 31, 1953. *Education:* Columbia University, A.B., 1950. *Home:* Milbridge, Me.

CAREER: New York Sun, New York, N.Y., copy boy, summers, 1947-49; Brooklyn Dodgers Baseball Club, Brooklyn, N.Y., publicity director, 1951-55; *Sport* (magazine), New York, N.Y., assistant managing editor, 1956-58; free-lance writer, 1958—. Board of trustees, New England Wild Flower Society. *Military service:* U.S. Navy, 1943-46; served as torpedoman's mate aboard escort carrier "Marcus Island," and saw action at Palau, Philippines, and Okinawa. *Member:* Authors Guild of the Authors League of America, National Audubon Society, American Ornithologists Union, American Association for the Advancement of Sci-

ence, Maine Audubon Society, Thoreau Fellowship (Old Town, Me.; president). *Awards, honors:* D.H.L., Colby College, 1976.

WRITINGS—Adult books: *Disaster By Default,* Evans, 1966; *Since Silent Spring,* Houghton, 1970; *Man's Dominion: The Story of Conservation in America,* Evans, 1971; *Where the Place Called Morning Lies,* Viking, 1974; *Gulls: A Social History,* Random House, 1975; *The Potomac: America's River,* Lippincott, 1976.

Juveniles: *Casey Stengel: His Half Century in Baseball,* John Day, 1958; (with Mel Allen) *It Takes Heart,* Harper, 1959; *Margaret Chase Smith: Woman of Courage,* John Day, 1964; *Austria,* Macmillan, 1964; *Great Pennant Races of the Major Leagues,* Random House, 1967; *Great No-Hit Games of the Major Leagues,* Random House, 1968; *Great Hitters of the Major Leagues,* Random House, 1969.

Juveniles with wife, Ada Graham: *The Great American Shopping Cart,* Simon & Schuster, 1969; *Wildlife Rescue,* Cowles, 1970; *Puffin Island,* Cowles, 1971; *The Mystery of the Everglades,* Random House, 1972; *Dooryard Garden,* Four Winds, 1974; four volumes of Golden/Audubon Primers: *The Floor of the Forest, Birds in our World, The Winter Woods, Changes Everywhere,* Golden Press, 1974; *The Careless Animal,* Doubleday, 1975; *Milkweed and Its World of Animals,* Doubleday, 1976; *Foxtails, Ferns and*

FRANK GRAHAM, JR.

Then one day she discovered that the tadpoles had changed. They had grown four legs. They had lost their tails. They had changed into frogs. ■ (From *Let's Discover Changes Everywhere* by Ada & Frank Graham. Photos by Susie Fitzhugh.)

Fish Scales: A Handbook of Art and Nature, Four Winds, 1976. Serves as field editor of *Audubon* magazine. Contributor to *American Heritage, Today's Health, Sports Illustrated, New York Times Magazine*, and other periodicals and newspapers.

WORK IN PROGRESS: A political history of the Adirondack Park.

SIDELIGHTS: "I was born in New York City, just about where Lincoln Center stands today. My father wrote a sports column for a New York newspaper, so it was natural that I became interested in both sports and writing. When I was still very young, we moved out of the city and I grew up in rural and suburban settings. I began to love the outdoor world, just as I loved sports.

"For a long time it never occurred to me that I could earn a living by writing about nature and the environment. Hiking, watching birds and studying botany were hobbies. When I became a free-lance writer I went back to the city to live and I wrote several books about sports. But I no longer enjoyed life in the city. Whenever my wife and I had some free time, we wanted to get out of the city and into the country. This was also true of the two years we lived in Europe, in Italy, France and Austria, writing and seeing the sights. The big European cities were interesting, but we preferred to settle in the country. When we came back to the United States in 1961 we moved to a small fishing town on the coast of Maine and we have lived there ever since.

"Now I write mostly about the natural world. My wife and I created nature programs for the children in our town, and we decided that we should share some of the things we learned with children everywhere. So we have written a number of books for young readers, and they are usually accompanied by photographs or drawings by friends of ours.

"My wife still does some teaching, while I also spend a good deal of my time writing for adults about nature and conservation. When I am not working, I take a sort of busman's holiday—I go for a walk in the woods."

HOBBIES AND OTHER INTERESTS: Hiking, sailing, tennis, chess.

GRAHAM, John 1926-

PERSONAL: Born September 1, 1926, in Washington, D.C.; son of John Thomas and Catherine (O'Neill) Graham; married Mary Washington (a teacher), August, 1954; children: Sarah, John, Christopher, Jane. *Education:* Georgetown University, A.B., 1949; Harvard University, M.A. (English literature), 1954; Johns Hopkins University, M.A. (American literature), 1959, Ph.D., 1960. *Politics:* None. *Religion:* None. *Home:* 701 Bolling Ave., Charlottesville, Va. 22903. *Office:* University of Virginia, Charlottesville, Va. 22903.

CAREER: Bullis School, Silver Spring, Md., member of Latin faculty, 1948; Georgetown University, Washington, D.C., instructor in English, 1949-50; English instructor at St. Paul's School, Concord, N.H., 1953, and Marquette University, Milwaukee, Wis., 1953-54; Johns Hopkins University, Baltimore, Md., junior instructor, 1954-57; University of Virginia, Charlottesville, instructor in English, 1958-61, assistant professor in Department of Speech and Drama, 1961-67, associate professor, 1967—, assistant dean of college, 1966-75. Director, "The Scholar's Bookshelf" (radio program), University of Virginia, 1965—. *Military service:* U.S. Army Air Corps, 1944-45. *Member:* Modern Language Association of America, Speech Association of America, American Society for Aesthetics, American Forensic Association, The Colonnade Club (faculty, past president), Raven Society (University of Virginia), Friday Club (University of Virginia), Blue Ridge Swimming Club Ltd. (vice-president), Farmington Hunt Club. *Awards, honors:* Fulbright fellowship to Germany, 1957-58.

WRITINGS: A Crowd of Cows (Child Study Association book list), Harcourt, 1968; (editor) *Great American Speeches, 1898-1963: Texts and Studies*, Appleton, 1970; (editor and contributor) *Studies in "A Farewell to Arms"* (by Ernest Hemingway), C. E. Merrill, 1971; (editor and contributor) *Studies in "Second Skin"* (by John Hawkes), C. E. Merrill, 1971; *Craft So Hard to Learn*, Morrow, 1972; *The Writer's Voice*, Morrow, 1973.

Contributor: Carlos Baker, editor, *Hemingway: Critiques of Four Major Novels*, Scribner, 1962; *The Dictionary of the History of Ideas*, Scribner, 1971 and 1972; Arthur Waldhorn, *Ernest Hemingway: A Collection of Criticism*, McGraw, 1973. Contributor of articles to *Massachusetts Review, Studies in Romanticism, Journal of the History of Ideas, Modern Fiction Studies, Speech Teacher*, and other literary journals.

Editor, for Caedmon Records, of "Anthologies of Great Speeches," including: "Great American Speeches," four volumes, 1970, "Great British Speeches," four volumes, 1971, "Great Black Speeches," two volumes, 1972, "The British Parliament Debates and the American Revolution," in press, and "The Burke-Paine Debate," in press..

JOHN GRAHAM

WORK IN PROGRESS: Study in the History of Ideas; Options to Language.

SIDELIGHTS: "I was born and reared in what now must be called 'old' Washington, a rather sleepy town in the 20's and 30's. It was, and I knew it then, too, the best of all possible worlds. Someone always had a canoe or flat-bottomed row boat for doping around on the river. There were plenty of woods for hiking. There were many vacant lots and playgrounds for interminable games of kick the can, baseball, and football. On long summer evenings we used a street light for home in hide and seek, quitting only after long insistence by parents. We trudged into the house, yawning 'we aren't tired.'

"The first house I can remember—a flat—was across from Montrose Park in Georgetown. I realize now that I was given a great deal of freedom from the age of three or four and played in the park all day most days, coming home, usually reluctantly, only for meals. Later we moved down near the river, and from eight or nine that was my playground. The banks were very undisciplined and therefore interesting. They were not yet cut off from boys by the highways and apartments that have replaced the paths and marshes. We most often (almost every weekend) went up the canal towpath simply because it was easy walking with no underbrush. There were wild flowers and the possibility of animals or the certitude of painted turtles and probably dangerous snakes. We wouldn't see another person all day.

"In other directions were Rock Creek Park and the great Washington Zoo or the Smithsonian Institution and Museum of Natural History. If nothing else, we could go up the Washington Monument one more time. Later these things remained happy and exciting and had added to them the art galleries and foreign films.

"I went across town to Gonzaga High School which I certainly respected and admired, but only, perhaps, loved. I studied very hard and was active in many extra-curriculars. But by my senior year I may have outgrown it or, since it was 1943, my consciousness of going into the service was too strong for me to see school as something even tolerable.

"While in high school I wrote a column for the newspaper, a column that was supposed to be rather witty. I also served as sports editor of the yearbook. We had no literary magazine at my high school. I believe that the existence of such a magazine would have encouraged me to do far more creative writing. I undoubtedly did learn something about organization and, above all, compression from the news work I did, but I do not think that I got as much as I could have.

"During my first year of high school, however, I wrote a number of short stories for a little news sheet turned out by the editors of a newspaper I delivered. I got $1.00 for each of these stories, so my first money for writing began when I was about fourteen. During my third year I wrote a great deal of poetry, much of it influenced by Stephen Vincent Benét and Emily Dickinson. I was in love with the woods and the wildlife at the time, so much of it was descriptive of scenes and feelings about nature.

"After a year in the Army Air Corps and the end of the war, I went to Georgetown College. Many of the same patterns of hiking and museums continued but by this time I was deeply committed to learning and my studies became increasingly important to me. I, quite simply, wanted to know everything.

"While in college I was associate editor of the college literary journal. This meant that I spent much time 'editing' or trying to round up good articles and short stories from talented students. I did write a few poems and short stories, as well as some articles, but I could hardly claim I was very productive. Again, I think I learned a good bit during these years about compression.

"At the same time, I was studying Latin, Greek, and French rather seriously, although I am not talented in languages. I am convinced that my attempts at good translations were an important part of my growing consciousness of language. Trying to beat one language into another remains as great a challenge as any writer can find.

"During these eight years of study with the Jesuits I learned much and feel deeply grateful. But in many ways it was a bourgeois education, one which was splendid in its insistence on reason and evidence and order but not really balanced with enough concern for the arts. There was no creative writing, studio arts, or the performing arts, and only accidental gestures toward supporting any interest in painting or music. I am not arguing there must be a 'course' in everything—surely the pleasures and 'values' of chording a guitar demonstrate this. But there seemed no context in which to place these interests except for nearly accidental encounters with other students, especially the staff of the college magazine. Even there, however, 'interest in' almost immediately translated into 'expert in' and I knew that wasn't true.

"Once into graduate school almost all my writing was analytic. Quite simply I had to turn out papers for my various classes. As a college professor the bulk of my writing remains along those lines. I have had to make certain choices. which meant that my creative writing was pushed to the back.

"The role books play is essential. I believe that my children are of great importance to me partially because I have such fun with them. I am certain I am excited by the potential I see in all children and their constant changes are an amazement and delight.

"I know part of the reason I write is because I read to my children. There is a closeness at that time, a sharing of experience that plunges very deeply. From this reading grew my telling of stories while we were driving. There is a little figure called a 'schwaepe' who grew out of my desperate attempts at entertaining very young children and someday I hope to do a book on this magical figure. This mischievous animal was born as much out of my children's demands for fun and excitement as out of my own imagination.

"I am convinced that the only way to learn anything about language is to write poetry. There is a demand for compression through seeking the exact word or phrase or image that fiction does not seem to insist on. I think I have also learned something about writing through working on very short book reviews where, again, compression is essential.

"I would like to write a really imaginative book, but I am not all convinced that I am capable of doing this. Although I write from my own experience I also write from my interest in language. The very words 'once upon a time' seem to me to jar us into dreaming about what could have happened at some time. I think from such dreams one extracts a good story, exciting people, and freedom of language. But at this point I believe I am a 'maker of books,' that my work is essentially analytic rather than genuinely creative.

"In writing books, I know that ideas can come from any place: a story is funny, a character is interesting or ambiguous, a place is rich with particular traditions. Or there may be those magic words 'once upon a time.' For me this magic of words is key. My first children's book *A Crowd of Cows* deals with the varied terms for groups of animals such as a 'flock' of sheep or a 'pod' of whales. My second book, *I Love You, Mouse*, is not so different in its basic concern. In it the diminutives and habitats of animals are the generative force. The diminutives range from the simple 'puppy' to the rarer 'duckling' and 'owlet.' The precision and variety of these terms fascinate me. Consider, too, the sounds of words. Go through, aloud, the names of fruits and vegetables and anyone can hear music in 'asparagus' and 'banana' and 'apple' and 'pomegranate.' There is a book, someplace, in those words.

"I was first drawn to children's books as a boy and, again, through my four children. I am certain that one major attraction of books for young children is their design and illustration. Children's books are simply more beautifully made than those for adults. My interest in painting (I cannot paint) is real and long lasting. I am certain that one thing that helps me in my writing is that I am constantly trying to envision what sort of illustration might function with my story or characters or ideas.

"When it comes to looking at children's books I am sure I could not do without *Treasure Island* and *Tom Sawyer*. Better books are *Alice In Wonderland* and *Gulliver's Travels*. I remain very fond of *Swiss Family Robinson* because I read it so often as a child, fascinated by their overcoming difficulties. I no longer think it's a particularly good book.

"One of the finest books I have read for young children is *The Rain Makes Applesauce*."

HOBBIES AND OTHER INTERESTS: Children's literature and illustrators; the relations between poetry and painting.

GRAHAM, Margaret Bloy 1920-

PERSONAL: Born November 2, 1920, in Toronto, Canada; daughter of Malcolm Robert (a physician) and Florence (Bloy) Graham; married first husband, Gene Zion, July, 1948 (divorced, 1968); married second husband, Oliver W. Holmes, Jr. (a merchant ship officer), August, 1972. *Education:* University of Toronto, B.A., 1943.

CAREER: Artist. Gibbs & Cox, New York, N.Y., draftsman, 1944-45; Condé Nast Publication, New York, N.Y., artist, 1946-56. *Awards, honors: All Falling Down* was a Caldecott honor book, 1952, *The Storm Book*, 1953.

WRITINGS: Be Nice to Spiders, Harper, 1968; *Benjy & the Barking Bird,* Harper, 1970; *Benjy's Dog House,* Harper, 1972.

Illustrator: Gene Zion, *All Falling Down,* Harper, 1951; Charlotte Zolotow, *The Storm Book,* Harper, 1952; Gene Zion, *Hide and Seek Day,* Harper, 1954; Gene Zion, *The*

MARGARET BLOY GRAHAM

"BOW WOW! BOW WOW!" squawked Tilly. "Gee," said Jimmy, "Tilly can bark better than Benjy." Benjy couldn't stand it. He went out into the backyard. ■ (From *Benjy and the Barking Bird* by Margaret Bloy Graham. Illustrated by the author.)

Summer Snowman, Harper, 1955; Gene Zion, *Really Spring,* Harper, 1956; Gene Zion, *Harry the Dirty Dog,* Harper, 1956; Gene Zion, *Dear Garbage Man,* Harper, 1957; Gene Zion, *No Roses for Harry!,* Harper, 1958; Gene Zion, *Harry and the Lady Next Door,* Harper, 1960; Gene Zion, *The Meanest Squirrel I Ever Met,* Scribner, 1962; Gene Zion, *The Sugar Mouse Cake,* Scribner, 1964; Gene Zion, *Harry By the Sea,* Harper, 1965; Shirley Gordon, *The Green Hornet Lunchbox,* Houghton, 1970; Jack Prelutsky, *The Pack Rat's Day,* Macmillan, 1974.

FOR MORE INFORMATION SEE: Illustrators of Children's Books: 1946-1956, Horn Book, 1958; *More Junior Authors,* edited by Muriel Fuller, H. W. Wilson, 1963; Diana Klemin, *The Art of Art for Children's Books,* Clarkson Potter, 1966; *Illustrators of Children's Books: 1957-1966,* Horn Book, 1968; *Saturday Review/World,* December 4, 1973; MacCann and Richard, *The Child's First Books,* H. W. Wilson, 1973.

GREEN, Mary Moore 1906-

PERSONAL: Born March 17, 1906, in Romulus, Mich.; daughter of George W. (a farmer) and Letitia (Bush) Moore; married A. Wendell Green (a horticulturist), June 30, 1937; children: George Arthur, James Wendell, Robert Moore. *Education:* Eastern Michigan University, B.S., 1931. *Home:* 37800 Fourteen Mile Rd., Walled Lake, Mich.

CAREER: Pontiac (Mich.) public schools, elementary teacher, 1936-43, 1950-55, elementary teacher consultant, 1955—. *Member:* National Education Association, Associa-

Farmer Green does not sell cider. He has only a small hand press which he uses to make cider for his own family. ■ (From *About Apples from Orchard to Market* by Mary Moore Green. Illustrated by Henry Luhrs.)

tion for Childhood Education, Michigan Education Association, Pontiac Education Association.

WRITINGS: About Apples From Orchard to Market, Melmont, 1960; (with Irma Johnson) *Three Feathers,* Follett, 1960; *Is it Hard, Is it Easy,* Addison-Wesley, 1960; *Everybody Has a House and Everybody Eats,* Addison-Wesley, 1961; *Whose Little Red Jacket,* F. Watts, 1965; *When Will I Whistle,* F. Watts, 1967; *Everybody Grows Up,* F. Watts, 1969.

Contributor of articles to *Science Review* and *Education.*

FOR MORE INFORMATION SEE: Pontiac Press, May 28, 1960; *Detroit Free Press,* November 5, 1960.

GREEN, Norma B(erger) 1925-

PERSONAL: Born September 15, 1925, in Providence, R.I.; daughter of C. Albert (an orthodontist) and Florence (Bomstein) Berger; married Norman S. Green, May 21, 1950 (divorced, 1969); children: John, William. *Education:* Rhode Island School of Design, B.F.A., 1945; also studied at Positano Art Workshop (Italy), Grande Chaumiere (Paris), and New School for Social Research. *Politics:* Democrat. *Home:* 5 Compo Beach Rd., Westport, Conn. 06880.

CAREER: Artist; paints in water color and designs textiles; had a solo show in New York, N.Y., 1970.

WRITINGS: (Self-illustrated) *Bears, Bees, Birch Trees* (juvenile), Doubleday, 1973; *The Hole in the Dike* (illustrated by Eric Carle), Scholastic, 1974, Crowell, 1975.

WORK IN PROGRESS: Research on Greek and Irish songs, verse, and superstitions, for a children's book; and obscure riddles from around the world.

All night long Peter kept his finger in the dike. His fingers grew cold and numb. He wanted to sleep but he couldn't give up. ■ (From *The Hole in the Dike* retold by Norma Green. Illustrated by Eric Carle.)

HOBBIES AND OTHER INTERESTS: Travel, photography, nature. "I am especially interested in other cultures as a way of understanding each other for friendship and peace."

NORMA B. GREEN

GREENE, Constance C(larke) 1924-

PERSONAL: Born October 27, 1924, in New York, N.Y.; daughter of Richard W. (a newspaper editor) and Mabel (a writer; maiden name, McElliott) Clarke; married Philip M. Greene (a radio station owner), June, 1946; children: Sheppard, Philippa, Stephanie, Matthew, Lucia. *Education:* Attended Skidmore College, 1942-44. *Politics:* Democrat. *Religion:* Roman Catholic. *Address:* R.F.D. #1, Poland Spring, Me. 04274. *Agent:* Marilyn Marlow, Curtis Brown Ltd., 60 East 56th St., New York, N.Y. 10022.

WRITINGS—Juveniles: *A Girl Called Al,* Viking, 1969; *Leo the Lioness,* Viking, 1970; *Good Luck Bogie Hat,* Viking, 1971; *The Unmaking of Rabbit,* Viking, 1972; *Isabelle the Itch,* Viking, 1973; *The Ears of Louis,* Viking, 1974; *I Know You, Al,* Viking, 1975; *Beat the Turtle Drum,* Viking, 1976.

WORK IN PROGRESS: A juvenile book dealing with a fourteen-year-old boy whose widowed father has remarried; short stories.

SIDELIGHTS: "I write to amuse and entertain children, but also to teach them to laugh at themselves and at the vagaries of life. My own childhood was extremely happy and my children say theirs was too. Still, there are always agonies, and a laugh or two helps.

"I live in Maine, where I moved several years ago when my husband, Phil, purchased a small radio station in Lewiston. We live in a large old house set on thirty-five acres. The house used to take the overflow of guests from a nearby inn, and although our five children are now all grown, some with families of their own, the extra space is perfect for large gatherings of family and friends. I miss the bustle of a large city, and during my first years in Maine, found writing difficult because of the lack of interruptions.

"My children and their friends, I guess you could say, were the original inspirations for my stories. Now my children are grown and I welcome a visit or an overheard conversation among children which sometimes triggers an idea. The song that Teddy, the narrator's brother in *I Know You, Al* sings, was brought home by my sister almost thirty years ago. I thought I'd forgotten it until, full blown, it popped into my mind when I started to write the sequel to *A Girl Called Al* and there was my final chapter dropped into my lap.

"I had a sister who died at the age of thirteen when I was eleven and for a long time had contemplated writing a story about a child's death. Thus came *Beat the Turtle Drum* which I found difficult to write and would never have done so while my mother and father were alive.

"I have been writing for many years. My grandfather, parents, and now a daughter, have all been newspaper people. My father, Richard Clarke, was executive editor of the New York *Daily News,* and my mother, Mabel Clarke, was the paper's first movie reviewer.

"The hardest part about being a writer is sticking to it. There are lots of times when it's terribly discouraging. I think a lot of people try to write books and aren't very successful, yet they keep on trying, which I think requires more courage than anything. Certainly, the most thrilling day in my life, was when *A Girl Called Al* was sold to Viking. As my husband says, 'Anyone can have a baby but not everyone can sell a book.' I thought that was nice of him. Anyway, to be paid to do what all your life you've wanted to do—be a writer—is surely the best of all possible worlds."

FOR MORE INFORMATION SEE: Horn Book, August, 1969, February, 1971, April, 1973, February, 1974, April,

"Isn't it icky in there?" Mary Eliza wrinkled her nose disdainfully. "Your mother'll have a fit when she finds out you were inside a garbage can." ■ (From *Isabelle the Itch* by Constance C. Greene. Illustrated by Emily A. McCully.)

1975; *New York Times Book Review,* November 4, 1973, November 15, 1975; *Booklist,* December 15, 1974; *Teacher,* April, 1975.

GREENE, Wade   1933-

PERSONAL: Born January 17, 1933, in Syracuse, N.Y.; son of Melville (in hardware business) and Nan (Wade) Greene; married Susanne Cavanagh (a carpenter); children: Nathaniel, Jennifer. *Education:* Princeton University, B.A., 1956; Columbia University, M.S., 1962; Stanford University, further graduate study, 1967-68. *Home and office:* 35 Charles St., New York, N.Y. 10014.

CONSTANCE C. GREENE

WADE GREENE

122

Something about the Author

CAREER: *American Heritage,* New York, N.Y., associate editor, 1962-64; *Newsweek,* New York, N.Y., associate editor, 1964-69; *New York Times* (magazine), New York, N.Y., articles editor, 1969; *Saturday Review,* New York, N.Y., assistant managing editor, 1972-73. *Military service:* U.S. Army, 1953-55.

WRITINGS: *Disarmament: The Challenge of Civilization,* Coward, 1966; *Youths' Agenda for the Seventies* (booklet), John D. Rockefeller III Fund, 1973. Contributor to popular journals, including *Saturday Review, New York Times, Reporter,* and *True.*

WORK IN PROGRESS: *Report of the Commission of Private Philanthropy and Public Needs.*

GREY, Jerry   1926-

PERSONAL: Born October 25, 1926, in New York, N.Y.; son of Abraham and Lillian (Danowitz) Grey; married Vivian Hoffman, June 27, 1948 (divorced); married Florence Maier (a fashion artist), 1974; children: (first marriage) Leslie Ann, Jacquelyn Eve (deceased). *Education:* Cornell University, B.M.E., 1947, M.S., 1949; California Institute of Technology, Ph.D., 1952. *Politics:* Registered Democrat. *Religion:* Hebrew. *Home:* Jobs Lane, Box 428, Bridgehampton, N.Y. 11932. *Office:* (Mail address) 1 Lincoln Plaza, 25-0, New York, N.Y. 10011.

CAREER: Cornell University, Ithaca, N.Y., instructor in thermodynamics, 1947-49; Fairchild Corp., Engine Division, Farmingdale, N.Y., development engineer, 1949-50; California Institute of Technology, Pasadena, hypersonic aerodynamicist at Guggenheim Aerospace Laboratory, 1950-51; Marquardt Aircraft Co., Van Nuys, Calif., senior engineer, 1951-52; Princeton University, School of Engineering and Applied Science, Princeton, N.J., research associate, 1952-56, assistant professor, 1956-59, associate professor of aerospace science, 1960-67, director of Nuclear Propulsion Research Laboratory, 1962-67; Greyrad Corp., Princeton, N.J., president, 1959-71; American Institute of Aeronautics and Astronautics, New York, N.Y., administrator for technical activities, communications, and public policy, 1971—; Calprobe Corp. (high-temperature instrumentation), New York, N.Y., president, 1972—. Chairman of solar power advisory panel, Office of Technology Assessment, U.S. Congress, 1974—; adjunct professor of environmental science, Long Island University, 1976—; presently consultant to the United Nations and the Office of Technology Assessment, U.S. Congress (on solar power and research development policy), Columbia University (on coal gasification), National Aeronautics and Space Administration, and Princeton University (on nuclear fusion and space power); previously consultant to Radio Corp. of America, General Electric Co., Boeing Airplane Co., and other firms and laboratories. Holds nine U.S. patents and foreign patents associated with them. *Military service:* U.S. Naval Reserve, active duty, 1943-46.

MEMBER: American Institute of Aeronautics and Astronautics (associate fellow; vice-president, 1966-71), American Astronautical Society (senior member), American Association for the Advancement of Science, American Nuclear Society, Institute of Electrical and Electronics Engineers, International Solar Energy Society, New York Academy of Sciences, Sigma Xi, Phi Kappa Phi, Tau Beta Pi, Bridge-

JERRY GREY

hampton Racquet and Surf Club, Midtown Tennis Club (New York).

WRITINGS: (Contributor) Angelo Miele, *Flight Mechanics: Theory of Flight Paths,* Volume I, Addison-Wesley, 1962; (technical editor with Vivian Grey) *Space Flight Report to the Nation,* Basic Books, 1962; (contributor) C. W. Watson, editor, *Nuclear Rocket Propulsion,* College of Engineering, University of Florida, 1964.

Nuclear Propulsion (audiovisual book), Educom, 1970; *The Race for Electric Power* (juvenile), Westminster, 1972; (editor with J. P. Layton) *New Space Transportation Systems: An AIAA Assessment,* American Institute of Aeronautics and Astronautics, 1973; *The Facts of Flight* (juvenile), Westminster, 1973; (editor with Arthur Henderson) *Solar System Exploration: An AIAA Review,* American Institute of Aeronautics and Astronautics, 1974; (editor) *Aircraft Fuel Conservation: An AIAA View,* American Institute of Aeronautics and Astronautics, 1974; *Noise! Noise! Noise!* (juvenile), Westminster, 1975; (editor with H. Killian and G. L. Dugger) *Solar Energy for Earth: An AIAA Assessment,* American Institute of Aeronautics and Astronautics, 1975.

Writer of more than thirty proprietary technical reports and collaborator on others. Contributor to *Encyclopedia of Science and Technology.* Publications include monographs, technical papers, and popular articles in periodicals, including *Journal of Spacecraft and Rockets, Astronautics and Aeronautics, Times* (London), and *L'Aerotecnica.*

WORK IN PROGRESS: Urban Energy, publication by Dekker expected in 1977.

SIDELIGHTS: "When I was young, I never expected to be a writer. From the time I was about four years old, I was crazy about airplanes. My earliest memories are of building models on the family's polished dining-room table, much to my mother's consternation! I went to a technical high school, an engineering college, a science graduate school, and studied thermodynamics, aeronautics, jet and rocket propulsion, power generation, mathematics—all the subjects I needed to be a first-rate aerospace scientist and engineer.

"As I worked in my chosen field of aerospace, I found myself writing thousands of pages—technical journal articles, reports, detailed letters explaining my research work to my colleagues, and so on. During this time, I became interested in other technologies, and changed my field of specialization several times; from jet propulsion to hypersonic aerodynamics to rocket propulsion to nuclear power to gas kinetics to research instrumentation to systems analysis to solar power—and found myself writing more and more pages about more and more subjects. So, one day just a few years ago, when the big hue and cry began about how technology was ruining the earth, I thought I'd try to explain to young people (and to those adults, too, who had never studied much science or engineering) some of the things *I'd* learned about the different technologies I'd worked on all my life. *That's* when I became a writer, although I still keep up my technical activities in solar power, aerospace, nuclear power, and research instrumentation.

"I am highly optimistic about man's ability to ensure his own survival and, indeed, his continued movement toward maturity, despite the apparent difficulties he keeps generating."

HOBBIES AND OTHER INTERESTS: Tennis, sailing, ice skating, and other sports.

GROSSMAN, Robert 1940-

PERSONAL: Born March 1, 1940, in New York, N.Y.; son of Joseph J. (silk screen printer) and Ethel (Stern) Grossman; married Donna Lundvall (an artist), October 28, 1963; children: Michael, Alexander, Leila. *Education:* Yale University, B.A., 1961. *Home:* Briarhill Rd., Williamsburg, Mass. 01096. *Office:* Robert Grossman Inc., 19 Crosby St., New York, N.Y. 10013.

ILLUSTRATOR: Betsy Byars, *The Eighteenth Emergency,* Viking, 1973; Mike Thaler, *What Can A Hippopotamus Be?,* Parents' Magazine Press, 1975.

FOR MORE INFORMATION SEE: Wilson Library Bulletin, December, 1975.

HAINES, Gail Kay 1943-

PERSONAL: Born March 15, 1943, in Mt. Vernon, Ill.; daughter of Samuel Glen (an atomic plant foreman) and Audrey (Goin) Beekman; married Michael Philip Haines (an oral surgeon), May 8, 1964; children: David Michael, Cindy Lynn. *Education:* Washington University, St. Louis, Mo., A.B., 1965. *Home:* 4145 Lorna Court, S.E., Olympia, Wash. 98503.

CAREER: Mallinckrodt Chemical Works, St. Louis, Mo., analytical chemist, 1965-66; full-time writer, 1970—. *Member:* American Chemical Society, Authors' Guild, Pacific Northwest Writers' Conference.

WRITINGS: The Elements (juvenile), Watts, 1972; *Fire* (juvenile), Morrow, 1975; *Explosives* (juvenile), Morrow, 1976; *Supercold/Superhot* (juvenile), Watts, 1976; *What Makes a Lemon Sour?* (juvenile), Morrow, 1977.

WORK IN PROGRESS: A book on poisons; chemical mysteries.

SIDELIGHTS: The best thing that ever happened to me was learning to read. Ever since then, reading has been my favorite thing to do. I have always enjoyed reading all kinds of books. But, as I was growing up, my favorites were books about science and the people who made scientific discov-

Watching the boys, Garbage Dog began to eat. He saw the boys disappear laughing behind the bakery, and after a moment he hurried to join them. ■ (From *The 18th Emergency* by Betsy Byars. Illustrated by Robert Grossman.)

Ask a parent or teacher to help, because fire can be very dangerous. . . ■ (From *Fire* by Gail Kay Haines. Illustrated by Jacqueline Chwast.)

GAIL KAY HAINES, and family

eries. I wanted to learn all about the things around me—what they are and what they are made of, and most of all I wanted to know how scientists managed to find out information about the world.

Chemistry seemed the most exciting field of all, to me, so I decided to become a chemist. I got my first chemistry set when I was eight years old. I studied chemistry in college, and I worked as a chemist for a while.

But I always wanted to be a writer, too, and I soon found that writing about science was the most interesting thing I could do. I get ideas from my children and from thinking about what I would want to know if I were a child again. There will always be new things to write about because science is always changing and growing.

HALL-QUEST, Olga W(ilbourne) 1899-

PERSONAL: Born August 30, 1899, in Willis, Tex.; daughter of William Shaw and Mollie (Derrick) Wilbourne; married Alfred Lawrence Hall-Quest (a university professor), June 4, 1931 (deceased). *Education:* Columbia University, B.S., 1933; New York University, M.A., 1934. *Home:* 209 Grove Pl., Apt. 201, San Antonio, Tex. 78209.

CAREER: Masters School, Dobbs Ferry, N.Y., teacher in English department, 1943-65. *Awards, honors:* Western Writers of America Spur Award, 1969, for *Conquistadors and Pueblos.*

WRITINGS—Youth books: *How the Pilgrims Came to Plymouth,* Dutton, 1946; *Shrine of Liberty: The Alamo,* Dutton, 1948; *Jamestown Adventure,* Dutton, 1950; *Wyatt Earp: Marshal of the Old West,* Farrar, Straus, 1956; *Powhatan and Captain Smith,* Farrar, Straus, 1957.

With Stanley in Africa, Dutton, 1961; *Guardians of Liberty: Sam Adams and John Hancock,* Dutton, 1963; *The Bell that Rang for Freedom: The Liberty Bell and Its Place in American History,* Dutton, 1965; *From Colony to Nation: With Washington and His Army in the War for Independence,* Dutton, 1966; *Flames Over New England: The Story of King Philip's War, 1675-1676,* Dutton, 1967; *Old New Orleans, the Creole City,* Dutton, 1968; *Conquistadors and Pueblos: The Story of the American Southwest 1540-1848,* Dutton, 1969. Contributor to *Collier's Encyclopedia.*

SIDELIGHTS: Olga Hall-Quest considers her books, mainly written in summer months, an avocation. Interest in historical subjects (and presenting them to young people) was spurred by cross-country travels with husband who taught four summers at University of Washington and eight other summers at University of Texas.

The green, flowering courtyards gave these old Spanish houses their private, interior charm—the balconies found on all houses of more than one story gave them their outward elegance. ■ (From *Old New Orleans, the Creole City* by Olga Hall-Quest. Illustrated by Victor Lazzaro.)

HALLSTEAD, William F(inn) III 1924-

PERSONAL: Born April 20, 1924, in Scranton, Pa.; son of William F. II, and Winifred (Mott) Hallstead; married Jean Little, October 9, 1948; children: William F. IV, Alyssa Jean. *Education:* Hill School, Pottstown, Pa., graduate, 1942. *Politics:* Republican. *Religion:* Episcopalian. *Home:* 2027 Skyline Rd., Ruxton, Md. 21204. *Office:* Maryland Center for Public Broadcasting, Owing Mills, Md. 21117.

CAREER: Scranton Municipal Airport Corp., Scranton, Pa., flight instructor, 1946-49; Pennsylvania Department of Highways, Scranton, draftsman, 1949-52; Whitman, Requardt & Associates (consulting engineers), Baltimore, Md., highway designer, 1952-58; free-lance writer, Baltimore, Md., 1958-61; Colony Publishing Corp., Baltimore, Md., president, 1961-65; James W. Rouse & Co. (real estate developers), Baltimore, Md., director of information services, 1965-68. The Maryland Center for Public Broadcasting, Baltimore, Md., director of development. *Military service:* U.S. Army Air Forces, 1942-45; radio operator-gunner on B-24 with 15th Air Force in Italy; became sergeant. *Member:* Authors Guild, Associated Business Writers of America.

OLGA W. HALL-QUEST

126 **Something about the Author**

WILLIAM F. HALLSTEAD, III

WRITINGS: Ev Kris, Aviation Detective, John Day, 1961; *Dirigible Scout,* McKay, 1967; *Sky Carnival* (Junior Literary Guild selection), McKay, 1969; *Missiles of Zajecar,* Chilton, 1969; *Ghost Plane of Blackwater,* Harcourt, 1974; *How to Make Money Writing Articles for the Free Lance Market,* Kirkley Press, 1976. Youth stories anthologized in several junior high school readers and textbooks; short stories in *Boy's Life* and other juvenile magazines; articles in engineering trade journals, other publications. Managing editor, *Architects' Report,* 1960-64, *Maryland Engineer,* 1963-64; editor, *Baltimore Scene* (bi-monthly magazine), 1963-64.

WORK IN PROGRESS: Aviation series.

SIDELIGHTS: "I have spent almost a decade in public television which is an audio and visual way of learning, but my great regret is that so many young people have turned toward television and away from books.

"If you get the chance, listen to a good radio drama. Notice how just a few simple sound effects—plus a good script—come to life even though radio is no more than sound; no fancy sets, no colors, no light or shadow. Why does radio work so well? Because it takes place in the greatest theater in the world: your own imagination.

"And books are a lot like radio. There is only the printed word, but the story is formed and lives in that great theater of your mind. Through no more than paper and an alphabet of twenty-six shapes, you can travel to the Florida Everglades, the Alaskan wilderness, Africa or Tibet. You can meet some of the most fascinating people, live through the most exciting adventures. You can journey to the stars on the wings of these twenty-six symbols. What a miracle is the understanding of print! What an incredible adventure is the ability to read.

"It began for me when I was very young and my father became one of the first suburbanites. We lived on a converted farm two miles from a small town which was thirteen miles from the nearest city of any size. There were no local children, aside from my brother and sister. Reading—and radio—were big entertainments in those days—the 1930's. I discovered high adventure with the grand old pulp magazines: *Doc Savage, The Lone Eagle, The Spider, G-8 and His Battle Aces.* . . . I actually knew the date each new magazine would be delivered to Fred Erb's variety store in nearby Dalton.

"I was fortunate to be able to go to private schools—two of them—where a lot of reading and writing was absolutely required. At The Hill School, where I was a boarding student for three years, we had to turn in a 'theme' each week on an assigned subject. These, as I recall, were about 2,500 words long. In the first year, I detested this Friday chore (I always waited until the last minute). The second year, one of my English masters (now you know what a formal school it was—and to a degree, still is) took the trouble to tell me that he found my writing interesting to read, even though he was unmerciful about grammar. I think that one comment was what planted the idea in my mind that I was perhaps just a bit more of a writer than I thought. From there on, the writing of the weekly theme was less of a chore and more of a satisfaction. In my final year at The Hill, I was editor of the literary magazine.

"While I served in the Army Air Forces during World War II, I struggled with poetry and a few stories that I didn't quite know where to send. Flying is a mystical experience. Flying in a heavy bomber off the coast of France as the sun rises out of the cold Atlantic is something you know you must remember for all time. Crouching on the floor of that bomber while flak bursts around you and punches five holes in the fuselage is something you know you will never forget. It all becomes part of the writer. . . .

"My first article sale was to *Flying* magazine, a short piece on crop dusting, after I'd spent a summer doing it. My first story sale was to *Boys' Life,* after that same summer. My first book sale came ten years later when I was lucky enough to have a collection of aviation stories published as an anthology. The first novel, *Dirigible Scout,* came six years after that and it was the first book to touch on the mystical side of flying. I can't explain it except to say that I know all pilots are poets when they leave the ground. Perhaps another and even more touching way to put this is to tell you that among glider pilots—those who know flying in its purest sense—there are very few bird hunters.

"My most successful book so far has been *Ghost Plane of Blackwater,* if you measure success by sales. But I think the best story is *Missiles of Zajecar.* It's a World War II adventure story, but to me its underlying theme is powerful and I've never written a scene that I think is more effective than the closing scene in that book. I don't take much credit for it;

it was one of those times when the right words just came along by themselves.

"That doesn't happen often. Writing is mostly uninspired determination. You have to consciously make time for it. The second most asked question of writers is, 'Where do you find the time?' The first is, 'Where do you get your ideas?' To the last, I say, 'Everywhere,' and that's true. To the first, I simply let them in on the secret that I have a twenty-eight hour day."

William F. Hallstead has written employee relations pamphlets which have sold more than 200,000 copies, and was the author of the 31st book in the "Hardy Boys" series.

HANFF, Helene

PERSONAL: Born in Philadelphia, Pa.; daughter of Arthur Joseph (a salesman) and Miriam (Levy) Hanff. *Education:* Attended Temple University, one year. *Politics:* Democrat. *Religion:* Jewish. *Home and office:* 305 East 72nd St., New York, N.Y. 10021. *Agent:* Flora Roberts, Inc., 65 East 55th St., New York, N.Y. 10022.

CAREER: Paramount Pictures, New York, N.Y., manuscript reader, 1946-52; free-lance writer of dramatic shows for Columbia Broadcasting System and National Broadcasting Co. television, 1952-58; free-lance writer, 1958—. Democratic county committeewoman, New York, N.Y. *Member:* Writers Guild of America East (executive council of Television and Screen Writers union, 1961-63), MacDowell Colonists Association, Lenox Hill Democratic Club (president, 1970). *Awards, honors:* Columbia Broadcasting System grant-in-aid for work on historic scripts for television.

■ (From the television production "84 Charing Cross Road," starring Anne Jackson, presented on PBS.)

She loved to study each face while she was told how rich and handsome and great each ruler was, and what a fine husband he would be. ■ (From *Queen of England* by Helene Hanff. Illustrated by Ronald Dorfman.)

WRITINGS: The Day the Constitution Was Signed, Doubleday, 1961; *The Battle for New Orleans,* Doubleday, 1961; *Underfoot in Show Business,* Harper, 1962; *Terrible Thomas,* Harper, 1964; *More Terrible Thomas,* Harper, 1964; (with L. L. Smith) *Early Settlers in America: Jamestown, Plymouth and Salem,* Grosset, 1965; *Religious Freedom,* Grosset, 1966; *Good Neighbors: The Peace Corps in Latin America,* Grosset, 1966; *John F. Kennedy, Young Man of Destiny,* Doubleday, 1966; *Our Nation's Capitol,* Doubleday, 1967; *The Unlikely Twins: Paraguay and Uruguay,* Doubleday, 1967; *Elizabeth I,* Doubleday, 1967; *The Movers and Shakers* (young adult book), Sidney Phillips, 1969; *84 Charing Cross Road,* Grossman, 1970; *The Duchess of Bloomsbury Street,* Lippincott, 1973. Thirty scripts for television's "Hallmark Hall of Fame" and "Matinee Theater"; scripts for eight U.S. Army training films. Contributor of articles to *Harper's, New Yorker, Reader's Digest.*

84 Charing Cross Road was televised for PBS in 1976.

HOBBIES AND OTHER INTERESTS: Theater, classical music, baseball (as spectator), cooking, reading "nonfiction."

They also know that newborn babies dream. What do you suppose they dream about? ■ (From *Your Busy Brain* by Louise Greep McNamara and Ada Bassett Litchfield. Illustrated by Ruth Hartshorn.)

HARTSHORN, Ruth M. 1928-

PERSONAL: Born April 4, 1928, in Boston, Mass.; daughter of Francis M. and Ruth N. (Herbert) Fonseca; married Earle C. Hartshorn (a machinist), February 7, 1959. *Education:* Boston University, school of fine & applied arts, B.S., 1952, school of education, B.A., 1953; University of Georgia, M.A., 1954; studied at Museum of Fine Arts, Boston, Mass., and with private teachers. *Home:* 250 Buckminister Drive, Norwood, Mass. 02062.

CAREER: Free-lance artist; Rust Craft Publishers, Dedham, Mass., art director, 1955—.

ILLUSTRATOR—All written by Ada Litchfield: *The Good-Morning Book,* Steck-Vaughn, 1966; *The Wonderful, Wonderful Book,* Steck-Vaughn, 1968; *Good-Night Sleep Tight,* Steck-Vaughn, 1969; *I Can, Can You?,* Steck-Vaughn, 1971; *Your Busy Brain,* Little, Brown, 1973. "All About You" eleven programs, black and white title and program drawings, 1964, thirty programs full-color and black and white titles and program drawings, WGBH Boston, 1974. Has also done a teachers guide.

WORK IN PROGRESS: Working with Ada Litchfield on some easy reading books and some human science concept books that are spin-offs from the "All About You" series.

HAYES, Carlton J. H. 1882-1964

PERSONAL: Born May 16, 1882, in Afton, N.Y.; son of Philetus A. and Permelia Mary (Huntley) Hayes; married Evelyn Carroll, 1920; children: Mary Elizabeth Hayes Tucker, Carroll J. J. *Education:* Columbia University, A.B., 1904, A.M., 1905, Ph.D., 1909. *Religion:* Catholic. *Home and office:* 88 Morningside Dr., New York, N.Y. 10027.

CAREER: Columbia University, New York, N.Y., 1907-50, started as lecturer, professor of history, 1919-35, Seth Low Professor, 1935-50, professor emeritus, 1950-64. U.S. Ambassador to Spain, 1942-45. *Military service:* U.S.

Army, Military Intelligence, 1918-19; became captain. Officers Reserve Corps, 1919-25; became major. *Member:* American Historical Association (past president), American Catholic Historical Association (past president), New York State Historical Association, Columbia University Club, Alpha Chi Rho. *Awards, honors:* Hamilton Medal. Honorary degrees from Williams College, Michigan State University, Notre Dame University, Marquette University, University of Detroit, Fordham University, LeMoyne College, Columbia University.

WRITINGS: An Introduction to the Sources Relating to the Germanic Invasions, Longmans, Green, 1909, AMS Press, 1967; (with Robert Livingston Schuyler) *A Syllabus of Modern History,* Columbia University Press, 1912, 3rd edition, 1916; *British Social Politics,* Ginn, 1913, Books for Libraries Press, 1972; *A Brief History of the Great War,* Macmillan, 1920; (with Parker T. Moon) *Modern History,* Macmillan, 1923, 4th edition, 1941, and *Teachers' Manual,* 1923, *Workbook,* 1930; *A Political and Social History of Modern Europe,* two volumes, Macmillan, 1924; *Essays on Nationalism,* Macmillan, 1926, Russell and Russell, 1966; (with Moon) *Ancient History,* Macmillan, 1929, and *Workbook,* Macmillan, 1931; (with Moon) *Ancient and Medieval History,* Macmillan, 1929, and *Workbook,* Macmillan, 1931; *France, a Nation of Patriots,* Columbia University Press, 1930; *The Historical Evolution of Modern Nationalism,* Farrar, 1931, Russell and Russell, 1968; (with Moon and John W. Wayland) *World History,* Macmillan, 1932, 3rd edition, 1955; *A Political and Cultural History of Modern Europe,* Volume I, *Three Centuries of Predominantly Agricultural Society, 1500-1830,* revised edition, Macmillan, 1932, Volume II, *A Century of Predominantly Industrial Society, 1830-1935,* Macmillan, 1939; *Outline of the History of Modern Europe, 1500-1932,* Part I, *1500-1830,* Eckhardt, 1935; (editor with Newton Baker) *American Way,* Willett, 1936; *Analytical Survey of Modern European History,* revised edition, Macmillan, 1938.

A Generation of Materialism, 1871-1900, Harper, 1941; *Wartime Mission in Spain, 1942-1945,* Macmillan, 1945; (with Marshall W. Baldwin and Charles W. Cole) *History of Europe,* Macmillan, 1949, revised edition, 1956, revised edition under title *History of Western Civilization,* 1962; *The U.S. and Spain: An Interpretation,* Sheed, 1951, Greenwood Press, 1970; *Modern Europe to 1870,* Macmillan, 1953; *Contemporary Europe since 1870,* Macmillan, 1953, revised edition, 1958; *Christianity and Western Civilization,* Stanford University Press, 1954; *Nationalism: A Religion,* Macmillan, 1960; (with Margareta Faissler) *Modern Times: The French Revolution to the Present,* Macmillan, 1963; (with Frederick F. Clark) *Medieval and Early Modern Times: The Age of Justinian to the Eighteenth Century,* Macmillan, 1966; (Edward Mead Earle, editor) *Nationalism and Internationalism: Essays Inscribed to Carlton J. H. Hayes,* Octagon Books, 1974. Author of pamphlets. Contributor to *Encyclopaedia Britannica, Encyclopedia of Social Sciences,* and journals.

(Died, September 3, 1964)

HAYES, John F. 1904-

PERSONAL: Born August 5, 1904, in Dryden, Ontario, Canada; son of John George (a merchant) and Jeannette (Houck) Hayes; married Helen Eleen Casselman; children:

JOHN F. HAYES

John Terrence, William Frederick, Nancy Diane (Mrs. J. Nicolson). *Education:* Attended University of Toronto evening classes for twelve years. *Politics:* Liberal. *Religion:* United Church of Canada. *Home and office:* 53 Bennington Heights Dr., Toronto, Ontario, Canada.

CAREER: Writer, Maclean-Hunter Publishing Co., Toronto, Ontario, 1925-27, Saturday Night Press, Toronto, 1928; General Motors of Canada, sales promotion writer, 1929-30; Brigdens Ltd., head of creative department, 1930-34, assistant sales manager, 1935; Moffats Ltd., sales promotion manager, 1937-40; Southam Press Ltd., Toronto, Ontario, 1940-54, sales manager, 1943-46, vice-president and general manager, 1947-50, vice-president and general manager of Montreal branch, 1950-54, later member of board of directors and of executive committee; Southam Printing Co., Toronto, Ontario, managing director, 1954-60; retired because of ill health, 1961. Member of board of directors, Toronto Graphic Arts Association.

MEMBER: Canadian Authors Association, Canadian Historical Society, National Club (Toronto). *Awards, honors:* Governor General's Literary Award for best juvenile book of the year, 1952, for *A Land Divided,* and, 1954, for *Rebels Ride at Night;* Quebec Scientific and Literary Award, 1955; Book-of-the-Year for Children Medal from Canadian Library Association, 1958, for *The Dangerous Cove;* Vicky Metcalf Award ($1,000), 1964, for inspirational writing for Canadian youth.

WRITINGS—Juvenile: *Buckskin Colonist,* Blackwell, 1949; *Treason at York,* Copp, 1949; *A Land Divided,* Copp, 1951; *Rebels Ride at Night,* Copp, 1953; *Bugles in the Hills,* Messner, 1956; *The Dangerous Cove: A Story of the Early*

Days in Newfoundland (Junior Literary Guild selection, Notable Canadian Children's book), Copp, 1957, Messner, 1960; *Quest in the Cariboo,* Copp, 1960; *The Flaming Prairie,* Copp, 1965; *The Steel Ribbon,* Copp, 1967; *The Nation Builders,* Copp, 1968; *Wilderness Mission: The Story of Sainte-Marie-Among-the-Hurons,* Ryerson, 1969; *On Loyalist Trails,* Copp, 1969.

Also author of *The Renovation Industry,* 1960, and *Bookkeeping for the Small Printer,* 1962. Writer of several school plays for Canadian Broadcasting Corp. and a six-month radio series on industry familiarization. Article anthologized in *The Atlas Christmas Anthology of Canadian Stories;* other articles contributed to ethnic newspapers in Canada.

SIDELIGHTS: Hayes's youth books have been published in United States, England, and West Germany, and in school editions for Canadian classroom study. They also have been dramatized on Canadian Broadcasting Corp. radio and television.

HEMMING, Roy   1928-

PERSONAL: Born May 27, 1928, in Hamden, Conn.; son of Benjamin Whitney (in cutlery manufacturing) and Anna (Sexton) Hemming. *Education:* Yale University, B.A., 1949; University of Geneva, graduate study, 1950; Stanford University, M.A., 1951. *Politics:* Independent Rupublican. *Home:* 1433 Boulevard, New Haven, Conn. 06511. *Office:* Whitney Communications, 150 East 58th St., New York, N.Y. 10022.

ROY HEMMING

CAREER: New Haven Journal-Courier, New Haven, Conn., reporter, 1947; WAVZ-Radio, New Haven, Conn., news editor, 1948-49, program director, 1949-50; Voice of America, New York, N.Y., writer, 1951-52; free-lance writer, 1952-53; National Broadcasting Corp. (NBC), New York, N.Y., researcher in news film library, 1953; Scholastic Magazines, Inc., New York, N.Y., writer, 1954-57, news editor, 1958, managing editor of Senior Scholastic, 1959, editor, 1960-72, editor of World Week, 1965-68, executive editor of social studies books and magazines, including Senior Scholastic, World Week, and Junior Scholastic, 1968-72, editor-at-large and director of publications for Scholastic International, 1972-75, music and record columnist, 1959-75; Whitney Communications, New York, N.Y., editor-in-chief of Retirement Living, 1975—. Member of preselection committee for Montreux International Record Award, 1971—. Member of board of directors of Eastern Music Festival, 1969-75, member of board of admissions, 1976—. Military service: U.S. Naval Reserve, active duty, 1945-46.

MEMBER: Overseas Press Club, Deadline Club, Yale Club (New York, N.Y.), Sigma Delta Chi, Commonwealth Club of California. Awards, honors: All-America Award from Educational Press Association of America, 1968, 1969.

WRITINGS: Discovering Music: Where to Start on Records and Tapes, the Great Composers and Their Works, Today's Major Recording Artists, Four Winds, 1974. Contributor to magazines and newspapers, sometimes under pseudonym Buzz Hamilton. Contributing editor of Stereo Review, 1973—; Opera News, 1974—.

WORK IN PROGRESS: Updating Discovering Music, publication expected about 1978; a special report on the state of concert music broadcasting in the United States.

SIDELIGHTS: "I have long divided my time professionally between writing and editing in international and national affairs with writing about the music field." Special assignments reporter in Viet Nam, 1964, Latin America, 1966, Berlin, 1967, Czechoslovakia, 1968, Russia, 1969, and Ethiopia, 1971.

HENRY, Marguerite

CAREER: Full-time professional writer. Awards, honors: Junior Scholastic Gold Seal Award and Award of the Friends of Literature, 1948, for Justin Morgan Had a Horse; Newbery Medal, 1949, for King of the Wind; William Allen White Award, 1956, for Brighty of the Grand Canyon; Sequoyah Children's Book Award, 1959, for Black Gold, 1969, for Mustang: Wild Spirit of the West; Society of Midland Author's Clara Ingram Judson Award, 1961, for Gaudenzia: Pride of the Palio, 1973, for San Domingo: The Medicine Hat Stallion; Western Heritage Award, 1967, for Mustang: Wild Spirit of the West; Kerlan Award, 1975.

WRITINGS: Auno and Tauno: A Story of Finland, Albert Whitman, 1940; Dilly Dally Sally, Saalfield, 1940; Birds at Home, Donohue, 1942, revised edition, Hubbard Press, 1972; Geraldine Belinda, Platt, 1942; (with Barbara True) Their First Igloo on Baffin Island, Albert Whitman, 1943; Boy and a Dog, Follett, 1944; Justin Morgan Had a Horse, Follett, 1945, revised edition, Rand McNally, 1954; Little Fellow (Junior Literary Guild selection), Winston, 1945;

MARGUERITE HENRY (center)

Robert Fulton: Boy Craftsman, Bobbs-Merrill, 1945; Misty of Chincoteague (Junior Literary Guild selection), Rand McNally, 1947; Always Reddy, McGraw, 1947; Benjamin West and His Cat, Grimalkin, Bobbs-Merrill, 1947; King of the Wind, Rand McNally, 1948; Little-or-Nothing from Nottingham, McGraw, 1949; Sea Star: Orphan of Chincoteague, Rand McNally, 1949.

Born to Trot, Rand McNally, 1950; Album of Horses (Junior Literary Guild selection), Rand McNally, 1951; (with Wesley Dennis) Portfolio of Horses (taken from Album of Horses), Rand McNally, 1952; Brighty of the Grand Canyon, Rand McNally, 1953; Wagging Tails: An Album of Dogs, Rand McNally, 1955; Cinnabar: The One O'Clock Fox, Rand McNally, 1956; Black Gold, Rand McNally, 1957; Muley-Ears, Nobody's Dog (Junior Literary Guild selection), Rand McNally, 1959.

Gaudenzia: Pride of the Palio, Rand McNally, 1960; Misty, the Wonder Pony, by Misty, Herself, Rand McNally, 1961; All About Horses, Random House, 1962; Five O'Clock Charlie, Rand McNally, 1962; Stormy, Misty's Foal, Rand McNally, 1963; White Stallion of Lipizza, Rand McNally, 1964; (with Dennis) Portfolio of Horse Paintings, Rand McNally, 1964; Mustang: Wild Spirit of the West, Rand McNally, 1966; Dear Readers and Riders, Rand McNally, 1969; San Domingo: The Medicine Hat Stallion, Rand McNally, 1972.

For Brighty the days followed one another in a dull sameness. All around him there was the blue of lupine and the pink of spring beauties, and meadow grass showing green. But he looked out of film-covered eyes and his days were gray. ■ (From *Brighty of the Grand Canyon* by Marguerite Henry. Illustrated by Wesley Dennis.)

"Pictured Geographies" series, published by Albert Whitman: *Alaska in Story and Pictures,* 1941, 2nd edition, 1942; *Argentina . . .,* 1941, 2nd edition, 1942; *Brazil . . .,* 1941, 2nd edition, 1942; *Canada . . .,* 1941, 2nd edition, 1942; *Chile . . .,* 1941, 2nd edition, 1942; *Mexico . . .,* 1941, 2nd edition, 1942; *Panama . . .,* 1941, 2nd edition, 1942; *West Indies . . .,* 1941, 2nd edition, 1942; *Australia . . .,* 1946; *Bahamas . . .,* 1946; *Bermuda , . .,* 1946; *British Honduras . . .,* 1946; *Dominican Republic . . .,* 1946; *Hawaii . . .,* 1946; *New Zealand . . .,* 1946; *Virgin Islands . . .,* 1946. Contributor of articles to magazines including *Nations' Business, Saturday Evening Post, Reader's Digest,* and *Forum.* Contributor to *World Book Encyclopedia.*

SIDELIGHTS: Marguerite Henry relates that in 1945 she received a letter "concerning the legend of the Spanish moor ponies that were washed into the sea, centuries ago, when a Spanish galleon was wrecked on a hidden reef." She read "how the ponies swam, unhurt, for the nearest shore, which happened to be Assateague Island off the coasts of Virginia and Maryland. Today, descendants of these ponies still run wild on that island. One day a year, called Pony Penning Day, oystermen and clam diggers from Chincoteague Island nearby turn cowboy. They round up the wild ponies, drive them into the sea, swim them over to their own island, and sell the colts in a big auction." With the illustrator, Wesley Dennis, she went to Pony Penning Day in search of a story. She returned with the story and a colt named Misty. This was the beginning of *Misty of Chincoteague* and of what M.

B. King called "one of the finest horse stories you'll find for the eight- to 12-year olds." It strengthened the author's already fine reputation as an outstanding author in this field.

She has proved, also, that she is adept in other areas. Her two books for Bobbs-Merrill's "Childhood of Famous Americans" Series, *Robert Fulton* and *Benjamin West and His Cat, Grimalkin,* were well received. "In adding the story of Robert Fulton to [this] series," wrote a *Book Week* reviewer, "Marguerite Henry had to match her skill against that of a number of illustrious predecessors who have contributed to the list. It is delightful to find that she has made good to the extent of writing one of the best of the series." Her writing has been deemed enchanting and rich in human values. "Miss Henry is frequently, unabashedly sentimental," wrote E. L. Buell, "but I have never known a horse-lover to object to that."

Misty of Chincoteague was made into the film "Misty" by 20th Century-Fox in 1961; *Brighty of Grand Canyon* was filmed by Stephen F. Booth in 1966; *Justin Morgan Had a Horse* was filmed by Walt Disney Productions in 1972.

FOR MORE INFORMATION SEE: Book Week, November 11, 1945; *Chicago Sun Book Week,* October 18, 1947; *Young Wings,* December, 1947; Miller and Field, *Newbery Medal Books: 1922-55,* Horn Book, 1955; *New York Times,* December 22, 1957.

HERRMANNS, Ralph 1933-

PERSONAL: Born January 31, 1933, in Berlin, Germany; now Swedish citizen; son of Otto (a chief justice) and Edith (Jacoby) Herrmanns. *Education:* University of Uppsala, B.A., 1953. *Religion:* Jewish. *Home:* Brännkyrkagatan 77, Stockholm, Sweden. *Office:* Bonniers, Stockholm.

CAREER: Journalist for Swedish newspapers, and foreign correspondent, 1953-1962; Ediciones Albon Medellin, Colombia (affiliate of the Bonnier Group, Stockholm), editor-in-chief and publisher, 1962-64; Åhlen & Åkerlunds Foerlag (The Bonnier Magazine Group), Stockholm, Sweden, editor-in-chief, 1964-66, served in Red China for Time-Life Books and Life International, 1966-67; scripts for film and TV, 1967—. *Military service:* Royal Swedish Horse Guards Reserve. *Member:* Publicistklubben, International P.E.N.

WRITINGS: Lee Lan, Hing och draken, Bonniers, 1961, translation by Annabelle Macmillan published as *Lee Lan Flies the Dragon Kite,* Harcourt, 1963; *Barnen vid Nordpolen,* Bonniers, 1963, translation by Annabelle Macmillan published as *Children of the North Pole,* Harcourt, 1964; *Bilen Julia,* Bonniers, 1963, translation by Annabelle Macmillan published as *Our Car Julia,* Harcourt, 1964; *Pojken och folden,* Bonniers, 1964, translation by Joan Tate published as *River Boy: Adventure on the Amazon,* Harcourt, 1965; *Flickan som hade braatom,* Bonniers, 1967; *Den förtrollade lådan,* Bonniers, 1967; *Den Förskräcklige snowmannen,* Bonniers, 1969, translation published under title *In Search of the Abominable Snowman,* Doubleday, 1970; *Världens vackraste tavla,* Bonniers, 1970; *Natten och drömmenatt måla som Miró,* Bonniers, 1972; *Biography on Joan Miró Liljevalchs,* Stockholm, 1972; *Biography on Count Carl Gustaf von Rosen,* Wahlström & Widstrand, 1975; *Stockholm's Royal Palace* (picture book), Bonniers, 1977. Contributor to several books on modern painting, also *Asia, A Natural History,* Random House, 1968 and *The Cooking of China,* Time-Life, 1968.

Most books have been published in nine languages and *Lee Lan Flies the Dragon Kite, Children of the North Pole, River Boy* and *Natten och drömmenatt måla som Miró* (U.S. title, *Joan Miro—the Man the Artist*) have been filmed by Stephen Bosustow Production, Los Angeles.

WORK IN PROGRESS: A musical on the early life of the painter Pablo Picasso.

SIDELIGHTS: "I came to write books for children when in Hong Kong on a job for a Swedish magazine. I saw the poverty (this was 1960-61), decided to try to do something about it, bought myself my first camera, took my first pictures and it turned into my first book. The idea was (and this worked) that part of my money and the publisher's money was to be spent on children in Hong Kong. This we kept up during a couple of books but then everybody had to get themselves cameras and make pictures from 'far-away-countries' so it was no fun anymore. Instead I used my dogs and somebody else's little girl and made a book explaining classical ballet and from there went on to books about painting like that of Tàpies and Miró. It is just the same as doing a book from Nepal or Greenland—showing children something new.

"I don't intend these books for any special group or age, however, and oddly enough some critics here have said sev-

RALPH HERRMANNS

"Just outside her home by the sea, she saw a baby bunting hopping around among the hillocks of heather. Ekaluk picked it up and held it in her hands. She felt that she could feel the presence of the summer." ■ (From *Children of the North Pole* by Ralph Herrmanns.)

eral times they are 'Americanized.' If there should be a 'message' in my books, which one of those Ph.D.'s insists there is, *I* would like it to be 'nobody is alike and everybody should have the right to be as different as she cares to be.' I am fond of travelling and guess I have done more so than most but do not think that my books necessarily need an exotic background (which, however, helps the sales).

"I find it pleasant and completely useable in our time to combine text with photographic pictures. However I don't think that photographic books are more suitable for children than otherwise illustrated books. My kind of books—if you make them the way I try to, writing a word you can't see illustrated in a picture—naturally tend to become duller, e.g. you can't put 'and then the boy had an elephant for lunch' if you don't show it. I try to do this too when I write for older people (not always adults) which is not considered 'good.'

"To start thinking of producing for television and film was natural. The ultimate of what my books have been."

HOBBIES AND OTHER INTERESTS: Modern paintings, antique Chinese bronzes, dogs and horses.

HITZ, Demi 1942-

PERSONAL: Born September 2, 1942, in Cambridge, Mass.; daughter of William Morris (an architect, actor, and entrepreneur) and Rosamond (an artist; maiden name Pier) Hunt; married John Rawlins Hitz (a teacher and writer), December 18, 1965; children: John. *Education:* Attended

Instituto Allende (Mexico) and Rhode Island School of Design; Immaculate Heart College, B.A., 1962; University of Baroda, M.S., 1963; further graduate study at China Institute. *Home and office:* 325 Riverside Dr., New York, N.Y. 10025. *Agent:* Pema Browne, 185 East 85th St., New York, N.Y. 10028.

CAREER: Artist; murals, paintings, mosaics, and silk screen prints have been exhibited in museums and galleries in California, New York, N.Y., and Massachusetts, as well as in India. *Member:* China Institute. *Awards, honors:* Fulbright scholarship to India, 1962; awards from *Boston Globe* scholastic competitions, 1961, California State Fair, 1962, Los Angeles County Museum, 1962, California Arts and Science Fair, 1962, and Los Angeles Outdoor Art Festival, 1962.

ILLUSTRATOR—For children, unless otherwise noted: Partap Sharma, *The Surangini Tales,* Harcourt, 1973; Lu Yu, *The Classic of Tea* (adult), Little, Brown, 1974; *Feelings,* Macmillan, 1975; *The Old China Trade,* Coward, 1976; *The Wonderful World of Cats,* Time/Life, 1976. Contributor to art, craft, and education journals.

WORK IN PROGRESS: Three children's books; Chinese calligraphy.

SIDELIGHTS: Demi Hitz has painted murals in Mexico,

DEMI HITZ

134   **Something about the Author**

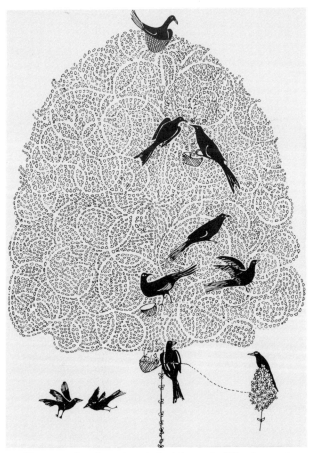

Kraw used to be exhausted at the end of the day and had no thought of playing and flying about in the evening wind. But Kree wanted to be taken out and shown new places. So she never kept any food in the nest. She would always want to eat out. ■ (From *The Surangini Tales* by Partap Sharma. Illustrated by Demi Hitz.)

walls for modern homes, and gold-leafed the dome of St. Peter's & Paul's Church in Wilmington, Calif.

HOBBIES AND OTHER INTERESTS: Travel (has traveled to Mexico, Guatemala, Chile, Canada, England, India, and Japan, and has lived in Sao Paulo, Brazil).

FOR MORE INFORMATION SEE: New York Times Book Review, May 6, 1973, December 8, 1974; *Dallas Morning News,* August 18, 1974; *Washington Post,* August 21, 1974; *Milton Record Transcript,* August 22, 1974; *Boston Herald American,* August 26, 1974, September 23, 1974, November 5, 1974; *Sunday Herald Advertiser,* October 20, 1974; *Boston Globe,* November 12, 1974; *Patriot Ledger,* November 13, 1974; *China Trade Register,* December, 1974.

HOCHSCHILD, Arlie Russell   1940-

PERSONAL: Born January 15, 1940, in Boston, Mass.; daughter of Francis Henry (a diplomat) and Ruth (Libbey) Russell; married Adam Marquand Hochschild (a magazine editor), June 26, 1965; children: David Russell, Gabriel Russell. *Education:* Swarthmore College, B.A., 1962; University of California, Berkeley, M.A., 1965, Ph.D., 1969.

Soon swings appeared in the city where there had never been swings before.
Bicycles with long handle bars appeared where there had never been bicycles before.
■ (From *Coleen the Question Girl* by Arlie Russell Hochschild. Illustrated by Gail Ashby.)

Politics: Socialist. *Religion:* Agnostic. *Home:* 2711 Virginia St., Apt. 4, Berkeley, Calif. 94709. *Office:* Department of Sociology, University of California, Berkeley, Calif. 94720.

CAREER: University of California at Santa Cruz, assistant

ARLIE RUSSELL HOCHSCHILD

professor of sociology, 1969-71; University of California, Berkeley, assistant professor, 1971-75, associate professor of sociology, 1975—. Guggenheim fellow, 1976-77. *Member:* American Sociological Association, Sociologists for Women in Society, American Gerontological Society, American Federation of Teachers.

WRITINGS: The Unexpected Community, Prentice-Hall, 1973; *Coleen, the Question Girl* (children's story), Feminist Press, 1973. Contributor to professional journals.

FOR MORE INFORMATION SEE: Ms., December, 1974.

HOFF, Carol 1900-

PERSONAL: Born February 24, 1900, in Tucson, Ariz.; daughter of Charles Frederick (a real estate dealer) and Helen (Eckhardt) Hoff. *Education:* University of Texas, LL.B., 1922; University of Colorado, summer graduate study; Texas Woman's University, M.L.S., 1954. *Politics:* Independent. *Religion:* Presbyterian. *Home:* 318 Delany Dr., Seguin, Tex. 78155.

CAREER: Yorktown (Tex.) public schools, high school teacher of English, 1924-50, school librarian, 1950-66; retired, 1966, but does substitute teaching and volunteer work in public library. Library Board, member, 1945-60, chairman, 1950-58. *Member:* Texas State Teachers Association, Texas Library Association, Texas Institute of Letters, Seguin Shakespeare Club, Seguin Delphian Club, Nogales Garden Club, Delta Kappa Gamma, Kappa Beta Pi, Beta Phi Mu, Key Allegro Landscape Club (secretary, 1967—). *Awards, honors:* Charles W. Follett Award and Cokesbury Award of Texas Institute of Letters, both for *Johnny Texas,*

1950; Boys' Clubs of America Junior Book Award for *Wilderness Pioneer,* 1956.

WRITINGS—Juveniles: *Johnny Texas,* 1950, *Johnny Texas on the San Antonio Road,* 1953, *Wilderness Pioneer,* 1955, *Head to the West,* 1957, *The Four Friends,* 1958, *Chris,* 1960 (all published by Follett).

Adult basic education books: *They Served America,* Steck, 1966; *Holidays and History,* Steck, 1967.

WORK IN PROGRESS: Another "Johnny Texas" book; two other juveniles set in early Texas; a book dealing with propaganda, and a reader, both for basic adult education.

SIDELIGHTS: "The first eight years of my life I lived in Tucson, Arizona, and I loved the mountains. The second six years of my life I lived in Rockport, Texas, and I loved the seashore. Now I live in Seguin, Texas, and I love the tall oak and pecan trees. But most of my life I lived in Yorktown, Texas, a small town about ninety miles south of San Antonio.

"I finished high school in Yorktown, and after I was graduated from the University of Texas I went back there to teach in high school. I hated school until my senior year, but I taught school for over thirty years and for the most part enjoyed it, perhaps because I always loved to read and I was teaching English and American literature and serving as the school librarian. I also enjoyed directing plays and sponsoring the school newspaper.

"Perhaps my writing began when I was a child. I used to make up stories to tell my little sister, and I made up plays and directed them for the neighborhood children. An old

Pulling his hand from Mama's, he stepped ahead of Papa from the boat to the little wharf, and the wooden floor seemed to rock under him. ▪ (From *Johnny Texas* by Carol Hoff. Illustrated by Bob Meyers.)

liked my books have added to that pleasure through the years."

HOBBIES AND OTHER INTERESTS: Reading, gardening, listening to symphonic music, playing bridge, collecting stamps, and designing clothes.

HOLLIDAY, Joseph 1910- (Joe Holliday; pseudonyms: Jack Bosco, Jack Dale)

PERSONAL: Born December 14, 1910, in Gibraltar, Brit.; son of Joseph (a laborer) and Julia Francis (Bosco) Holliday; married Gladys Muriel Squier, November 30, 1935; children: Anne June (Mrs. Stanley Hotchkiss), Marilyn Jane (Mrs. Tony Cucci). *Education:* Attended public schools in Toronto, Ontario, and took night classes in art, advertising, and other subjects. *Politics:* Liberal ("generally—not firm"). *Religion:* Anglican ("generally—not firm"). *Home:* 26 Porter Crescent, Scarborough, Ontario, Canada.

CAREER: Prior to 1940 was associate editor of *Sporting News,* did publicity for a radio station, and was manager of a theater, all in Toronto, Ontario; de Havilland Aircraft, Toronto, publicity staff and chief photographer, 1940-45; Imperial Oil, Ltd., Toronto, publicity and editorial work, 1945-56; Weston Publishing Co., Toronto, Ontario, editor, 1956-70; Wadham Publications Ltd., Toronto, Ontario, editor, 1970—; Canadian Authors Association, Toronto, chairman of headquarters committee, 1959-71. *Member:* Canadian Business Press Association (member of board of directors, 1960), Canadian Aviation Historical Society. *Awards,*

CAROL HOFF

piano crate was our stage, and we charged five pins' admission. I also loved to listen to my grandmother and great-aunt tell stories about the experiences of their parents, who came to Texas as pioneers in 1834. Many of these family tales I have woven into my books, especially in *Johnny Texas* and *Head to the West.*

"My first little published story was a surprise to me. It was a tale based on an incident in a pioneer town in Arizona written as an English theme. My father sent it to a newspaper in Tucson, which published it. What a happy surprise when he handed it to me!

"My second published story was a little fairy tale I wrote shortly after I finished the University and sent to *The Youth's Companion,* a magazine I had grown up with. Encouraged, I sent a second story to our church magazine. It was also accepted. Then I sent a third story. It was rejected and I was so discouraged that I foolishly did not try again for years.

"When my two nephews were growing up, they used to spend the summers with me. They were always interested in the old family tales I told them. Thinking that other boys and girls would also enjoy these adventures, I wove them into a book, *Johnny Texas.* Imagine my delight when *Johnny Texas* won the first Charles W. Follett Award!

"My writing has always been a pleasure to me, and the many fan letters I've had from boys and girls telling me that they

JOSEPH HOLLIDAY

honors: Centennial Medal from Canadian Government, 1967; Allan Sangstor Memorial Award, 1973.

WRITINGS: "Dale of the Mounted" juvenile series, Thomas Allen (Toronto) and Pennington Press (Cleveland), 1950-62, with titles including *Dale of the Mounted, Dale of the Mounted on the West Coast, Dale of the Mounted in Newfoundland, Dale of the Mounted: Dew Line Duty, Dale of the Mounted Submarine Hunt, Dale of the Mounted Atlantic Assignment, Dale of the Mounted: Atomic Plot, Dale of the Mounted in Hong Kong, Dale of the Mounted in the Northwest, Dale of the Mounted in the Arctic, Dale of the Mounted on the St. Lawrence, Dale of the Mounted at the U.N.*

Other books: *Oil Trails in Headless Valley* (juvenile), Longmans, Green, 1954; *Mosquito: The Wooden Wonder Aircraft of World War II,* Doubleday, 1970. Contributor of articles on a variety of subjects to magazines, trade journals, and newspapers in Canada and the United States; some of the articles were published under Joe Holliday and the pseudonyms Jack Bosco and Jack Dale. Editor, *Canadian Author & Bookman Quarterly,* 1955-60, 1976.

SIDELIGHTS: "Although I received a certificate in public school for 100 per cent in spelling, for a complete year I never entertained any ideas about writing. In 1931, when I was only 21, I witnessed an incident of police brutality. I was so incensed that I offered to write a petition for the parties involved and witnessed by neighborhood people and storekeepers. It went to three daily newspapers, a scandal weekly, and to the Mayor of Toronto, not to the Chief of Police!"

"The resulting furor and banner headlines gave me an inkling of the power of the pen (or the typewriter!) in that the accused police sergeant was suspended for three months after a police commission inquiry. I found out that I had a way with words and the gift of description. I started to contribute sports stories to a local tabloid and over the next five years became quite a local sportswriter, but my chief speciality became amateur and professional boxing. I got paid now and then, but was so fired with ambition to be a writer the money did not matter. I lived at home with understanding parents who gave me the green light to pursue my objectives.

"Later I got into weekly journalism, more sports writing, some radio work and kept building contacts, getting story bylines and making my way gradually. I became many things in the interim, trying to learn to write, such as truck driver, laborer in airport work, sign painter, salesman, jail guard, radio commercial writer, lecture manager for a well known radio commentator, etc. During World War II I got into aircraft work, and eventually looked after the plant's publicity, house organ and all photography."

"After the war I joined Imperial Oil (ESSO) for twelve years and here started to write my 'Dale of the Mounted' books which ended after Book 12. I always had a yen for exciting adventure, but wanted to do a series that included a fifty-fifty mix of adventure and education. I weaved in historical happenings in Canada, industrial and geographic, etc., of the 1950's and 1960's to let my youthful readers know what was being accomplished. A thirteenth volume, not related to the Dale set, was about oil exploration, etc. in northern Canada. My book *Mosquito* evolved from my ex-

periences in aircraft work, being a documentary effort. I have completed my autobiography *Frantic Til Fifty* but no publisher yet!"

HOBBIES AND OTHER INTERESTS: Photography (has a collection of 3,500 color slides taken on travels in Europe, Japan, Hong Kong, and elsewhere), wood carving, metal sculpture, making tape recordings.

HOLMQUIST, Eve   1921-

PERSONAL: Born January 29, 1921, in Minnesota; daughter of Fred J. (a musician and farmer) and Olive (a teacher; maiden name, Seager) Holmquist; married Russell W. Smith, March, 1944 (divorced January, 1968); children: Heidi (Mrs. Alan C. Sweeney), Gene, Joel, Robin. *Education:* University of Minnesota, B.A., 1947, graduate sutdy, 1954; Fresno State University, M.S.W., 1973. *Politics:* Independent. *Religion:* Protestant. *Home:* 13408 Christie Dr., Saratoga, Calif. 95070. *Agent:* Ruth Cantor, 156 Fifth Ave., New York, N.Y. 10010. *Office:* Santa Clara County Department of Social Services, 55 West Younger, San Jose, Calif.

CAREER: Bruce Publishing Co., St. Paul, Minn., clerical work, 1956; University of Minnesota Press, Minneapolis, proofreader, 1956-58; Santa Clara County Department of Social Services, San Jose, Calif., social worker, 1966—. *Member:* National Association of Social Workers, National Writers Club.

WRITINGS: *The Giant Giraffe* (juvenile), Carolrhoda Books, 1973. Contributor to *Poetry Digest, Velvet Glove,* and *Four Quarters.*

EVE HOLMQUIST

And since this is so,
it obviously follows
that there are no giant giraffes
entangled in trees
or
elsewhere."
And with that,
he went back to his coffee.

■ (From *The Giant Giraffe* by Eve Holmquist. Illustrated by Joan Hanson.)

WORK IN PROGRESS: The Very Stubborn Stork; No Certain Time; a novel, as yet untitled; short stories.

SIDELIGHTS: "As a social worker I spend a lot of time driving from point to point in my car. Since driving is pretty automatic, the field of the mind is open for daydreams, thoughts, worries, plans, words, phrases to enter, dance about and leave or to be caught and held.

"My first children's book, *The Giant Giraffe,* came about when the first line simply came out of nowhere and announced itself as I drove about on my rounds, and I thought, 'Aha! That sounds like a children's book to me.' From then on lines and phrases had a habit of appearing from time to time, and gradually most of the story had come. After that, some adding, subtracting, re-shaping, and the thing was finished.

"I had raised four children and knew their fascination with sounds and their delight in nonsense, so I let the alliteration and the nonsense stand as they had come. As to the big words, they were perhaps a reaction to the painful 'See Jane, see Jane run' kind of thing which my children were subjected to in their early years. It amazes me that children learn to read at all when such muck is forced upon them.

"Basically, I wrote the kind of book I knew my own children would have enjoyed. But for the most part the story announced itself. I did not do much besides write it down."

HOBBIES AND OTHER INTERESTS: Travel; classical music, both as consumer and performer.

HOOPES, Roy 1922-

PERSONAL: Born May 17, 1922, in Salt Lake City, Utah; son of Roy H. (a lawyer) and Lydia Hoopes; married; wife's name Cora; children: Spencer, Sallie, Tommy. *Education:* George Washington University, A.B., 1946, M.A., 1949. *Politics:* Democrat. *Home:* 7708 Hackamore Dr., Potomac, Md. 20854.

CAREER: U.S. Department of State, Washington, D.C., research analyst, 1946-48; *Pathfinder* (magazine), assistant world editor, 1949-52; Time, Inc., New York, N.Y., general promotion manager of *Time-Life* International, 1952-53; managing editor of *High Fidelity,* 1953-56, and *Democratic Digest,* 1956-61; *National Geographic,* Washington, D.C., editor and writer, 1963-65; *Washingtonian* (magazine), Washington, D.C., associate editor, 1965-66; Department of Health, Education and Welfare in the Public Information Office, 1967-73; *Newsday,* Long Island, N.Y., National affairs editorial writer, 1973-74; free-lance writer, 1966—. *Member:* Authors League of America, National Press Club (Washington, D.C.).

WRITINGS: (Editor) *Wit From Overseas,* Avon, 1953; (editor) *Building Your Record Library,* McGraw, 1958; (editor) *The "High Fidelity" Reader,* Hanover House, 1958; *The Complete Peace Corps Guide,* introduction by R. Sargent Shriver, Dial, 1961, 4th edition, 1968; *The Steel Crisis: 72 Hours That Shook the Nation,* John Day, 1962; *What the President Does All Day,* John Day, 1962; (editor) *State Colleges and Universities,* Robert B. Luce, 1962; *A Report on Fallout in Your Food,* New American Library, 1962; (editor) *The Peace Corps Experience,* preface by Hubert Hum-

phrey, C. N. Potter, 1968; *Getting with Politics: A Young Person's Guide to Political Action,* Delacorte, 1968.

What a United States Senator Does, John Day, 1970, revised, 1975; (with son, Spencer) *What a Baseball Manager Does,* John Day, 1970; *What a United States Congressman Does,* John Day, 1972; *What a Pro Football Coach Does,* John Day, 1972; *What a State Governor Does,* John Day, 1973; *What the President of the United States Does,* John Day, 1974; (with Erwin Hargrove) *The Presidency: A Question of Power,* Little, Brown, 1975. Contributor to magazines and newspapers including *Esquire, Seventeen, Nation, New Republic, America Illustrated, Writer's Digest, Better Living, Washington Post,* and *Washington Star Magazine;* weekly newspaper columnist for several years under an undisclosed pseudonym.

SIDELIGHTS: "I was born in Salt Lake City, Utah, but when I was four, my parents moved to Washington, D.C. so that my father could work and attend law school at night. This must account for my interest in writing about government and public affairs. Having grown up in Washington, it seemed to me for years that government and politics were the only subjects worth writing about. However, that feeling is changing now and I am becoming more interested in history, personal experiences, literature and fiction.

"I did not think seriously about being a writer until World War II, when I spent two years at sea on an LST reading constantly and, incidentally, helping our ship, the 559, get through the war in one piece, which it did. While in the Navy, I kept a diary (against Naval Regulations) and on the first page I noted that, if nothing else, it would prove 'whether I have any ability in the literary field' and if I decide I do I will give up my plans to go to law school after the war and 'look forward to a busy life . . . turning out six or seven Books of the Month a year.'

"A re-reading of my diary recently confirms my decision after the war to enroll in Georgetown law school, where I remained two whole *weeks.* The trouble was that I had majored in history in college and because of the war I had become intensely interested in international affairs. And through friends, I had a job offer with the United States Delegation to the United Nations, which was just getting into operation in New York. It seemed like an opportunity too good to pass up, so I accepted.

"This took me first to New York, then to Washington to work in the division of the State Department concerned with United Nations affairs and then back to George Washington University where I completed my master's degree in history. I was supposed to return to the State Department after I had completed work on my Master's Degree in 1949, but the government was suffering one of its periodic job freezes, which included mine. Also, I wanted to get married.

"So, there I was at age 27, having abandoned my writing career, stymied in my diplomatic career and eager to get married. Naturally, I did what many frustrated young men of that era—or any era—did; I went into journalism. This experience is outlined in the *Career* entry under my name, and it eventually led to my first book—an anthology of anecdotes and cartoons taken from a column I had edited for the old *Pathfinder* magazine called 'Wit From Overseas.' From this point on, I realized that although journalism was all right for making a living and that sort of thing, there was only one

Something about the Author

ROY HOOPES, with Vice-President Mondale

thing that really counted for a writer—books. I have been writing them ever since.

"The thing about writing books is that I can always go down to the Library of Congress and look in the card catalogue under my name and know that those sixteen entries and the books that go with them are going to be there forever—unless someone drops a hydrogen bomb on Washington, which is always a possibility. These books and their cards in the Library of Congress are a much more satisfactory monument for my brief shining moment here on earth than a gravestone or even an obit in the *Times*. And, who knows—someday I might even write a good book or a 'great' book entering me in the 'Shakespeare Sweepstakes', as the late Ian Fleming, creator of James Bond, used to call it—a book that will be read years, decades or centuries from now. But there is nothing I can do about that; history, not the critics, or even today's readers decides which books will live and which will not.

"The main problem—for a man, at least—in writing books is that 99.9 per cent of them do not make enough money for one person let alone a family, to live on. So you have to do other things, which is where journalism comes in. And if you really want to write and enjoy it, writing newspaper and magazine articles is the next best thing to writing books. And today, it does not hurt to know how to use a camera and a tape recorder.

"When my son Spencer and I started out to do our picture book on a baseball manager, Ted Williams had just begun his

career as manager of the Washington Senators. So, naturally, there were no photographs available of him managing. It would have been very expensive to hire a professional photographer to take as many photographs of Williams as we needed. So I took up photography myself, and so did Spencer. We eventually took one thousand photographs of Ted Williams, about sixty-five of which were used in our book, *What a Baseball Manager Does*. For my current 'work in progress,' as we writers say, I am learning to use a tape recorder. The book, to be published by Hawthorn Books, is about the homefront during World War II and will entail interviewing maybe a couple of hundred people, to get their first-hand recollections of what life was like in America in the years 1941-45.

"So you can see, there is more to writing books than sitting alone in a room in front of your typewriter—but that's still mostly what you do. And anyone who is thinking about maybe being a writer someday, should not forget it."

HOPKINS, Joseph G(erard) E(dward) 1909-

PERSONAL: Born September 12, 1909, in Brooklyn, N.Y.; son of Joseph Henry and Florence (Brady) Hopkins; married Virginia Appleton, 1944; children: Virginia, Joseph, Margaret, James. *Education:* Fordham University, A.B., 1929, law school student, 1930-31; Columbia University, M.A., 1939. *Politics:* Democrat. *Religion:* Roman Catholic. *Home:* 4 Pine Brook Dr., Larchmont, N.Y. .

CAREER: Teacher at preparatory schools and colleges, including Loyola, New York City, Notre Dame College, Staten Island, N.Y., Fordham University and Columbia University, 1931-42; Charles Scribner's Sons, New York, N.Y., editor, 1946-75. *Military service:* U.S. Merchant Marine, 1943-45, attaining rank of lieutenant, junior grade. *Member:* New York Historical Society, Century Association (New York), Grolier Club (New York).

WRITINGS: (Editor) *Album of American History,* Volumes IV, V, Scribner, 1948, 1960; (editor) *The Scribner Treasury,* Scribner, 1953; *Colonial Governor* (juvenile biography), Kenedy, 1957; *Blackrobe Peacemaker* (juvenile biography), Kenedy, 1958; *Patriot's Progress,* Scribner, 1961; (editor) *Concise Dictionary of American Biography,* Scribner, 1964; *Retreat and Recall,* Scribner, 1966; *The Price of Liberty,* Scribner, 1976.

WORK IN PROGRESS: A novel about 19th-century immigrants to the United States; a revised edition of *Concise Dictionary of American Biography.*

SIDELIGHTS: "My stories, as will be apparent from their titles, have been a natural development out of my work as editor of historical treatises and reference books. I have tried to make the stories faithful accounts of the period of the American Revolution by basing their psychology and vocabulary on diaries, letters, and personal narratives by people of that time—the plain folk equally with the great and famous. I have made a special effort to avoid reading the present into the past. The ideas and motivations of the various characters are, so far as I could make them, just such ideas and motives as would have been entertained by men and women of the late 18th century who had been circumstanced as my fictional people are circumstanced. Physical descriptions of places are drawn from descriptions by contemporary travelers and considerable study of old maps."

HOBBIES AND OTHER INTERESTS: Collects rare Americana, books and manuscripts.

HORWICH, Frances R(appaport)   1908-
(Miss Frances)

PERSONAL: Born July 16, 1908, in Ottawa, Ohio; daughter of Samuel and Rosa (Gratz) Rappaport; married Harvey L. Horwich (an attorney), June 11, 1931. *Education:* University of Chicago, Ph.B., 1929; Columbia University, M.A., 1933; Northwestern University, Ph.D., 1942. *Home and office:* 6801 E. Camelback Rd., G-103, Scottsdale, Ariz. 85251.

CAREER: Primary teacher, nursery schools supervisor, and director of junior kindergarten in Chicago, Ill., and suburbs, 1929-38; Pestolozzi Froebel Teachers College, Chicago, Ill., dean of education, 1938-40; Chicago Teachers College, Chicago, Ill., counselor of student teachers, 1940-43; Hessian Hills School, Croton-on-Hudson, N.Y., director, 1943-45; University of North Carolina, Chapel Hill, visiting professor of education, 1945-46; Roosevelt University, Chicago, Ill., associate professor, 1946-47, professor of education and chairman of department, 1947-52; National Broadcasting Co., New York, N.Y., supervisor of children's programs, 1955-56; Curtis Publishing Co., Philadelphia, Pa., director of children's activities, 1962-63, educational director and author of bimonthly letter to parents,

1963-64, consultant, 1965; television personality as Miss Frances, conducting, writing, and producing "Ding Dong School," beginning 1952, and "Parents Time With Miss Frances," 1955; Educational consultant, Field Enterprises Educational Corp., beginning 1965. Visiting summer professor or lecturer at Northwestern University, University of North Carolina, University of California, and other universities, 1942-60; conductor of workshops and lecturer for organizations throughout America. Member of board of directors, Girl Scouts of Chicago, beginning 1965.

MEMBER: National Association for the Education of Young Children (secretary, 1944-47; director, 1944-56; president, 1948-51), National Society for the Study of Education, Association for Childhood Education International, Association for Supervision and Curriculum Development, International Reading Association, National Association of Educational Broadcasters, American Association for Gifted Children, National Association for Mental Health, National Academy of Television Arts and Sciences (director, Chicago chapter, 1958-59), American Federation of Television and Radio Artists, American Women in Radio and Television, International Platform Association, Authors League of America, Chicago Unlimited (director, beginning 1965), Delta Kappa Gamma.

AWARDS, HONORS: More than sixty awards and citations for "Ding Dong School," including Woman of the Year in Education, Associated Press, 1953, George Foster Peabody Award, 1953, National Association for Better Radio and Television Award, 1953, 1954, *Parents' Magazine* Medal Award, 1955, Silver Trophy Award of National Audience Board, 1956; P.D. (Doctor of Pedagogy), Bowling

FRANCES R. HORWICH

Green State University, 1954; Alumni Award of Merit, Northwestern University, 1954; Alumni Medal, University of Chicago, 1957.

WRITINGS: Nursery School First, Then Kindergarten (curriculum material), Hinds, 1947; (contributor) *Portfolio on More and Better Schools for Children Under Six,* Association for Childhood Education, 1949; *Have Fun With Your Children,* Prentice-Hall, 1954; (contributor) *Understanding Yourself and Your Child,* National Society for Crippled Children and Adults, 1955; (author of foreword) Winthrop M. Phelps, Thomas W. Hopkins, and Robert Cousins, editors, *The Cerebral-Palsied Child: A Guide for Parents,* Simon & Schuster, 1958; *The Magic of Bringing Up Your Child,* McGraw, 1959.

Children's books: *Miss Frances' Ding Dong School Book,* Rand McNally, 1953, and twenty-six other "Ding Dong School Books," Rand McNally, 1953-56; *Miss Frances' All-Day-Long Book,* Rand McNally, 1954; *Miss Frances' Ding Dong School Piano Book,* Hanson Music Corp., 1954; *Miss Frances' Storybook of Manners for the Very Young,* Rand McNally, 1955; *Miss Frances' Storybook of Pets for the Very Young,* Rand McNally, 1956; *Stories and Poems to Enjoy,* Doubleday, 1962.

Writer and narrator for "Ding Dong School Records," issued by RCA-Victor, 1953-56, Golden Records, 1960.

Associate editor, "Junior Life Series" of *Teacher Guides,* Science Research Associates, 1951-52; member of editorial advisory board, *Childcraft,* 1956-60. Contributor to *Jack and Jill, Chicago Sunday Tribune Magazine,* and to educational and television periodicals.

SIDELIGHTS: "Ding Dong School," which was nominated for television's Emmy Awards four times, 1954-59, provided material for the nation's cartoonists for many years. A "Peanuts" comic strip character found solace in "Miss Frances likes me!" in 1954, and its creator, Charles M. Schulz, continued to draw on the Miss Frances' theme for other United Feature Syndicate cartoons. Cartoonists for the *New Yorker,* Post-Hall Syndicate, New York Herald Tribune Syndicate, and other syndicates also have used "Ding Dong School."

HOBBIES AND OTHER INTERESTS: Knitting, working in ceramics and other crafts, cooking and baking.

IRWIN, Keith Gordon   1885-1964

PERSONAL: Born March 13, 1885, in Galesburg, Ill.; son of John N. and Angie (McMaster) Irwin; married Mary Kent, August 15, 1906; children: Beth (Mrs. W. E. Burleson), Jane (Mrs. P. S. Lanphear), Jean (Mrs. R. C. Othberg), Margery (Mrs. R. J. Mueller), Amy (Mrs. D. L. Ghent). *Education:* Knox College, B.S.; University of Chicago, M.S.; additional study at University of Missouri, University of Wisconsin. *Religion:* Presbyterian. *Home and office:* 510 Peterson, Fort Collins, Colo.

CAREER: Knox College, Galesburg, Ill., mathematics teacher, one year; Penn College, Oskaloosa, Iowa, chemistry teacher, three years; Cleveland High School, St. Louis, Mo., head of physics department, twelve years; Arkansas City Junior College, Arkansas City, Kan., instructor in

"If I understand anything, greater wealth lies hidden beneath the ground in the mountainous parts of our country than has ever been rumored." — Georgius Agricola. ■ (From *The Romance of Chemistry* by Keith Gordon Irwin. Illustrated by Anthony Ravielli.)

chemistry, one year; Colorado State University, Fort Collins, professor of chemistry, 1925 until retirement in 1955.

WRITINGS: (Self-illustrated) *The Romance of Writing: From Egyptian Hieroglyphics to Modern Letters, Numbers, and Signs,* Viking, 1956; *The Romance of Chemistry: From Ancient Alchemy to Nuclear Fission,* Viking, 1959; *The Romance of Weights and Measures,* Viking, 1960; *Chemistry: First S-t-e-p-s,* Watts, 1963; *The 365 Days: The Story of Our Calendar,* Crowell, 1963; *Man Learns to Measure,* Dobson, 1963; *The Romance of Physics,* Scribner, 1966.

Contributor of introductions, notes: Michael Faraday, *The Chemical History of a Candle,* Crowell, 1957; Faraday, *On the Various Forces of Nature,* Viking, 1960; John Tyndall, *Faraday as a Discoverer,* Crowell, 1961; C. V. Boys, *Soap Bubbles,* Crowell, 1962; A. M. Worthington, *A Study of Splashes,* Macmillan, 1963. Contributor of more than three hundred educational and scientific articles to magazines and scientific journals, 1923—. Illustrator of chemistry text and bulletins.

SIDELIGHTS: All of Irwin's books were written after retirement at the age of seventy; they have been published in Canada and England, and translated into other languages, including Danish and Urdu.

HOBBIES AND OTHER INTERESTS: Bird drawings and bird walks, study of weather.

FOR MORE INFORMATION SEE: Colorado State Collegian, December 9, 1949; Fort Collins Coloradan, August 17, 1956, January 23, 1961, June 24, 1963; Christian Science Monitor, May 4, 1967; Times Literary Supplement, June 29, 1967.

(Died 1964)

ISH-KISHOR, Judith   1892-1972.

PERSONAL: Born March 26, 1892, in Boston, Mass.; daughter of Ephraim and Fanny (Berlin) Ish-Kishor; married Herbert Lapides, 1949. Education: Attended Hunter College, one year. Home and office: 1001 President St., Brooklyn, N.Y.

CAREER: Edited children's weekly and worked as staff writer for food magazine before becoming free-lance writer in 1920s. Worked at occasional part-time jobs, including resident chaplain in home for girls, critic for literary agent. Member: Dramatists Guild of America (associate), Authors League of America, American Association for the United Nations, United World Federalists, American Civil Liberties Union, Congress on Racial Equality.

WRITINGS: Adventure in Palestine, Messner, 1947; (contributor) Norton Belth, The World Over Story Book, Bloch, 1952; Joel is the Youngest, Messner, 1954; Tales From the Wise Men of Israel, Lippincott, 1962.

WORK IN PROGRESS: A 3-act play; two books, one historical, one fiction.

HOBBIES AND OTHER INTERESTS: Books and the theater, neighborhood movies, and gardening in pots.

(Died, 1972)

JAMES, Harry Clebourne   1896-

PERSONAL: Born April 25, 1896, in Ottawa, Ontario, Canada; son of Alfred Edgar (a veterinary surgeon) and Clara Lena (Wright) James; married Grace Kammerer Clifford (a teacher), March 30, 1927. Education: Studied at Ottawa Collegiate Institute; University of California, Los Angeles and University of Southern California. Politics: Democrat. Home and office: Lolomi Lodge, P.O. Box 716, Banning, Calif. 92220.

CAREER: Formerly writer for Citizen, in Ottawa, Ontario, Canada, camera boy at Triangle Motion Picture Studio, Hollywood, Calif., production assistant for Paramount Studios, Hollywood, Calif., assistant director for Universal Studios, Hollywood, Calif. Trailfinders (outdoor organization for boys), Hollywood, Calif., founder and chief executive; Trailfinders School for Boys, Altadena, Calif., founder and headmaster. President's Committee on Juvenile Delinquency and Youth Crime, member of advisory council. Desert Protective Council, Inc., founder; active in other conservation work and in projects to help American Indians. Military service: Canadian Army, Signal Corps, World War I. Member: Swiss and Austrian Alpine Clubs; Westerners, Federation of Western Outdoors Clubs (past president). Awards, honors: American Motors Conservation Award; Award of Merit, Desert Protective Council, 1964.

WRITINGS: Treasure of the Hopitu, Young & McAllister, 1927; Haliksai! A Book of Hopi Legends, Desert Magazine Publishing, 1940; The Hopi Indians, Caxton, 1956; A Day with Honau, a Hopi Indian Boy, Melmont, 1957; A Day with Poli, a Hopi Indian Girl, Melmont, 1957; Red Man, White Man, Naylor, 1958; A Hopi Indian Butterfly Dance, Melmont, 1959; A Day at Oraibi, A Hopi Indian Village, Melmont, 1959; The Cahuilla Indians, Westernlore, 1960; Grizzly Adams, Children's Press, 1963; Ovada, Ritchie, 1969; The First Americans, Children's Press, 1971; Western Campfires, Northland Press, 1973; Pages from Hopi History, University of Arizona Press, 1974. Author of motion picture scripts. Contributor of short stories and articles to magazines and newspapers.

WORK IN PROGRESS: A biography of James Willard Schultz.

SIDELIGHTS: "Before coming to the United States in 1913 I worked as a reporter for the Ottawa Citizen and managed concerts by well-known artists of that time. During my early years in Los Angeles I worked at a variety of jobs; cameraboy, property-man, assistant director, and script writer at the D. W. Griffith, Famous Players Lasky, and Universal Studios. At the Griffith studio, Lillian Gish suggested I be tested as an actor. It was no go!

"During those studio days I went on hikes in the Hollywood hills with Tahamount (Dark Cloud), who had been model and advisor for Frederick Remington and was then employed as an actor at the Griffith studio. On these trips we often met Hollywood youngsters who joined in exploring the then wild canyons and ridges overlooking Los Angeles. These boys were the nucleus of a club which met every Friday night in the basement auditorium of the Hollywood Public Library. This organization developed into The Trailfinders.

"My interest in the American Indians began while a small boy in Canada, largely as a result of the long-term concern of my mother's family, one of whose ancestors, Philemon Wright, became the actual 'White Chief' of the Ottawa as a result of his willingness to share with the local Algonquin Indians the lands alloted to him by the Crown.

"Shortly after my arrival in California I became well acquainted with Charles Fletcher Lummis, James Willard Schultz, and Stewart Edward White, all well known authors of the time who were deeply interested in the welfare of the Indian. Later I also came to know Frederick Webb Hodge, the authority on the American Indian, as well as on the history of the entire Southwest. These men all became life-long friends.

"In the early 1920's I joined James Willard Schultz, Stewart Edward White, Marah Ellis Ryan, Frederick Webb Hodge, Emerson Hough, Edward S. Curtis and others in forming The Indian Welfare League and The National Association To Help the Indian. Virtual starvation conditions among the Montana Blackfeet and the determined campaign by the Indian Bureau to end Indian ceremonials were matters of grave concern at that time.

"At the prompting of Lummis I took a small party of boys into the Grand Canyon and Hopi Country shortly after the end of the first World War. A cloudburst marooned us at Old Oraibi where we remained for over two weeks. The gener-

HARRY CLEBOURNE JAMES, with Hopi Indian boys

osity of the Hopi in supplying us with food when our own supply gave out and the long talks I had with leaders at Hotevila, Mishongnovi as well as Old Oraibi whom we met on our innumerable hikes through the area developed in me a lasting interest in the Hopi as well as lasting friendships with many of their important leaders.

"As years passed I became more and more involved in the struggle of the Hopi to preserve their culture, particularly their religion and its ceremonies, from pressure to abolish them by missionaries and the federal government, I felt strongly that the Hopi could maintain their own way of life and at the same time be excellent participating citizens of the United States. I was even sure that they could be good Christians and participants in their own religious life at the same time! Naturally this brought me and my associates into a certain amount of disagreement with some missionaries, reservation officials, and converted Hopi, as well as with the lunatic fringe of strange white Indian-lovers. The Little People of Peace seem to have a curious attraction for the latter!

"In 1926 I organized the Trailfinders School for Boys, a private school for super-bright younsters, stressing an extensive outdoor program. In 1950 we sold the school to Mr. Thomas Chandler who renamed it The Chandler Day School. During all these years we maintained an extensive year-round camping program, and we continued our summer camps until 1965.

"In 1970 The Trailfinders was dissolved as a non-profit corporation and reorganized into a conservation organization particularly interested in the preservation of places of scenic, scientific, historic, or recreational value. The organization is directed by its Life Members Association, an alumni group of about seven hundred former boy members, its Conservation Committee, and an advisory council of men and women of prominence who are interested in the objectives of the organization, many members of this advisory council being early participants in our school and camps.

"Before we sold the school we had begun construction of a large log cabin on property in the San Jacinto Mountains given us by the late M. Amelia Foshay, well-known principal of 24th Street School in Los Angeles, where Mrs. James (Grace) had taught and where I had the Hopi Council of The Trailfinders. By careful selection we were able to fell about 150 Ponderosa pines for building without in any way destroying the beauty of the place.

"Shortly after we moved in, a party of Hopi from Old Oraibi, Moenkopi, and Shongopovi came to visit us. We climbed through the snow to the top of a small mountain nearby from which they could see the ocean, 'mother of rains' and home of *Hurung Whuti* of the West. After appropriate prayers the Hopi had a wild time sliding down the mountain side on the toboggans nature had provided. At the bottom they at once scrambled back to the top to try the slide all over again. Back at the log cabin they inquired as to our water supply and when I showed them the spring we had developed by driving a tunnel into the hillside they planted prayer-plumes, scattered sacred cornmeal, and made appropriate prayers. The spring has never gone dry even in years of severe drought that dried up many similar springs in the San Jacintos! Prayer-plumes were also attached to the rafters inside the house as protection against its destruction.

"As at our earlier home in Altadena, we are frequently visited by Hopi friends. Before dinner the Hopi drum made for us by Tewaquaptewa is put by the fireplace to warm up. After dinner and late into the night they sing Hopi songs and we talk of Hopi affairs past, present and future.

"It was Tewaquaptewa, or rather his wife Nasayungsee of the Kachina Clan, who in the 1920's adopted me giving me the name Honaywayma (Walking Bear) because of the long walks I used to so often make through the Hopi country.

"My interest in Indians has not been limited to the Hopi but has come to include the Blackfeet of Montana and the Cahuilla of Southern California. I have also had very pleasant experiences and developed lasting friendships among the people of San Ildefonso Pueblo in New Mexico.

"My reasons for writing my various books about Indians have been in the hope that they might help develop a pride among Indian young people in their own history and culture and to acquaint white readers with the great variety that exists among the numerous tribes of the Americas.

"I am often asked, 'Do you speak Indian?' and I have to reply, 'No, there is no such language—as every tribe has its own language.'

"In our country Indian children were usually forbidden to speak their own language or develop an appreciation of their own culture including their own religion. In recent years such unfortunate restrictions have been largely abolished. Nowadays young Indians try to be good Indians and not poor imitation white men and women. I hope that in some small way my books may have helped bring about this change.

"On June 4, 1972 the property where we have lived for many years was dedicated by the University of California as the James San Jacinto Mountain Reserve 'In recognition of the devotion of Harry and Grace James to the preservation of our outdoor heritage.' We are privileged to live here at Lolomi Lodge as long as we wish.''

CHARLES R. JOHNSON

JOHNSON, Charles R.   1925- (Chuck Johnson)

PERSONAL: Born September 16, 1925, in Williston, N.D.; son of Charles A. (a grain elevator manager) and Lena (Quick) Johnson; married Lillian Hilmo, August 21, 1949; children: Linda, Eric, Paul, Thomas. *Education:* Attended Mississippi College, 1944, Massachusetts Institute of Technology, 1944-45; University of North Dakota, journalism, PHB, 1948. *Religion:* Lutheran. *Home:* 1722 North 58th St., Milwaukee, Wis. 53208. *Agent:* Larry Sternig, 742 Robertson, Milwaukee, Wis. 53213. *Office:* Milwaukee Journal, Milwaukee, Wis. 53201.

CAREER: Newspaperman. *Fargo Forum,* Fargo, N.D., assistant sports editor, 1948-52; *Milwaukee Journal,* Milwaukee, Wis., sports writer, 1952-58, assistant sports editor, 1958-68, sports editor, 1968-75, assistant news editor,

1975—. *Member:* Milwaukee Press Club (president, 1972-74), Sigma Delta Chi, Society of Professional Journalists, Wisconsin Associated Press Sports Writers (president, 1971-72). *Awards, honors:* Story included in *Greatest Sports Stories,* 1968.

WRITINGS: The Green Bay Packers: Pro Football's Pioneer Team, Nelson, 1961; *The Greatest Packers of Them All,* Putnam, 1968.

WORK IN PROGRESS: Another sports book for Putnam; a textbook on sports writing.

JOYCE, J(ames) Avery

PERSONAL: Born in London, England; married Barbara Escombe (died, 1971). *Education:* London School of Economics, B.Sc., 1942; University of London, Ph.D., 1953, LL.D., 1970; attended Geneva School of International Studies, 1935-38. *Politics:* Labour Party (Parliamentary candidate). *Religion:* Methodist. *Agent:* Anne Harrel, Bolt & Watson, 8 Sterling's Gate, London S.W.1, England. *Office:* Palaides Nations, Geneva, Switzerland. *Law chambers:* 3, King's Bench Walk, Temple, London, England.

CAREER: Lawyer, London, England, 1943—. Visiting lecturer at University of Chicago, Columbia University, University of New York, Washington University, Cornell University, Vanderbilt University, Howard University, and University of California; International Association for Social Progress in London, secretary, 1937-38; League of Nations Assemblies, Geneva, Switzerland, special correspondent, 1935-38; International Labor Office, Geneva, Switzerland, staff member, 1956-63; United Nations Economics Security Council, consultant, 1953-56; Fletcher School of Law and Diplomacy, Tufts University, senior research associate, 1968-71. *Member:* American Association of University Professors.

WRITINGS: Youth Faces the New World, Pelican Press, 1931; *Peacemaking for Beginners,* Herbert Joseph (London), 1938; *The Phantom Broadcast,* Herbert Joseph, 1939; (editor) *Three Peace Classics,* Herbert Joseph, 1940; *Bring Me My Bow,* printed for private circulation (London), 1942; (editor) *World Unity Booklets,* World Unity Movement (London), 1944-49; *World Organisation: Federal or Functional?,* Watts (London), 1945; *Chicago Commentary: Case for World Airways,* World Citizenship Movement (London), 1946; *Education for a World Society,* World Citizenship Movement, 1947; (with Ithel Davies) *World Law,* World Citizenship Movement, 1949.

Now is the Time, World Calendar Association (London), 1951; *Justice at Work,* Chapman (London), 1952; *World in the Making,* Schuman, 1953; *Economic and Social Advantages of Calendar Reform,* World Calendar Association (Geneva), 1954; *Studies in Charter Revision,* Council for United Nations Charter Review (London), 1955; *Revolution on East River,* Abelard, 1956; *Red Cross International,* Oceana, 1959; *The Right to Life,* Gollancz (London), 1961; *Capital Punishment: A World View,* Nelson, 1961; *Human Rights: The Dignity of Man,* Oceana, 1963; *Education and Training,* United Nations (Geneva), 1963; *The Story of International Co-Operation,* Watts, 1964; *World of Promise,* Oceana, 1965; *Labour Faces the New Age,* International Labour Office (Geneva), 1965; *Decade of Development,*

JAMES AVERY JOYCE

Coward, 1966; *End of an Illusion,* Bobbs, 1968; *Jobs Versus People,* International Labour Office, 1974; editor, *Population Documents* (four volumes), Oceana, 1975; *Broken Star,* Christopher Davies, 1976. Articles have appeared in *Saturday Review, Nation, Christian Century* and other American journals.

WORK IN PROGRESS: Fourth World Perspectives.

SIDELIGHTS: "For many years I have served with groups promoting civil liberties, penal reform, and adult education on both sides of the Atlantic. I have twice contested marginal seats as a parliamentary candidate in England."

KAKIMOTO, Kozo 1915-

PERSONAL: Born November 30, 1915, in Hiroshima, Japan; son of Hirokichi (a rice-shop owner) and Kuni (Doi) Kakimoto; married Hiro Takeda, January 20, 1943; children: Machi (Mrs. Hidetaka Iwasaki), Izumi (Mrs. Kiyotaka Nozaki). *Education:* Attended several private art schools. *Religion:* Buddhism. *Home:* 836 Jyuniso Akashi, Kamakura City, Kanagawa Pref., Japan.

CAREER: Planning and arranging for exhibitions, etc. for children. Work on publishing of art for children. *Member:* Association of Artists of Childrens' Books (Jido Bijutsu Renmei), A Group of Painters for Children (Doga Shudan). *Awards, honors:* Art work prize from Shogaku-Kan (publisher), 1959; *Mr. Bear Goes to Sea,* Children's Cultural Prize, Sankei Press, 1968.

ILLUSTRATOR: Chizuko Kuratomi, *Remember Mr. Bear,* Shiko-Sha, 1966, Parents', 1968; K. I. Tucker, *The Lion's Nose,* Hawthorn, 1966; Chizuko Kuratomi, *Mr. Bear Goes to Sea,* Shiko-Sha, 1967, Judson, 1969; Hirosuke Hamada, *The Ogre Who Cried,* Shyuei-sha, 1967; Chizuko Kuratomi, *Mr. Bear in the Air,* Shiko-sha, 1968, Judson, 1970; Chizuko Kuratomi, *Mr. Bear's Trumpet,* Shiko-Sha, 1969, Judson, 1970; Morihisa Yamashita, *The Adventures of Sinbad,* Reader's Digest, 1969; K. Tsutsui, *Saint-Saens' Carnival of the Animals,* Gakken, 1970; Chizuko Kuratomi, *Mr. Bear and the Robbers,* Shiko-Sha, 1970, Dial, 1972; Chizuko Kuratomi, *Mr. Bear, the Station Master,* Shiko-Sha, 1972; *Dictionary of Picture Books,* Gakken, 1972; Hirosuke Hamanda, *Konezumi Choro Choro,* Kaisei-sha, 1972, translated, *The Little Mouse who Tarried,* Parents', 1972; Chizuko Kuratomi, *Mr. Bear's Apple Jam,* Shiko-Sha, 1973; Chizuko Kuratomi, *Mr. Bear's Christmas,* Shiko-Sha, 1973; Chizuko Kuratomi, *Mr. Bear Can Paint, Too,* Shiko-Sha, 1975.

WORK IN PROGRESS: Working on the "Mr. Bear series" with Y. Takeichi and C. Kuratomi.

SIDELIGHTS: "I started drawing for childrens' picture books about 1954 and ever since then have concentrated my work on pictures for children. I think it is the work that suits me most and that I would like to do most. I consider the Mr. Bear series my life work and hope to produce one Mr. Bear book each year.

"I enjoy gardening and living with small wild creatures. At present I live in the ancient city of Kamakura with my wife and bees, two chickens, six squirrels and fish. I like drinking and also going for walks."

KOZO KAKIMOTO

KENDALL, Carol (Seeger) 1917-

PERSONAL: Born September 13, 1917, in Bucyrus, Ohio; daughter of John Adam (a cabinetmaker) and Laura (Price) Seeger; married Paul Murray Kendall (a college professor and writer), June 15, 1939 (died, November 21, 1973); children: Carol Seeger, Gillian Murray. *Education:* Ohio University, A.B., 1939. *Home:* 928 Holiday Drive, Lawrence, Kansas 66044.

Now Little Dog had been sleeping himself, and he was right in the middle of a beautiful dream when Grandma Mouse woke him. ■ (From *The Little Mouse Who Tarried* by Hirosuke Hamada. Pictures by Kozo Kakimoto.)

148   Something about the Author

CAROL KENDALL

CAREER: Writer. *Member:* Phi Beta Kappa, Phi Mu. *Awards, honors:* Ohioana Award, and runner-up for Newbery Award, both for *The Gammage Cup,* 1960.

WRITINGS—Adult: *The Black Seven,* Harper, 1946; *The Baby-Snatcher,* Lane, 1952.

Children's books: *The Other Side of the Tunnel,* Abelard, 1957; *The Gammage Cup,* Harcourt, 1959; *The Big Splash,* Viking, 1960; *The Whisper of Glocken,* Harcourt, 1965.

WORK IN PROGRESS: A fantasy; *The Firelings;* Chinese folk tales.

SIDELIGHTS: "I am one to live quietly and to myself because the things I like to do best are of a quiet-and-to-oneself nature: writing, reading, studying Chinese, hiking, mowing the lawn; for a change of pace I go traveling, but even that I do in a rather quiet and inner way. It's not that I mean to be aloof; I just turned out that way.

"My family was large and happy and mainly boys, and I was the baby. By the time I learned to read, most of my brothers had grown up and drifted away, but they left me a legacy at the top of the house: their old books. The attic was stifling in summer, freezing in winter; no matter. Like the salmon called upstream, periodically I climbed my way up to the bookcases to see what was there. No bland diet of Elsie Dinsmoor or the Little Colonel for me: I raised myself on

the Hardy boys and Shakespeare; Tarzan and Joe Strong the Boy Fish; Andersonville Prison; Stover at Yale, the McGuffey Readers, and even *Petits Contes de France,* which I laboriously and joyously translated from the vocabulary at the back. Although I never wanted to be a boy—I had too strong a sense of my own identity for that—it was clear from the start of my reading that it was boys who *did,* and girls who *didn't.* Fortunately, coming at the end of a raft of brothers, I had not been forced into the hateful mold of endlessly playing house. Along with the usual roller-skating, rope-jumping, and a modicum of doll-dressing, I climbed trees, hunkered on the garage roof eating cherries and green apples, played baseball, marbles, mumblety-peg, cowboys and indians, and tennis. A lot of the time, though, I was stretched flat out on the floor reading, reading, reading.

"The summer before I entered fourth grade, it came to me that I was going to be a writer, and I lost no time starting my career. I wrote the first page of what might be titled 'The Girl Pickpocket Who Wouldn't Pick Pockets' while sitting cross-legged in front of the attic bookshelves. By the time school started in the fall, I had nineteen pages written in an exercise book. I was so excited that I simply had to share my novel's beginning with somebody—and who more understanding than my smiling new teacher! She kept the book for three days (surely a teacher could read faster than *that!*), until I was forced to ask her, finally, if she had finished. She had. With two disdainful fingers she handed the exercise

Walter the Earl thrust his sword into the air. "Sound the trumpets! Advance the host! Death to the invaders!" ■ (From *The Gammage Cup* by Carol Kendall. Illustrated by Erik Blegvad.)

book down to me. She said, with the first curled lip I had seen outside the movies, 'Carol, don't be so silly!' I was utterly stricken by her contempt. SILLY!? I had never been more serious in all my nine years. That was a long time ago, but I never have to dredge for that scene. Even now it springs before me and I remember the hot rush of blood to my head. I suddenly realize why I dislike a particular shade of blue. It's the blue of my teacher's dress that day.

"The year before this devastating experience, my father had died, and we started the slide from comfortably-enough-off to rather-badly-off; when the stock market crashed a few years later, we became, in fact, extremely hard-up. We began to 'make-do,' a creative form of living frequently missed by those who have also missed poverty. It is an art that stimulates and teaches.

"*Item:* When clothes are cleverly remade from expensive hand-me-downs, they never quite conform to the 'going thing.' The wearer looks like nobody else. She stands out from the crowd. The dresses, after all, are originals.

"*Item:* If the only bike available to you in a world of spanking new girls' bikes is your brother's burnt-out, fenderless, flat-tired, wonky-seated, rusty Silver King, you think only of how lucky you are to have an older brother, and get to work with sandpaper, paint, and tire patches to create your own machine. Having an open mind (the first requirement of 'making-do'), you discover that a boy's bike is far superior to a girl's, for it can be steered with the feet or with no hands at all, and it can carry a passenger on the crossbar. Even the missing fenders become an asset. The bike is lighter to handle, faster on the road, and is never never taken by mistake, for it is the only one of its kind.

"*Item:* You learn about sexual inequality the hard, sure way when you help out your older brother one day by mowing one of his lawns, and Mrs. Bennett pays you only 25¢ instead of your brother's 50¢—because you're a girl.

"*Item:* When one of the two roomers in your house is a rotten apple, but a necessary paying fixture, you make of her a case study, writing up her foibles at intervals as you would a character in a story. Every vinegar word she speaks becomes sweet, for it is grist to your writing mill. You have a stock of villainy to last a lifetime of writing.

"*Item:* When 'making-do' has become a way of life, you realize that nothing is impossible if you want it badly enough. I started college with a scholarship, a National Youth Administration job (my gratitude to FDR is boundless), and $70 from an insurance policy. Four years later I had earned my BA degree and met the man I wanted to share my life. We were both penniless, both determined—determined to live happily, travel the world, and write books. And we did. We even stopped being penniless after awhile and so had two marvelous children to write and travel and live happily with."

HOBBIES AND OTHER INTERESTS: Hiking, travel and translating Chinese into English.

FOR MORE INFORMATION SEE: Eleanor Cameron, *The Green and Burning Tree,* Atlantic-Little, Brown, 1969; *Third Book of Junior Authors,* edited by de Montreville and Hill, H. W. Wilson, 1972; Margery Fisher, *Who's Who in Children's Books,* Holt, 1975.

KENNEDY, John Fitzgerald   1917-1963

PERSONAL: Born May 29, 1917, in Brookline, Mass.; son of Joseph P. and Rose (Fitzgerald) Kennedy; married Jacqueline Leė Bouvier, 1953; children: Caroline, John F., Jr., Patrick Bouvier (deceased). *Education:* London School of Economics, student, 1935-36; Harvard University, B.A. (with honors), 1940; Stanford University, graduate work, 1940.

CAREER: Before and immediately following World War II, John F. Kennedy was a correspondent for Hearstpaper's *Chicago Herald-American* and the International News Service, covering the San Francisco United Nations Conference, the Potsdam Conference, and the British elections of 1945; U. S. House of Representatives, congressman from the 11th Congressional District of Massachusetts, 1946-52; United States Senator from Massachusetts, 1952-60; President of the United States, 1960-63. While a senator, he was a member of the Foreign Relations, Labor and Public Welfare, and the Joint Economic Committees, and the Select Committee to Investigate Improper Activities in the Labor-Management Field; he was also chairman of the Subcommittee on Labor. *Military service:* U.S. Navy, 1941-45, with rank of lieutenant at the time he was retired for injuries; served as PT boat commander in the South Pacific during World War II; decorated twice by the Navy for the serious injuries he suffered when his boat was cut in two by ramming while attacking a Japanese destroyer during a night action in the Solomons, and for "his courage, endurance and excellent leadership" in towing injured members of his crew to safety, and bringing them through Japanese lines after nine days.

AWARDS, HONORS: Received eighteen honorary doctor of law degrees while a senator, received numerous others as President. Citations awarded to him when a senator included his having been designated "One of the Ten Most Outstanding Young Men in America" by the National Junior Chamber of Commerce. Other awards include: Annual Brotherhood Award of the National Conference of Christians and Jews; the 1956 Patriotism Award as "Outstanding Statesman of the Year" from Notre Dame University; the Italian Star of Solidarity of the First Order, the highest honor that the Italian government can bestow on any individual; the title of "Grande Official" of the Italian government; and the Greek Cross of the Commander of the Royal Order of the Phoenix. *Profiles in Courage* was awarded a Pulitzer Prize in 1956, as well as the Notable Book Award of the American Library Association, the Christopher Book Award for 1956, and the Book Award of the Secondary Education Board.

WRITINGS: Why England Slept, Funk, 1940; (editor and contributor) *As We Remember Joe,* privately printed (Cambridge, Mass.), 1945; *Profiles in Courage,* Harper, 1956, inauguration edition, Harper, 1961, abridged edition for young readers, Harper, 1961; *A Nation of Immigrants,* Anti-Defamation League of B'nai B'rith, 1959; *The Strategy of Peace,* edited by Allan Nevins, Harper, 1960; *President Kennedy Speaks,* U.S. Information Service, 1961?; (contributor) *Creative America,* Ridge Press, c. 1962; *To Turn the Tide,* edited by John W. Gardner, foreword by Carl Sandburg, Harper, 1962; *The Quotable Mr. Kennedy,* edited by Gerald C. Gardner, Popular Library, 1963; *America the Beautiful,* Country Beautiful Foundation, 1964; *The Burden*

JOHN FITZGERALD KENNEDY

and the Glory, edited by Allan Nevins, Harper, 1964; *John F. Kennedy: 1917-1963,* edited by Urs Schwarz, P. Hamlyn (London), 1964; *John F. Kennedy's Inaugural Address,* proclamation by Lyndon B. Johnson, Watts, 1964; *The Kennedy Wit,* edited by Bill Adler, Bantam, 1965; *Memorable Quotations of John F. Kennedy,* edited by Maxwell Meyersohn, Crowell, 1965; *Kennedy and Africa,* edited by Robert A. Marshall, Pyramid, 1967; *The Complete Kennedy Wit,* edited by Bill Adler, Citadel, 1967; *Living in the Age of Crisis,* Nan'un-do (Tokyo), 1967; *John F. Kennedy Talks to Young People,* compiled and edited by Nicholas Schneider and Nathalie S. Rockhill, Hawthorn, 1968; *Sam Huston and the Senate,* Pemberton Press, 1970.

Author of preface or foreword: Robert Johns Bulkley, *At Close Quarters: PT Boats in the World War,* Government Printing Office, 1962; Adlai E. Stevenson, *Looking Outward: Years of Crisis at the United Nations,* Harper, 1963; Theodore C. Sorensen, *Decision-making in the White House,* Columbia University Press, 1963.

SIDELIGHTS: President Kennedy was the second eldest of nine children. His father served under Franklin Roosevelt as Ambassador to Great Britain, chairman of the Securities and Exchange Commission, and chairman of the U.S. Maritime Commission. His mother is the daughter of the late John F. Fitzgerald, onetime mayor of Boston, who more than fifty years ago represented in Congress the same district later served by the President. His paternal grandfather, Patrick J., served in both houses of the Massachusetts legislature. The President's election in 1952 marked the third time a Democrat was ever elected to the Senate from Massachusetts. In 1958 he was reelected by the largest margin ever accorded a candidate for any office in either party in the history of Massachusetts, and the largest margin received by any candidate in the United States in 1958. At the Democratic National Convention in 1956, he came within twenty and one-half votes of capturing the nomination for Vice-President of the United States.

One of his lost hopes was to write the memoirs of his years as President. The *Saturday Review* reports that "no honor more delighted him than his Pulitzer Prize; nothing angered him more than the unfounded charge that *Profiles in Courage* was ghost-written."

"John Fitzgerald Kennedy: A History of Our Times" was filmed by Audio Brandon Films in 1967; "The Spoken Arts Treasury of John F. Kennedy's Addresses," edited by Arthur Luce Klein was recorded by Spoken Arts in 1972; "Profiles in Courage" was adapted for television as a series; "PT-109" was filmed by Warner Bros., 1963; "Johnny We Hardly Knew Ye," was televised by NBC, 1977.

FOR MORE INFORMATION SEE: John Francis Dinneen, *The Kennedy Family,* Little, 1959; James MacGregor

■ (From the television production "Johnny We Hardly Knew Ye," starring Paul Rudd and Burgess Meredith. Courtesy of NBC Television.)

Burns, *John Kennedy: A Political Profile,* Harcourt, 1960; Joseph Weston McCarthy, *The Remarkable Kennedys,* Dial, 1960; Robert John Donovan, *PT 109: John F. Kennedy in World War II,* McGraw, 1961; Jacques Lowe, *Portrait: The Emergence of John F. Kennedy,* McGraw, 1961; Alfred Kazin, *Contemporaries,* Little, 1962; Norman Mailer, *The Presidential Papers,* Putnam, 1963; Benjamin Bradlee, *That Special Grace,* Lippincott, 1964; Jim Bishop, *A Day in the Life of President Kennedy,* Random, 1964; T. G. Buchanan, *Who Killed Kennedy?,* Putnam, 1964; Tom Wicker, *Kennedy Without Tears,* Morrow, 1964; E. A. Glikes and P. Schwaber, editors, *Of Poetry and Power: Poems Occasioned by the Presidency and by the Death of John F. Kennedy,* Basic Books, 1964; The New York Times, *The Kennedy Years,* Viking, 1964; United Nations, *Homage to a Friend,* U.S. committee for the United Nations, 1964; Arthur M. Schlesinger, Jr., *A Thousand Days,* Houghton, 1965; Theodore C. Sorensen, *Kennedy,* Harper, 1965; *John Fitzgerald Kennedy . . . As We Remember Him,* by his family and friends, edited by Goddard Lieberson, Atheneum, 1965; Kenneth O'Donnell ånd David Powers, *Johnny We Hardly Knew Ye,* Little, 1972.

Juvenile books: Boys' Life of John F. Kennedy, by Bruce Lee, Sterling, 1961; *John Fitzgerald Kennedy, Youngest President,* by Edward H. Sammis, Scholastic Book Service, 1961; *John F. Kennedy and PT-109,* by Richard William Tregaskis, Random, 1962.

(Assassinated in Dallas, Tex., November 22, 1963)

KLASS, Morton 1927-

PERSONAL: Born June 24, 1927, in Brooklyn, N.Y.; son of David A. and Milly (Fisher) Klass; married Sheila Solomon, 1953; children: Perri Elizabeth, David Arnold, Judith Alexandra. *Education:* Brooklyn College, B.A., 1955; Columbia University, Ph.D., 1959. *Home:* 403 West 115th St., New York, N.Y. 10025.

CAREER: Bennington College, Bennington, Vt., member of faculty, 1959-64; Columbia University, New York, N.Y., visiting assistant professor of anthropology, 1962-65; Barnard College, New York, N.Y., associate professor of anthropology, 1965-1969, professor of anthropology, 1969—. Research Institute for the Study of Man, research associate. Conducted study of East Indians in Trinidad and other West Indian groups, 1957-58; researcher on effects of industrialization on Indian villages, as co-principal investigator of Columbia University and National Institute of Mental Health India Project, 1963-64. *Military service:* U.S. Maritime Service, Merchant Marine, 1945-48, becoming warrant officer. *Member:* American Anthropological Association (fellow), Association for Asian Studies, Asiatic Society (Bengal). *Awards, honors:* Social Science Research Council Fellow, 1957-58.

WRITINGS: East Indians in Trinidad: A Study of Cultural Persistence, Columbia University Press, 1961; (with H. Hellman) *The Kinds of Mankind: An Introduction to Race and Racism,* Lippincott, 1971, *Gondogram: Village and Factory in West Bengal,* in press.

WORK IN PROGRESS: The Emergence of Caste in South Asia.

HOBBIES AND OTHER INTERESTS: Writing fiction.

Two young schoolgirls in India. ■ (From *The Kinds of Mankind* by Morton Klass and Hal Hellman. Illustrated with drawings by Visa-Direction, Inc.)

LAIMGRUBER, Monika 1946-

PERSONAL: Born 1946, in Klagenfurt, Austria; daughter of Otto (a scene painter) and Gertrud Laimgruber. *Education:* Attended Hochschule für Bildende künste, Hamburg, Germany, 1963-68. *Home:* Einschlagstr. 17, CH-3065 Bolligen, Switzerland.

CAREER: Graphic artist and illustrator for children's books; scenic designer for children's theater. *Awards, honors: Der standhafte Zinnsoldat (The Steadfast Tin Soldier),* Die Schönsten Schweizer Bücher (the most beautiful Swiss books), 1970; Society of Illustrators, citation of merit, 1972; *Childcraft Annual* award, 1972.

ILLUSTRATOR: Hans Christian Andersen, *Der Schneemann* (title means *The Snowman*), Atlantis Verlag, 1970; Hans Christian Andersen, *Der standhafte Zinnsoldat,* Artemis Verlag, 1970, translated as *The Steadfast Tin Soldier,* Atheneum, 1971; Manfred Kyber, *Das Pantoffelmännchen,* Artemis Verlag, 1971, translated as *The Little Slipperman,* Scroll, 1973; Hans Christian Andersen, *Des Kaisers neue Kleider,* Artemis Verlag, 1973, translated as *The Emperor's New Clothes,* Addison, 1973; Wilhelm Hauff, *Der Kleine Muck,* Artemis Verlag, 1974, translated as *The Adventures of Little Mouk,* Macmillan, 1975; Kathe Recheis, *Kleiner Bruder Watomi,* Herder Verlag, 1974; Max Bolliger, *Das Riesenfest,* Artemis Verlag, 1975, translation published as *The Giant's Feast,* Addison-Wesley, 1976.

SIDELIGHTS: "I was born in Klagenfurt, Austria, in 1946.

MONIKA LAIMGRUBER

My father painted and drew a lot (he is a scene-painter in the theatre), and at the age of two and a half I started to do the same, very enthusiastically especially pictures with figures from fairy tales.

"In 1956 my family moved to Hamburg, and there, after school, I studied graphic arts and book design at the College

She gave him a surly look and asked grumpily what he was doing there. "You said, 'Come all and eat,'" Mouk replied. "And I'm so hungry." ■ (From *The Adventures of Little Mouk* by Wilhelm Hauff. Illustrated by Monika Laimgruber.)

of Art for five years. At that time I illustrated my first book, a bibliophile edition of *Antike Tierfabeln (Antique Animal Fables)*. Since 1968 I have lived in Berne, Switzerland, and enjoy doing picture books for children. I also do scenery for children's theatre.

"Besides drawing, reading and listening to music, I like to travel as much as possible."

FOR MORE INFORMATION SEE: New York Times Book Review, November 4, 1973.

LEE, (Nelle) Harper   1926-

PERSONAL: Born April 28, 1926, in Monroeville, Ala.; daughter of Amasa Coleman (a lawyer) and Frances (Finch) Lee. *Education:* Attended Huntington College, 1944-45; studied law at University of Alabama, 1945-49; studied one year at Oxford University. *Politics:* Republican. *Religion:* Methodist. *Home:* Monroeville, Ala. *Office:* c/o McIntosh & Otis, Inc., 18 East 41st St., New York, N.Y. 10017.

CAREER: Airline reservation clerk with Eastern Air Lines and British Overseas Airways, New York, N.Y., during the fifties; left to devote full time to writing. Member, National Council on Arts, 1966-72. *Awards, honors:* Pulitzer Prize, 1961, Alabama Library Association award, 1961, Brotherhood Award of National Conference of Christians and Jews, 1961, *Bestsellers'* paperback of the year award, 1962, all for *To Kill a Mockingbird.*

WRITINGS: To Kill a Mockingbird (Literary Guild selection, Book-of-the-Month Club alternate, *Reader's Digest* condensed book), Lippincott, 1960, Popular Library, 1962, large print edition, National Aid to Visually Handicapped, 1965. Contributor to *Vogue.*

WORK IN PROGRESS: A second novel.

SIDELIGHTS: To Kill a Mockingbird, a first novel, received almost unanimous critical acclaim. It is a story narrated by a six-year-old Southern girl whose father, an attorney, defends a Negro accused of the rape of a white woman. Told with "a rare blend of wit and compassion" (*Booklist*),

You can pet him, Mr. Arthur, he's asleep. You couldn't if he was awake, though, he wouldn't let you. . ." ■ (From the movie "To Kill a Mockingbird," starring Gregory Peck, Mary Badham and Robert Duvall. © 1962 by Universal Pictures.)

Something about the Author

HARPER LEE

FOR MORE INFORMATION SEE: *New York Times Book Review,* July 10, 1960, April 8, 1962; *New York Herald Tribune Book Review,* July 10, 1960; *Chicago Sunday Tribune,* July 17, 1960; *Saturday Review,* July 23, 1960; *Atlantic,* August, 1960; *Booklist,* September 1, 1960; *New Yorker,* September 10, 1960; *New Statesman,* October 15, 1960; *Times Literary Supplement,* October 28, 1960; *Commonweal,* December 9, 1960; *Newsweek,* January 9, 1961.

LEITCH, Patricia 1933-

PERSONAL: Born July 13, 1933, in Paisley, Renfrewshire, Scotland; daughter of James Ritchie (an engineer) and Anna (Mitchell) Leitch. *Education:* Craigie College of Education, primary teacher's diploma, 1967. *Home:* 11 Argyll Ter., Dunoon, Argyll, Scotland. *Agent:* A. M. Heath & Co. Ltd., 40-42 William IV St., London WC2N 4DD, England.

CAREER: Glasgow Corporation and Renfrewshire County Library, library assistant, 1954-59; Kilmacolm Riding School, riding school instructor, 1960-61; shop assistant in various book shops, 1962-63; Troon Primary School, Ayrshire, Scotland, 1968-70; typist, 1971-73; writer, 1974—.

WRITINGS—Juveniles: *A Pony of Our Own,* Blackie & Son, 1960; *To Save a Pony,* Hutchinson, 1960; *Rosette for Royal,* Blackie & Son, 1963; *Janet Young Rider,* Constable, 1963, published in the United States as *Last Summer to Ride,* Funk, 1965; *The Black Loch,* Collins, 1963, Funk, 1968; *Highland Pony Trek,* Collins, 1964; *Riding Course Summer,* Collins, 1965; *Cross Country Pony,* Blackie & Son, 1965; *Treasure to the East,* Gollancz, 1966; *Jacky Jumps to the Top,* Collins, 1973; *First Pony,* Collins, 1973;

it moves "unconcernedly and irresistibly back and forth between being sentimental, tough, melodramatic, acute, and funny," according to the *New Yorker.* Keith Waterhouse, a British novelist, believes that "Miss Lee does well what so many American writers do appallingly: she paints a true and lively picture of life in an American small town. And she gives freshness to a stock situation." Richard Sullivan writes: ". . . the unaffected young narrator uses adult language to render the matter she deals with, but the point of view is cunningly restricted to that of a perceptive, independent child. . . . Casually, on the side, as it were, *To Kill a Mockingbird* is a novel of strong contemporary national significance. . . . But first of all it is a story so admirably done that it must be called both honorable and engrossing." The author considers the novel to be a simple love story.

Harper Lee, whose family is related to Robert E. Lee, writes slowly from noon until evening, completing a page or two a day. She considers the law, with its emphasis on logical thought, an excellent training for a writer.

To Kill a Mockingbird has been translated into ten languages. A screenplay adaptation by Horton Foote was filmed in 1962; was issued on records and cassettes by Miller-Brody Productions, narrated by Maureen Stapleton.

HOBBIES AND OTHER INTERESTS: Golf and music.

PATRICIA LEITCH

Afraid to Ride, Collins, 1973; *Rebel Pony,* Collins, 1973; *Pony Surprise,* Collins, 1974; *Dream of Fair Horses,* Collins, 1975.

WORK IN PROGRESS: A series for Collins, for children; *The Lordly Ones,* a juvenile novel.

SIDELIGHTS: "I have always had a vivid imagination being typical of the Jungian category of introverted intuitive. . . . I have neither a visual nor an aural imagination. It is something else. Most of my books are 'pony books,' some are fantasies but really they all say the same thing—'Sin is behovely, but all shall be well, and all manner of thing shall be well'. . . . I am a vegetarian and am enthused by the growing synthesis of Eastern and Western cultures."

LERNER, Marguerite Rush   1924-

PERSONAL: Born May 17, 1924, in Minneapolis, Minn.; daughter of Harry Harold (a salesman) and Sophia (Goldstein) Rush; married Aaron Lerner (now a physician), June 21, 1945; children: Peter, Michael, Ethan, Seth. *Education:* University of Minnesota, B.A. (summa cum laude), 1945; graduate study at Barnard College, 1945-46, and Johns Hopkins University, 1946-48; Western Reserve University, M.D., 1950. *Religion:* Jewish. *Home:* Old Mill Rd., Woodbridge, Conn. 06525.

CAREER: Physician, specializing in dermatology. Yale University Medical School, New Haven, Conn., professor of clinical dermatology. *Member:* American Academy of Dermatology, New England Dermatologic Association, Phi Beta Kappa.

WRITINGS: Dear Little Mumps Child, Lerner, 1959; *Michael Gets the Measles,* Lerner, 1959; *Peter Gets the Chickenpox,* Lerner, 1959; *Doctor's Tools,* Lerner, 1960; *Lefty,* Lerner, 1960; *Red Man, White Man, African Chief,* Lerner, 1960; (with husband, Aaron Lerner) *Dermatologic Medica-*

MARGUERITE RUSH LERNER

About one week later Ethan had no more bumps."
■ (From *Dear Little Mumps Child* by Marguerite Rush Lerner, M.D. Illustrated by George Overlie.)

tions, Year Book, 1960; *Twins,* Lerner, 1961; *Fur, Feathers, Hair,* Lerner, 1962; *Who Do You Think You Are?,* Prentice-Hall, 1963; *Hucket-a-Bucket Down the Street,* Lerner, 1965; *Horns, Hoofs, Nails,* Lerner, 1966; *Where Do You Come From?,* Lerner, 1967; *Hucket-a-Bucket Again,* Lerner, 1967; *Color and People,* Lerner, 1971. Contributor of articles to medical journals.

LERNER, Sharon (Ruth) 1938-

PERSONAL: Born November 9, 1938, in Chicago, Ill.; daughter of Julius N. (a salesman) and Ethel Goldman (a teacher); married Harry J. Lerner (a publisher), June 25, 1961; children: Adam, Mia, Daniel. *Education:* University of Minnesota, B.S., 1960. *Home:* 2215 N. Willow Lane, Minneapolis, Minn. 55416.

CAREER: Public school art teacher in Minneapolis and White Bear, Minn., 1960-62; Lerner Publications Co., Minneapolis, Minn., art director, 1961—, Carolrhoda Books, president, 1969—. Book illustrator. Art educator and tour guide at Walker Art Center, 1963—, and Minneapolis Institute of Art.

WRITINGS: Places of Musical Fame, 1962, (author and illustrator) *I Found a Leaf,* 1964, *The Self-Portrait in Art,* 1965, (author and illustrator) *I Picked a Flower,* 1966, (author and illustrator) *I Like Vegetables,* 1966, (author and illustrator) *Who Will Wake Up Spring?,* 1967, *Orange is a Color,* 1970, *Straight is a Line,* 1970, *Square is a Shape,* 1970, *The Fruit Book,* 1975, *The Flower Book,* 1975, *The Vegetable Book,* 1975, *The Leaf Book,* 1975 (all published by Lerner).

Illustrator: Ruth Brin, *Interpretations,* Lerner, 1965; Ethel Goldman, *I Like Fruit,* Lerner, 1969; Ruth Brin, *Butterflies Are Beautiful,* Lerner, 1974.

WORK IN PROGRESS: Jewelry Making.

SHARON LERNER

I LIKE TOMATOES!
I like spaghetti and pizza.
Whoever heard of these foods made without
tomato sauce?
Tomato juice is good, too.
And so are sliced fresh tomatoes in a salad.
■ (From *I Like Vegetables* by Sharon Lerner. Illustrated by the author.)

SIDELIGHTS: Sharon Lerner's published works combine her love of nature, art, and writing. As an artist she has been recognized for her watercolors, collages and jewelry.

HOBBIES AND OTHER INTERESTS: "I am actively involved in designing and making jewelry, which is being marketed in many places around the country. I spend time biking and I enjoy cross-country skiing, cooking, reading, hiking and traveling."

FOR MORE INFORMATION SEE: Christian Science Monitor, May 1, 1974.

LEVINE, Joan Goldman

PERSONAL: Born in New York, N.Y.; daughter of Edward and Ethel (Schwartz) Goldman; married James A. Levine; children: Jessica, Joshua. *Education:* Attended University of Wisconsin; New York University, B.A.; University of California, Berkeley, secondary teaching credential. *Residence:* Wellesley, Mass.

CAREER: Has taught English, film, and drama in high schools in California and Massachusetts; Wellesley High School, Wellesley, Mass., teacher of English, film, and drama. *Member:* Public Action Coalition for Toys, Action for Children's Television, New England Association of Authors and Illustrators, Wellesley League of Women Voters.

WRITINGS: A Bedtime Story (juvenile), Dutton, 1975; *The Santa Claus Mystery* (juvenile), Dutton, 1975. Reviewer for *Voice for Children* and *New York Times.*

There, on the back of the second shelf, in plastic wrap, sat my sandwich for Santa. My heart thumped. ■ (From *The Santa Claus Mystery* by Joan Goldman Levine. Illustrated by Gail Owens.)

JOAN GOLDMAN LEVINE

SIDELIGHTS: "As a child books always were a great source of pleasure and comfort for me. I can remember crouching under my covers with a flashlight at night, trying to read when I was supposed to be sleeping. When my daughter, Jessica, was born I revisited the world of children's literature and experienced that delight again. I think my writing springs from these two sources: my own childish love of books and my daughter's newly awakened interest."

FOR MORE INFORMATION SEE: New York Times Book Review, May 4, 1975; *Woman's Day,* December, 1975.

LIETZ, Gerald S. 1918-

PERSONAL: Born August 9, 1918, in Bellwood, Ill.; son of Edwin (a laborer) and Ermentine (Stout) Lietz; married Kathryn Zoeller (a dietician), June 13, 1942; children: Ronald, Greg, Gary. *Education:* University of Illinois, B.S.; University of Illinois School of Medicine, M.D., 1944. *Religion:* Protestant. *Home:* 1002 West Armory, Champaign, Ill. 61820. *Agent:* Garrard Publishing Company, Champaign, Ill. 61820. *Office:* 401 E. Springfield, Champaign, Ill. 61820.

CAREER: Private Medical Practitioner, Champaign, Ill., 1944—. *Military service:* U.S. Navy, Medical Corps, became lieutenant. *Member:* American Medical Association, American Academy of Family Practice.

WRITINGS: Bacteria, Garrard, 1962. Co-author of five books in series under the title of "The Wonder of Wonders: Man."

SIDELIGHTS: "I became interested in writing children's books after reading some of the books that my ten-year-old son was reading. On investigation I found that there were very few, if any, books being written on medical subjects. And if they were, I felt they did not convey the story and information that I thought young people would really like to know. In the beginning, I was particularly interested in writing about the subject of bacteria. When mentioning the word bacteria, people usually infer that this represents germs or those micro-organisms that cause disease. Germs actually represent a very small, yet important, segment of the whole world of bacteria. The majority of bacteria, however, are beneficial. As the book relates, all the original antibiotics that were used were derivatives of bacteria. Secondly, I wanted to stress the importance of the organic material that grows in the world and that we would soon have a planet overrun by these materials if it weren't for the rotting effect of bacteria. The most interesting fact is that I was writing a book on ecology in 1961 and didn't realize how important that subject would become. Consequently this book continues to be a very popular one.

"The remaining books and their medical substance came about by my investigation of the amount of material that is placed in the children's text books in fourth, fifth and sixth grades. For example: Subjects concerning the heart and blood vessels may take up three paragraphs. I was able to write an entire book on the subject covering broad elements, not necessarily every aspect. The book on the heart and blood system was one of the five books, entitled *The Wonders of Wonders: Man.* The subject matter concerns the organ systems of the body. The brain being the 'key' to all their functions. Because the human brain has developed into such an important organ, man is where he is today."

Something about the Author

The animals with which man competed are all here, stuffed and harmless now. ■ (From *Man the Thinker* by Anne Terry White and Gerald S. Lietz, M.D. Illustrated by Ted Schroeder.)

LLEWELLYN LLOYD, Richard Dafydd Vyvyan 1906- . (Richard Llewellyn)

PERSONAL: Born December 8, 1906, in St. David's, Pembrokeshire, Wales; son of William (a hotelier) and Sarah Anne (Thomas) Llewellyn Lloyd; married Nona Theresa Sonsteby, 1952 (divorced, 1968); married Susan Frances Heimann (an editor), March 29, 1974. *Education:* Educated in Great Britain. *Politics:* Plaid Cymru (Welsh Nationalist). *Religion:* Roman Catholic. *Residence:* Dublin, Ireland.

CAREER: Novelist, playwright, scriptwriter, and journalist. *Military service:* Indian Army, 1925-31. British Army, Welsh Guards, 1940-46; became captain. *Awards, honors:* National Book Award, 1940, for *How Green Was My Valley.*

WRITINGS—All under name Richard Llewellyn: *How Green Was My Valley* (first volume of tetralogy), M. Joseph, 1939, Macmillan, 1940; *None But the Lonely Heart,* Macmillan, 1943, new edition, 1969; *A Few Flowers for Shiner,* Macmillan, 1950; *A Flame for Doubting Thomas,* Macmillan, 1953; *The Witch of Merthyn,* Doubleday, 1954; *The Flame of Hercules,* Doubleday, 1955; *Mr. Hamish Gleave,* Doubleday, 1956; *Chez Pavan,* Doubleday, 1958; *Warden of the Smoke and Bells,* Doubleday, 1956.

Up, into the Singing Mountain (second volume of tetralogy), Doubleday, 1960; *A Man in a Mirror,* Doubleday, 1961; *Sweet Morn of Judas' Day,* Doubleday, 1964; *Down Where the Moon is Small* (title is sometimes listed *And I Shall Sleep . . . Down Where the Moon Is Small;* third volume of tetral-

ogy), Doubleday, 1966; *The End of the Rug,* Doubleday, 1968; *But We Didn't Get the Fox,* Doubleday, 1969; *White Horse to Banbury Cross,* Doubleday, 1970; *The Night Is a Child,* Doubleday, 1972; *Bride of Israel, My Love,* Doubleday, 1973; *A Hill of Many Dreams,* Doubleday, 1974; *Green, Green My Valley Now* (fourth volume of tetralogy), Doubleday, 1975; *At Sunrise, The Rough Music,* Doubleday, 1976.

Also author of plays, "Poison Pen," 1938; "Noose," 1946; "The Scarlet Suit," 1962; "Ecce," 1972.

WORK IN PROGRESS: An untitled novel of London.

SIDELIGHTS: "I suppose the first thing to say about why I write is that I like it. It is often the hardest sort of work imaginable, and it is all the other things every writer says it is, but I don't feel quite right or comfortable—happy—when I'm not doing it.

"I really don't know what made me a writer, but there was something that I had to say and knew I could say better than anyone else could. Still, I tore up five novels before *How Green Was My Valley* was accepted by a publisher. That was in 1939—a long time ago—but I haven't stopped wishing I hadn't destroyed them. They had a certain truth, and reflected a kind of reality that is no longer part of life today.

"It might be correct to say that the characters in my books tell their *own* stories—my job is to find the words in which they can do it. Only by communicating do people ever discover who they are."

Before leaving for military service in the Second World War, Llewellyn left the manuscript of *None But the Lonely Heart*

■ (From the movie "How Green Was My Valley," starring Roddy McDowell and Walter Pidgeon. Copyright 1942 by 20th-Century Fox Film Corp.)

■ (From the movie "None But the Lonely Heart," starring Cary Grant and Ethel Barrymore. Copyright 1944 by RKO Radio Pictures, Inc.)

■ (From the television production "How Green was My Valley," starring Stanley Baker. "Masterpiece Theatre" series presented on PBS.)

RICHARD LLEWELLYN LLOYD

on his desk. The unfinished novel was published in the author's absence (he first learned of its publication from a correspondent in Italy who showed him a review of the novel in *Time* magazine), subsequently became a bestseller and was made into a movie starring Cary Grant and Ethel Barrymore. A quarter of a century later, Llewellyn completed the novel (adding 160 pages of manuscript) for a new edition.

"Important to most of my books has been—and will ever remain—writing *in situ*. Whatever truths my characters tell me about themselves they tell me, as it were, at home. They couldn't do it—as I could not—elsewhere."

How Green Was My Valley, was filmed in 1941. It starred Walter Pidgeon and Maureen O'Hara, and was directed by John Ford. It was also a six-part television dramatization for PBS's "Masterpiece Theatre," 1976. The play, "Noose," was filmed in 1948.

LOSS, Joan 1933-

PERSONAL: Born August 10, 1933, in Baltimore, Md.; daughter of Harry A. (a tool and die inspector) and Ruth (Heinz) Loss. *Education:* Towson State College, B.S., 1955, M.Ed., 1965; attended University of Colorado, 1960, University of Maryland, 1961-63, Western Maryland College, 1964, University of Washington, Seattle, Wash., 1970, Maryland Institute, College of Art, 1971.

CAREER: Board of Education of Baltimore County, Towson, Md., elementary school teacher, 1955-62, librarian/audio-visual coordinator, 1962—. *Member:* Baltimore County School Librarians' Association (treasurer, 1968-69), Educational Media Association of Maryland,

American Library Association, Association for Educational Communications & Technology; Teachers Association of Baltimore County, Maryland Teachers Association, National Education Association.

WRITINGS: What Is It? A Book of Photographic Puzzles, Doubleday, 1974. Contributor to *Maryland English Journal.*

SIDELIGHTS: "Ever since I was a little girl, I have had a camera of some kind taking pictures on trips or special occasions. But it was not until 1971 that I took a course in basic photography and discovered a whole new world, the darkroom. As part of the required number of prints for the course, I took some extreme close-up pictures called photomacrographs. It was these photographs that sparked the idea of a book of photographic puzzles.

"I am still fascinated with extreme close-ups and think they are my favorite kind of photograph. Often things right at hand take on an interesting new appearance when viewed closely. There is a whole world of infinite variety and unnoticed beauty in a host of common and insignificant items. If you have ever seen hickory seeds in their pod, you may have noticed the lovely packing design created by nature, but have you looked at one of the tiny individual seeds? It is delicately fluted around the edges. The air trapped in ice cubes creates a multitude of different designs. Green peas do not have smooth skins but are slightly bumpy. Thus, it is with each new photomacrograph comes the delight in sharing with others a new way to look at things."

HOBBIES AND OTHER INTERESTS: All types of craft work and nature study.

Toothbrush bristles. ■ (From *What Is It?: A Book of Photographic Puzzlers* by Joan Loss. Photos by the author.)

LOW, Alice 1926-

PERSONAL: Born June 5, 1926, in New York, N.Y.; daughter of Harold (in textiles) and Anna (a writer of children's books; maiden name, Epstein) Bernstein; married Martin Low (owner of a film studio), March 25, 1949; children: Andrew, Katherine, David. *Education:* Smith College, B.A., 1947; also attended Columbia University. *Residence:* Briarcliff Manor, N.Y. *Agent:* Russell & Volkening, Inc., 551 Fifth Ave., New York, N.Y. 10017.

CAREER: Warren Schloat Productions, Tarrytown, N.Y., writer and producer of educational filmstrips, 1968-72; Birch Wathen School, New York, N.Y., teacher of creative writing, 1972-73; Random House, New York, N.Y., free-lance editor, 1975—. Guide to the Museum of the City of New York. *Member:* Authors Guild of Authors League of America, American Society of Composers, Authors, and Publishers.

WRITINGS—Juveniles: *Open My Suitcase,* Simon & Schuster, 1954; *Out of My Window,* Random House, 1962; *Grandmas and Grandpas,* Random House, 1962; *Summer,* Random House, 1963; *Taro and the Bamboo Shoot* (adaptation of a folk tale), Pantheon, 1964; *A Day of Your Own, Your Birthday,* Random House, 1964; *What's in Mommy's Pocketbook?,* Golden Press, 1965; *Kallie's Corner,* Pantheon, 1966; *At Jasper's House and Other Stories,* Pantheon, 1968; *Witches' Holiday,* Pantheon, 1971; *Herbert's Treasure,* Putnam, 1971; *David's Windows,* Putnam, 1974.

JOAN LOSS

Work has been anthologized in *Captain Kangaroo's Read Aloud Book,* Random House, 1962; *Captain Kangaroo's Sleepytime Book,* Random House, 1963.

Filmstrips—author of scripts for "Folk Songs and the American Flag," "Folk Songs and the Declaration of Independence," "Folk Songs and Abraham Lincoln," and "Folk Songs and Frederick Douglas," all for Warren Schloat Productions, 1968-70; "First Things, Social Reasoning" (series of eight filmstrips), Guidance Associates, 1973-74; "You Can Be Anything," Teaching Resource Films, 1975; "Bringing Home the Beach," Guidance Associates, 1975. Author of scripts and producer of "Folk Songs and the Railroad," "Cowboys," and "Whaling," all for Warren Schloat Productions, 1970-72; "History of the City," Warren Schloat Productions, 1972.

Author of operetta for elementary school children and of material for UNICEF. Contributor of stories to young adult magazines, including *Ingenue* and *Seventeen.*

WORK IN PROGRESS: A children's book; short stories.

SIDELIGHTS: "My mother wrote children's books and many of her friends were in the arts and publishing. Birch Wathen School also encouraged creativity—we made books, puppets, gave plays, painted, sang, etc. under the guidance of people in the arts.

"Painting and ceramics were my first interests, and I still make ceramics in between books, and sing in a local chorus. Travel stimulates, and many a line has come to me on a tennis court or a walk."

FOR MORE INFORMATION SEE: New York Times Book Review, November 6, 1966, November 3, 1968; *Junior Literary Guild Catalog,* March, 1971; *Christian Science Monitor,* November 11, 1971.

ALICE LOW

They stretched and yawned, kicked off their shoes,
Rubbed their necks, and blinked their eyes.
"Space at last!" the head witch said,
"Come on, let's get some exercise."
■ (From *Witches' Holiday* by Alice Low. Illustrated by Tony Walton.)

LUHRMANN, Winifred B(ruce) 1934-

PERSONAL: Born November 19, 1934, in Greenfield, Mass.; daughter of Frederick R. (a clergyman) and Mildred (a minister; maiden name, Blair) Bruce; married George W. Luhrmann (a psychiatrist), June 16, 1956; children: Tanya, Anna, Alice. *Education:* Boston University, B.A., 1956. *Home and office:* 157 Winthrop Pl., Englewood, N.J. 07631.

CAREER: Free-lance writer, 1956-62; Pitman Publishing Co., New York, N.Y., assistant editor, 1962; American Book Co., New York, N.Y., assistant editor, 1963; Grolier, Inc., New York, N.Y., editorial re-writer for *The Book of Knowledge,* 1964-65; free-lance writer, 1965—. *Member:* American Association of University Women, Englewood League of Women Voters.

WRITINGS: The First Book of Gold, F. Watts, 1968. Contributor to *Baby and Child Care Encyclopedia;* author of assorted short stories.

WORK IN PROGRESS: A children's book; a gothic novel of the American pre-revolutionary period; a juvenile biography of Anne Hutchinson; research on early American history.

SIDELIGHTS: "Am fascinated by early development of America—especially the New England area—the integration with and death of the Indians and the early concepts of discipline and sin. I am myself descended from early Americans and am part Indian. Have also inherited a fascination for theology which extends my sympathies."

LUIS, Earlene W. 1929-

PERSONAL: Born October 21, 1929, in Alabama; daughter of Paul A. (a farmer) and Millie O. (Robinson) Woods; married Reinaldo Luis, June 24, 1950 (divorced, 1969); children: Paul, Rebecca (Mrs. Phillip Mydelski), Kathleen, John. *Education:* King College, Bristol, Tenn., student, 1948-50; University of Alabama, B.S.Ed., 1952. *Home:* 23 Treasure Dr., Tampa, Fla. 33609. *Office:* Hillsborough High School, Tampa, Fla.

CAREER: Sunland Training Center, Gainesville, Fla., teacher, 1955-58; elementary school teacher, 1960-69; Hillsborough High School, Tampa, Fla., teacher of English, 1969—. Social worker in Hillsborough County, Fla., 1960. *Member:* Bonsai Clubs International, Bonsai Societies of Florida. *Awards, honors:* Edith Busby Award from Dodd, Mead, 1966, for *Wheels for Ginny's Chariot.*

WRITINGS: (With Barbara Miller) *Wheels for Ginny's Chariot,* Dodd, 1966; (with Miller) *Listen, Lissa!,* Dodd, 1969. Contributor to English and education journals, and to *Florida Bonsai.*

WORK IN PROGRESS: No Visa for Roberto, with Barbara Miller, a book about a Cuban refugee youth; another book with Miller about a Vietnamese refugee child.

SIDELIGHTS: "The first two [books] are concerned with handicapped persons—we felt these young people have few fictional characters with whom they can identify. . . . I speak

EARLENE W. LUIS

Spanish fluently, and have been very much interested in the problems of people who must adapt to a new culture. . . ."

HOBBIES AND OTHER INTERESTS: Growing Bonsai trees, gardening.

FOR MORE INFORMATION SEE: Young Reader's Review, May, 1966.

LYDON, Michael 1942-

PERSONAL: Born September 14, 1942, in Boston, Mass.; son of Patrick J. and Auce (Joyce) Lydon; married; children: Shuna. *Education:* Yale University, B.A. (cum laude), 1965. *Home:* 1807 Bonita, Berkeley, Calif. 94709.

CAREER: Writer and musician. *Newsweek Magazine,* San Francisco and London, bureau correspondent, 1965-68.

WRITINGS: Rock Folk (ALA Notable book), Dial, 1971; *Boogie Lighting,* Dial, 1974.

WORK IN PROGRESS: A book on contemporary show business; an introduction to music; many songs and musical compositions.

SIDELIGHTS: "My motivations for my writings have been my enjoyment in writing, my love of music, and the need to earn my living.

"I am proud of my books and proud to be a writer. I am very happy when people like and are moved by what I write."

LYSTAD, Mary (Hanemann)   1928-

PERSONAL: Born April 11, 1928, in New Orleans, La.; daughter of James and Mary (Douglass) Hanemann; married Robert Lystad, June 20, 1953; children: Lisa Douglas, Anne Hanemann, Mary Lunde, Robert Douglass, James Hanemann. *Education:* Newcomb College, A.B. (cum laude), 1949; Columbia University, M.A., 1951; Tulane University, Ph.D., 1955. *Home:* 4900 Scarsdale Rd., Washington, D.C. 20016. *Office:* National Institute of Mental Health, 5600 Fishers Lane, Rockville, Md. 20852.

CAREER: Southeast Louisiana Hospital, Mandeville, fellow in social psychology, 1955-57; conducted field research in social psychology in Ghana, 1957-58; Charity Hospital of Louisiana, New Orleans, chief psychologist on collaborative child development project, 1958-61; American University, Washington, D.C., consultant to special operations research office, 1962; Voice of America, Washington, D.C., feature writer for African Division, 1964-73; National Institute of Mental Health, Rockville, Md., special assistant to director of Division of Special Mental Health Programs, 1973—. Consultant to White House national goals research staff on youth, 1969-70.

"It is time for the Halloween parade," said Miss Reiley to the class." ■ (From *Halloween Parade* by Mary Lystad. Pictures by Cyndy Szekeres.)

MARY LYSTAD

MEMBER: American Sociological Society (fellow). *Awards, honors: Millicent the Monster* was chosen as one of the children's books of the year, 1968, by Child Study Association of America, *James the Jaguar* was chosen in 1972, and *Halloween Parade* in 1973.

WRITINGS: *Social Aspects of Alienation,* U.S. Public Health Service, 1969; *As They See It: Changing Values of College Youth,* Schenkman, 1973; *A Child's World As Seen in His Stories and Drawings,* U.S. Department of Health, Education and Welfare, 1974; *Violence at Home,* U.S. Department of Health, Education and Welfare, 1974.

Juveniles—All with social psychological themes: *Millicent the Monster,* Harlin Quist, 1968; *Jennifer Takes Over P.S. 94,* Putnam, 1972; *James the Jaguar* (Weekly Reader Book Club selection), Putnam, 1972; *That New Boy,* Crown, 1973; *The Halloween Parade,* Putnam, 1973. Contributor to academic journals.

SIDELIGHTS: *Millicent the Monster* has had editions in French, German, and Danish.

FOR MORE INFORMATION SEE: *Washington Post Children's Book World,* November 5, 1972.

MACDONALD, Zillah K(atherine) 1885-
(Zillah)

PERSONAL: Born January 15, 1885, in Halifax, Nova Scotia, Canada; daughter of Charles John (a lieutenant colonel) and Annie (MacLearn) Macdonald; married Colin Macdonald. *Education:* Studied at Dalhousie University and Columbia University. *Home address:* P.O. Box 1293, Wolfville, Nova Scotia, Canada; and (summer) Blinkbonnie, Swan's Island, Me. 04685. *Agent:* Howard Moorepark, 444 East 82nd St., New York, N.Y. 10021.

CAREER: Dalhousie University, Halifax, Nova Scotia, secretary, 1906-13; Columbia University, University Extension, General Studies, and School of Business, New York, N.Y., teacher and lecturer, 1919-49; writer for children. *Member:* Women's National Book Association, Women's Faculty Club of Columbia University.

WRITINGS: *Eileen's Adventures in Wordland: The Life Story of Our Word Friends,* Stokes, 1920; *Cobblecorners,* Appleton, 1926; *The Bluenose Express,* Appleton, 1928; *Spindlespooks,* Appleton, 1928; *Windywhistle,* Appleton, 1929; *Mic Mac on the Track,* Appleton, 1930; *Haunthouse,* Appleton, 1931; (under pseudonym Zillah) *Little Travelers,* Whitman Publishing, 1937; *The Tin Tin Car,* William Penn, 1937; *Two on a Tow,* Houghton, 1942; *Flower of the Fortress,* Westminster, 1944, reissued as *Prisoner in Louisbourg,* Macmillan (Toronto), 1966; *Marcia, Private Secretary,* Messner, 1949.

A Cap for Corinne, Messner, 1952 (published in England as *Nurse Fairchild's Decision,* Transworld Publishers, 1959); *Fireman for a Day,* Messner, 1952, revised edition, Melmont, 1964; *Courage to Command, a Story of the Capture of Louisbourg,* Winston, 1953; *A Tugboat Toots for Terry,* Messner, 1953, revised edition, Melmont, 1964; *The Mystery of the Piper's Ghost,* Winston, 1954; (with Josie Johnston) *Rosemary Wins Her Cap,* Messner, 1955; (with Johnston) *Roxanne, Industrial Nurse,* Messner, 1957; (with Vivian J. Ahl) *Nurse Todd's Strange Summer,* Messner, 1960.

Plays: (With Estelle Davis) "Dad's Turn"; "The Royal Romance"; (with Victor O'Dwyer) "Two Gentlemen of the Bench"; "Our John"; "The Long Box"; "The Featherfisher"; "Circumventin' Sandy"; "Markheim"; and others.

Contributor: *Day In and Day Out,* Row, Peterson & Co.; *Luck and Pluck,* Heath; *Yesterday and Today,* Silver Burdette; *Over Hill and Plain,* Silver Burdette; *With New Friends,* Silver Burdette; *Finding New Neighbors,* Ginn. Contributor of a dozen serials and several score short stories to juvenile publications, including *American Girl, Children's Activities, Child Life, Gateway, Jack and Jill, St. Nicholas, Story Parade, Venture, Girls Today.*

WORK IN PROGRESS: A book for girls about growing up; a story set in Prince Edward Island, Canada.

SIDELIGHTS: "I was barely six years old, when I was dropped at the door of my father's office in the old post office building in Halifax, N.S., Canada, to be delivered home when he left.

"To my delight he picked me up in his arms and dropped me

ZILLAH K. MACDONALD, age six

on the blue blotter of his desk. Sinking back into his big swivel desk chair, he pushed a knee under my feet to make sure I did not fall.

"'Now,' he announced, 'we can talk comfortably and on a level.'

"His hand went into his open top drawer, looking for something to amuse me. It came out with a long blue, ruled, sheet of fresh writing paper. There was on it the ivory sheen which Ottawa provided for her servants, OHMS (On Her Majesty's Service).

"He swung around in his chair. His hand held aloft the sheet to the light of the big window behind him.

"Like magic, there appeared in the centre of the sheet, a gleaming translucent outline of a Jester's cap and bells! I recognized the cap of my beloved six foot high portable puppet show, 'Punch and Judy,' seen at Country Fairs and Harvest Homes. Its secret presence in the paper thrilled me.

"'Paper-making is a very old art,' my father said. 'I believe it began with the Chinese, years and years ago and was a carefully guarded secret. There are many stories as to when and how this knowledge came into the hands of the paper makers of the Middle Ages in France, Italy, Holland and England. They carried it into the machine age.'

"'Great pieces of pap were run over a great roller which helped to squeeze the water out of it. A wire jacket, called the Dandy Roll was placed about the big roller. On it at regular intervals was fixed an outline of bright copper wire. Later, when the paper pap was cut into small sheets, each piece bore the impression of the cap and bells. Today it is still used as a trade mark of the longer size of Fool's Cap paper.'

"'When the boy comes around with his supply cart, he will ask me, "How many packages of square paper do you wish, Sir? And how many reams of Long Fool's Cap paper?"'

"Then my father added wistfully, 'I do not know why the Jester's cap and bells was chosen for this mark in the first place. I have often wished I knew. I think there must have been some reason, and I wish I knew.'

"The question was to lie in my small thought-box for years and years, until one day, searching for an appropriate mystery for *Marcia,* I remembered my father's question, and I found a possible answer.

"Years passed. I was teaching on the campus of Columbia University, New York, and enrolled in one of the new writing courses, when I met Helen Diehl Olds, and made a life-long friend. She was writing juveniles then and selling them to the Julian Messner Publishing House, New York. She offered to get me an interview with them. Two days later I received a letter from the juvenile editor, asking me to come down for an interview.

"Gertrude Blumenthal was the tiniest woman I ever saw working in business, an exquisitely proportioned Meussen Figurine. But I found she carried a terrific torch for her job, and her 'writers.'

"Gertrude had discovered a gap in the usual reading program for juveniles. There was a definite gap between the teenager's needs and the adults. She was bridging it with her new list, by injecting into a glamorous, richly authentic career background, a compelling love interest.

"She drew out of her desk two lists. One contained the titles of books already published, and the other, possible careers to come. She read them over to me.

"Alas, the careers proposed were completely beyond both my knowledge and my experience. I did not dare attempt a single one. Gertrude buried both lists. I prepared to leave.

"'Tell me,' she said, 'What career you would like to pursue?'

"'I feel I know everything there is to know,' I replied, 'about how to train for, how to get, how to hold a secretarial job, and how to move up and out of it into a career of executive status.'

"Gertrude's face fell. 'Who,' she demanded, 'wants to be a steno? Who wants to pound a typewriter, eight hours a day, six and a half days a week, fifty weeks in a year, turning out other people's thoughts and ideas, and brainwork. No glamour in that! I have to have glamour to catch their interest.'

"Her words stung me.

"'I can give it glamour,' I insisted.

"'A career on a college campus like Columbia!' I cried. 'It began as King's College, a colorful history. I'd make the locale Butler Hall. You ascend a flight of steps wide as a city street, to a tiled plaza with fountains and pines, climb an Aztec stairway to a pillared entrance. A building within a building. The centre a vast rotunda, its perimeter a series of deep alcoves to galleries five stories high, jammed with books, secret stairways, and travelling ladders, rising to a lantern roof. Outside a squarish Romanesque lump, capped

"By the way, Michael"—the Mountie put his hand in his jacket and brought out the muffler— "is this yours?" The Mountie held it out to him. "Cy found it," he added, eyeing Michael shrewdly. ■ (From *Mystery of the Piper's Ghost* by Zillah K. MacDonald. Illustrations by Charles Beck.)

with a mosque-like dome. It's cellar floor circles the whole campus with doors and stairways like a village street. It's built on the site of an Insane Asylum and the students swear that—'

"Gertrude stopped me, smiling.

"'You've made your point! You go back home and write me a synopsis, and if I like your outline, I'll give you a contract, a bonus above royalties that may accrue, and a sliding scale, if the book makes good. O.K.?'

"In my experience, it was munificent. I had to get that contract!

"*Marcia, Private Secretary,* owed its inception to a clipping from the *New York Sun.* I quote:

> *Psalm Book at 35¢*
> In 1737 the ministers and elders of the Bay Colony asked to have the 'Bay Psalm Book' abolished. A copy of this sold at auction lately for $151,000. The original cost in 1737 was 35 cents.

My attention was caught.

"The following bits and scraps of research went into my notebook for consideration. The *Bay Psalm Book* was continually referred to as the 'First book published in America.'

"Publication took place in the Harvard Yard in 1640. I had studied in the Harvard Summer School for three summer classes, three consecutive years, hall marking me for a career in writing.

"In 1947 only eleven copies of the *Bay Psalm Book* were extant. Three copies, including the one sold at auction, were still perfect in private collections, the remaining eight ranged from 'slightly imperfect' to 'noble wrecks.'

"Here, my mind imposed a question. How had a paperback survived the centuries in such perfect condition? What had authenticated it? Why the high price?

"My mind flew back to my childhood. Was it possible the *Bay Psalm Book* had been printed on watermarked paper?

"My interest changed to excitement. I researched watermarks, and found the first known watermark was dated to

1282! I had to see a copy! My luck held.

"The copy which had commanded such a price, the perfect copy, was in the New York Public Library, at 42nd and Fifth Avenue, a bus ride away. I was frantic to get there. But first I had to know more about watermarks.

"Columbia provided two fascinating books: William Churchill's *Watermarks of the Sixteenth and Seventeenth Centuries,* and Harold Bayley's *Lost Language of Symbolism.*

"The Churchill Book consisted of pages spotted with watermarks identified by year. 1640 was there! And every year before and after, for the century.

"Was the *Bay Psalm Book* watermarked? I had to Know.

"There is a story that the watermarked Cap and Bell inside the paper was a message that at the next county fair the pastor of the flock might be found in the crowd in a costume of a Jester and would have a message for them.

"My father was right. Watermarks had a meaning.

"As I left for the library on 42nd Street and Fifth Avenue it seemed almost too pat, when the frosted door of an office caught my attention. It was marked *Columbiana.*

"Campus gossip had it that *Columbiana* housed all the trash and treasure of departing Faculty, and successful student alumni. I knew instinctively that I had found the locale for my story.

"The thermometer registered over 100° that afternoon when I reached the library and secured my ticket of admittance to the Rare Book room, on the basis of my Columbia identification card. I reached the room and found the door open but guarded by a heavy locked grill. I rang the bell, and waited. The Curator came and gazed through the grill at the card I held up. He unlocked the door and I explained my errand. He made no move. 'No one,' he said, 'is to be allowed to handle that book.' I was ready to weep. My whole body wilted. I turned to go.

"'What,' he said to my back, 'what is your interest in the *Bay Psalm Book?*' I poured out my story. I held up the traceries, I had made, and suddenly I saw a strange gleam, the light of the bibliophile shine in his face.

"'Wait,' he said. 'This copy we have is known as the Prince-Crownenshield-Stevens-Brimly-Vanderbilt-Whitney copy. We are seventh owners. One of the previous owners, had the book rebound in a new, beautiful cover of tooled, flawless scarlet morocco, elaborately embossed in gold. It was our feeling that the moisture of the human hand, especially in this weather, might start decay in the binding.' He paused a moment. 'How would it be if I put a light on this high file, and held the pages up to the light for you to see? Would that help you?'

"I was overjoyed.

"He fixed the light and returned with the book. I understood at once his concern, when I saw the priceless beauty of the binding.

"He held it up and showed me page by page the device which appeared on every ivory page, still flawless. Page after page of the *Bay Psalm Book* was watermarked with the Pillars of Solomon, supporting a huge bunch of grapes, according to Harold Bayley, urging our forefathers to seek strength, and beauty if we would have abundant life. On the very last page was a change, one of the so-called 'Pot Designs,' symbolic of the Holy Grail, the cup that Joseph of Arimathea, raised to Christ's bleeding side on the cross, to catch his blood. The cup that Michelangelo painted in his *Last Supper,* the cup that only the pure in heart could see. Was it a message from the founding fathers of the first thirteen states, that we, as a Christian Nation should remember the Atonement, or (as the Albigenses put it, according to Bayley) remember our at-one-ment with Christ.

"One other angle of this to me curious story, came to me. The Vaughn Library of Acadia University handed me recently another book of Harold Bayley's 'New Light on the Renaissance.'

"In it Bayley further establishes his beliefs that the watermarks had a meaning. He claims many of them are similar to those used in Free Masonry.

"I knew at once that was the source of my father's interest. He was a thirty-second Degree Mason, a Knight Templar, and a Grand Master of the order in Halifax, N.S., Charles John Macdonald, Athol Lodge.

MacFARLANE, Iris   1922-

PERSONAL: Born July 22, 1922, in Quetta, Pakistan; daughter of William Rhodes and Violet Juxon (Jones) James; married Donald MacFarlane, March 1, 1941; children: Alan Donald, Fiona Stirling (Mrs. John Pearson), Anne Elizabeth (Mrs. Erik Pearse). *Politics:* Socialist. *Home:* Sidinish, Isle of North Uist, Outer Hebrides.

CAREER: Writer.

WRITINGS: Tales and Legends from India, Chatto, 1965; *The Children of Bird God Hill,* Chatto, 1967, McGraw, 1968; *The Summer of the Lame Seagull,* Chatto, 1970; *The Mouth of the Night,* Chatto, 1973; *The Black Hole,* Allen & Unwin, 1975. Regular contributor to *The Scotsmen,* short stories to British Broadcasting Company, other occasional journalism.

WORK IN PROGRESS: Research, with son, Dr. Alan MacFarlane, of Kings College, Cambridge, into 17th-Century parish history. Also study of Gaelic with view to working on Gaelic.

SIDELIGHTS: "It is difficult to say exactly why one writes, especially why one writes for children. I suspect in my case its because I want to try to get back to a time when the world was a vastly exciting and wonderful-smelling place.

"Smells seem to figure a lot in my books, because when I try to get back into childhood, I smell the world very vividly—leaves, and the pages of books, and window glass, and morning, and people's skin—all these were very strong and particular smelling. I always remember the smell of the sea when we drove down for our summer holidays to Cornwall,

. . .she had known he was her Rochester, Darcy,
Galahad, Peter O'Toole, the star to her moth. Or was
it flame? ■ (From *The Summer of the Lame Seagull*
by Iris Macfarlane. Illustrated by Mary Dinsdale.)

and perhaps that is why I always wanted to live by the sea.
Now I do, in a tiny grey stone house on a small island off the
west coast of Scotland. Water and enormous skies, sheep,
goats and seabirds, these share my life, and in the clean air
my sense of smell has partly returned. Because of that, and
the beautiful restful silence, I feel like writing here more than
in any other place I have lived in. Also there is, in the Hebrides, a great tradition of story telling, and a great stock of
folklore and ballad. This I find stimulating to my imagination.

"Most of my life has been spent in India, another beautiful-
smelling country, and also full of folklore. It provided me
with one of the great passions of my life, animals; they were
inside and outside the house, and were one of my most constant pleasures. It also gave me time, and this one needs for
writing. Although I write very fast, with little correction, it
still needs time to get into a state of concentration and unless
one can be sure of at least two uninterrupted hours ahead, it
never seems worth starting.

"Though I write a little history, and short stories for broadcasting to adults, I enjoy my work for children most. My
seven grandchildren keep me in touch with that world I almost remember. When I am with them I am happiest, seeing
through their eyes, smelling through their noses. We create
the world for each other, and it seems to me that this relationship is almost the most rewarding there is. Being with
them, writing for them, makes of middle age a very happy
time.

"My interests are in history and folklore. Also, recently, in
wild flowers. I have done quite a bit of research in Indian
history for my recent book, *The Black Hole.*"

MAHON, Julia C(unha) 1916-

PERSONAL: Born February 20, 1916, in Phenix City, Ala.;
daughter of Francis Cornelius (a textiles worker) and Ferol
(Smith) Cunha; married Edmund Mahon (a machine repair-
man), November 14, 1936; children: John, Paul, Rosemary
(Mrs. John Adamec), Thomas, Elizabeth Ann (deceased).
Education: Attended Willimantic State College, 1960-62,
Harvard University, 1963, and University of Rhode Island,
1972-73. *Politics:* Independent. *Religion:* Roman Catholic.
Home address: Route 193, Thompson, Conn. 06277. *Office:*
Tourtellotte Memorial High School, North Grosvenordale,
Conn. 06255.

CAREER: Tourtellotte Memorial High School, North
Grosvenordale, Conn., librarian, 1960—. Conducted crea-
tive writing workshops in student leadership conferences at
University of New Hampshire and at Rhode Island College.
Member: New England Educational Media Association,
Northeastern Connecticut Librarians' Swap Group.

WRITINGS: His Name is Jesus (juvenile), Grail, 1953;
Mystery at Old Sturbridge Village (juvenile), Albert Whitman, 1966; *The First Book of Creative Writing* (juvenile),
Watts, 1968. Contributor to articles, stories, and poems to
religious and popular magazines.

WORK IN PROGRESS: A collection of famous American
trials, *Principals and Principles;* the story of a runaway slave

JULIA C. MAHON

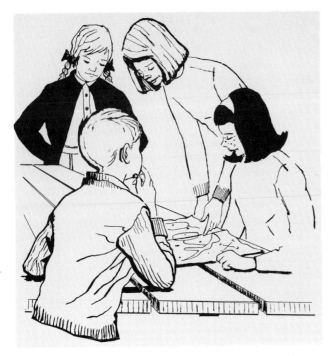

"Then Mr. Easton could have been coming up this road." said Sue, pointing. "If he turned around there and scooted back, he could have gone to any spot over here, the sawmill, the gristmill, the blacksmith shop. . ." ▪ (From *Mystery at Old Sturbridge Village* by Julia C. Mahon. Illustrated by Sidney Rafilson.)

girl during the American Revolution, *Mystery at the Vernon Stiles Inn*.

SIDELIGHTS: "My writing career began about the age of eleven. At this time, I was living with my grandmother, Mrs. Margaret Smith, in a big, old house in Phenix City, Alabama. It provided an ideal setting for a youthful, romantic imagination. There were fireplaces in the bedrooms which threw wonderful, mysterious shadows on the walls and ceilings at night. There were pomegranate bushes under the windows where one could watch humming-birds hovering at the crinkled blossoms. There was a nest of sparrows under the roof outside my upstairs bedroom where, at the expense of danger to life and limb, I could watch the exciting progress from egg to fledgling to adult bird.

"My imagination having been sparked by what I learned of Michael I of Romania, who became king while still a child, I proceeded to fill composition books with stories of a boy king whose exploits rivaled those of *The Perils of Pauline* for excitement and derring-do. In this period, I was doing my own illustrations. One thing about my youthful monarch never varied: whatever the situation, no matter if he was tied to railroad tracks or hanging from a cliff, his crown was always perched squarely on his head. The idea of a king without a crown would have been unthinkable to me.

"These being depression years, and our situation being that of genteel poverty, with the accent on the second word, my first desk consisted of boards resting across two sawhorses, and the whole covered with a bedsheet. However, this unorthodox arrangement disturbed me not in the least. It was a place to write, and that was all I needed.

"Immediately after graduation from Columbus High School in Columbus, Georgia, I had to follow my family to New England, to which my father had returned because of the scarcity of work in the South. I hated the drastic change at first, but with the passage of time, I gradually found myself metamorphosed into a New Englander, which I am and shall remain.

"As the second oldest of ten children, I had ample opportunity through the years to exercise my talents as a storyteller for the younger children. One was a series of humorous tales concerning the misadventures of a bumbling character named Itty Artic, which the little ones found vastly entertaining.

"Although I continued to write after I started to work, then got married, it was several years before I felt ready for publication. In the meantime, my husband, Ed Mahon, and I had five children of our own. I had sold short pieces—stories, articles, poems—to various magazines, but it was 1953 when my first children's book was published. By one of those strange ironies of life, it appeared about the time our baby, Betty, died of leukemia.

"Two other children's books appeared after I had taken on the job of librarian at Tourtellotte Memorial High School in North Grosvenordale, Connecticut, where I still am. I now find myself looking forward to retirement when I can devote more time to the writing which has been such a vital part of my being virtually all of my life. And, as long as I am wanted, I shall continue to teach in the Confraternity of Christian Doctrine, which I think represents one of the greatest needs of our children today."

MARSHALL, Evelyn 1897-
(Lesley Bourne, Jean Marsh, J. E. Marsh)

PERSONAL: Born December 2, 1897, in Pershore, England; married Gerald Eric Marshall (a civil servant, now retired), June 26, 1918; children: Harold William (killed in World War II), Jean (Mrs. Clarence Davies). *Home:* The Spinney, Bewdley, Worcestershire, England. *Agent:* Rupert Crew Ltd., King's Mews, Gray's Inn Rd., London WC1 N2JA, England.

CAREER: Writer, now in semi-retirement and working only on serious novels and countryside articles illustrated by her daughter.

WRITINGS: The Shore House Mystery, J. Hamilton, 1931; *Murder Next Door* (Crime Book Society selection), J. Long, 1933; *Death Stalks the Bride,* J. Long, 1945; *On the Trail of the Albatross* (juvenile), Burke Publishing, 1950; *Identity Unwanted,* J. Long, 1950; *Secret of the Pygmy Herd* (juvenile), Burke Publishing, 1951; *Death Visits the Circus,* J. Long, 1953; *The Pattern is Murder,* J. Long, 1954; *Death at Peak Hour,* J. Long, 1954; *Death Among the Stars,* J. Long, 1955; *Trouble for Tembo* (juvenile), University of London Press, 1958; *Adventure with a Boffin* (juvenile), University of London Press, 1962; *Valley of Silent Sound* (juvenile), University of London Press, 1962; *Sand Against the Wind,* Robert Hale, 1972.

Paperbacks: *Forest Bride, Beloved Heritage, Trouble at Deepacres, Story of Jan Appleby, Storm over Corfu,* about a dozen other original publications. Writer of regular page,

EVELYN MARSHALL

"At Home," in *Home Companion* for many years, also magazine serials, short stories, radio plays, and a radio adventure series.

WORK IN PROGRESS: Operation Hydra.

SIDELIGHTS: "My father was a policeman, an excellent police officer who became the chief superintendent of the Worcestershire County Constabulary. This was in the days before the English reorganisation of the police forces into larger units. Because of this police background, it was perhaps inevitable that my first novels were the conventional mystery stories so popular during the rather depressing period following World War I.

"I married a young officer in the newly-formed Machine Gun Corps, long since incorporated into other army units. The war left him partially incapacitated, so that I was immensely glad of my flair for writing. But books in those days were not very profitable, so that I had to spend much more writing time churning out romantic serials for the women's magazines. Often I would be writing two at the same time, for different magazines and under different pen-names. Once, when a new magazine was about to be launched, a fellow writer and myself wrote all the serials and the short stories for the first issues in order to help preserve the secrecy until the new magazine was ready to be launched. It was great fun.

"But before long, after making up countless bedtime stories for my children, I started to type them up, and found a fresh outlet. The second war interrupted this form of writing. I found myself roped in to giving regular broadcasts on what was known as 'The Kitchen Front,' and also giving some overseas broadcasts. It was an extremely tiring war for me, and also an immensely sad one. I lost my only son, who was shot down over Berlin in his Lancaster bomber; and many, many friends.

"As soon as the war ended, the B.B.C. resumed its special broadcasts for children in a daily programme called Children's Hour. One of my talks producers was appointed Children's Hour producer and she immediately asked me to start writing children's stories for the programme. I found them delightful to write, and scripted a six-part serial for almost every year until Children's Hour was dropped from radio with the growing popularity of television. Most of my radio serials were adventure thrillers: 'Mystery at Castle Rock Zoo,' 'On the Trail of the Albatross,' 'Meet Johnny Pilgrim,' and a dozen others. There were several Johnny Pilgrim serials which were very popular, and I loved writing them.

"But alas one grows old, and from 1955 onwards, I found little time for writing. My husband, a semi-invalid for many years, needed the peace and quiet of the country. So we bought an old-world walled garden in the delightful, ancient river town of Bewdley, and built a small bungalow up on one of its several terraces. The garden overlooks the River Severn, and is a sanctuary for birds and some animal wild-life. My husband spent the last years of his life happily restoring the once famous old garden, with the help of local ancients who knew its long history. Naturally the historical old town, and the lovely garden gave me material for the occasional radio documentary such as 'Sanctuary Town,' and a large number of articles for the country magazines.

"I should like to preserve the garden intact for my family. My grandsons love it. When they were small boys, they built tree houses, and played out their own jungle adventures in the bamboo thicket. It is rare for bamboos to grow freely in the English Midlands, and mine have been mentioned in many gardening talks. But alas, politics creep into every paradise. Both central government and local authorities want to grab even the landscaped treasures of our beautiful countryside. I have already had to put up a long battle to hold on to my garden, and soon someone will wrest it away for a housing site. It isn't only the Russian authors who have their problems. What a pity writers from all over the world can't form a militant union! Perhaps the young writers coming along will do so."

MAXWELL, Arthur S. 1896-1970

PERSONAL: Born January 14, 1896, in London, England; came to United States, 1936; son of George Thomas and Alice Maud (Crowder) Maxwell; married Rachel E. Joyce, May 3, 1917; children: Maureen, Graham, Mervyn, Lawrence, Malcolm, Deirdre. *Education:* Educated in England. *Home:* 24301 Elise Ct., Los Altos Hills, Calif. 94022. *Office:* Pacific Press Publishing Association, Mountain View, Calif. 94040.

CAREER: Stanborough Press Ltd., Watford, Hertfordshire, England, editor of *Present Truth*, 1920-36, general

ARTHUR S. MAXWELL

manager of company, 1925-32; Pacific Press Publishing Association, editor of *Signs of the Times,* and member of board of directors, 1937-70. *Awards, honors:* D.Lett., Andrew University, 1970.

WRITINGS: After Many Days, Review & Herald, 1921; *Looking Beyond World Problems,* Stanborough Press, 1923, revised edition, 1926; *Christ's Glorious Return,* Stanborough Press, 1924; *Protestantism Imperilled!,* Stanborough Press, 1926, revised edition, Signs Publishing Co. (Australia), 1943; *Great Issues of the Ages: Has Christ a Solution?,* Stanborough Press, 1927; (editor) *The Bible and the Wonders of Our Age,* Stanborough Press, 1930; (editor) *The Bible and the Wonder of Christ's Return,* Stanborough Press, 1931; *The Mighty Hour: The Message of These Stirring Times,* Stanborough Press, 1933, 2nd edition, Signs Publishing Co., 1934; *The Book That Changed the World,* Stanborough Press, 1933; *Back to God: The Call and the Way,* Pacific Press Publishing Association, 1935, reissued as *Back to God: The World's Most Urgent Need,* 1946; *Discovering London,* Skeffington & Son, 1935; *Our Wonderful Bible,* Stanborough Press, 1935; *These Tremendous Times: What Do They Mean? Where Are We Heading?,* Review & Herald, 1938; (with W. O. Edwards) *Great Fundamentals of Our Wonderful Bible,* Pacific Press Publishing Association, c.1939.

History's Crowded Climax: Prophecy Speaks to Our Time, Pacific Press Publishing Association, 1940; *Power and Prophecy: Who Shall Rule the World,* Pacific Press Publishing Association, 1940 (published in Australia as *World Power and Prophecy: Who Shall Rule the World?,* Signs Publishing Co., 1941); *Challenge of the Tempest,* Pacific

Press Publishing Association, 1941; *Qui l'emportera* (pamphlet), Rose-Hill, 1941; *War of the Worlds,* Review & Herald, 1941; *Great Prophecies for Our Time,* Pacific Press Publishing Association, 1943; *Nuestro porvenir descifrado,* Pacific Press Publishing Association, 1943; *So Little Time: The Atom and the End,* Pacific Press Publishing Association, 1946; *Forever Heaven,* Review & Herald, 1948; *Time's Last Hour,* Pacific Press Publishing Association, 1948; *God and the Future,* Review & Herald, 1952; *Christ and Tomorrow,* Review & Herald, 1952; *The Coming King: Ten Great Signs of Christ's Return,* Pacific Press Publishing Association, 1953; *Your Bible and You: Priceless Treasures in the Holy Scriptures,* Review & Herald, 1959; *You and Your Future,* Pacific Press Publishing Association, 1959.

How to Read the Bible, Review & Herald, 1960; *Your Friends, The Adventists,* Pacific Press Publishing Association, 1960; *Courage for the Crisis: Strength for Today, Hope for Tomorrow,* Pacific Press Publishing Association, 1962; *Time Running Out: New Evidence of the Approaching Climax,* Pacific Press Publishing Association, 1963; *Under the Southern Cross,* Southern Publishing, 1966; *Good News for You,* Review & Herald, 1966; *This Is the End!,* Pacific Press Publishing Association, 1967; *Man the World Needs Most,* Pacific Press Publishing Association, 1970.

Juveniles: *The Secret of the Cave: A Thrilling Mystery Story for Boys and Girls,* Pacific Press Publishing Association, 1920, revised edition, 1951; *Uncle Arthur's Bedtime Stories,* forty-eight volumes, Stanborough Press, 1924-71; *Uncle Jim's Visitors,* Pacific Press Publishing Association, 1927; *Little Angels Unawares: The Adventures of "Denver N Company Ltd."* Stanborough Press, 1930; *The Children's Hour with Uncle Arthur,* five volumes, Review & Herald, 1945-49; *Uncle Arthur's Bible Stories,* two volumes, Stanborough Press, 1949, 1953; *The Bible Story,* ten volumes, Review & Herald, 1953-57; *Uncle Arthur's Bible Book,* Review & Herald, 1968; *Uncle Arthur's Storytime,* Review & Herald, Volumes 1-2, 1970, Volume 3, 1972.

SIDELIGHTS—Written by the author's son, C. Mervyn Maxwell: "The icy waters of the Atlantic Ocean surrounded him on all sides up to his chin. Teenager Arthur Maxwell was selling religious books during the summer of 1912 to help pay for his college education. His assignment was to the barren, windy Outer Hebrides islands off the west coast of Scotland.

"After visiting all the homes on one island he was glad to learn that, to save expense, he could reach the next island by walking across the sand when the tide was out. As he walked across he wondered why other people were going so much faster than he was. He soon learned. The tide turned when he had gone only half the distance, and almost instantly the long sandy space between the islands was covered with water. Deep places here and there were treacherous now, for he could not see them and might drown if he stepped into one. He rolled up his trousers to keep them dry, but the waves quickly lapped his waist. He held his books above his head as the breakers splashed his face.

"When at last he reached dry land, cold and soaked but alive, an old shepherd who had watched him said he hadn't expected him to survive. Many men who knew the waters well had drowned there.

"Arthur S. Maxwell was born sixteen years earlier in London, England, on January 14, 1896. Soon the family had moved south to Hove, near Brighton. There he and his brother once built canoes apiece in their attic, only to find that they couldn't get them down the stairs! They had to lower them to the ground through a window.

"Arthur once lowered *himself* to the ground through a window. After his father's death in 1910 his mother was converted to the Seventh-day Adventist faith. Arthur resisted religion, however, even climbing out of a second-story window to avoid the minister's visits. But later, after studying the promises in the Bible about the second coming of Jesus and after his experience in the Outer Hebrides, he decided to give his life to the Lord and in time became an ordained minister in the Seventh-day Adventist church. In his Bible he underlined God's promise, 'When thou passest through the waters, I will be with thee; and through the rivers, they shall not overflow thee.' Isaiah 43:2. As long as he lived he believed that God protected him on that occasion because He had a special work for him to do. He also believed that God is a heavenly Father who always takes a warm personal interest in young people.

"Arthur Maxwell took a warm interest in young people himself. It is said that even at his engagement party he dressed in a bearskin and gave the children rides on his back.

"In 1917 he married Rachel Joyce. They had six children.

"For fifty years he edited religious family-type magazines. From 1920 to 1936 he edited *Present Truth* and other journals in England; from 1936 until just before his death he edited *Signs of the Times* in Mountain View, California. When he became editor of the *Signs,* its weekly circulation stood near 55,000. After ten years of enthusiastic promotion, it passed 300,000.

"His earliest stories for children were fictional, but he came to believe that stories about real children would be even more enjoyable as well as more helpful. *Uncle Arthur's Bedtime Stories* was born in 1924, when he had two children of his own. The first paperback volume of 96 pages sold easily and there was a demand for more. He wrote another volume the following year, and went on to complete forty-eight annual editions that have sold 37,000,000 copies and have led millions of children around the world to think of him as 'Uncle Arthur.'

"In writing these stories Maxwell's motive was to help children to be loyal to their families and to think of God—as he did himself—as a heavenly Father who takes a warm interest in children. One of his frequent themes was, 'God loves to answer little children's prayers.'

"For seven years (1951-1958) Maxwell used his spare time and weekends to write out the entire Bible as a story book. He wrote the ten-volume set, *The Bible Story,* to help children 'not only to understand the Bible but to love it.' He hoped, he said, that it would help them to see the Bible as the Word of God and to exalt Jesus as their Creator and Redeemer. Determined that *The Bible Story* should be true to the Bible, he read no commentaries of any sort during the years he spent working on it. Instead, he read and reread Bible passages in various translations 'until they glowed.' He believed that his final product was virtually a 'translation of the Bible for children.'

"Altogether he produced 79 books for children; but he also wrote 33 books for adults, making a total of 112 volumes with a combined sale of 60,000,000. They became popular in many different countries and have been translated into a total of 32 different languages. One of his adult books, *Your Bible and You,* has sold nearly 2,000,000.

"Maxwell lived life to the full, bubbling with enthusiasm and often praising God for fulfilling His promises. He traveled vigorously in Europe, North America, and Australasia preaching on the second coming of Christ and telling stories to children. His infectious chuckle and hearty laugh were characteristic. One of his great pleasures was playing Santa Claus. His principle hobby was writing stories, but he also enjoyed gardening and now and then a few hours of fishing or golf.

"Having devoted his life to working with children, it was a satisfaction to him in his later years that all his own children became active in Christian work.

"In June, 1970, Arthur S. Maxwell was awarded an honorary Doctor of Letters degree by Andrews University in Michigan. He completed his last book, *Bedtime Stories* volume 48, a week before his death. He died on November 13, 1970, after a brief illness."

MAY, Julian 1931-
(John Feilen, Matthew G. Grant, Ian Thorne)

PERSONAL: Born July 10, 1931, in Chicago, Ill.; daughter of Matthew M. and Julia (Feilen) May; married T. E. Dikty, 1953; children: Alan Samuel, David Bernard, Barbara Ellen. *Education:* Attended Rosary College, 1949-52. *Address:* Box E, West Linn, Ore. 97068.

JULIAN MAY, with her Japanese Akita, Susie

CAREER: Free-lance writer, editor; owner of book production and design service, Publication Associates, together with husband, since 1957. In addition to her writing and editing, has done book design, art direction, commercial art, photography.

WRITINGS: *There's Adventure in Atomic Energy*, *There's Adventure in Chemistry*, *There's Adventure in Electronics*, *There's Adventure in Rockets*, *There's Adventure in Geology*, *There's Adventure in Marine Science*, *There's Adventure in Jet Aircraft*, *There's Adventure in Automobiles*, *There's Adventure in Astronautics* (all published by Popular. Mechanics Press), 1957-60.

You and the Earth Beneath Us, Childrens, 1958; *The World of Astronomy*, Pennington, 1960; *The World of Modern Airplanes*, Pennington, 1960; *The World of Electronics*, Pennington, 1960; *The World of Space Travel*, Pennington, 1960; *Real Book of Robots and Thinking Machines*, Doubleday, 1961; *Motion*, Accelerated Instruction Methods, 1962; *Every Boy's Book of American Heroes*, Frederick Fell, 1963; *Catholic Programmed Instruction*, Franciscan Herald, 1964; *They Turned to Stone*, Holiday, 1965; *Rockets, Deer, Squirrels*, Follett, 1967; *They Lived in the Ice Age*, Holiday, 1967; *Weather, Astronautics*, Follett, 1968; *The Big Island*, Follett, 1968; *Horses—How They Came to Be*, Holiday, 1968; *Climate*, Follett, 1969; *Follett Family Life Education Program: Living Things and Their Young, How We are Born, Man and Woman*, Follett, 1969; *Alligator Hole*, Follett, 1969; *Moving Hills of Sand*, Hawthorn, 1969; *The First Men*, Holiday, 1969; *Before the Indians*, Holiday, 1969; *Why the Earth Quakes*, Holiday, 1969.

The First Living Things, Holiday, 1970; *Why Birds Migrate*, Holiday, 1970; *Millions of Years of Eggs*, Creative Education, 1970; *Do You Have Your Father's Nose?*, Creative Education, 1970; *A New Baby Comes*, Creative Education, 1970; *How to Build a Body*, Creative Education, 1970; *Dodos and Dinosaurs are Extinct*, Creative Education, 1970; *Tiger Stripes and Zebra Stripes*, Creative Education, 1970; *Wildlife in the City*, Creative Education, 1970; *Why Plants are Green Instead of Pink*, Creative Education, 1970; *Ecology of North America*, Creative Education, 1970; *These Islands Are Alive*, Hawthorn, 1971; *A Walk in the Mountains*, Reilly & Lee, 1971; *Why People are Different Colors*, Holiday, 1971; *Blue River: The Land Beneath the Sea*, Holiday, 1971; *Plankton*, Holiday, 1972; *Islands of the Tiny Deer*, Young Scott, 1972; *The Mysterious Evergreen Forest*, Creative Education, 1972; *Forests that Change Color*, Creative Education, 1972; *Deserts—Hot and Cold*, Creative Education, 1972; *Rainbows Clouds and Foggy Dew*, Creative Education, 1972; *The Land is Disappearing*, Creative Education, 1972; *Living Blanket on the Land*, Creative Education, 1972; *What Will the Weather Be?*, Creative Education, 1972; *The Prairie Has an Endless Sky*, Creative Education, 1972.

Snowfall, Creative Education, 1972; *The Arctic—Top of the World*, Creative Education, 1972; *Antarctica—Bottom of the World*, Creative Education, 1972; *Cactus Fox*, Creative Education, 1972; *Cascade Cougar*, Creative Education, 1972; *Prairie Pronghorn*, Creative Education, 1972; *Sea Lion Island*, Creative Education, 1972; *Glacier Grizzly*, Creative Education, 1972; *Giant Condor of California*, Creative Education, 1972; *Sea Otter*, Creative Education, 1972; *Eagles of the Valley*, Creative Education, 1972; *Captain*

Cousteau, Creative Education, 1972; *Matthew Henson*, Creative Education, 1972; *Sojourner Truth*, Creative Education, 1972; *Sitting Bull*, Creative Education, 1972; *Willie Mays*, Crestwood, 1972; *Hank Aaron*, Crestwood, 1972; *Mickey Mantle*, Crestwood, 1972; *Jim Brown*, Crestwood, 1972; *Johnny Unitas*, Crestwood, 1972.

Wild Turkeys, Holiday, 1973; *Opossum*, Creative Education, 1973; *Red Fox*, Creative Education, 1973; *Cottontail Rabbit*, Creative Education, 1973; *Raccoon*, Creative Education, 1973; *Snapping Turtle*, Creative Education, 1973; *Bullfrog*, Creative Education, 1973; *Polyphemus Moth*, Creative Education, 1973; *Monarch Butterfly*, Creative Education, 1973; *Mammals We Know*, Creative Education, 1973; *Birds We Know*, Creative Education, 1973; *Reptiles We Know*, Creative Education, 1973; *Fishes We Know*, Creative Education, 1973; *Insects We Know*, Creative Education, 1973; *Quanah*, Creative Education, 1973; *Hillary and Tenzing*, Creative Education, 1973; *Thor Heyerdahl*, Creative Education, 1973; *Amelia Earhart*, Creative Education, 1973; *Ernie Banks*, Crestwood, 1973; *Gale Sayers*, Crestwood, 1973; *Kareem Abdul-Jabbar*, Crestwood, 1973; *Fran Tarkenton*, Crestwood, 1973; *Roberto Clemente*, Crestwood, 1973; *Bobby Orr*, Crestwood, 1973; *How the Animals Came to North America*, Holiday, 1974; *Baltimore Colts*, Creative Education, 1974; *Kansas City Chiefs*, Creative Education, 1974; *Dallas Cowboys*, Creative Education, 1974; *Green Bay Packers*, Creative Education, 1974; *New York Jets*, Creative Education, 1974; *Miami Dolphins*, Creative-Childrens, 1974; *O. J. Simpson*, Crestwood, 1974; *Bobby Hull*, Crestwood, 1974; *Lee Trevino*, Crestwood, 1974; *Roy Campanella*, Crestwood, 1974; *Billie Jean King*, Crestwood, 1974.

Geronimo, Childrens, 1974; *Crazy Horse*, Childrens, 1974; *Chief Joseph*, Childrens, 1974; *Pontiac*, Childrens, 1974; *Squanto*, Childrens, 1974; *Osceola*, Childrens, 1974; *Columbus*, Childrens, 1974; *Leif Ericson*, Childrens, 1974; *DeSoto*, Childrens, 1974; *Lewis and Clark*, Childrens, 1974; *Champlain*, Childrens, 1974; *Coronado*, Childrens, 1974; *Daniel Boone*, Childrens, 1974; *Buffalo Bill*, Childrens, 1974; *Jim Bridger*, Childrens, 1974; *Francis Marion*, Childrens, 1974; *Davy Crockett*, Childrens, 1974; *Kit Carson*, Childrens, 1974; *John Paul Jones*, Childrens, 1974; *Paul Revere*, Childrens, 1974; *Robert E. Lee*, Childrens, 1974; *Ulysses S. Grant*, Childrens, 1974; *Sam Houston*, Childrens, 1974; *Lafayette*, Childrens, 1974; *Clara Barton*, Childrens, 1974; *Jane Addams*, Childrens, 1974; *Elizabeth Blackwell*, Childrens, 1974; *Harriet Tubman*, Childrens, 1974; *Susan B. Anthony*, Childrens, 1974; *Dolly Madison*, Childrens, 1974; *Pittsburgh Steelers*, Creative-Children, 1975; *The World Series*, Creative-Children, 1975; *The U.S. Open Golf Championship*, Creative-Children, 1975; *The Wimbledon Tennis Tournament*, Creative-Children, 1975; *The Kentucky Derby*, Creative-Children, 1975; *The Indianapolis 500*, Creative Children, 1975; *The Olympic Games*, Creative-Children, 1975; *The Super Bowl*, Creative-Children, 1975.

The Masters Tournament of Golf, Creative-Children, 1975; *The Stanley Cup*, Creative-Children, 1975; *The NBA Playoffs*, Creative-Children, 1975; *Meet the Running Backs*, Creative-Children, 1975; *Meet the Quarterbacks*, Creative-Children, 1975; *Meet the Coaches*, Creative-Children, 1975; *Meet the Linebackers*, Creative-Children, 1975; *Phil Esposito*, Crestwood, 1975; *Evonne Goolagong*, Crestwood,

1975; *Evel Knievel,* Crestwood, 1975; *Vince Lombardi,* Crestwood, 1975; *Frank Robinson,* Crestwood, 1976; *Joe Namath,* Crestwood, 1975; *Muhammad Ali,* Crestwood, 1975; *The Goalies,* Creative-Children, 1976; *The Centers,* Creative-Children, 1976; *The Right Wings,* Creative-Children, 1976; *The Left Wings,* Creative-Children, 1976; *Pelé,* Crestwood, 1976; *Chris Evert,* Crestwood, 1976; *Janet Lynn,* Crestwood, 1976; *A. J. Foyt,* Crestwood, 1976; *Arthur Ashe,* Crestwood, 1976; *Bobby Clarke,* Crestwood, 1976; *America's Cup Yacht Races,* Childrens, 1976; *The Winter Olympics,* Childrens, 1976; *The Forest Hills Tennis Championship,* Childrens, 1976; *Grand Prix Auto Championships,* Childrens, 1976; *World Heavyweight Championship,* Childrens, 1976; *Daytona 500 Stock Car Champion-

ship,* Childrens, 1976; *The Rose Bowl,* Childrens, 1976; *PGA Golf Championship,* Childrens, 1976; *Great Horse Races,* Childrens, 1976; *New York Giants,* Creative-Children, 1976; *Los Angeles Rams,* Creative-Children, 1976; *Minnesota Vikings,* Creative-Children, 1976; *Detroit Lions,* Creative-Children, 1976; *San Francisco 49ers,* Creative-Children, 1976; *Washington Redskins,* Creative-Children, 1976.

SIDELIGHTS: "Among my first writings were grammar-school plays, usually funny, and similar dramas done in high school. During my teenage years I developed an incurable urge to write as an outgrowth of a rather solitary and over-imaginative personality. Voluminous reading, especially in

And there were mysteries, too. In the river valleys of the East and Midwest, settlers found mounds of earth built by men. The Indians said that the mounds had been made by "old people"—their ancestors who lived there long before the Indians. ■ (From *Before the Indians* by Julian May. Illustrated by Symeon Shimin.)

the field of science, eventually led me to science-fiction—which remains my first love. My first story, *Dune Roller,* is a science-fiction novelette that became a sort of minor classic. Someday I hope to be able to return to writing science-fiction.

"Writing has been to me a way of earning a living. After college I became an encyclopedia editor and wrote 7,000 articles on science and natural history. This background led me to write my first juvenile books, for Popular Mechanics Press. I made the interesting discovery that I was able to write books much faster than most of the other authors of my acquaintance. This encouraged me to strike out as a freelance juvenile writer, a career I have continuously pursued now since 1957. My avalanche of juveniles includes many books on science and natural history, biographies, and sports books. My choice of topic is usually dictated by the needs of the publisher.

"I have had all kinds of hobbies, including amateur delving into many different sciences. At present I make jewelry, stained glass windows, and costumes; my husband and I share the care of a giant rose garden with over 1,000 bushes; I canoe with my grown daughter, Barbara; during more tranquil moments, I play my theatre organ, pull weeds, prowl flea markets and antique shops, clean the gutters, sew or read.

"My researches have taken me to every state except one, to most of Canada, Mexico and the Bahamas. Some of my experiences have been hilarious and some perilous—and most of the time, my family accompanied me. (From the beginning, my husband and I shared the care of house and children and pursued overlapping careers.)

"Because my writing has been a job rather than a pasttime or a sideline, I have never been anxious to talk about my work. I have little emotional involvement in my books and this tends to disappoint readers and librarians who have romantic ideas of authorship. I don't write because I love it, but because I am good at it and it pays the bills. My joy comes from the endless acquisition of knowledge and from learning how to do new things."

First published work, novelette *Dune Roller,* 1951, has been anthologized six times (latest 1976), adapted for television and radio. Her books have been translated into many languages and published in numerous foreign editions.

FOR MORE INFORMATION SEE: Horn Book, December, 1969, June, 1972; *Redbook,* August, 1974; *Library Journal,* December 15, 1974.

McCLINTON, Leon   1933-

PERSONAL: Born January 29, 1933, in Des Moines, Iowa; son of John Keith (an engineer) and Leona (Stamp) McClinton; married Joan Elinor Cox, February 23, 1957; children: Cheryl Lee, Mark James, Scott Eugene. *Education:* Arkansas Polytechnic College, student, 1952-53, 1956; University of Central Arkansas, B.S.Ed., 1959; Wisconsin State University—Stevens Point, M.A.Ed., 1968. *Religion:* Methodist. *Home:* 413 Lincoln St., Antigo, Wis. 54409. *Office:* Antigo High School, Antigo, Wis. 54409.

LEON McCLINTON

CAREER: Professional baseball player with Cleveland Indians, 1951-52, and St. Louis Cardinals, 1953-57; high school English teacher and athletic coach in Winnipeg, Manitoba, 1960-65, and Osceola, Ark., 1959-60; Antigo High School, Antigo, Wis., English teacher and athletic coach, 1965-76. Has pitched for minor league baseball teams in Green Bay, Wis., 1951, Winnipeg, Manitoba, 1956-57, Fort Smith, Ark., 1951-52, Peoria, Ill., 1955, and Lynchburg, Va. 1955. *Military service:* U.S. Army, 1953-55, member of Ninth Corps battalion rifle team in Korean Far East championships; served in Korea and Japan. *Member:* Council for Wisconsin Writers. *Awards, honors: Cross-Country Runner* was named "top juvenile book" by Wisconsin Writers Council, 1974.

WRITINGS: Cross-Country Runner (juvenile), Dutton, 1974. Author of "Sideline Slants," column in *Echo,* University of Central Arkansas, 1957-58. Contributor to college newspapers.

WORK IN PROGRESS: A juvenile novel based on legends and old stories of baseball.

SIDELIGHTS: "Both as an athlete and a coach, I have been interested in the talent and motivation which go into the

"I'll tell you one thing, Mansfield, you had better not go out for cross-country or any other sport in this school if you quit football. You won't have a friend in this town, if you have any left now." ■ (From *Cross-Country Runner* by Leon McClinton.)

making of a successful athlete, particularly the individual drive necessary to produce a long-distance runner.''

FOR MORE INFORMATION SEE: Kirkus Review, April, 1974; *School Library Journal,* September, 1974; *Milwaukee Journal,* April 13, 1975; *Bulletin of the Center for Children's Books,* April, 1975.

McDERMOTT, Beverly Brodsky 1941-

PERSONAL: Born August 16, 1941, in Brooklyn, N.Y.; married Gerald McDermott (a graphic artist and filmmaker). *Education:* Brooklyn College, B.A., 1965; attended School of Visual Arts, one year. *Residence:* Litchfield County, Ct.

CAREER: Author and illustrator of children's books. Teacher for three years, textile designer and colorist, assistant gallery director.

WRITINGS—All self-illustrated: *The Crystal Apple: A Russian Tale,* Viking, 1974; *Sedna: An Eskimo Myth,* Viking, 1975; *The Golem,* Lippincott, 1976.

Illustrator: John R. Townsend, *Forest of the Night,* Lippincott, 1975. Work has appeared in *Print Magazine, Horn Book, Times Book Review, Booklist, Library Journal,* and as the cover illustration of the *Wilson Library Bulletin,* Jan., 1976.

BEVERLY BRODSKY McDERMOTT

■ (From the filmstrip "The Crystal Apple," produced by Weston Woods.)

**Sasha, Masha, and Marusha were sisters.
They worked in the fields each day.
They collected the sunflower seeds
and gathered the wheat.**
■ (From *The Crystal Apple* by Beverly Brodsky McDermott. Illustrated by the author.)

SIDELIGHTS: "While living in the south of France several years ago, I saw the German version of the film *The Golem* which was made in the 1920's. It was then that I decided to do my own adaptation for a picture book. Research for the story and its development took two years during which time I studied the symbols of the Hebrew alphabet and their corresponding magical qualities.

FOR MORE INFORMATION SEE: Horn Book, February, 1975; *Wilson Library Bulletin,* February, 1975; *Teacher,* March, 1975.

McFARLAND, Kenton D(ean)   1920-

PERSONAL: Born October 11, 1920, in Branson, Mo.; son of Ira C. (a blacksmith) and Mamie (Cox) McFarland; married Sadako Aoki, April 9, 1958; children: Amy, Betsy. *Education:* Sacramento Junior College, A.A., 1940; San Jose State College, student, 1940-41; Syracuse University, B.A., 1961. *Politics:* Independent. *Religion:* Church of Religious Science. *Home:* 28315 South Ella Rd., Rancho Palos Verdes, Calif. 90274. *Office:* The Ralph M. Parsons Company, 100 West Walnut St., Pasadena, Calif. 91124.

CAREER: United Press International (UPI), Los Angeles, Calif., writer, 1946-48; U.S. Army Air Forces (now U.S. Air Force), career officer, 1942-64, pilot, 1962-64, information officer, 1954-64, serving in Europe and the Caribbean, retiring as colonel; public relations manager, at the Ralph M. Parsons Company, 1964—. *Member:* Quiet Birdmen. *Awards, honors*—Military: Distinguished Service Cross, Distinguished Flying Cross, Air Medal with four oak leaf clusters, eleven medals.

WRITINGS—Juveniles: (With James C. Sparks) *Midget Motoring and Karting,* Dutton, 1961; *Airplanes: How They Work,* Putnam, 1966. Has worked as ghost writer.

SIDELIGHTS: "During my growing up years, being a writer was the last thing in the world I ever thought about doing—I wanted to fly an airplane. As it happened, my

KENTON D. McFARLAND

...has his own small auto geared down to run at a very low speed. [He] confines his driving to the backyard.
■ (From *Midget Motoring and Karting* by Kenton D. McFarland and James C. Sparks, Jr.)

senior year in college was interrupted by World War Two and within one month I found myself taking my first airplane ride. . . . Later, after the war was over and I returned to civilian life, I was practically thrust into the news business almost as abruptly as my entrance into the flying business. . . . It was during my assignment in New York City starting in 1958 that I started to take a serious look at doing something besides writing news releases for the Air Force, and as often has been the case in my life, again I rather inadvertently got involved in writing the book about midget motoring.''

MEYER, Jean Shepherd 1929-
(Jean Berwick)

PERSONAL: Born September 3, 1929; daughter of Otis Floyd (a bank vice-president) and Dorothy (Steelman) Shepherd; married Keith B. Berwick (an assistant professor of American history), May 3, 1952; married second husband, Donald Meyer; children: (first marriage) Rebecca, Sarah, Jeffery, Rachel; (second marriage) William. *Education:* Syracuse University, B.F.A., 1951; Art Institute of Chicago, graduate study, 1955-56. *Politics:* Democrat. *Religion:* Presbyterian. *Home:* Norwich Rd., East Haddam, Conn. 06423.

CAREER: Free-lance illustrator of children's books and textbooks.

WRITINGS: (Self-illustrated) *Arthur and the Golden Guinea,* Golden Gate, 1963.

Illustrator: *Land of the Free,* Franklin, 1965; (compiler) *Abbie D's Cookbook* (adult), 1976.

WORK IN PROGRESS: Children's books with historical settings and background.

SIDELIGHTS: Jean Meyer gathered material for her book, and others underway, from Williamsburg (Va.) sources during a year's residence there.

FOR MORE INFORMATION SEE: Gazette (Old Lyme, Conn.), February 12, 1976.

■ (From *Abbie D's Cookbook* by Jean S. Meyer.)

MILOTTE, Alfred G(eorge) 1904-

PERSONAL: Born November 24, 1904, in Appleton, Wis.; married Elma Moore Jolly, June 15, 1934. *Education:* Studied at University of Washington and Cornish Art School, both Seattle, and Art Institute of Chicago and Chicago Academy of Fine Arts. *Office:* 9710 Angeline Rd. E., Sumner, Wash. 98390.

CAREER: Began as commercial artist in Chicago, Ill.; owner and operator of photographic studio in Ketchikan, Alaska, 1934-39; professional lecturer (with wife) on Alaska, 1939-42; producer of war and educational films, 1942-45; photographer for Walt Disney's ''True Life Adventure'' and ''People and Places'' series, 1946-57; writer and film producer, 1957—. Milotte and wife returned to the lecture circuit, 1966-69, for a tour with the film, ''Background of Adventure.'' Films for Walt Disney include ''The Grand Canyon Country and the Colorado River,'' 1947, ''Seal Island,'' 1948, ''Alaska Eskimo,'' 1950, ''Beaver Valley,'' 1950, ''Prowlers of the Everglades,'' 1952, ''The African Lion,'' 1955, ''Nature's Strangest Creatures'' (Australia), 1959. Teacher at University of Puget Sound, winter, 1972, 1973, and trustee of university natural history museum board. Member of Board of Allied Arts, Tacoma, 1963-66.

For seconds the pool was quiet, then Masiki Moja, annoyed by the little newcomer raised his head to the surface and snorted: "Rumppfff! haw, haw, haw, haw, haw." ∎ (From *The Story of a Hippopotamus* by Alfred G. Milotte. Illustrated by Helen Damrosch Tee-Van.)

Something about the Author

ALFRED G. MILOTTE

Awards, honors: Several of his films for Walt Disney, including "Seal Island" and "Alaska Eskimo," won Academy of Motion Picture Arts and Sciences "Oscars"; U.S. Camera Achievement Award for "Beaver Valley."

WRITINGS: The Story of the Platypus, Knopf, 1959; *The Story of a Hippopotamus,* Knopf, 1964; (with wife, Elma Milotte) *The Story of an Alaska Grizzly Bear,* Knopf, 1969. Illustrator (color stills) of a number of Disney nature books. Contributor to *Rotarian, Smithsonian Magazine,* and *Reader's Digest.*

WORK IN PROGRESS: A book on the personal experiences of Milotte and his wife; a television special, "Christmas Nature Fantasy"; an art exhibit for Frye Art Museum, Seattle.

SIDELIGHTS: Milotte designed the structure to be built for First Church of Christ, Scientist, in Puyallup, Washington.

FOR MORE INFORMATION SEE: Rotarian, November, 1941, August, 1955; *Vogue,* February 1, 1952; *Life,* November 2, 1953; *Reader's Digest,* February, 1955, and October, 1971; *National Geographic,* August, 1963; Christopher Finch, *The Art of Walt Disney,* Abrams, 1973.

MINER, Lewis S.   1909-

PERSONAL: Born November 18, 1909, in Waterloo, Iowa; son of Lewis S. and Marguerite (Roeschlaub) Miner; married Frederika Mueller, February 2, 1934; children: Mark S., Marcia S. *Education:* University of Minnesota, B.B.A.,

1931. *Home:* 3615 Albemarle St. N.W., Washington, D.C. 20008.

CAREER: One-time music and drama critic on *St. Paul Daily News,* St. Paul, Minn., and editor of weekly sales magazine; U.S. Army, Comptroller of the Army, Washington, D.C., 1941-70, civilian systems accountant and writer and editor of army regulations on property accounting.

WRITINGS—All juvenile books: *Mightier Than the Sword: The Story of Richard Harding Davis,* Whitman, 1940; *Pilot on the River* (historical novel), Whitman, 1940; *Wild Waters* (Junior Literary Guild selection), Messner, 1946; *Front Lines and Headlines: The Story of Richard Harding Davis,* Messner, 1959; *King of the Hawaiian Islands, Kamehameha I,* Messner, 1963; *Industrial Genius: Samuel Slater,* Messner, 1968. Contributor of stories and articles to newspapers and magazines.

HOBBIES AND OTHER INTERESTS: Reading, music, theatre.

FOR MORE INFORMATION SEE: Writing Books for Boys and Girls, Doubleday, 1952; *Best Sellers,* April 1, 1968.

MOSS, Don(ald)   1920-

PERSONAL: Born January 20, 1920, in Somerville, Mass.; son of Frank A. and Eva M. (Bowen) Moss; married Virginia Hardesty (a designer and painter), June 25, 1949; children: Donald H., Elisabeth P., Margaret B. *Education:* Attended Vesper George School of Art, Boston, Mass.; Pratt Institute, Brooklyn, N.Y.; Art Students League, New York, N.Y. *Home and Office:* 78 Haights Cross Road, Chappaqua, N.Y. 10514.

DONALD MOSS

■ Oil painting for the 1969 Open Golf Tournament.

CAREER: Free-lance illustrator, 1948—. *Exhibitions:* Watercolor exhibitions (one-man show), designed Fire Island home, 1960-70 (featured in *Sports Illustrated* and *New York Times*); one-man sports exhibition, Society of Illustrators Gallery, 1968; paintings at Katonah Gallery, other Westchester galleries and in the Pentagon and U.S. Air Force Academy. *Military service:* U.S. Marine Corps, became sergeant, 1942-46. *Member:* Society of Illustrators (vice-president, 1964-68, chairman, 1964); U.S. Air Force Art Program (chairman), Graphic Art Guild. *Awards, honors:* American Institute of Graphic Artists, award of excellence, 1974; Society of Illustrators Exhibitions, several citations; Chicago Art Directors Show, 100 Best Posters of Year award, 1960.

ILLUSTRATOR: Question and Answer Book of Nature, Random House, *The Art of Watercolor,* Golden Book Encyclopedia. Paintings included in *The Best of Sports Illustrated, 18 Best Golf Holes, Northlight* magazine, *Lithopinions, Colliers, Saturday Evening Post, Reader's Digest, Boys' Life, World Book* and *Time-Life* Books. Paintings have also appeared regularly in *Sports Illustrated* for over twenty years. Designed twelve stamps for United States Postal Service including 1976 Olympic set.

SIDELIGHTS: "Briefly, my national recognition has been for my sports paintings, mostly for *Sports Illustrated.* I work in tempera, acrylics and oils. I have been influenced by Paul Rand as a student, John Atherton as an artist and the French impressionists. I grew up playing hockey, but am a long-time skier and play as much tennis as possible."

EDYTHE NEWELL

184

NEWELL, Edythe W. 1910-

PERSONAL: Born October 28, 1910, in Arlington, Ore.; daughter of Marion Earl (a farmer) and Minnie Clara (a teacher; maiden name, Snell) Weatherford; married George L. Newell (an electronics engineer), September 2, 1931; children: Lora Joan (Mrs. David P. Moller), Susan Clara (Mrs. Ben L. Bachulis). *Education:* Attended University of Maryland, Overseas Extension, and University of Alaska. *Religion:* Protestant. *Residence:* Prineville, Ore.

CAREER: University of Alaska, Fairbanks, technical librarian in periodicals, 1964-67; librarian in public elementary school in Fairbanks, Alaska, 1967-69. Trustee of Crook County Library, 1971-74.

WRITINGS: Rescue of the Sun and Other Tales from the Far North, Albert Whitman, 1970.

WORK IN PROGRESS: A series of nature tales for first readers, set in the desert; a tenth-century legend for teenagers.

SIDELIGHTS: "I've been a full-time wife and mother, following my husband as he pursued his career in electronics.

The coat was called a parka and it had a hood so big and so deep that a child could hide his face behind the long fur ruff that trimmed it. ■ (From *The Rescue of the Sun and Other Tales From the North* by Edythe W. Newell. Illustrated by Franz Altschuler.)

This has forced me to develop many interests while allowing me to discover for myself the richness and variety of many cultures, both old world and primitive. I was fascinated most by the Indian and Eskimo peoples, the lore and legends of the far north. I have more of their tales to tell."

HOBBIES AND OTHER INTERESTS: Travel, art, music.

NICKELSBURG, Janet 1893-

PERSONAL: Born March 1, 1893, in San Francisco, Calif.; daughter of Jacob Jackson (a merchant) and Edith (Brandenstein) Jacobi; married Melvil S. Nickelsburg, December 9, 1917 (deceased); children: Stephen L., Ruth Denmark, Edith Parker. *Education:* Attended University of California, Stanford, and San Francisco State College (now University). *Home and office:* 2585 Union St., San Francisco, Calif. 94123.

CAREER: Josephene Randall Junior Museum, curator of science room for five years; Child Care Center, head teacher during World War II; elementary school science teacher in San Francisco at Presidio Open Air School for eight years; director of nature services in children's camps in the 1950's. Conducted television and radio programs in the San Francisco area, including "Signposts for Young Scientists," 1947-52, "Stop, Look and Listen," on NBC-Television for two years, KQED-Television for two years, and "Children's Forum," on KPFA-Radio. Docent of California Academy of Sciences, 1976—; extension lecturer at San Francisco State College (now University) and Sonoma State College (now California State College, Sonoma); volunteer science teacher in elementary schools in California cities. Feature speaker at nursery school, child care, and recreation and camp conferences. Former education chairman at Audubon Canyon Ranch. Chairman of local committee on recreation for the handicapped.

MEMBER: Golden Gate Audubon Society, Hearing Society for the San Francisco Bay Area (past president; current member of executive committee). *Awards, honors:* Gulick Award from National Camp Fire Girls, 1927; National award from Chicago School Broadcast Council, 1948, for radio program "Children's Forum"; award from California Conservation Society, 1955.

WRITINGS: The Nature Program at Camp, Burgess, 1960; *Stargazing: A Group Leader's Guide,* Burgess, 1964; *California from the Mountains to the Sea* (juvenile), Volume I: *California Climates,* Volume II: *California's Mountains,* Volume III: *California: Water and Land,* Volume IV: *California's Natural Resources,* Lippincott, 1964; *Field Trips: Ecology for Youth Leaders,* Burgess, 1966; *Ecology: Habitats, Niches, and Food Chains,* Lippincott, 1969; *Nature Activities for Early Childhood.* Author of a series of about two hundred fifty radio scripts and of scripts for a ten-record album series for Educational Activities, Inc., 1964, both titled "Signposts for Young Scientists." Editor of *Cygnet* (children's leaflet from local Audubon Society), 1965-68.

WORK IN PROGRESS: Fiction; memoirs.

SIDELIGHTS: Janet Nickelsburg continues her education at California Academy of Sciences, most recently having studied spiders and fish. "I am interested in seeing that chil-

JANET NICKELSBURG

dren become once more in tune with the outdoors, with an ecological and conservational outlook.''

OBRANT, Susan 1946-

PERSONAL: Born August 24, 1946, in Philadelphia, Pa.; daughter of Joseph (an art director) and Rae (Folstin; a painter) Obrant; married Steven K. Meier (an attorney) February 24, 1972; children: Sarah Elyse. *Education:* Attended State University of New York, Buffalo, N.Y., 1964-65; Parsons School of Design, Brooklyn, N.Y., 1966-67. *Politics:* Liberal. *Religion:* Jewish. *Home:* 222 Cleveland Dr., Croton-on-Hudson, N.Y. 10520.

CAREER: Illustrator. *Exhibitions:* J. Walter Thompson, New York, N.Y., 1968; Foote Cone Belding, New York, N.Y., 1971; D'arcy McManus, New York, N.Y., 1972. *Awards, honors:* Society of Illustrators, citation, 1970-72, 1974, award of excellence, 1972; Best Album Cover, *Naras* nomination, 1971.

ILLUSTRATOR: David Fletcher, *Mother O'Pearl: Three Tales,* Random, 1970; Joan Aiken, *Cuckoo Tree,* Doubleday, 1971; Joan Aiken, *Not What You Expected,* Doubleday, 1975.

SIDELIGHTS: ''After a period of thought it has become clear to me that I draw because I must. It seems to be an integral part of my makeup, dormant at times, but continually emerging with different needs and different results. For this reason I work in many different mèdia. Materials vary as does dimension. Line is integral but unless there is generated movement, the drawing is deadly. For this reason, understanding my own nature is my largest work and responsibility. A drawing is like a photographic portrait—nothing is hidden. That reality keeps the imagination full.

''I have been influenced by Paul Klee, Wassily Kandinsky, Mozart, Japanese print, Chinese painting, Tai Chi Chuan.''

Half seriously, half not, she put out both hands and shut her eyes. She remembered Chris saying, "When we first start talking I can feel him put his hands in mine."
"Aswell?" said Dido. "Is you there, poor old Aswell? Can you hear me?" ■ (From *The Cuckoo Tree* by Joan Aiken. Illustrated by Susan Obrant.)

SUSAN OBRANT

ODENWALD, Robert P(aul)   1899-1965

PERSONAL: Born June 25, 1899, in Karlsruhe, Germany; son of Ferdinand and Mathilda (Straus) Odenwald; married Margaret Scharf (died 1954); married Dorothy Quirin, 1956; children: John F., Robert Paul, Jr., Francis J. *Education:* Pre-medical studies at University of Strasbourg, Germany, 1917; University of Heidelberg, B.S., 1920; University of Munich, student, 1920-21; University of Leipzig, student, 1921-22; University of Frankfort, M.D., 1923. *Religion:* Roman Catholic. *Home:* 5500 Chevy Chase Parkway, N.W., Washington, D.C. *Office:* 3701 Livingston St., N.W., Washington, D.C.

CAREER: Studied and worked in various psychiatric clinics and hospitals in Germany, 1923-26; Hospital of Neurology and Psychiatry, Berlin, clinical director, 1927-28; Veterans Administration in North Bavaria, consultant psychiatrist, 1929-35; St. Mary's Hospital, Passaic, N.J., resident in psychiatry, 1936-37; Good Samaritan Hospital, Suffern, N.Y., chief neuro-psychiatrist, 1938-48; St. Vincent's Hospital, New York, N.Y., neuro-psychiatrist, 1946-49; Catholic University of America, Washington, D.C., assistant professor of psychiatry, director of child center, 1948-52; private psychiatric practice, 1953-65; consultant neuro-psychiatrist for various hospitals and organizations. Diplomate, American Board of Psychiatry and Neurology, 1947. *Military service:* U.S. Army, Medical Corps, 1943-56, became major. *Member:* Academy of Religion and Mental Health (chairman, 1959), American Medical Writers' Association (chairman, 1958-61), St. Luke's Physician's Guild (director), Guild of Catholic Psychiatrists (director of executive committee), Knights of Columbus, Holy Name Society. *Awards and honors:* Latern Cross, Family Catholic Action Award, 1952.

WRITINGS: (With James H. Van der Veldt) *Psychiatry and Catholicism,* McGraw, 1952, 2nd edition, 1957; (translator) *Medical Guide to Vocations,* Newman, 1956; *Your Child's World,* Random, 1958; *How God Made You,* Kenedy, 1960; *How You Were Born,* Kenedy, 1962. Wrote

more than 150 articles in professional and religious magazines. Contributed regularly to *The Sign* and *Ava Maria* magazines. Consultant, *Jubilee* and *St. Jude* magazines.

WORK IN PROGRESS: How God Made You, second of a series of three; *What to Do With Our Older Citizens.*

FOR MORE INFORMATION SEE: St. Jude Magazine, September, 1961.

(Died, 1965)

ORMSBY, Virginia H(aire)

PERSONAL: Born in Atlanta, Ga.; daughter of Robert Lee and Juliet (Milmow) Haire; children: Eric Linn, Alan Robert. *Education:* Atlanta Art Institute, completed three-year course, 1936; Oglethorpe University, A.B., 1939. *Politics:* Democrat. *Religion:* Protestant. *Home:* 1336 Obispo Ave., Coral Gables, Fla. 33134.

CAREER: Elementary school teacher, on and off, in southern states and Idaho, 1939-48, in Miami, Fla., 1949—; now retired. Writer and illustrator; lecturer-cartoonist. *Member:* National Education Association, Classroom Teachers Association. *Awards, honors:* Delta Kappa Gamma certificate of achievement in field of literature, 1960; National Education Association journal writing award, 1964, 1965, 1966.

WRITINGS—Self-illustrated juveniles, all published by Lippincott: *Here We Go,* 1955, *It's Saturday,* 1956, *Twenty-*

"What's wrong with Julio?" we all
    wanted to know.
"He's always bad.
And he's ALWAYS mad."
But nobody knew.
■ (From *What's Wrong with Julio* by Virginia H. Ormsby. Illustrated by the author.)

VIRGINIA H. ORMSBY

One Children, 1957, *The Little Country Schoolhouse,* 1958, *Cunning is Better Than Strong,* 1960, *Long Lonesome Train Whistle,* 1961, *The Right-Handed Horse,* 1963, *The Big Banyan Tree,* 1964, *What's Wrong with Julio?* (Spanish-English picture book), 1965, *Twenty-One Children Plus Ten,* 1971. Also author of *Mountain Magic for Rosy,* illustrated by Paul E. Kennedy, Crown, 1969. Contributor of articles to *Today's Education* and of fictionalized experience stories to a National Education Association anthology. Cartoonist in local Florida magazine.

WORK IN PROGRESS: Little Monster Meets the Humans, a picture book; *Summertime Girl,* for ages 8-to-10.

SIDELIGHTS: "My writing career grew out of my two greatest interests, children and drawing. When my own children were small, creative activities went along with the household chores. There were always paints and modeling clay in the kitchen. When drawing paper was hard to come by, the butcher sent a pound of butcher paper along with a pound of hamburger so the Ormsbys could paint. Many unpublished picture books evolved for the neighborhood children during that period.

"One of the best ways to keep the creative spark alive, I believe, is to teach young children. Children, if encouraged to express their emotions in writing, painting and music, can generate the same creativity in the teacher. My earlier books came directly from the charged atmosphere of the elementary school where I taught. At first my cartoons of children and their hardworking teachers were designed to give my colleagues a laugh. Later these ideas grew into my first picture book for children about a day in an elementary school and appeared in 1954 as *Here We Go.*

"The regional books which I now write evolved almost by chance. I wanted to do a slight picture book with a country background. But when Eunice Blake, my editor, saw the fragmentary ideas she remarked, 'I think this would make a good book of about thirty-thousand words.' This opened up a new vein and with it childhood memories of Georgia. I credit my father with most of the material I used to create the scenes and characters in my books about the rural South. It was from songs and stories I heard from him in my childhood that I was able to write in the authentic idiom of the region I depict."

OSBORNE, Chester G.   1915-

PERSONAL: Born September 18, 1915, in Portsmouth, N.H.; son of James Chester (a pianist and composer) and Viola (also a musician; maiden name, Cofman) Osborne; married Mary Rooney, April 26, 1943; children: Maureen (Mrs. Frank Pagano), Patricia (Mrs. Donald Feiler), Virginia (Mrs. Mark Mesiano), James, Kevin. *Education:* New England Conservatory of Music, Mus. B., 1937; Northwestern University, Mus. M., 1950. *Home address:* Box 517, Center Moriches, Long Island, N.Y. 11934.

CAREER: Boston Symphony Orchestra, and other orchestras, Boston, Mass., trumpeter, 1935-38; Center Moriches High School, Center Moriches, N.Y., member of faculty, 1938-70. Writer of children's books. Curator of manuscripts, Manor of St. George (public museum), Mastic, N.Y., 1955-76. Founder of Center Moriches Music Award Association. *Military service:* U.S. Army, 1942-46; became staff sergeant. *Member:* Music Educators National Conference

CHESTER G. OSBORNE

(life), New York State School Music Association (adjudicator). *Awards, honors:* Gold Medal, Boys' Clubs of America, for *The First Lake Dwellers.*

WRITINGS: *The First Bow and Arrow,* Follett, 1951; *The First Puppy,* Follett, 1953; *The First Lake Dwellers,* Follett, 1956; *The First Wheel,* Follett, 1959; *The Wind and the Fire,* Prentice-Hall, 1959; *The Silver Anchor,* Follett, 1967. Contributor to *Encyclopedia Americana;* contributor of articles on regional history, stories, and plays to *Children's Playmate, Instructor, Junior Natural History,* and other periodicals. Contributing editor, *Long Island Forum.* Musical compositions: "Treasure Island" (overture for band), Mills Music; "British Eighth" (march), National Educational Music Publishers; "Connemara Sketches" (suite for band), William Allen Music, "Solos and Ensembles for Snare Drum," Elkan-Vogel.

WORK IN PROGRESS: *Nathan Hale;* a novel with working title, *The White Tree.*

SIDELIGHTS: "My interest in literature dates to kindergarten, when an excellent teacher read aloud very dramatically to the class. I've been writing ever since the Worcester, Massachusetts *Sunday Telegram* printed my four-sentence account of a policeman catching a rabid dog; I was six at the time and wrote with the help of my baby-sitter. Children's pages of Worcester papers continued to print my efforts; I won a serial contest in high school and had a science-fiction story published in a national magazine when I was seventeen.

"Preparation for a professional music career took my attention for a while; my father, was a composer and pianist and sometime accompanist for tenor John McCormack, and my grandfather, Henry I. Osborne, was a composer and once played with Sousa's Band. My mother was a concert violinist—so music was a heritage.

"At one time I was researching the origins of the harp for an article, discovered it may have begun with the sounds of bow strings being plucked as a 'musical' accompaniment to stories around a campfire in the days of primitive man—an evocative scene!—and the result was my first book, an adventure novel called *The First Bow and Arrow.*

"Boyhood hikes in rural Massachusetts with John Farnon, the prototype of '01' in my first two novels, and summers in a Scout camp in the New Hampshire hills gave me a life-long love of the out-of-doors and nature, and great respect for our earliest ancestors who had to live with nature at its wildest; perhaps these attitudes can be observed in my writing.

"I write for young people because I like to, with both books and music: the band and choral and solo compositions in the summary are performed not only by professionals, but also by junior and senior high groups."

HOBBIES AND OTHER INTERESTS: "Fishing, collecting certain kinds of old records (recently found one of a tune my father had written fifty or more years ago) and the repairing of my ancient but stalwart house overlooking the sea."

FOR MORE INFORMATION SEE: *New York Sunday News,* October 4, 1964.

PAHZ, (Anne) Cheryl Suzanne 1949- (Cheryl Goldfeder, Zan Paz)

PERSONAL: Born January 29, 1949, in Ypsilanti, Mich.; daughter of Morris (a businessman) and Shirley (Bender) McConnell; married James Alon Pahz (a consultant for programs for the deaf), August 27, 1969. *Education:* Attended Ringling Art School; University of Tennessee, B.A., 1972. *Home:* 1611 Laurel Ave., #807, Knoxville, Tenn. 37916.

CAREER: Illustrator, writer, teacher. Poster designs are on display in the United States and abroad. *Member:* Society of Children's Book Writers, International Association of Parents of the Deaf, National Association of the Deaf, National Association of the Deaf and Mute in Israel, National Congress of Jewish Deaf. *Awards, honors:* First place in design from Jewish Agency in Israel, 1974, for a poster design made for World Union of Jewish Students Institute.

WRITINGS—Self-illustrated: (With husband, Jim Goldfeder, now Pahz) *The Girl Who Wouldn't Talk,* National Association of the Deaf, 1975; (with husband) *Robin Sees a Song,* National Association of the Deaf, 1976; (with husband) *Will Love Be Enough,* National Association of the Deaf, 1976.

WORK IN PROGRESS: *Total Communication* and *Right as Can Be,* with husband, James Pahz; with Shirley McConnell, *General Watie,* for Dillon Press.

SIDELIGHTS: "In the children's books, which my husband and I write together, we hope to show that a physical handicap need not mean defeat. Most of our experience

CHERYL SUZANNE PAHZ

being with hearing impaired children, we decided to begin a series about a little deaf girl named Robin. Since Robin cannot achieve communication skills auditorily, her parents do not think she will ever be able to talk—until SHE teaches THEM to 'talk' via the sign language and manual alphabet. The only thing more rewarding than writing and illustrating these stories is discovering that it has brought pleasure and hope to other parents and children throughout the country.

"Aside from writing children's books, I also enjoy writing poetry which has been published in several small magazines. My husband and I are very interested in the small press movement and have begun our own publishing enterprise, Moondog Press. We review small press publications in our bi-weekly book review column for the University of Tennessee *Daily Beacon*."

FOR MORE INFORMATION SEE: The Tennessee Alumnus, Volume 55, Number 2, Spring, 1975; *The Deaf American,* April, 1975.

PAHZ, James Alon 1943-
(Jim Goldfeder, A. Paz)

PERSONAL: Name legally changed; born September 11, 1943, in Chattanooga, Tenn.; son of Abraham (a physician) and Katherine (Suggs) Goldfeder; married Cheryl McConnell (a writer/illustrator), August 27, 1969. *Education:* Ohio Wesleyan University, student, 1961-63; Tennessee Temple College, B.A., 1967; University of Tennessee, M.S., 1972, M.P.H., 1975, Ed.D. candidate, 1976. *Home:*

JAMES ALON PAHZ

1611 Laurel Ave., Apt. 807, Knoxville, Tenn. 37916. *Office:* East Tennessee Health Improvement Council, 10901½ Lake Ridge Rd., Concord, Tenn. 37720.

CAREER: Comprehensive Service for the Deaf, Nashville, Tenn., director, 1973-74; Tennessee School for the Deaf, Knoxville, coordinator of Title I projects, 1974-75, University of Tennessee, Knoxville, teaching assistant in public health, 1975—. *Member:* National Association of the Deaf, National Association of the Deaf and Mute in Israel, Professional Rehabilitation Workers with Adult Deaf, Convention of American Instructors of the Deaf, American Association for Comprehensive Health Planning, Congress of Jewish Deaf, American Public Health Association, American School Health Association, Association for the Advancement of Health Education. *Awards, honors:* Community service awards.

WRITINGS: (Under name Jim Goldfeder; with wife, Cheryl Goldfeder) *The Girl Who Wouldn't Talk,* National Association of the Deaf, 1975; *Will Love Be Enough: A Deaf Child and the Family,* National Association of the Deaf, 1976; (with wife) *Robin Sees a Song,* National Association of the Deaf, 1976. Contributor to professional journals. Tennessee editor of *Silent News,* 1975—; author of bi-weekly column entitled "Small Press Review" for University of Tennessee *Daily Beacon,* 1976—; editor and founder with wife of Moondog Press, 1976—.

WORK IN PROGRESS: Total Communication, Charles C. Thomas, Publishers.

SIDELIGHTS: "I began writing as a natural consequence of my work with deaf children. In the course of this work I saw countless instances of the love and understanding required to help a child overcome an auditory disability. I thought these stories of courage needed telling and with the encouragement and assistance of my wife Cheryl, we tried to relate some of them in our books.

"Our first story, *The Girl Who Wouldn't Talk* concerned a deaf child who was born into a world where 'everybody talked,' and the problems she encountered while adjusting to a 'hearing world.' This was followed by *Robin Sees a Song* and *Right as Can Be*—the beginnings of our 'People Potential Series.' In all of these stories we tried to emphasize what could be accomplished through a spirit of acceptance and understanding.

"I have always been an advocate of TOTAL COMMUNICATION which is a method of instruction for deaf children which encourages a healthy atmosphere in which a child can learn. Implicit in the philosophy behind the method is acceptance of the child in every respect. My wife and I try to illustrate this aspect of TOTAL COMMUNICATION in our children's stories.

"Most of my writing activity has been directed at educational journals toward an adult audience. These projects, however, do not begin to give me the sense of satisfaction that is derived upon the completion of a children's book. The greatest sense of pleasure comes after a communication from a parent who has found some measure of meaning or insight in one of our narratives and felt strongly enough to communicate his or her feelings.

"In 1975 my wife and I started the Moondog Press in Knoxville, Tennessee, with the intent of publishing notable works of poetry as well as creative children's materials. At the present time this project is still in its earliest stages of development. Our first collection of poetry, *Periphery,* is expected to be published in 1976. Other writing activities which would fall under the heading of 'hobbies,' are the bi-weekly book review column that my wife and I write for the University of Tennessee *Daily Beacon*."

FOR MORE INFORMATION SEE: ("The Music of Sound," by Richard Smith Green) *The Tennessee Alumnus,* Volume 55, Number 2, Spring, 1975; ("The Girl Who Wouldn't Talk Has a Lot to Say," by Lee McCartt) *The Deaf American,* April, 1975 (reprinted, *The Deaf Spectrum,* Volume 6, Number 3, Summer, 1975).

**HE CHECKED HER AND SOON
IT BECAME QUITE CLEAR.
THE PROBLEM WAS THAT
ROBIN COULD NOT HEAR!**
■ (From *The Girl Who Wouldn't Talk* by Cheryl and Jim Goldfeder. Illustrated by Cheryl Goldfeder.)

PALMER, (Ruth) Candida 1926-

PERSONAL: Born June 19, 1926, in Germany; grew up in New Zealand and came to United States, 1953, became U.S. citizen, 1959; daughter of Volker (a doctor of law and ceramics researcher) and Maria (Carstens) Heine: married T. Vail Palmer, Jr. (a professor of religion and philosophy), December 6, 1952; children: Logan, Crystal. *Education:* New Zealand College of Pharmacy, M.P.S. Ph.C., 1947; attended Woodbrooke College, 1952 and 1975, Kentucky Wesleyan College, 1968, Ohio University, 1973, Rio Grande College, 1975, U.S. Department of Agriculture Graduate School, 1976. *Politics:* Independent. *Religion:* Society of Friends (Quaker). *Home address:* P.O. Box 176, Rio Grande, Ohio 45674; 1729 19th St., N.W., Washington, D.C. 20009. *Agent:* Ruth Cantor, 156 Fifth Ave., New York, N.Y. 10010. *Office:* Ranger Rick's Nature Magazine, National Wildlife Federation, 1412 16th St. N.W., Washington, D.C. 20009.

CAREER: Pharmacist in New Zealand, 1944-52; free-lance writer and publisher, 1962-74; *Small World* (magazine of U.S. committe for UNICEF), Philadelphia, Pa., associate editor, 1974; *Ranger Rick's Nature Magazine* (children's publication of National Wildlife Federation), Washington, D.C., associate editor for production, 1975—. Delegate from New Zealand to Friends World Conference in England, 1952. *Member:* Authors Guild, Authors League of America, Women's International League for Peace and Freedom, National League of American Pen Women, Faculty Women's Club (Rio Grande College).

WRITINGS—All juveniles: *Snow Storm Before Christmas,* Lippincott, 1965; *A Ride on High,* Lippincott, 1966; (with others) *All Sorts of Things* (reading text), Ginn, 1969; (with T. Clymer and others) *On the Edge* (reading text), Ginn, 1970; (with W. K. Durr and others) *Fiesta* (reading text), Houghton, 1971; *Kim Ann and the Yellow Machine,* Ginn,

CANDIDA PALMER

The workmen knew that Kim Ann wanted to learn more about machines. Whenever they had time, they talked about the machines they were using. ∎ (From *Kim Ann and the Yellow Machine* by Candida Palmer. Illustrated by Mercer Mayer.)

1972; *The Soapsuds Fairy,* Ginn, 1972; (self-illustrated) *Sidings* (poetry), privately printed, 1972; (self-illustrated) *Extra Cranks Free,* privately printed, 1973; (with others) *Windchimes,* Houghton, 1976. Wrote weekly column, "Life Is Full of Surprises," for *Owensboro Star* (Ky.), 1968. Regular contributor to *Friends Journal* and *Quaker Life;* contributor of poems, stories, essays, and articles to periodicals, including *Green River Review, One/Two, Three/Four, The Vine, Highlights for Children, Home Life, Quaker Religious Thought,* and *Ranger Rick's Nature Magazine.*

WORK IN PROGRESS: Poetry for children and adults; *Sidings II,* another anthology of poems; two stories for children; an adult short story.

SIDELIGHTS: "As a young person I had a strong urge to write and had some work published in pharmaceutical magazines, some religious newsletters, etc. Not till my own children started in school did I seriously take up writing for publication. Our children started school in the large city schools in Chicago and Philadelphia among black youngsters who had rarely been outside the ghetto and had no reading materials which depicted the city or them. It seemed an impossible expectation of both teachers and students to teach reading to these youngsters from white, suburban, middle-class oriented materials, such as the 'Dick and Jane' series. In the early 1960's there was little editorial sympathy or daring in this area; when my first book came out depicting the inner city minority-group children the first mildly integrated readers were coming on the market also. The first review of my *Snow Storm Before Christmas* could have been written by a hate group instead of by a recognized reviewing medium, so negative was the reception. However, it wasn't long before educational reviews and library reviews, as well as the *New York Times,* credited the positive contribution this necessary reading material for non-white children represented."

PARKINSON, Ethelyn M(inerva)   1906-

PERSONAL: Born September 13, 1906, in Oconto County, Wis.; daughter of James Nelson (a salesman) and Ethel (a teacher; maiden name, Bigelow) Parkinson. *Education:* Oconto County Normal School, first grade teaching certificate, 1923; Bellin Memorial Hospital School of Nursing, R.N., 1928. *Religion:* Presbyterian. *Residence:* Green Bay, Wis.

CAREER: Has taught in elementary school and practiced private nursing; writer. *Awards, honors:* First place in playwriting from Wisconsin Dramatic Society, 1933, for "Shepherd's Queen"; first place for children's short fiction from Scholastic Book Services, 1957, for "A Man or a Mouse"; Abingdon Press Award, 1970, for *Never Go Anywhere with Digby;* award of merit from Wisconsin Historical Society, 1971.

*WRITINGS—*For children: *Double Trouble for Rupert,* Scholastic Book Services, 1958; *Triple Trouble for Rupert,* Scholastic Book Services, 1960; *The Terrible Troubles of Rupert Piper,* Abingdon, 1963; *The Operation that Happened to Rupert Piper,* Abingdon, 1966; *Today I am a Ham,*

ETHELYN PARKINSON

Abingdon, 1968; *Higgins of the Railroad Museum,* Abingdon, 1970; *Elf King Joe,* Abingdon, 1970; *Never Go Anywhere with Digby,* Abingdon, 1971; *Rupert Piper and Megan, the Valuable Girl,* Abingdon, 1972; *Rupert Piper and the Dear, Dear Birds* (Junior Literary Guild selection), Abingdon, 1976. Also author of play, "Shepherd's Queen," and of short juvenile fiction.

SIDELIGHTS: "I grew up in the country, in northern Wisconsin. On winter days my parents worried about my brothers, sister and me because we had to trudge a mile to school on a snowy road. Had they watched the ditches closely, they might have seen that we didn't bother about the road. Instead, we took to the roadsides, where we made 'angels.' You just lie flat on your back in the snow, spread your arms and move them up and down against the snow, with a swinging motion. You rise carefully, and there lies your 'angel,' wings outspread. After every fresh storm, we left our marks.

"The schoolhouse was red brick, quite new. We had one room, one teacher. There I learned to concentrate, no matter what funny thing might be going on up front, where a class would be reciting, and no matter how cold my feet might be.

"Summers were heavenly. We weren't farmers, but we had one of everything. One cow, named Nancy. One hen, named Hoover. One rooster, named Dainty. One dog, named Smig. No cat. We loved the birds, and cats love them for just one thing. We did have horses, and I spent my summers on a horse's back—when I hadn't sneaked a book outdoors, or wasn't practicing my music lesson. Always, I wrote. My poems and stories went into a notebook which looked something like granite. Nobody ever saw what I wrote.

"At twelve, I was ready for high school. After that, I was never at home much, and never in the country again. I missed it.

"I wrote throughout my school life, including the years in the school of nursing. There I was with girls of my own age for the first time in my life, and there I had a wonderful time. However, there was the writing. When I completed my nursing education, and got my R.N., I knew that my career would be writing, not nursing. I have a profound respect and true affection for that profession, and the happiest memories of the school life, but I had to be a writer.

"Poetry and plays came first. Then I had a go at syndicated newspaper fiction. I learned to cram a strong plot with a surprise ending, a good background, great characters, and terrific dialog into one thousand words—for from five to twenty dollars.

"When I had had enough of that, a conversation with a thirteen year old girl did something for me. I wrote a new kind of story for a new market. I was doing a great deal of youth work with boys and girls of this age. Why not tell their stories the way they told them, using their language? I knew it well. I had found part of my field.

"A few dozen stories later a thought came home to me that since there is nothing more alive, more interesting, more appealing, more lovable and delightful—albeit more maddening—than an eleven-year-old boy, I should be writing

"Our Univac will be just about the best Univac in the U.S.A. It will answer all questions correctly within five minutes—or your money back." ■ (From *Triple Trouble for Rupert* by Ethelyn M. Parkinson. Illustrated by Mary Stevens.)

about one and for one. I should be telling it the way it is, in the boy's own language.

"When I realized this, I was holding in my hand a cardboard box, left for safekeeping in my home, and posted with dire warnings:

"KEEP OUT. HANDS OFF! DO NOT OPEN ON PANE OF DEATH—YOU WILL DYE A HORRIBLE DEATH! THIS MEANS YOU!

"I stood there with the box in my hand and joy filled me. Rupert Piper came into being, along with his friends, including eleven-year-old girls, who are surely next most delightful.

"So I wrote about Rupert, and Scholastic published two paperbacks—*Double Trouble for Rupert* and *Triple Trouble for Rupert.* Then I sent *Good Old Archibald* to Abingdon Press. Abingdon became my publisher.

"Sometimes I have a feeling about my writing—a feeling that I haven't done things, but rather that things have happened to me. Perhaps that's because people—children included—have helped me all the way. Nieces and nephews and their friends have been an inexhaustible source of inspiration. I am thankful.

"My books are funny. I'm dedicated to giving as much happiness as I can to children through my writing, and in other ways."

FOR MORE INFORMATION SEE: Horn Book, August, 1971; *Washington Post Children's Book World,* November 5, 1972.

PATON, Alan (Stewart)   1903-

PERSONAL: Surname rhymes with "Dayton"; born January 11, 1903, in Pietermaritzburg, South Africa; son of James (a civil servant) and Eunice (James) Paton; married Doris Olive Francis, July 2, 1928 (died, October 23, 1967); married Anne Hopkins, January 30, 1969; children: (first marriage) David Francis, Jonathan Stewart. *Education:* Attended Maritzburg College, 1914-18; University of Natal, B.Sc., 1923. *Religion:* Anglican. *Address:* P.O. Box 278, Hillcrest, Natal, South Africa.

CAREER: Ixopo High School, Ixopo, Natal, South Africa, teacher of mathematics and physics, 1925-28; Maritzburg College, Pietermaritzburg, Natal, South Africa, teacher of mathematics, physics, and English, 1928-35; Diepkloff Reformatory, near Johannesburg, South Africa, principal, 1935-48; Toc H Tuberculosis Settlement, Botha's Hill, Na-

The King of Beasts acknowledges admirers in Kruger National Park. ▪ (From *The Land and People of South Africa* by Alan Paton.)

tal, South Africa, honorary commissioner, 1949-58; University of Natal, Natal, South Africa, president of the Convocation, 1951-55, 1957-59; co-founder and president, Liberal Party of South Africa (originally the Liberal Association of South Africa before emergence as a political party; declared an illegal organization, 1968), 1958-68. Non-European Boys' Clubs, president of Transvaal association, 1935-48. *Member:* Royal Society of Literature (fellow), Free Academy of Arts (Hamburg; honorary member). *Awards, honors:* Anisfield-Wolf *Saturday Review* Award, 1948, Newspaper Guild of New York Page One Award, 1949, and London Sunday *Times* Special Award for Literature, 1949, all for *Cry, the Beloved Country;* Freedom House Award (U.S.), 1960; Medal for Literature, Free Academy of Arts, 1961; L.H.D., Kenyon College, 1962; C.N.A. Literary Award for the year's best book in English in South Africa, for *Hofmeyr,* 1965, *Apartheid and the Archbishop,* 1974. L.H.D., Yale University, 1954; D.Litt., Kenyon College, 1962, University of Natal, 1968, Trent University, 1971, Harvard University, 1971, Rhodes University, 1972, Willamette University, 1974; D.D., University of Edinburgh, 1971; L.L.B., Witwatersrand University, 1975.

WRITINGS: Cry, the Beloved Country, Scribner, 1948; *Too Late the Phalarope* (Book-of-the-Month Club selection), Scribner, 1953; *The Land and the People of South Africa,* Lippincott, 1955, reprinted with title *South Africa and Her People,* Lutterworth, 1957, revised edition (under original title), Lippincott, 1972; *South Africa in Transition,* Scribner, 1956; *The People Wept,* 1958; *Hope for South Africa,* Praeger, 1959; *Debbie Go Home* (stories), J. Cape, 1961; *Tales From a Troubled Land* (stories), Scribner, 1961; *Hofmeyr* (biography), Oxford University Press, 1964, abridged edition under title *South African Tragedy: The Life and Times of Jan Hofmeyr,* Scribner, 1965; (with Krishna Shah) *Sponono* (play; based on three stories from *Tales From a Troubled Land*), Scribner, 1965; *Instrument of Thy Peace,* Seabury, 1968; *The Long View,* edited by Edward Callan, Praeger, 1968; *Kontakion For You Departed,* J. Cape, 1969, published as *For You Departed,* Scribner, 1969; *Apartheid and the Archbishop,* Scribner, 1973; *Knocking on the Door,* Scribner, 1976.

WORK IN PROGRESS: An autobiography.

ALAN PATON

It would seem that a native, probably with two accomplices, entered by the kitchen, thinking no doubt there would be no one in the house. The native servant in the kitchen was knocked unconscious, and it would appear that Mr. Jarvis heard the disturbance and came down to investigate. ■ (From the movie "Cry, the Beloved Country," starring Sidney Poitier and Canada Lee. Copyright 1952 by London Films.)

SIDELIGHTS: "I was born in Pietermaritzburg, South Africa in 1903. I was educated at Maritzburg College and the University of Natal, where I graduated with a B.Sc. In 1935 I accepted the principalship of Diepkloff Reformatory which had in 1934 been transferred from the Department of Prisons to the Department of Education. The reforms which I initiated, being of an educational not a penal character, earned for me a certain reputation as both an administrator and prison reformer. At the close of World War II, I set off to study the prisons of Scandinavia, Great Britain and the United States. While on this tour, I turned seriously to writing. In the next three months I produced, *Cry, the Beloved Country*.

"Circumstances compelled me to take a leading part in the (South African) Liberal Party. This is not a good thing for a writer. He may be 'committed,' as they say, but not that far. I would have withdrawn from politics had it not been for the actions of the Government, who had restricted the movements and activities of Liberals on the grounds that they 'further the aims of Communism.' This is called a 'banning,'

and a banned person (who is usually restricted for five years) is never charged, never brought to court, nor can he himself contest the order. Under these circumstances I did not feel able to retire to the ivory tower, if I had one. After a trip to the United States, my passport was revoked in 1960 due to outspoken criticism of my government, it was restored to me in 1971."

Maxwell Anderson adapted *Cry, the Beloved Country* into an opera, *Lost in the Stars* (Sloane, 1950), with music by Kurt Weill. London Films also made a movie, "Cry, the Beloved Country," based on the novel. *Too Late the Phalarope* has also been made into a play. Film and stage rights to *Kontakian For You Departed* have been sold.

FOR MORE INFORMATION SEE: Harvey Breit, *The Writer Observed*, World, 1956; *Saturday Review*, August 1, 1959; *New Republic*, September 21, 1959; *Chicago Sunday Tribune*, April 9, 1961; *New York Herald Tribune*, April 9, 1961; *Atlantic*, May, 1961; *Christian Century*, May 24, 1961; *New Statesman*, April 30, 1965; *New York Times*, August 11, 1965, August 4, 1974.

PHILLIPS, Irving W. 1908-
(Irv Phillips, Sabuso)

PERSONAL: Born October 29, 1908, in Wilton, Wis., son of Mary Ellen (Willis) Phillips; married Lucille D. Defnet, October 2, 1910; children: Arden (Mrs. Able Bomberault). *Education:* Attended Chicago Academy of Fine Arts; Columbia Music College. *Home:* 2807 E. Sylvia Street, Phoenix, Arizona 85032.

CAREER: Cartoonist, illustrator, writer. *Esquire Magazine,* New York, N.Y., cartoon humor editor, 1937-39; Chicago *Sun-Times* Syndicate, Chicago, Ill., cartoon staff, 1940-52; Phoenix College, Phoenix, Ariz., instructor; motion picture assignments with Warner Brothers, RKO, Charles Rodgers Productions and United Artists; author-illustrator of syndicated strip appearing in one-hundred eighty papers in twenty-two countries, *The Strange World of Bordighera. Exhibitions:* National Cartoonist Society Exhibits; Arizona State University (one-man show), "Comedy in Art"; New York Worlds Fair Exhibits; Cartoon Council traveling exhibits; Smithsonian Institution, permanant collection; El Prado Gallery, Sedona, Ariz.; Phoenix College Gallery, Phoenix, Ariz.; Studio Gallery, Southbury, Conn. *Awards, honors:* Salone dell'Umorismo of Bordighera, Italy, international first prize and cup, 1969. *Member:* Writers Guild, Dramatists Guild, National Cartoonists Society, Magazine Cartoonists Guild, Newspaper Cartoon Council, American Society of Composers, Authors and Publishers.

WRITINGS: (Self-illustrated) *The Strange World of Mr. Mum,* Putnam, 1965; *The Twin Witches of Fingle Fu,* Random House, 1969; *No Comment by Mr. Mum,* Popular Library, 1971. Author and co-author of two-hundred sixty television scripts; contributor of scripts and animation to ABC television children's program, *Curiosity Shop;* contributor to *Saturday Evening Post* and others.

SIDELIGHTS: Paints under the name of Sabuso.

POHLMANN, Lillian (Grenfell) 1902-

PERSONAL: Born March 31, 1902, in Grass Valley, Calif.; daughter of William Albert and Myrtle (Massie) Grenfell; married second husband, George Russell Pohlmann, May 16, 1947; children: (previous marriage) Iris Twigg Mac-Innes, Hal Grenfell Twigg. *Education:* Special courses at Universities of California, Colorado, and Mexico, and at Free University, Amsterdam, Netherlands. *Home:* 15 Mesa Ave., Mill Valley, Calif. 94941.

WRITINGS: Myrtle Albertina's Secret, Coward, 1956; *Myrtle Albertina's Song,* Coward, 1958; *Calypso Holiday,* Coward, 1959; *Owls and Answers* (Junior Literary Guild selection), Westminster, 1964; *The Summer of the White Reindeer,* Westminster, 1965; *Love Can Say No,* Westminster, 1966; *Wolfs,* Norton, 1968; *Sing Loose,* Westminster, 1968; *The Bethlehem Mouse,* Stone Educational Publications, 1970; *Tall, Skinny, Towheaded and Miserable,* Westminster, 1975; *American Martin,* Westminster, 1976.

FOR MORE INFORMATION SEE: Book World, November 3, 1968.

The deer kept running and so did Heikki. ■ (From *The Summer of the White Reindeer* by Lillian Pohlmann. Illustrated by Beth and Joe Krush.)

GERALD RAFTERY

RAFTERY, Gerald (Bransfield) 1905-

PERSONAL: Born October 30, 1905, in Elizabeth, N.J.; son of Timothy Edward (an attorney) and Mary (Bransfield) Raftery; married Eleanor M. Murnin, August 5, 1933. *Education:* Seton Hall University, A.B., 1929; New York University, M.A., 1937; Columbia University, library courses. *Politics:* Independent Democrat. *Religion:* Roman Catholic. *Home address:* R.D. 2, Arlington, Vt. 05250.

CAREER: Elizabeth (N.J.) Board of Education, junior high school teacher, 1930-46, librarian, 1947-64; Martha Canfield Memorial Library, Arlington, Vt., librarian, 1964—. *Military service:* U.S. Army, Signal Intelligence Service, 1942-45; served in European theatre; became sergeant; received five battle stars.

WRITINGS: Gray Lance (juvenile), Morrow, 1950; *Snow Cloud* (juvenile), Morrow, 1951; *Copperhead Hollow* (juvenile), Morrow, 1952; *City Dog* (juvenile), Morrow, 1953; *Twenty-Dollar Horse* (juvenile), Messner, 1955; *The Natives Are Always Restless,* Vanguard, 1964; *Slaver's Gold* (juvenile), Vanguard, 1967. Author of weekly column, "If I May Say So," in *Bennington Banner* (Vermont) and *Berkshire Eagle* (Pittsfield, Mass.), 1966—.

WORK IN PROGRESS: An adult comic novel.

SIDELIGHTS: "I have been interested in writing for as long as I can remember, and I started my first book when I was in the first grade, printing the words on one of those little cardboard oblongs which used to come in Shredded Wheat boxes. The project bogged down when I discovered, halfway through the first sentence, that I didn't know how to spell 'train.'

"My first commercial writing venture came a dozen years later, when I sold several very old jokes to some magazines. On a more artistic level, I started writing poetry, and selling it, when I was in college. In those days, there were a lot of magazine and newspaper markets for verse, most of which have disappeared. Because I was lazy, I found writing such stuff to my taste, because I could produce a finished product quite rapidly.

"There were years when I sold $200 or $300 worth of verse, and in those times it was possible to live on that amount for a couple of months. When I started teaching school, this added income made it possible for me to take the summer off and write more verse, instead of getting a regular job as most of my friends had to do.

"The verse I wrote in those days was very formal stuff, which rhymed and followed a precise meter. I even used to write sonnets, which almost no one does any more. It was excellent training, and I gradually got more ambitious and wrote a few stories and magazine articles. Most of what I wrote found its way into print, because if I couldn't sell it, I could usually give it away to professional education magazines (which paid in free copies), or to the little magazines and poetry journals.

"Oddly enough, my writing habit probably got its biggest practical boost during World War II. I served in Europe with Signal Intelligence and I tried to write regularly to my wife. Often it was impossible to find a dry or warm place to sit down and write, but a typewriter was always available in our Control Room, because we had to make regular intelligence reports. I learned to compose on the typewriter, using the GI model which had all capitals.

"After the war, I realized that the basic rule for successful writing is simply to apply the seat of the pants to the seat of the chair, so I spent one summer writing a book of juvenile fiction. It sold to the first publisher who saw it, and then for the next five or six years, I wrote almost one a year.

"Some were good and some were not. Some practically wrote themselves and others I really had to sweat over. I wrote one in three months in the evenings, by the simple expedient of sitting down at the typewriter after supper every night and staring at it for two hours, whether any ideas came or not. It should have been a lemon, but that book has never been out of print in England over a period of 25 years.

"When I retired, after 34 years as a teacher and school librarian, I had always expected to write an adult novel, but I have been working on it now for more than ten years, and I keep revising and discarding bits which don't quite come up to my expectations. In addition, I am running the local library, writing a weekly column for two area newspapers, and writing publicity and news for half a dozen local organizations. This seems to satisfy my life-long desire to see myself in print.

"Just a few weeks ago, though, I turned up a new slant on my adult comic novel, so I'm going back to work on it, just as soon as I find the time."

Four of Raftery's juvenile books have been published in England, Holland, Germany, and Sweden.

RAIFF, Stan 1930-

PERSONAL: Born July 28, 1930, in New York, N.Y.; son of Samuel J. (a lawyer and certified public accountant) and Betty (an artist) Raiff. *Education:* Syracuse University, M.A., 1952. *Politics:* "Equal rights for all." *Home:* 438 West 20th St., New York, N.Y. 10011. *Office:* Youth Education, 10 East 40th St., New York, N.Y. 10016.

CAREER: Arlington County School System, Arlington, Va., special teacher, 1952-55; Western Pacific Railroad, San Francisco, Calif., community relations department, 1955-57; National Association of Broadcasters, Washington, D.C., youth director, 1957-60; European Travel Commission, New York, N.Y., vice-president of travel promotions, 1960-68; Inter-Public Group of Companies, New York, N.Y., marketing specialist (accounts supervisor at McCann Erikson, Erwin Wayzey and Jack Tinker & Partners), 1968-69; Youth Education (multi-media education company), New York, N.Y., president, 1970—. Vice-president of Industry Education Corp.

WRITINGS: Get Ready! Get Set! Go!: A European Travel Guide for Young People, Doubleday, 1970. Author of more than a hundred television scripts for young people and of scripts for two sound recordings.

SIDELIGHTS: "All of my professional time is spent helping young people explore with their teachers and parents how they can find out all the potential they may have. These explorations are done in a simple yet sophisticated manner. There is never any condescension in terms of being directed toward young people." His firm creates, produces, and distributes multi-media programs to schools, homes, and communities. "The programs are open-ended allowing people to examine their options, trade-offs, and risks and then make their own personal choices." Raiff has directed and produced children's theater productions.

"Bienvenue!" Welcome to Paris, for centuries the center of enlightenment, art, and learning. That is why it is called "la ville lumiere," the city of light. ■ (From get ready! get set! go! by Stan Raiff. Illustrated by William Accorsi.)

RATHJEN, Carl H(enry) 1909-
(Charlotte Russell)

PERSONAL: Born August 28, 1909, in Jersey City, N.J.; son of Carl Martin Henry (a retail and wholesale food dealer) and Agnes (Liechtenstein) Rathjen; married Olive Minerva Stretch (an osteopathic physician), May 14, 1958 (died March 27, 1971); stepchildren: Barbara Joy (Mrs. Herbert C. Miller). Education: New York University, B.C.S., 1931. Politics: "Vote issues and man." Home and office: 1140 West Eighth St., Meridian, Idaho 83642. Agent: Larry Sternig, 742 Robertson St., Milwaukee, Wis.

CAREER: During depression years worked at variety of jobs, including copywriter for advertising agency, laborer, counselor at boy's camp; full-time writer, 1932—, except for period as cutter in rubber company, Los Angeles, Calif., 1941-44. Served as executive secretary for Idaho Osteopathic Medical Association, 1971-75; trustee, Meridian Library Board, 1975—; executive secretary of Cranial Academy and Sutherland Cranial Teaching Foundation. Member: Idaho Writers League, Oregon Trail Writers, California Writers Guild. Awards, honors: Honorable mention, Boys' Life—Dodd Mead Writing Award, 1954, for Smoke-Eater; "Runaway Rig" named among twenty best Saturday Evening Post stories, 1957; Rotary International Service Award, for conspicuous service to youth, 1965; Idaho Governor's certificate, 1967; Idaho Writer of the Year, 1972.

WRITINGS—Youth novels: Smoke-Eater, Dodd, 1954; Ken Tompkins, Animal Doctor, Dodd, 1956; Haunted Highway, Funk, 1960; Cruise of the Catalyst, Funk, 1962; Wild Wheels, Grosset, 1965; Hot Rod Road, Whitman, 1968; Smoke River Mystery, Lantern, 1968; Flight of Fear, Whitman, 1969; Saddle Patrol, Whitman, 1970; Race of the Hours, Grosset, 1974; Shadow on the Ice, Whitman, 1975; The Waltons, The Treasures, Whitman, 1975; The Waltons, The Puzzle, Whitman, 1975.

Adult novel: (Under pseudonym Charlotte Russell) Dark Music, Lancer, 1972.

Contributor: Teen-Age Outdoor Stories, Lantern, 1947; Post Stories, 1957, Random, 1957; Teen-age Frontier Stories, Lantern, 1958; Boys' Life Treasury, Simon and Schuster, 1958; Reading for Significance, American Book Co., 1959; Reading with Purpose, American Book Co., 1959; Teen-Age Ghost Stories, Lantern, 1961; Adventures for Today, Harcourt, 1962; More Teen-Age Ghost Stories, Lantern, 1963; Everygirl's Dog Stories, Lantern, 1963; Boys' Life Book of Horse Stories, Random, 1963; Stories for Teen-Agers, Globe, 1963; Boys' Life Book of Flying Stories, Random, 1964; Behind the Wheel, Morrow, 1964; Teen-Age Great Rescue Stories, Lantern, 1964; Scope/Reading 2, Harper, 1965; Teen-Age Haunted Stories, Lantern, 1965; American Girl Book of Short Stories, Random, 1965; Masters of Mayhem, Morrow, 1965; Open Throttle, Morrow, 1966; In Orbit, Scott, 1966; More Teen-Age Hunted Stories, Lantern, 1967; Adventure Calling, Whitman, 1969; Crime Without Murder, Scribners, 1970; Desperate Moments, Morrow, 1971; Like It Is, Whitman, 1972; Where Speed is King, Morrow, 1972; Consider the Evidence, Morrow, 1973; Adventure and Suspense, Scholastic, 1973; Combo 501, Scott, 1975.

CARL HENRY RATHJEN

Contributor of short stories to young people's mystery, and general magazines, including *Argosy, Boys' Life, Saturday Evening Post, Alfred Hitchcock Mystery Magazine, American Girl, Ellery Queen's Mystery Magazine, Writer's Digest, New York Daily News.* Editor of *News Letter* of Cranial Academy.

WORK IN PROGRESS: Research for young people's books and research and short stories about a small-town police department.

SIDELIGHTS: "I guess I was destined to become a writer before I gave any thought to it. I grew up in a neighborhood where the other children were either much older or younger, so I had to learn to amuse myself, which I did by making up dramatic, exciting stories involving the use of my toys. When I was twelve a well-known successful writer, Carroll John Daly, told me I should become a writer. I paid no attention then.

"I'd hoped to become a mechanical engineer—machinery still intrigues me and I love to get my hands greasy working on it—but in high school higher mathematics—trigonometry—thwarted that ambition. So at New York University School of Commerce I studied to become an advertising copywriter. Unfortunately for that ambition, I was graduated in the midst of the Great Depression of the 1930's. My family, recalling my boyhood and the advice given me by

Daly, suggested I try writing stories. At last I took the advice, and stuck with it, writing stories for three years before I made my first sale. I drew on that background when I was asked in 1974 to do a book, two of them in fact, based on the characters of "The Waltons" television series. John-Boy, in the midst of the Great Depression, was trying to become a writer, so I had a great rapport with that character.

"You notice from the above that I've had several ambitions thwarted, and as it turned out they were for the best. So I've learned to have the attitude of taking disappointments gracefully for often one will look back and be pleased that a 'disappointment' did occur.

"In my writing classes a student frequently asks what sort of story he should attempt to write. My answer is the same one which has ruled my writing career since 1932: 'Write the kind of stories you like to read.'"

Carl Rathjen's short stories have been transcribed into Braille, and published in periodicals in Sweden, Norway, Germany, Holland, Belgium, Denmark, Australia. He likes to write about the everyday man on his everyday job.

RAZZELL, Arthur (George) 1925-

PERSONAL: Born October 17, 1925, in Welling, Kent, England; son of William Lewin (a designer) and Alice (Wakefield) Razzell; married Daphne Jean Patten (a dress designer), August 12, 1950; children: Philip, Simon, Margaret. *Education:* Attended London University, 1949-51. *Politics:* Liberal. *Religion:* Anglican. *Home:* Veryan, Kettlewell Close, Horsell, Surrey, England. *Office:* Ravenscote Middle School, Frimley, Surrey, England.

CAREER: University of London Institute of Education, London, England, lecturer in education, 1964-69; University of Lancaster, Lancaster, England, senior researcher, 1969-72; Scholastic Publication Ltd., London, England, director (non-executive), 1965-75; Ravenscote County Middle School, Frimley, Surrey, England, headmaster, 1972—. Macmillan Publishers, London, England, educational consultant. *Military service:* Royal Navy, lieutenant, staff of Admiral Lord Fraser. *Member:* William Morris Society, Society of Authors (England).

WRITINGS: Circles and Curves, Doubleday, 1964; *Symmetry,* Doubleday, 1964; *Probability,* Doubleday, 1964; *A Question of Accuracy,* Doubleday, 1964; *Four and the Story of Four,* Doubleday, 1964; *Three and the Story of Three,* Doubleday, 1964; *Juniors,* Penguin (England), 1967; *Have We Got Time?,* Hart Davis (United Kingdom), 1968; *Signs and Symbols,* Hart Davis, 1968; *The Lie of the Land,* Hart Davis, 1968; *Shapes and Numbers,* Hart Davis, 1968; (with Professor Alec Ross) *The Middle Years of Schooling,* Schools Council (United Kingdom), 1969; (with Professor Alec Ross) *The Curriculum for the Middle Years,* Schools Council, 1975; *Ways of Knowing,* Macmillan, 1976; *Awarenesses One,* Macmillan, 1976; *Awarenesses Two,* Macmillan, 1976; *You Need to Know Your Tables,* Macmillan, 1976. Television scriptwriter, twenty-two programmes in series "Summing it up" nationally networked in United Kingdom, forty programmes in Primary Mathematics Programmes, 1959-63. Board of "New Education," 1964-67.

SIDELIGHTS: "After ten years in the academic work lecturing and undertaking research at London and Lancaster Universities, I achieved my ambition to open a new Middle School with 700 pupils aged from eight to twelve years old in a delightful part of Surrey, England. The school opened in 1972 and has been pioneering new approaches to parent involvement in education."

RENLIE, Frank H. 1936-

PERSONAL: Born April 17, 1936, in Ketchikan, Alaska; son of Frank O. (a fisherman) and Anna E. (Hanson) Renlie; married Beverly S. Koons, April 19, 1958; children: Kimberley, Jeff, Kristin. Education: Western Washington State College, 1955; Burnley School of Professional Art, graduated in 1962. Religion: Protestant (Lutheran). Home: 4726 North East 178th, Seattle, Wash. 98155. Office: 500 Aurora North, #204, Seattle, Wash. 98109.

CAREER: Freelance illustrator/designer. The Boeing Co., Seattle, Wash., graphic illustrator, 1956-1963. Military service: U.S. Navy Reserve, seaman, 1962. Awards, honors: Advertising Association of the West Creative Competition Awards, second award in Transit Outside Posters, 1965; Thirty-seventh Outdoor Advertising Competition, National Institute of Outdoor Advertising, third award for Campaign Local, 1969.

EXHIBITIONS: Northwest Annual, Seattle Art Museum, 1962, 1974; Changing Scene in Washington, Museum of History & Industry, Seattle, Wash., 1963, 1964, 1965, 1966, 1967; Northwest Watercolor Society, Seattle Art Museum

Someone filled our swimming pool with live piranha. If we don't swim there anymore, the piranha will starve. ■ (From *The Big Book of Gleeb* by Paul B. Lowney. Illustrated by Frank Renlie.)

Pavilion, 1973; Illustrators 16, New York Society of Illustrators, 1974; Seventeenth Annual Puget Sound Area Exhibition, Frye Art Museum, Seattle, Wash., 1975.

ILLUSTRATOR: Illustrated Games, Rhythms & Stunts For Children, Prentice, 1957; Gleeb, Dodd, 1968; The Big Book of Gleeb, Dodd, 1975.

SIDELIGHTS: "I specialize in humorous illustration and work in pen and ink. I also like to experiment and work in different directions of contemporary illustration and at the present I am exploring new illustrative approaches other than humorous. I guess, basically, I just like to draw and as long as I can remember, I have been an artist, inspired and encouraged by my father and mother.

"I illustrated the nationally syndicated (NEA) comic strip *Tom Trick*, 1965-1970. It was a children's oriented strip, puzzles, games, etc.

"I was not influenced by anyone in particular, just many in general both fine artists and commercial types, more of the stylized or humorous types. I'm trying to find my own individuality I guess."

HOBBIES AND OTHER INTERESTS: Antiques (buying and refinishing), woodworking, sailing, skiing, fishing and family.

ROBINSON, Maudie (Millian Oller) 1914-

PERSONAL: Born August 4, 1914, in Norris, Okla.; daughter of William Randolph (a farmer and merchant) and Fannie Elizabeth (Kimbrough) Oller; married William Cole Lewis, May 5, 1933 (divorced, 1940); married Charles Hugh Robinson (an educator and administrator of schools in New Mexico), September 6, 1942; children: (first marriage) Betty Carole (Mrs. Donald George Worrall). Education: Attended

FRANK H. RENLIE

Highlands University, 1950-58. *Politics:* Republican. *Religion:* Presbyterian. *Home and office:* 152 Crescent Dr., Clovis, N.M. 88101. *Agent:* August Lenniger, Lenniger Literary Agency, Inc., 437 Fifth Ave., New York, N.Y. 10016; Jody Ellis, Sunstone Press, Santa Fe, N.M.

CAREER: Vaughn municipal schools, Vaughn, N.M., bookkeeper, 1943-1958; bookkeeper, secretary at Montgomery Ward, General Motors, Murphy's drugstore, and Veterans Administration at Las Vegas, N.M.; writer, 1958—; Navajo Lodge, Las Vegas, N.M., manager, 1963-1973. Member of Friends of the Clovis Library. *Member:* New Mexico Book League, Order of the Eastern Star.

WRITINGS: Children of the Sun: The Pueblos, Navajos, and Apaches of New Mexico (juvenile), Messner, 1973; *White Husband, Kit Carson,* Western Heritage Press, in press. Contributor of articles and stories to popular magazines, including *She, Reader's Digest,* and *Homemaker.*

WORK IN PROGRESS: The Proverbial Way; A Do-It-Yourself Book on How To Do Nothing; Unvarnished (novel); *Jimson Weed* (novel); *Mystery of the Squash Blossom Necklace* (juvenile).

SIDELIGHTS: "I grew up in a very close-knit family in the eastern hills of Oklahoma. The small place where I was born was originally called Bugscuffle! My father was a mixture of English and German and a perfectionist in all his endeavors.

MAUDIE ROBINSON

When the pot is dry, she polishes it inside and out with small stones until it has a smooth surface and is ready to paint. ■ (From *Children of the Sun* by Maudie Robinson. Photo by New Mexico Dept. of Development.)

My mother was a delightful mixture of Irish and Cherokee. We grew up among the Choctaws and Cherokees, and my father was always their friend and champion.

"New Mexico has been my home since 1930, and for me, it is truly a Land of Enchantment. I am vitally interested in Southwest history and the Indians who inhabit the land now and those of long ago. I enjoy tramping through the hills and over the prairies, visiting old ruins, and searching through junk shops and second-hand stores for that rare Old West Book that has long been out of print."

ROLAND, Albert 1925-

PERSONAL: Born December 9, 1925, in Pinerolo, Italy; son of Carlo and Mary (Bellini) Roland; married Jo Ann Alkire (a teacher), December 20, 1950; children: Ann Claire, Kathryn Lei, Daniel Arnaud, Paul Alkire, Carl Albert. *Education:* Attended University of Rome and University of Turin, 1944-47; Bethel College, Newton, Kan., B.A., 1948; University of Kansas, M.A., 1951. *Religion:* "Grew up in Waldensian family." *Home:* 3717 Underwood St., Chevy Chase, Md. 20015. *Office:* U.S. Information Agency, 1776 Pennsylvania Ave., Washington, D.C. 20547.

CAREER: Capper Publications, Topeka, Kan., editor, 1951-57; U.S. Information Agency, Washington, D.C., magazine editor in Washington, D.C., 1957-64, editorial director in Manila, the Philippines, 1964-69, and in charge of overall publications program in Washington, D.C., 1969—.

WRITINGS: Christian Values in Recent Fiction, University Press of Kansas, 1951; (editor with Richard Wilson and Michael Rahill) *Adlai Stevenson of the United Nations,* Free Asia Press, 1965; *Great Indian Chiefs* (juvenile), Crowell-Collier, 1966, revised edition, 1972; *The Philippines* (juvenile), Macmillan, 1967; (contributor) Hennig Cohen, editor, *The American Culture,* Houghton, 1968; *Profiles from the New Asia* (juvenile), Macmillan, 1970. Contributor to literary journals, including *Antioch Review, Western Humanities Review, American Quarterly,* and *Quill.*

WORK IN PROGRESS: A book of profiles of immigrants.

SIDELIGHTS: "The first magazine I edited was a four-page, poorly mimeographed job some friends and I started publishing in high school—a rather unusual venture in the northern Italian town where I was born. Still a teenager, in Italian magazines, I grappled with semi-philosophical and political issues—and wrote love poems. . . . Later I did quite a bit of travel writing. A lifelong fascination with the American Indians—going back to the summer days in the foothills of the Alps when, decked out in full turkey-feather bonnet, I was 'Powerful Jaguar'—resulted eventually in my first book for Macmillan, *Great Indian Chiefs.* . . . Three of my books are classed as 'juveniles' but there was no conscious effort on my part to single out an audience, except for the deliberate avoidance of useless big words and overly involved sentences."

HOBBIES AND OTHER INTERESTS: Travel, tennis.

ROSENBLUM, Richard   1928-

PERSONAL: Born January 24, 1928, in Brooklyn, N.Y.; son of Archie (a retired tailor) and Anna Rosenblum; married Barbara Rhode (a secretary), May 5, 1959; children: Anne. *Education:* Cooper Union, three years, diploma. *Politics:* Liberal/Democratic/Independent. *Religion:* Jewish. *Home:* 2 Grace Ct., Brooklyn, N.Y. 11201. *Office:* 370 Lexington Ave., New York, N.Y. 10017.

CAREER: Freelance illustrator. *New York Herald Tribune,* New York, N.Y., art apprentice, 1950-51; CBS-TV News,

RICHARD ROSENBLUM

New York, N.Y., staff artist, 1951-52, UPA Films, New York, N.Y., animation designer, 1955-57. Teacher of illustration at Parsons School of Design; Grace Court Association, executive board. *Exhibitions:* Art Director Club, New York, N.Y., Society of Illustrators, New York, N.Y. *Military service:* U.S. Army, 1946.

WRITINGS: (Self-illustrated) *Tugboats,* Holt, 1976.

Illustrator: L. Frank Baum, *Kidnapped Santa Claus,* Bobbs, 1969; *Ecidujerp-Prejudice,* Watts, 1974.

SIDELIGHTS: "I work in pen and ink—water color and dye. Have a studio in Manhattan. Don't like to work home. Find I get more realistic as I get older."

Santa Claus lives in the Laughing Valley, where stands the big, rambling castle in which his toys are manufactured. His workmen, selected from the ryls, knooks, pixies and fairies, live with him, and every one is as busy as can be from one year's end to another. ■ (From *A Kidnapped Santa Claus* by L. Frank Baum. Illustrated by Richard Rosenblum.)

202

FRANKLIN RUSSELL

RUSSELL, Franklin   1926-

PERSONAL: Born October 9, 1926, in Christchurch, Canterbury, New Zealand; son of Alexander Grant and Vida (McKay) Russell. *Education:* Educated in New Zealand at Nelson College and Victoria University of Wellington. *Politics:* None. *Religion:* None. *Home and office:* Swann's Way Out, Warsaw Rd., Frenchtown, N.J. 08825. *Agent:* John Cushman Associates, Inc., 24 East 38th St., New York, N.Y. 10016.

CAREER: Professional writer. *Awards, honors:* Guggenheim fellow, 1964-65.

WRITINGS: Watchers at the Pond, Knopf, 1961; *Argen the Gull,* Knopf, 1964; *The Frightened Hare* (juvenile), Holt, 1965; *Hawk in the Sky* (juvenile), Holt, 1965; *The Secret Islands,* Norton, 1966; *The Honeybees* (juvenile), Pantheon, 1967; *Searchers at the Gulf,* Norton, 1970; *The Atlantic Coast,* Natural Science of Canada Ltd., 1970; *The Sea Has Wings,* Dutton, 1973; *The Okefenokee Swamp,* Time-Life Books, 1974; *Season on the Plain,* Dutton, 1974; *The Secret Life of Animals,* Dutton, 1975; (with Lorus and Margery Milne) *Mountains of America,* Abrams, 1975; *Wild Creatures,* Simon and Schuster, 1975.

SIDELIGHTS: "Although born in New Zealand, I was brought up in Australia, Europe, England as well as New Zealand and have lived longer in the United States than any other country. My parents were wanderers and it would seem that I have been almost everywhere. I cannot remember being in Peking in the early 1930's, but I was there,

and I have these pictures of me as a kid, Warsaw, 1931, Sault Ste. Marie, Canada, 1932, Singapore, 1929, Buenos Aires, 1930, which suggest that as a preschooler, I spent most of my time traveling.

"My interest in natural history, however, came from a number of years spent on a New Zealand farm, in the province of Nelson, where we grew all kinds of crops and raised sheep. Because of family difficulties, I had to leave the farm, but I stayed out there in the country, inside my head anyway, even though I later became a newspaperman, magazine writer in New Zealand, Australia, England, Europe, Canada and then the United States. I suppose I have written more than a million words on the natural historical world.

"After World War II was over, I left New Zealand and have traveled even more widely than my parents. I like to write about interesting places around the globe and have included some of my own experiences and observations in books and magazine articles about Antarctica, Asia, Japan, the Arctic, the Atlantic Ocean, Europe, Mesopotamia (Babylon and Nineveh), Egypt (which I have visited many times) and most parts of Africa.

"Although a lot of my material is factual, I have had some success in taking factual situations, involving animals, or worlds that animals occupy and turning the material into fictional stories which try to give the natural history another dimension for both adult and young readers. The response to this work has been very rewarding for me because at last people are beginning to realize what I have known for many years: we cannot live on this planet, despite our technology, without conforming to most of the laws of natural history. Understanding these laws is difficult. Providing that understanding has been a lot of my work."

One morning half the bees in the hive gather together around the queen bee.
Suddenly they rush out toward the bright sun their queen with them.
■ (From *The Honeybees* by Franklin Russell. Illustrated by Colette Portal.)

SANDERLIN, Owenita (Harrah) 1916-

PERSONAL: Born June 2, 1916, in Los Angeles, Calif.; daughter of Owen Melville (a physician and surgeon) and Marigold (Whitford) Harrah; married George William Sanderlin (a professor; writer), May 30, 1936; children: Frea Elizabeth (Mrs. Frank Sladek), Sheila Mary (Mrs. Roland Buska), David George, John Owen (died, 1963). *Education:* The American University, B.A. (summa cum laude), 1937; University of Maine, graduate study, 1938; San Diego State University, graduate study, 1969; University of California, graduate work in gifted education, 1972. *Politics:* Democrat or independent. *Religion:* Catholic. *Home:* El Cajon, California.

CAREER: During student years worked as a restaurant cashier ("cashiered my way through college") and with a professional marionette company in Washington, D.C.; did free-lance writing, 1938—. Taught English part time at University of Maine, Orono, 1943, 1947; Academy of Our Lady of Peace, San Diego, Calif., head of speech and drama department, 1961-62, 1963-68. *Member:* National Forensic League, San Diego Tennis Patrons Association, Mortarboard. *Awards, honors:* Radcliffe Award for most outstanding junior girl; Alpha Chi Omega Award (poetry); National Forensic League Double Ruby (Speech Coaching).

WRITINGS: Jeanie O'Brien (junior novel), Watts, 1965; *Johnny,* A.S. Barnes, 1968; *Creative Teaching,* A.S. Barnes, 1971; *Teaching Gifted Children,* A.S. Barnes, 1973. Stories, plays, verse and articles have appeared in a number of magazines, including *Parents' Magazine, Saturday Evening Post, Seventeen, Catholic Digest, Jack and Jill,* and *Catholic World.*

WORK IN PROGRESS: A novel about family life; juvenile sports novels.

OWENITA SANDERLIN

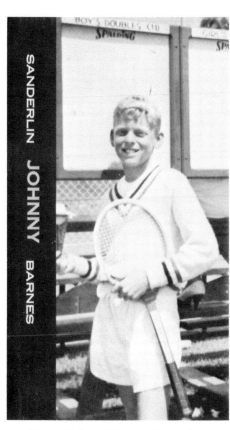

They said I could do anything as long as my red count stayed up, but they had to keep checking. [They] did that at the hospital clinic every other Saturday, unless my mom could argue Dr. Evans into letting me off for a tournament. It wasn't that they wouldn't let me play tennis. Dr. Evans was an internationally known hematologist so you could hardly expect him to arrange his hours to suit an internationally unknown boy. But my mom did. ■ (From *Johnny* by Owenita Sanderlin.)

SIDELIGHTS: "I decided to become a 'famous authoress' when I was six, and read my first book; at twelve I approached the local newspaper, *The Lamanda Park* (California) *Herald* and offered to sell them some of my poetry. They didn't pay, but printed a poem of mine on the front page every week till I had to move to Washington, D.C. I couldn't make the *Washington Post* but was editor-in-chief of the creative magazine at Central High School, and when there was no literary journal in college I founded one.

"My childhood was torn up by divorce (when I was eight), alcoholism, stepmothers and stepfathers, moving (back and forth across the United States several times), the death of my father when I was thirteen, and the Depression, so we had no money. But I did get to college (work and a scholarship) and there as a freshman I met the man I'm still married to, forty years later; we had four children, two girls and two boys and they had the happy childhood I missed—so I can write about both the problems and the joys. That's what I want to write about—family life. Both my husband and I took up writing 'for money' (!)—but that's fun, too—to help support the children on a professor's salary, very low in the 1940's. I sold an article about that to the *Saturday Evening Post,* also some light verse. Mostly I sold children's stories and articles about raising children to less well-known magazines for an average of $20.00 each. I've sold over 1,700 of these, and when people ask if I ever get any of my writing published I tell them this, and they say 'Oh? What name do you write under?' I say 'Owenita Sanderlin—my own!' So my childhood ambition is only half fulfilled. I'm an authoress all right, but not very famous. I am also a grandmother, with twelve wonderful grandchildren—one in every grade of school.

"The best book I've written is *Johnny,* the story of our youngest son, who died in 1963 of leukemia. When he was eleven, doctors said he couldn't possibly live more than a year, but two years later he won the United States doubles championship in thirteen and under Boys' Tennis, and lived to be a senior in high school, having fun all the way. He really 'collaborated' with me in writing the book because I was able to use his own writings, his school papers, diary, and a weekly newspaper he kept the last year. So the story is told in his own words, and when I go to schools to talk to the boys and girls they say, 'He must have been a pretty neat guy. I would like to have had him for a friend.' I wrote the book to help people—children with illnesses and their parents—and it has. I hear it has also helped in other ways. Kids who 'don't like to read' have read *Johnny* and liked it so much, they tell me, that now they are reading other books, too. You never know, when you're a writer, what may come of it."

HOBBIES AND OTHER INTERESTS: Playing tennis and working with local juniors (son, David, was also a ranking national tennis player); acting in and directing plays.

SARGENT, Shirley 1927-

PERSONAL: Born July 12, 1927, in Los Angeles, Calif.; daughter of Robert Chester (an engineer) and Alice

SHIRLEY SARGENT

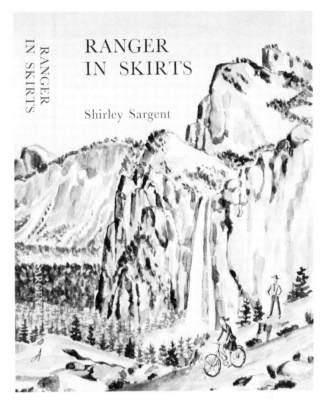

"Entering Yosemite National Park," read the wood, roughhewn sign. To Molly Bishop, the carved words said "heaven on earth." ■ (From *Ranger in Skirts* by Shirley Sargent. Illustrated by Anne Marie Jauss.)

(Fletcher) Sargent. *Education:* Pasadena City College, A.A., 1947. *Home:* Flying Spur, Box 278, Yosemite National Park, Calif. 95389.

CAREER: Topsy-Turvy Nursery School, Pasadena, Calif., head teacher, 1948-59; free-lance writer. Foresta Property Owners Association, board member, historian, 1959—. *Member:* California Historical Society, Mariposa County Historical Society (co-editor, 1960-62, librarian, 1960), Sierra Club. *Awards, honors:* Dodd, Mead Prize Competition, honorable mention, 1955, for *Pipeline Down the Valley;* James D. Phalen Awards, 1964, honorable mention for *Galen Clark, Yosemite Guardian;* Award of Merit from California Historical Societies, 1971.

WRITINGS: Pipeline Down the Valley, Dodd, 1955; *Pat Hawley: Pre-School Teacher,* Dodd, 1958; (with Hannah Smith) *Three Names for Katherine,* Messner, 1960; *The Heart-Holding Mountains,* Messner, 1961; *Wawona's Yesterdays,* Yosemite Natural History Association, 1961; *Stop the Typewriters,* Abelard, 1963; *Galen Clark, Yosemite Guardian,* Sierra Club, 1964; *Treasure at Flying Spur,* Abelard, 1965; *Pioneers in Petticoats,* Trans-Anglo, 1966; *Ranger in Skirts,* Abingdon, 1966; *Yosemite Tomboy,* Abelard, 1967; *John Muir in Yosemite,* 1972; *Yosemite's Famous Guests,* 1973; *Yosemite and Its Innkeepers,* 1975. Weekly columnist, *Mariposa Gazette;* contributor of more than one hundred articles, stories and essays to periodicals.

WORK IN PROGRESS: A guidebook to Mariposa County.

SIDELIGHTS: "I had a moving life, because my father was a highway engineer and the family moved from job to job during the Great Depression.

"We lived in twenty-four places including tents and a log cabin, in ten years, during which time I attended twelve schools. The smallest school had nine students in eight grades—the largest a thousand. My favorite school, and my favorite place—then, now and forever—was in Yosemite National Park, the world's best place.

"When I was ten, I decided to become a rich famous author, and when I was fourteen, I decided I wanted to live in Yosemite and become a rich famous author. A number of years later, I built a house on a mountain top in the forest about a hundred feet outside the national park boundary. Here I write books for adults and children, feed the wild birds and a fairly tame cat—but I do not feed the wild deer, bear, raccoons or coyotes. I am still waiting to be rich.

"Writers are supposed to write about what they know, and I do. I write about kids and rangers, mountains and mountaineers like John Muir, and about Yosemite history. Most of the time I love my work, and I am at my desk all morning long. Some days I spend hours writing, cutting and rewriting one single page. Ugh!

"Despite the work and discipline, I think I am one of the luckiest people in the world, because I live where I want to, and do what I want to."

HOBBIES AND OTHER INTERESTS: Mountains, children, reading and collecting books, camping and traveling, and riding a three-wheel bike.

SCANLON, Marion Stephany

PERSONAL: Born in Lanesboro, Minn.; daughter of Cornelius (a businessman) and Margaret (Rafferty) Scanlon. *Education:* Ripon College, B.Ph.; University of Minnesota, graduate study in Medical School; University of Wisconsin, M.S., postgraduate study; University of Michigan, postgraduate study. *Home:* Box 183, Lanesboro, Minn. 55949.

CAREER: Marygrove College, Detroit, Mich., professor of health education (retired). *Member:* American Association of University Women, American Association of Health, Physical Education, and Recreation, National League of American Pen Women (president, Michigan branch and Detroit chapter, 1958), Theta Upsilon, Alpha Lambda Delta. *Awards, honors:* Avery Hopwood award for drama, 1942, from the University of Michigan; National League of American Pen Women, third place for juveniles, 1964.

WRITINGS: Trails of the French Explorers, Naylor, 1956; *Hygiene for College Freshman,* Edwards, 1963; *Sports and Ballroom Dancing for College Freshman,* Edwards, 1963; *White Beaver,* 1974.

Small books for children, in verse: *Wiggly Nell,* 1949, *Calm and Cool was Penguin Row, a Ferry-Boat I'd Like to Ride,* 1953, *Seven Frisky Lambs,* 1954, *Pudgie Pat's Pets,* 1958, *Freddie the Froggie,* 1959, *Mister Roberto R. Robot,* 1960 (all published by Edwards).

MARION STEPHANY SCANLON

Children's books in prose: *Three Little Clouds,* Denison, 1959; *Little Johnnie Trout,* Denison, 1962.

WORK IN PROGRESS: An historical novel, *Dr. Samuel Todd.*

SIDELIGHTS: "My first ambition had been to become a medical doctor. After completing half of the required courses a lack of funds made me change my first ambition. Having always had a yen for writing several courses in creative writing helped me decide the contents and age levels that would be best for me.

"Being a lover of history and true facts I traveled to the places that would be involved in my stories. I also did research in the libraries of State Historical Societies.

"Having always enjoyed writing in light verse I decided to experiment in writing some stories for young children. I found that children seemed to enjoy them. All of the experimenting had been preceded by such courses as 'Literature for Children.' I also read most of the past and present accepted good stories for children.

"I seem to cater to home situations of a boy or girl or animal, who craves adventures, and after finding it, rediscovers the joys of home and togetherness. I do not believe in talking down to children. An increase in vocabulary should always be present for every age level. I studied the vocabularies for each age level.

"Last but not least there must be enthusiasm for what one is doing. I have enjoyed every inch of the way the struggles as well as a bit of success."

SCOTT, Cora Annett (Pipitone)   1931-
(Cora Annett)

PERSONAL: Born April 15, 1931, in Boston, Mass.; daughter of Salvatore (a tile contractor) and Concettina (Pepi) Pipitone; divorced; children: Clifford Duane Scott. *Education:* Boston University, B.A., 1968; University of Massachusetts, M.S., 1973, Ph.D., 1974. *Home:* 49 Constitution Way, Methuen, Mass. 01844.

CAREER: Clinical psychologist at a community mental health center; author of children's books. *Member:* Phi Beta Kappa, Americal Psychological Association, Association for Research and Enlightenment.

WRITINGS—Under name Cora Annett: *The Dog Who Thought He Was a Boy,* Houghton, 1965; *Homerhenry,* Addison-Wesley, 1970; *When the Porcupine Moved In,* Watts, 1971; *How the Witch Got Alf,* Watts, 1975.

SIDELIGHTS: "I began writing at the age of eight, and my first undertaking was a mystery novel, of which I completed three chapters. Like many people, I daydreamed a lot, but unlike most people, I never daydreamed about myself. I always had a continually running serial in my head about beautiful, improbable people. I read constantly, from early grade school on, and remember when I was quite young de-

They brought him inside (for he was shivering with wet and cold) where the Old Man sat him in the rocking chair and covered him with a blanket while the Old Woman made him hot chocolate. ■ (From *How the Witch Got Alf* by Cora Annett. Illustrated by Steven Kellogg.)

ploring the dearth of good humorous stories. Perhaps this is one reason why, when I grew up, I tried to write a few.

"My interest in psychology and fascination with the human mind have, however, led me away from writing children's books. I am now a psychotherapist, and my avocational interests lie in the areas of meditation, higher states of consciousness and psychic phenomena."

SHIRREFFS, Gordon D(onald)   1914-
(Gordon Donalds, Jackson Flynn, Stewart Gordon)

PERSONAL: Born January 15, 1914, in Chicago, Ill.; son of George and Rose (Warden) Shirreffs; married Alice Johanna Gutwein, February 8, 1941; children: Carole Alice, Brian Allen. *Education:* Northwestern University, student, 1946-49; California State University at Northridge, B.A., 1967,

CORA ANNETT SCOTT

GORDON D. SHIRREFFS

M.A., 1973. *Home and office:* 17427 San Jose St., Granada Hills, Calif. 91344. *Agent:* Donald MacCampbell, Inc., 12 East 41st St., New York, N.Y. 10017.

CAREER: Union Tank Car Co., Chicago, Ill., clerk, 1935-40, 1946; Brown & Bigelow, Chicago, Ill., salesman, 1946-47; Shirreffs Gadgets and Toys, Chicago, Ill., owner, 1948-52; professional writer, 1952—. *Military service:* U.S. Army, 1940-45, 1948; became captain. *Member:* Veterans of Foreign Wars, National Rifle Association, Western Writers of America. *Awards, honors:* Commonwealth Club of California Silver Medal Award for *The Gray Sea Raiders,* 1962.

WRITINGS: Rio Bravo, Gold Medal Books, 1956; *Code of the Gun,* Crest Books, 1956; (under pseudonym Gordon Donalds) *Arizona Justice,* Avalon, 1956; *Range Rebel,* Pyramid Books, 1956; *Fort Vengeance,* Popular Library, 1957; (under pseudonym Stewart Gordon) *Gunswift,* Avalon, 1957; *Bugles on the Prairie,* Gold Medal Books, 1957; *Massacre Creek,* Popular Library, 1957; *Son of the Thunder People,* Westminster, 1957; (under pseudonym Gordon Donalds) *Top Gun,* Avalon, 1957; *Shadow Valley,* Popular Library, 1958; *Ambush on the Mesa,* Gold Medal Books, 1958; *Swiftwagon,* Westminster, 1958; *Last Train from Gun Hill,* Signet Books, 1958; *The Brave Rifles,* Gold Medal Books, 1959; *The Lonely Gun,* Avon, 1959; *Roanoke Raiders,* Westminster, 1959; *Fort Suicide,* Avon, 1959; *Trail's End,* Avalon, 1959; *Shadow of a Gunman,* Ace Books, 1959; *Renegade Lawman,* Avon, 1959.

Apache Butte, Ace Books, 1960; *They Met Danger,* Whitman, 1960; *The Mosquito Fleet,* Chilton, 1961; *The Rebel Trumpet,* Westminster, 1961; *The Proud Gun,* Avon, 1961;

Hangin' Pards, Ace Books, 1961; *Ride a Lone Trail,* Ace Books, 1961; *The Gray Sea Raiders,* Chilton, 1961; *Powder Boy of the Monitor* (Child Study Association book list), Westminster, 1961; *The Valiant Bugles,* Signet Books, 1962; *Tumbleweed Trigger,* Ace Books, 1962; *The Haunted Treasure of the Espectros,* Chilton, 1962; *Voice of the Gun,* Ace Books, 1962; *Rio Desperado,* Ace Books, 1962; *Action Front!,* Westminster, 1962; *The Border Guidon,* Signet Books, 1962; *Mystery of Lost Canyon,* Chilton, 1963; *Slaughter at Broken Bow,* Avon, 1963; *The Cold Seas Beyond,* Westminster, 1963; *The Secret of the Spanish Desert,* Chilton, 1964; *Quicktrigger,* Ace Books, 1964; *Too Tough to Die,* Avon, 1964; *The Nevada Gun,* World Distributors, 1964; *The Hostile Beaches,* Westminster, 1964; *The Hidden Rider of Dark Mountain,* Ace Books, 1964; *Blood Justice,* Signet Books, 1964; *Gunslingers Three,* World Distributors, 1964; *Judas Gun,* Gold Medal Books, 1964; *Last Man Alive,* Avon, 1964; *Now He Is Legend,* Gold Medal Books, 1965; *The Lone Rifle,* Signet Books, 1965; *The Enemy Seas,* Westminster, 1965; *Barranca,* Signet Books, 1965; *The Bolo Battalion,* Westminster, 1966; *Torpedoes Away!,* Westminster, 1967; *Southwest Drifter,* Gold Medal Books, 1967; *The Mystery of the Lost Cliffdwelling,* Prentice-Hall, 1968; *Five Graves to Boothill,* Avon, 1968; *The Godless Breed,* Gold Medal Books, 1968; *The Killer Sea,* Westminster, 1968; *Showdown in Sonora,* Gold Medal Books, 1969.

Jack of Spades, Dell, 1970; *The Manhunter,* Gold Medal Books, 1970; *Brasada,* Dell, 1972; *Bowman's Kid,* Gold Medal Books, 1973; *Renegade's Trail,* Gold Medal Books, 1974; (under pseudonym Jackson Flynn) *Shootout,* Award Books, 1974; *Apache Hunter,* Gold Medal Books, 1975.

Contributor of over 150 short stories and novelettes to periodicals.

SIDELIGHTS: "I have always had an interest in history and reactions of people to historical circumstances. I had a father who was a skilled story-teller and was self-educated in literature. Perhaps the Scot's blood in me has contributed to the story telling ability, as I feel that the Scots and Irish are the best tellers of tales. I was raised on stories of the Highlanders and the Irish gallow-glasses and the Scots and Irish mercenaries who fought all over Europe for any king or nation who would hire them as professionals. Also *Kidnapped, Robinson Crusoe, The Red Badge of Courage,* Kipling's great yarns, Joseph Altsheler's great Civil War stories, *Battles and Leaders of the Civil War,* and many other such books developed my interest in history and writing.

"I think also the background in my earlier life has contributed a great deal to my writing—working as a deck hand on the Great Lakes, as an itinerant farm hand in Minnesota, serving in the army as an artilleryman throughout the Aleutian Campaign, and later serving as a Ship's Transportation Officer in the Mediterranean. My latter service as an assistant historian compiling, researching and editing military history also helped further my interest in writing.

"I was fortunate enough right after WW II to study under several fine professors at Medill School of Journalism, Northwestern University, in particular Frederic Nelson Litten for the short story and the novel, and Elmo Scott Watson for non-fiction writing. My lifelong interest in history, war, adventure, the sea and its lore, antique weapons and uniforms, lost treasures and other such fields have helped my writing immeasurably. I have files of research

■ (From the movie "Oregon Passage," starring John Ericson and Lola Albright. Copyright 1958 by Allied Artists Pictures Corp.)

gathered on many subjects for the past thirty years, books relative to these subjects, and the added advantage of actually visiting many of the places about which I write, has often set the scenes for some of my books. If I write about hunting buffalo, I have actually fired buffalo hunting rifles from my own collection. If I write about hunting a lost treasure, I have also hunted lost treasures . . . and so on.

"My books are intended for anyone interested in the subjects about which I write. I have always tried to avoid stereotyped styles of writing. My Westerns are usually called 'off the trail', which probably means they do not follow the standard fight for the waterhole, cowboy against rustler or Indian, or other standard and worn-out formats for the Western. I have developed, after fifty published Western novels a man who hunts men, a true professional, dedicated to his work, who leavens humanism into his life and work, but always accomplishes that which he sets out to do—find a man, or men—the most dangerous business in the world.

"I never read any other writer's Westerns and do not pattern any of my books on the style of another writer. I think each writer has his own unique way of presenting his material, doing his research and fashioning his book. I start out with what is professionally called 'a germinal idea', usually garnered from history or biography, and develop it from there,

but only in my mind. I do not touch the typewriter until the story, at least the major part of it is clear in my mind, as well as the major characters. I add the minor characters and scenes as I go along, and as I need them. I rarely write a synopsis and *never* write character sketches: I draw on my characters from people I have known in my life, for the most part, or a facsimile of some historical character. I rarely rewrite any material. Usually the first written draft is sufficient. I have sold virtually everything I have ever written, a total of about four and a half million words at the last count. For a period of ten years I sold one novel almost every two months on the average, and yet there are other writers who do *more* than that. . . . ???

"After twenty years of professional writing, I have slowed down in my production, for a number of reasons—the markets are much tighter than they have been for years and everything, at least in the Western field must be very, very good; my royalties have built up my annual income to a point where I can take more time to write slower; I have been busy in adapting my material to films in some cases, which sometimes necessitates working in Europe, Italy in particular, and also in Mexico.

"I am asked (invariably), by people I meet, one standard question; it *never* varies—'Where do you get your ideas?'

The ideas are everywhere, easily found, but the trick is to *find* them, and further—the ability to *see* a story situation in perhaps one single item, a chance remark, an incident in one's life, and then take it from there to build up forty to sixty thousand published words. It's a developed sense, perhaps a gift. *Quien sabe?* Coupled with a lively imagination, a great deal of knowledge of humans (psychology), the discipline of writing; the ability to work alone and like it, these all add up to being a writer, at least a 'selling' writer.''

Western books have been published in Norway, Sweden, Denmark, Finland, Germany, France, Italy, Spain, England, Canada, and Australia. *Massacre Creek* was filmed as "Galvanized Yankee" for "Playhouse 90" (television), *Rio Bravo* as "Oregon Passage" by Allied Artists, *Silent Reckoning* as "The Lonesome Trail" by Lippert Productions, *Judas Gun,* filmed in Italy as "The Trail to Hell."

HOBBIES AND OTHER INTERESTS: Arms collecting, model making, marksmanship (pistol, rifle, and bow), fishing, hunting, travel, Southwest legends, and sea lore.

SIMON, Shirley (Schwartz)   1921-

PERSONAL: Born March 21, 1921, in Cleveland, Ohio; daughter of Bernard H. (a salesman) and Sylvia (Silverman) Schwartz; married Edgar H. Simon (an interior designer), March 1, 1942; children: Allen Harold, Ruth Esther. *Education:* Spencerian Business College, student, 1938-39; Cleveland College, student, 1939-40; Goddard College, B.A., 1973. *Religion:* Jewish. *Home:* 3630 Cedarbrook Rd., Cleveland, Ohio. *Agent:* McIntosh & Otis, Inc., 18 East

SHIRLEY SIMON

41st St., New York, N.Y. 10017. *Office:* Ed Simon Interiors, 27149 Chagrin Blvd., Cleveland, Ohio.

CAREER: Author of junior novels and classroom materials, 1956—. Cleveland Book Fair, Cleveland Public Library, lecturer, 1963-68; Case Western Reserve University (Cleveland College), lecturer, instructor, 1965-67; Dayton Book Fair, lecturer, 1968; Mount Union College, Alliance, Ohio, workshop in Creative Writing, 1968, 1972; John Carroll University, University College of Continuing Education, lecturer, instructor, 1969—; Ohio University, instructor, 1972-75; Glen Oak School (independent high school for girls), Gates Mills, Ohio, instructor, 1973—. *Awards, honors:* Cousins at Camm Corners selected for list of one hundred outstanding 1963 books for young readers by the *New York Times.*

WRITINGS: Molly's Cottage, Lothrop, 1959; *Molly and the Rooftop Mystery,* Lothrop, 1961; *Cousins at Camm Corners* (Calling All Girls Book Club selection), Lothrop, 1963; *Best Friend,* Lothrop, 1964; *Libby's Stepfamily,* Lothrop, 1966; (with Beat Stadtler) *Once Upon a Jewish Holiday,* Ktav, 1966. Contributor of stories, serials, and plays to national juvenile and teachers' publications, including *Jack and Jill, Calling All Girls, Child Life, Plays, Grade Teacher,* and *Instructor.*

Plays and stories included in the following: Sylvia Kamerman, editor, *Children's Plays from Favorite Stories,* Plays, Inc., 1959; Sylvia Kamerman, editor, *Fifty Plays for Junior Actors,* Plays, Inc., 1966; P. R. Wise, *Patterns of English: A Book of Pattern Practices for Chinese Students* (used in Chinese universities in Hong Kong and Singapore); Leo Fay, Paul S. Anderson, *The Young America Basic Reading Program, Level 12* (fifth grade reader), Lyons & Carnahan, 1972; *Reading Laboratory Inc.* (Philippine Edition), Science Research Associates, Inc.

WORK IN PROGRESS: A junior novel set in the 1940's, dealing with relationships between women of all ages.

SIDELIGHTS: "I have always loved children's stories. My mother read to me endlessly. At age eight I was writing (bad) poetry. My mother gathered up some of my 'poems' and shipped them off to the editor of the local newspaper, along with a letter submitting them for publication. The editor returned my poems with a very kind letter. He explained that newspapers seldom buy poetry, almost never from little girls. He picked out the least bad poem and declared that to be his favorite of the group. He advised me to keep on writing—and to read poetry and novels and stories. I did all of these. About thirty years later I began to sell what I wrote.

"As I grew into adulthood I never lost my passion for children's books. I still read them. All of my novels are about my own childhood—or that of my children, friends' children or children's friends. I receive many letters from readers all over the country. Most of them ask whether Marcy (or Molly or Jenny) is a real person. The answer is 'Not really,' but many of the things that happen in my books happened to our family or to our friends or neighbors. *Best Friend* is based on my own experiences and feelings when I was Jenny's age. I had a friend very much like Dot, who was delightful and fickle, and I learned that I needed more than one friend.

Aunt Helen turned toward the stairs, and Marcy suddenly ran and flung her arms around her aunt. "I . . . I hope everything will be all right," Marcy cried.
■ (From *Cousins at Camm Corners* by Shirley Simon. Illustrated by Reisie Lonette.)

"When my husband was a boy about Sandy's age, he and his friends built a raft like the one in *Cousins at Camm Corners,* and it did not stay afloat, either. We once saw a talking crow at school (just like the crow in *Cousins*) that kept saying, 'What is Charles going outside for?' Imogene is exactly like a poodle that belonged to one of our neighbors, and a boy who lived next door had a catfish like Louis Cats. We even listened to the same records that Molly enjoyed.

"One of the greatest joys of writing . . . for me . . . is receiving the letters from girls who read my books. Readers send snapshots, tell me about themselves and their families and friends. The largest number of letters are about *Best Friend.* I can't tell you how many girls have written to say they have had the same experience that Jenny had and experienced the same pain and frustration that Jenny felt.

"My interest in children's literature has led me into two second careers—writing and adapting material for classroom use, designing course material, and most recently, teaching a course in children's literature at an independent high school for girls.

"I am particularly interested in the ways in which books for very young children depict girls and women, and I enjoy helping my students to understand the ways in which this early conditioning affects their values and expectations as young women."

HOBBIES AND OTHER INTERESTS: "When I am not working my husband and I enjoy all kinds of travel—from trailering in New England to visits to London and Tel Aviv. We enjoy visiting our son and daughter, who live in Boston and New York respectively. We love music, especially folk music and Dixieland Jazz."

SISSON, Rosemary Anne 1923-

PERSONAL: Surname is pronounced to rhyme with "listen"; born October 13, 1923, in London, England; daughter of Charles Jasper (a professor) and Vera (Ginn) Sisson. *Education:* University College, London, B.A. (honors), 1946; Cambridge University, M.Lit., 1948. *Politics:* Conservative. *Religion:* Church of England. *Agent:* Andrew Mann, Ltd., 32 Wigmore St., London W.1, England.

CAREER: University of Wisconsin, Madison, instructor in English, 1949-50; University College, University of London, London, England, assistant lecturer in American literature, 1950-54; University of Birmingham, Birmingham, England, assistant lecturer in English, 1954-55. *Stratford-upon-Avon Herald,* drama critic, 1955-57. Coventry Cathedral Drama Council, member. *Military service:* Royal Observer Corps, 1943-45. *Member:* Writers Guild of Great Britain, Writers Guild of America, Dramatists' Club. *Awards, honors:* Repertory Players Award, 1964, for "The Royal Captivity."

ROSEMARY ANNE SISSON

■ (From the movie "Ride a Wild Pony," copyright © Walt Disney Productions.)

WRITINGS—Children's books: *The Adventures of Ambrose*, Harrap, 1951, Dutton, 1952; *The Impractical Chimney-Sweep*, Macmillan, 1956, F. Watts, 1957; *The Isle of Dogs*, Macmillan, 1959; *The Young Shakespeare*, Parrish, 1959; *The Young Jane Austen*, Parrish, 1962; *The Young Shaftesbury*, Parrish, 1964; *The Exciseman*, R. Hale, 1973; *The Killer of Horseman's Flats*, R. Hale, 1973; *The Stratford Story*, W. H. Allen, 1975; *Escape from the Dark*, W. H. Allen, 1976 (published in America as *The Littlest Horse Thieves*, Pocket Books, 1976).

Plays: *The Queen and the Welshman* (acting edition), Samuel French, 1958; *Fear Came to Supper* (acting edition), Samuel French, 1959. Other plays produced: "The Splendid Outcasts"; "Home and the Heart"; "The Royal Captivity"; "Bitter Sanctuary"; (with Robert Morley) "A Ghost on Tiptoe."

Screenplays: *Anstice*; *Ride a Wild Pony* (from the novel *A Sporting Proposition* by James Aldridge), Walt Disney Productions; *Pit Ponies*, Walt Disney Productions.

Television plays: "The Vagrant Heart"; "The Man from Brooklyn"; (adapted from the novel by Meredith) "The Ordeal of Richard Feverel"; (adapted from the novel by Eliot) "The Mill on the Floss"; "Catherine of Aragon" ("Six Wives of Henry VIII" series); "The Marriage Game" ("Elizabeth R." series); "Beyond Our Means"; "Let's Marry Liz." Plays anthologized in *Plays of the Year*, Flek Books, 1958, 1959, and in "Heritage of Literature" series, Longmans Green, 1962.

Script writer of episodes in British Broadcasting Corp. television series, "Compact," "Upstairs, Downstairs," "The Duchess of Duke Street," and "Within These Walls." Contributor of poetry and short stories to magazines, and articles to *Sunday Times*.

WORK IN PROGRESS: Animation film for Walt Disney; novel trilogy, *The Coming of the Tudors*.

SIDELIGHTS: "I was born in London, the second daughter of the Shakespearean scholar, the late Professor C. J. Sisson. An early ambition to go on the stage being frustrated by the war, I lectured in Universities in the United States and England, until the production of my first play, *The Queen and the Welshman* on the fringe of the Edinburgh Festival in 1957. Since then, I have had six more plays

212   **Something about the Author**

William went by himself up Welcombe Hill. He thought how strange it was that while all the rest of them would grow up and go out into the world, and become, in a way, different people, Nan would never change. ■ (From *The Young Shakespeare* by Rosemary Anne Sisson. Illustrated by Denise Brown.)

produced on the stage, and have written extensively for television, including plays for the B.B.C.'s *The Six Wives of Henry VIII* and *Elizabeth R.* and for "Upstairs, Downstairs" on London Weekend. My first two novels, *The Exiseman* and a Western novel, *The Killer of Horseman's Flats,* were published in 1973, and I have also written several films, including two for Walt Disney.

"I live in a late Victorian house in London which is rapidly falling victim to a passion for souvenirs and a total inability to throw anything away. Western riding boots jostle piles of theatre programmes, and a bone once owned by a beloved dog nestles behind a group of production photographs. I love riding, gardening, cooking and housework—but very rarely have time for any of them."

SMITH, Vian (Crocker) 1919-1969

PERSONAL: Born February 2, 1919, in Totnes, Devon, England; son of Albert George Smith (a carpenter) and Mary Laura (Crocker) Smith; married Susan Spark, Aug. 6, 1942; children: Robert, Stroma, Mark, Penelope, Andrew. *Education:* Attended King Edward VI Grammar School, Totnes, Devon. *Politics:* "No orthodox party—generally radical." *Religion:* Protestant. *Home:* Netherton Farmhouse, Berry Pomeroy, Totnes, Devon, England. *Agent:* Winant Towers of Clifford's Inn, London, England; Monica McCall, 667 Madison Ave., New York, N.Y. 10021.

CAREER: British army, 1939-46; traveled widely through England, Ireland, and northern France; worked as freelance journalist until 1950; feature and news editor of South Devon newspapers until 1963, when he quit journalism for full-time writing.

WRITINGS: Song of the Unsung, Hodder & Stoughton, 1945; *Candles to the Dawn,* Hodder & Stoughton, 1946; *Hungry Waters,* Hodder & Stoughton, 1947; *Hand of the Wind,* Hodder & Stoughton, 1948; *Holiday for Laughter,* Hodder & Stoughton, 1948; *So Many Worlds,* Hodder &

Stoughton, 1949; *Press Gang,* P. Davies, 1961; *Question Mark,* P. Davies, 1961 (under title *Pride of Moor,* Doubleday, 1962 [Literary Guild selection]); *Genesis Down,* P. Davies, 1962, Doubleday, 1963; *Green Heart* (Literary Guild selection), Doubleday, 1964; *Martin Rides the Moor* (novel for children), Constable, 1964, Doubleday, 1965; *The First Thunder,* Doubleday, 1965, P. Davies, 1966; *The Horses of Petrock* (novel for adolescents), Constable, 1965; *A Second Chance,* Doubleday, 1966; *Tall and Proud* (formerly *King Sam,* novel for children), Doubleday, 1966, P. Davies, 1966, Archway, 1968; *Portrait of Dartmoor* (nonfiction), Robert Hale, 1966, revised 1972, 1976; *Tall and Proud* (juvenile), Doubleday, 1966; *A Horse Called Freddie* (nonfiction), Stanley Paul, 1967; *Come Down the Mountain* (juvenile), Constable, 1967, Doubleday, 1967; *The Lord Mayor's Show* (juvenile), Longman's, 1968; *Point to Point* (nonfiction), Stanley Paul, 1968; *The Wind Blows Free* (adult), Doubleday, 1968, P. Davies, 1968; *The Grand National* (non-fiction), Stanley Paul, 1968, A. S. Barnes, 1969; *Moon in the River* (juvenile), Longman's, 1969; *The Minstrel Boy* (adult), Doubleday, 1970, P. Davies, 1970; *Parade of Horses* (juvenile), Longman's, 1970 (under title *Horses in the Green Valley,* Doubleday, 1971).

Radio plays: "Inherit the Earth," "Come Down the Mountain," "The Boy Who Made It," "When Sam was King," "The White Stallion," "Green Heart," "Three 'O' Clock on the Sixteenth," "Sunday Morning on the Hill" (all on B.B.C., London).

Television plays: "Giants on Saturday," B.B.C., London; "The First Thunder," I.T.V., Bristol.

VIAN SMITH

They had made progress. People in towns and cities were expressing disgust of all blood sports. ■ (From *Martin Rides the Moor* by Vian Smith. Illustrated by Ray Houlihan.)

SIDELIGHTS: His wife, Susan Vian Smith wrote: "When he left the South Devon newspaper, he came to live at Netherton where he realised his life's ambition, to keep horses. He held a jockey club permit to train steeple chasers; his horses ran at many English courses and were ridden by his son Mark wearing the Vian Smith colours; scarlet with a huge yellow question mark. He wrote non-fiction about horses from personal knowledge and experience: *Point to Point, The Grand National, A Horse Called Freddie,* and non-fiction about his beloved Dartmoor—*Portrait of Dartmoor.*

"Vian Smith was a dynamic personality and a perfectionist, he rewrote many of his works as many as nine times; he said that 'the skill lay in knowing what to cut out.' He was a real family man, passionately fond of both family and horses, yet he would stand no nonsense. The dogs and cats followed him everywhere. He had a great sense of humour and an even greater sense of fun. On December 9, 1969 Vian Smith died very suddenly of a pulmonary thrombosis, he literally dropped dead outside his stables. He was fifty. A sad loss to all who knew him and to literature."

Boston University is collecting his manuscripts and correspondence.

HOBBIES AND OTHER INTERESTS: The nineteenth century, especially the middle years, horses, steeplechase racing and sport of all kinds.

SOTOMAYOR, Antonio   1902-

PERSONAL: Born May 13, 1902, in Chulumani, Bolivia; son of Juan and Carmen (Meza) Sotomayor; married Grace Andrews, May 13, 1926. *Education:* Educated at School of Fine Arts, La Paz, Bolivia, and Hopkins Institute, San Francisco, Calif. *Home and studio:* 3 LeRoy Pl., San Francisco, Calif. 94109.

CAREER: San Franciscan Magazine, art director, 1926-1932; Palace Hotel, San Francisco, Calif., art consultant, 1928-1955; Mills College, artist in residence, 1942, 1943; California School of Fine Arts, instructor, 1946-1950; San Francisco Art Commission, commissioner, 1948-1955, 1967-1975. *Exhibitions:* Exhibited in numerous one-man shows in North and South America and Europe; mural paintings; magazine and newspaper drawings and caricatures. *Member:* Royal Society of Arts, London, England; Bohemian Club, San Francisco, Calif.; Family Club, San Francisco, Calif. *Awards, honors:* First prize, National Exposition of Painting, 1921.

WRITINGS: Khasa Goes to the Fiesta, Doubleday, 1967; *Balloons: The First Two Hundred Years,* Putnam, 1972. Contributor to *Encyclopedia Americana* and *Arts and Architecture* (magazine).

Illustrator: Leslie B. Simpson, *Indian Tales from Guatemala,* Scribner, 1936; Victor von Hagen, *Quetzal Quest,*

Balloon ascensions became so popular that they were the central attractions at all important fairs and festivals throughout Europe. Circus and carnival showmen gave spectacular performances from them. ■ (From *Balloons: The First Two Hundred Years* by Antonio Sotomayor. Illustrated by the author.)

Harcourt, 1939; Carl O. Sauer, *Man in Nature,* Scribner, 1939; Victor von Hagen, *Treasure of the Tortoise Islands,* Harcourt, 1940; Robert O'Brien, *This is San Francisco,* McGraw, 1948; Robert O'Brien, *California Called Them,* McGraw, 1951; Quail Hawkins, *Best Birthday,* Doubleday, 1954; Arturo Torres Rioscco, *Relatos Chilenos,* Harper, 1956; Stanton Delaplane, *Stan Delaplane's Mexico,* Chronicle Books, 1976.

SIDELIGHTS: "I was born in South America, in a small town in one of those deep, hot valleys of the Bolivian Andes called 'Yungas.' The town had an Aymara Indian name—Chulumani, which means 'cougar drinking water.' It had been, before the Spanish Conquest, an outpost of the Inca Empire where such things as exotic fruits and feathers were collected from the vast Amazon region for the Incas. The Yungas still supply Bolivia's capital city, La Paz, with tropical products like bananas, oranges, coffee and fragrant jasmine.

"When I was a small boy in Chulumani, I was surrounded with color. On Sundays and holidays, the Indians came in from their farms to dance in the square in front of the church. Groups of them, wearing grotesque masks and costumes of brilliant colors would mimic jungle animals—monkeys and jaguars—while others, in gold-embroidered uniforms, would poke fun at the early Spanish Conquistadores.

"Many of these festivals would be celebrated far into the night; then there were fireworks. I can still vividly recall the dazzling bursts of color of pinwheels and roman candles exploding in the night sky. After one of these fiestas, I would spend the rest of the week making drawings of what I had seen. But best of all, from my point of view, were the special occasions when the townspeople made big, colored, paper balloons. These were twice as tall as a man. They had been inflated by the hot air and smoke from a straw fire, and had started to rise, a small ball of cotton, hung underneath the opening, was soaked in kerosene and ignited to keep the air inside warm so the balloon would stay aloft longer. I was so fascinated with these balloons that my grandmother bought me a tablecover with reproductions of historic balloons printed on it, and I proceeded to copy each of them. These drawings of mine were shown off proudly to all the neighbors.

"When I was about eleven, some of our Indian neighbors asked me to help them with a 'miracle.' They had found an odd-shaped stone in the river. It vaguely resembled the statue of St. Anthony in the church; and they said that since my name was Anthony, and I was always drawing and painting, I could touch up the stone so everyone would recognize it as the saint.

"Books for children, apart from school texts, were virtually non-existent in Chulumani. But storytelling was almost an art. In the evenings, after dinner, the grownups would sit around telling stories. They told tales and fables from mediaeval Spain and Indian myths and legends; and sometimes a more gifted story-teller would weave the Spanish and Indian stories together to make new ones. Occasionally I fell asleep before a story session ended. But I would be up early the next morning making illustrations of the stories as I remembered them.

ANTONIO SOTOMAYOR

"When my family moved to La Paz, there were many changes. Besides the physical adjustment to the very high altitude, there was the visual adjustment to the new landscape, from the warm, lush greens of the tropics to the grays and browns of the barren, high plateau and the majestic, snowcovered mountains all around. Then there was the excitement of the new school. I was determined to do well; but my first assignment was almost a disaster—I got an inkblot on it! Then I remembered the stone and St. Anthony; so I touched up the blot and made it into an illustration of the lesson. The teacher was pleased with it and held it up as an example to the rest of the class.

"In the city there were books and magazines and newspapers. I read them all. I read about politicians and made sketches of them. I began to develop a knack for making caricatures; and by the time I was fifteen, the magazines of La Paz were regularly publishing my caricatures and commentaries.

"Since the age of twenty-two, when I came to the United States, I have had a career as a painter while still doing drawings and caricatures for periodicals. I have illustrated technical works and some textbooks; I have designed sets and costumes for the ballet; but the illustrations I have done for children's books have given me a special pleasure. Remembering the fiestas of my childhood in Bolivia, I decided to share them with other children in a book. *Khasa Goes to the Fiesta* was the result. Because I never got over my enthusiasm for balloons, *Balloons the First Hundred Years* was written.

"Artists have always painted pictures that tell stories. As an artist it is natural for me to visualize a story in pictures. I have developed the illustrations of my stories first, and then gone back to work out the text.

"My wife and I love to travel. We have visited the pre-historic caves of Altamira, in Spain and Lascaux, in France, The Etruscan tombs in Italy, the pyramids of Egypt and Mexico, and the awe-inspiring Inca city of Macchu Picchu. I find the world is full of wonders, and they are all material for stories or paintings."

SPECKING, Inez   1890-196?

PERSONAL: Born April 8, 1890, in Washington, Mo.; daughter of Bernard Joseph and Ann (Comer) Specking. *Education:* University of Colorado, A.B., 1922; Stanford University, M.A., 1923; Washington University, St. Louis, Mo., postgraduate study, 1924-25; Oxford University, research, 1928; St. Louis University, Ph.D., 1931. *Religion:* Catholic. *Home:* 4135 Begg Blvd., St. Louis, Mo.

CAREER: Public school teacher in Dolores, Colo., 1910-14, St. Louis, Mo., 1916-22; Harris Teachers College, St. Louis, Mo., started as instructor, 1925, became professor of English, became chairman of department, 1950. Graduate lecturer on Shakespeare, St. Louis University, for fifteen years; summer professor at University of Toledo for five years. *Member:* Shakespeare Association of America, French Language and Literature Society, Royal Society of Arts (fellow), National Education Association, Modern Language Association of America, American Pen Women, Sigma Tau Delta, St. Louis Newman Club (founder), St. Louis Teachers Club. *Awards, honors:* Litt.D., St. Louis University, 1940.

WRITINGS: Missy, Benziger, 1924; *The Awakening of Edith,* Benziger, 1924; *Mirage,* Benziger, 1925; *Martha Jane,* Benziger, 1925; *Martha Jane at College,* Benziger, 1926; *Boy: The Story of a Real Boy from His First Day at School,* Benzinger, 1928; *What Else Is There?,* Herder, 1929, 2nd edition, Exposition, 1961; *So That's That,* Herder, 1929; *Martha Jane, Sophomore,* Herder, 1929; *It's All Right,* Herder, 1929; (compiler) *Literary Readings in English Prose,* Bruce, 1935; *Go West, Young Lady,* Catholic Literary Guild, 1941; (adapter) Nina Brown Baker, *Simon Bolivar,* Webster Publishing, 1947; *A Shakespeare for Children,* Vantage, 1954; *Boy: The Story of Missy's Brother,* Benziger, 1955.

WORK IN PROGRESS: A novel.

HOBBIES AND OTHER INTERESTS: Travel, riding, reading, and walking.

(Deceased)

SPINK, Reginald (William)   1905-

PERSONAL: Born December 9, 1905, in York, England; son of William and Lillian Annie (Newbold) Spink; married Else Marie Buus, 1932; children: Allan Olaf, Karen Margaret Ann. *Education:* Educated in England. *Home and office:* 6 Deane Way, Eastcote, Ruislip, Middlesex HA4 8SU, England.

CAREER: Self-employed journalist, editor, translator and author of books both for children and adults. *Member:* Society of Authors (London), Translators Association (London). *Awards, honors:* Freedom Medal of King Christian X, Denmark, 1945; Knight's Cross of the Order of the Dannebrog, 1966.

WRITINGS: (With Jens Otto Krag) *England bygger op* (title means "Britain Rebuilds"), Det danske Forlag, 1947; *The Land and People of Denmark* (juvenile), Macmillan, 1953; *Fairy Tales of Denmark* (juvenile), Dutton, 1961; *The Young Hans Andersen* (juvenile), Roy, 1962; *Hans Chris-*

REGINALD SPINK

tian Andersen and His World, Thames & Hudson, 1972; *Hans Christian Andersen: The Man and His Work,* Hoest, 1972.

Translator: Carl Nielsen, *My Childhood,* Hutchinson, 1953; Nielsen, *Living Music,* Hutchinson, 1953; Palle Lauring, *The Roman,* Museum Press; 1956; Anton Bruun and others, *The Galathea Deep Sea Expedition,* Allen & Unwin, 1956; Lauring, *Land of the Tollund Man,* Lutterworth, 1957; Ludvig Holberg, *Three Comedies,* Theatre Arts, 1957; Poul Borchsenius, *Behind the Wall,* Simon & Schuster, 1957; Hans Christian Andersen, *Fairy Tales,* Dutton, 1958; Frank Wenzel, *The Buzzard,* Allen & Unwin, 1959.

Andersen, *Fairy Tales and Stories,* Dutton, 1960; Rolf Blomberg, *Chavante,* Allen & Unwin, 1960; Bengt Danielsson, *Terry in the South Seas* (juvenile), Allen & Unwin, 1960; Danielsson, *Terry in Australia* (juvenile), Allen & Unwin, 1961; Joergen Bisch, *Ulu: The World's End,* Dutton, 1961; Borchsenius, *And It Was Morning,* Simon & Schuster, 1962; Bisch, *Behind the Veil of Arabia,* Dutton, 1962; Bisch, *Mongolia: Unknown Land,* Dutton, 1963; Einar Rud, *Vasari's Life and Lives,* Thames & Hudson, 1963; Danielsson, *Gauguin in the South Seas,* Doubleday, 1965; Knud Soenderby, *The Blue Flashes,* Danish Ministry of Foreign Affairs, 1966; Poul Abrahamsen, *Royal Wedding,* Danish Ministry of Foreign Affairs, 1967.

Translator or editor of several editions of *Denmark: An Official Handbook,* Danish Ministry of Foreign Affairs, 1946—. Scandinavian correspondent for *New Leader,* 1935-39, 1945-50.

"Just look in the glass, Gerda!" he said. And when she did each snowflake grew much bigger and looked like a beautiful flower or a ten-sided star. It was lovely to look at. ■ (From *Hans Andersen's Fairy Tales* translated by Reginald Spink. Illustrated by Hans Baumhauer.)

Contributor to American, British, Canadian, Australian, New Zealand, and Danish journals. Translator and English text editor of *Danish Foreign Office Journal* (now *Danish Journal*), 1946—; editor of *Denmark: A Quarterly Review of Anglo-Danish Relations*, 1961-74.

SIDELIGHTS: "There were no books in my childhood home and very few in the library box of my elementary school, but I read them all eagerly on Friday afternoons when teacher was making up the register. I joined the local public library and was soon hardly ever without a book under my arm, except when playing games, which I also went in for. I can remember once being told to 'get that book out of your hand; you'll read your eyeballs out!' However, my optician told me recently that my eyesight is better than average for my age. As a teenager, too, I started taking literary journals, got commendations and quotations in one of them, and my first check, for the week's best letter (about a now rather forgotten English poet and dramatist), from another.

"I tried my hand at various literary compositions then, but it was not until years later that I turned again to authorship,

through journalism and translating. I have translated mainly from Danish, which is the foreign language I know best (and can speak fluently). I lived for some years in Denmark and my wife is Danish. Our children both speak the language. I have also translated from Swedish and Norwegian, and I read books in these three languages for British publishers, in order to report on their possibilities in English translation. I am fluent in German and can make my way in several other languages.

"Perhaps all this linguistic effort has diverted me from my original intention to write more myself. During the Second World War, I worked mainly in London as a senior member of the Danish section Special Operation Executive (SOE), the British sister organization of the American OSS, and during the latter part of the war, when our respective sections were integrated, had an American secretary."

STREET, Julia Montgomery 1898-

PERSONAL: Born January 19, 1898, in Concord, N.C.; daughter of Samuel Lewis (a physician) and Elizabeth (Norris) Montgomery; married Claudius A. Street (a pediatrician), September 13, 1924; children: Carol Street McMillan, Claudius A., Jr. *Education:* Women's College of the University of North Carolina, A.B., 1923. *Religion:* Methodist. *Home:* 545 Oaklawn Ave., Winston-Salem, N.C.

CAREER: Edgecomb County (N.C.) schools, teacher, 1917-18; Woman's College of the University of North Carolina, Greensboro, instructor of primary teachers, 1920; North Carolina Children's Home, Greensboro, N.C., field worker, 1921-23; Winston-Salem (N.C.) schools, primary

JULIA MONTGOMERY STREET

teacher, 1923-24. Script writer and script-writing teacher, WSJS Radio Council, Winston-Salem, N.C., 1942-45; consultant on North Carolina history, for radio series for fourth grades, 1970-76. *Member:* American Association of University Women, North Carolina Writer's Conference (secretary, 1960-62), Alumnae Association of Woman's College of the University of North Carolina (vice-president, 1935), North Carolina Folklore Society, North Carolina Literary and Historical Association, Forsyth-Stores Medical Auxiliary, American Medical Association Medical Auxiliary. *Awards, honors:* American Association of University Women award for juvenile fiction for *Fiddler's Fancy,* 1956; American Association of University Women awards for *Dulcie's Whale,* 1963, and *North Carolina Parade,* 1966.

WRITINGS—Books for young readers: *Fiddler's Fancy,* Follett, 1955; *Moccasin Tracks,* Dodd, 1958; *Candle Love Feast,* Coward, 1959; *Drover's Gold,* Dodd, 1961; *Dulcie's Whale,* Bobbs, 1963; (with Richard Walser) *North Carolina Parade,* University of North Carolina Press, 1966; *Judacalla's Handprint,* Hogan, 1976. More than one hundred radio scripts for WSJS Radio Council; contributor of plays to *Plays Magazine,* historical puppet plays for the Junior League, articles on welfare and baby care to numerous magazines, articles on North Carolina to *State Magazine* and on North Carolina history to *Raleigh News and Observer* and *North Carolina Folklore Magazine.*

WORK IN PROGRESS: Songs in the Wilderness, a Moravian story; *Armour of Light,* a biographical novel for adults.

SIDELIGHTS: "Since my father died when I was a baby, I grew up in the household of my mother's father, surrounded by unmarried aunts, uncles and servants, in the little town of Apex, North Carolina. A small southern town is a good place to grow up, with its friendliness, hospitality, and the interests of its inhabitants. I fished in the millpond, picked blackberries, chased wild rabbits, had lots of pets, and with my grandfather, rode over the farms. But one child in a house full of grown-ups is necessarily lonely.

"I started reading when I was five, and devoured everything printed I could get my hands on, suitable for my age, or not. Reading has always been my refuge, joy and delight. In my grandfather's front yard were two summerhouses—I believe they are called gazebos, now—one of which I claimed as mine; and woe to anyone who invaded my sanctum and touched my pencils, paper, paints and books. I scribbled long before I could write, and painted and drew incessantly.

"Another fascinating occupation of my childhood was that of sitting in 'my' tree and watching the trains go by on the railroad that ran in front of our house. I counted the cars on the freight trains and marveled at the far-away place names painted on their sides; and, in my imagination, traveled on the passenger trains to who knows where. I was adventuresome, in my mind.

"One memorable day a small train-transported circus unloaded near our house, and from my tree, I got to see all its exotic wonders at first hand. I was enthralled with the wild animals, and greatly astonished at the long eyelashes of the giraffe. None of my thirteen cats had eyelashes.

"At times, I lived with my adored mother in Raleigh, N.C., and those were halcyon days. During one period I saw Halley's Comet streak across the dawn sky—an awesome and unforgettable experience. And I saw Teddy Roosevelt, then President, ride down our street in an open carriage, high silk hat in hand, bowing right and left, on his way to our State Fair.

"My mother loved pets, as I did, and we had dogs, cats, guinea pigs, an alligator, bantam chickens, white mice, and once, for a wonderful two days, a cuddly baby lion cub. But alas! The city would not allow wild beasts, and we had to return Leo to the circus. Another time the 'Dog and Pony Show' abducted our bulldog pup, named *Lucky;* and lucky he was for we got him back when they returned the next year!

"All these experiences and many more furnished seeds for some of my stories.

"In high school I had a marvelous teacher who encouraged me to write and draw; and who proved a rock of consolation when my mother died when I was sixteen. This wonderful woman, now at the age of 91, still writes to me urging me to 'keep on writing.'"

"College was a joy and delight, where I worked on the year book, wrote papers and generally enjoyed the entire experience. I loved teaching school—I taught on both college and primary levels, and doing welfare work; but I loved, even more, being a wife and mother.

"My kind, warm-hearted, compassionate, loving, doctor-husband of forty-three years, always applauded and encouraged me in everything I tried to do; and he was enthusiastically proud of my writing accomplishments. He went on many a long trip of research with me, and helped me gather material for books. While the children were growing up, and he was at his busiest period, I just wrote now and then, newspaper features, magazine articles, stories and poems for Sunday School papers, and radio scripts. It was only when my last child married that I started writing books.

"I have no idea why I started writing for young readers, except that the subjects I chose seemed to fit that category. I find, however, that adults enjoy my books as well as children.

"My first book, *Fiddler's Fancy* is based on a day in the life of my husband's mother. Happily, she lived to read 'her book,' at the age of 92, and loved it.

"My husband was a mountain man, and mountains are my favorite haunts. Over the years we must have traveled every back road and byway in the hills of North Carolina, and from these wanderings have come much of the material that has gone into my books. We also traveled rather widely to other places, but our own mountains drew us more often.

"North Carolina history, which I have studied in depth, is my greatest interest, which accounts for the settings of all my books, which I call historical fiction for young readers.

"I demand of myself absolute authenticity of locales, customs and manners, and I spend much time in research. It takes me a minimum of two years to write a book.

"My husband died suddenly in 1968, and I could not write for a long time; but for the last few years I have spent my time at the typewriter, supervised by my calico cat, Sister. Cats and cat-animals are my favorite creatures. Aside from writing I paint landscapes, work as a hospital volunteer, do church work, hold writing workshops for the Y.W.C.A., read, knit, sew, play my mountain dulcimer—a fascinating instrument—and entertain my friends and nine grandchildren. My life is full, and interesting; and the core of it is my writing.

"One last word: I have never considered writing a 'lonely business' as so many people claim it to be. How can I be lonely when I am surrounded by all those fascinating people I have conjured up, and travel with them to all the places I love best?"

TERRY, Luther L(eonidas)   1911-

PERSONAL: Born September 15, 1911, in Red Level, Ala.; son of James Edward (a physician) and Lula M. (Durham) Terry; married Beryl Janet Reynolds, June 29, 1940; children: Janet Terry Kollock, Luther Leonidas, Jr., Michael D. *Education:* Birmingham-Southern College, B.S., 1931; Tulane University, M.D., 1935. *Office:* College Hall, University of Pennsylvania, Philadelphia, Pa. 19104.

LUTHER L. TERRY

CAREER: Hillman Hospital, Birmingham, Ala., intern, 1935-36; University Hospital, Cleveland, Ohio, assistant resident, 1936-37; City Hospital, Cleveland, Ohio, resident in medicine, 1937-38, intern in pathology and assistant admitting officer, 1938-39; Washington University, St. Louis, Mo., instructor in medicine and research fellow in pneumonia, 1939-40; University of Texas, Medical Branch, Galveston, instructor, 1940-41, assistant professor, 1941-42, associate professor of medicine and preventive medicine, 1942-46 (on military leave, 1943-46); U.S. Public Health Service Hospital, Baltimore, Md., medical service staff, 1942-43, chief of medical services 1943-53; Johns Hopkins University, School of Medicine, Baltimore, Md., part-time instructor, 1944-53, assistant professor of medicine, 1953-61; National Heart Institute, Bethesda, Md., chief of general medicine and experimental therapeutics, 1950-58, assistant director of Institute, 1958-61; U.S. Public Health Service, Washington, D.C., surgeon general, 1961-65; University of Pennsylvania, Philadelphia, vice-president for medical affairs, 1965—, and professor of medicine and of community medicine in School of Medicine. American Board of Internal Medicine, diplomate, 1943. U.S. Strategic Bombing Survey to Japan, member of Medical Division, 1945-46; U.S. Public Health Service, member of committee on civilian health requirements, 1955-58, and of advisory committee on nutrition, Division of Indian Health, 1957-61; World Health Organization, chief of U.S. delegation, 1957-61; National Board of Medical Examiners, member; National Interagency Council on Smoking and Health, chairman, 1967; National Academy of Sciences, chairman of committee on veterinary medicine, research, and education. Member of board of directors of Medic Alert Foundation, and United Health Services, among others; trustee of American Fund for Dental Education, Institute for Advancement of Medical Communication, and Institute for Medical Research, Camden, N.J.; public trustee, Nutrition Foundation. Member at large of national council, Boy Scouts of America; honorary vice-president, National Tuberculosis Association.

MEMBER: American College of Cardiology (fellow), American College of Physicians (former governor), American Heart Association, American Public Health Association, American Social Health Association (member of board of directors), Association of American Physicians, National Society for Medical Research (member of board of directors), Pan American Medical Association, U.S. Public Health Service Clinical Society (past president), National Resuscitation Society, Royal Society of Health (England; honorary fellow), American College of Chest Physicians, and other medical associations; Alpha Kappa Kappa, Pi Kappa Alpha, Omicron Delta Kappa.

AWARDS, HONORS: Fourteen honorary degrees, 1961-70; including D.Sc. from Birmingham-Southern College, 1961, Tulane University, 1964, University of Rhode Island, 1964, McGill University, 1966, University of Alabama, 1966, and LL.D. from University of Alaska, 1964, and Marquette University, 1968; Distinguished Achievement Award of Pi Kappa Alpha, 1962; Robert D. Bruce Award of American College of Physicians, 1965; Distinguished Service Medal of U.S. Public Health Service, 1965.

WRITINGS: (Contributor) Lewis Herker, editor, *Crisis in Our Cities,* Prentice-Hall, 1965; (contributor) Seymour Tilson, editor, *Toward Environments Fit for Men,* Johns Hopkins Press, 1968; (with Daniel Horn) *To Smoke Or Not to Smoke* (youth book), Lothrop, 1969; (contributor) Gerald

And what about the cough and the sinus trouble most smokers complain of? Do they mean anything? Is the smokers's body trying to tell him something? ■ (From *To Smoke or Not to Smoke* by Luther L. Terry and Daniel Horn. Illustrated by Robert Quackenbush.)

Leinwand, editor, *Air and Water Pollution,* Washington Square Press, 1969. Contributor to *Encyclopedia of Careers and Vocational Guidance* and *New Book of Knowledge;* contributor of more than one hundred articles to medical journals.

SIDELIGHTS: "I am a physician who is broadly interested in the field of public health and community medicine. Most of my publications have been articles published in either the medical or the general press. In these publications I have attempted to advance the knowledge and appreciation of the need for good medical care and for improving our system for the delivery of medical care.

"There are many specific medical areas in which I have been involved and the principal one is the subject of smoking and health. I was the Surgeon General of the Public Health Service who released the famous report on this subject on January 11, 1964. I have continued to be active in this field because I think it represents one of our major preventable public health problems."

FOR MORE INFORMATION SEE: Library Journal, March 15, 1970.

TODD, H(erbert) E(atton) 1908-

PERSONAL: Born February 22, 1908, in London, England; son of Henry Graves (a headmaster) and Minnie Elizabeth Todd; married Bertha Joyce Hughes, 1936 (died, 1968); children: Jonathan (died, 1964), Mark, Stephen. *Education:*

Christ's Hospital, Horsham, England, student, 1919-25. *Religion:* Church of England. *Home:* St. Nicholas, 2 Brownlow Rd., Berkhamsted, Hertfordshire HP4 1HB, England. *Agent:* Winant Towers Ltd., 1 Furnival St., London E.C.4, England.

CAREER: Houlder Brothers Ltd., London, England, shipping clerk, 1925-27; British Foreign and Colonial Corp., London, England, investment clerk, 1927-29; Bourne & Hollingsworth Ltd., London, England, hosiery underbuyer, 1929-31; F. G. Wigley & Co. Ltd., London, England, traveler, later director, 1931—. Children's Book Week storyteller in libraries and schools, 1953—; broadcaster of "Bobby Brewster" stories on radio and television; broadcaster of children's musical programs; performer in local operatic productions, 1945-62. *Military service:* Royal Air Force, 1940-45; became squadron leader. *Member:* Berkhamsted Amateur Operatic and Dramatic Society (choir master, 1948-52; chairman, 1956-60; president, 1961—). *Awards, Honors:* The White Rose Award, 1971, for *Bobby Brewster and the Ghost.*

WRITINGS—"Bobby Brewster" series; all published by Brockhampton Press, except as indicated: *Bobby Brewster*

H. E. TODD

and the Winkers Club, Edmund Ward, 1949; *Bobby Brewster,* 1954; *Bobby Brewster—Bus Conductor,* 1955; *Bobby Brewster's Shadow,* 1956; *Bobby Brewster's Bicycle,* 1957; *Bobby Brewster's Camera,* 1959; *Bobby Brewster's Wallpaper,* 1961; *Bobby Brewster's Conker,* 1963; *Bobby Brewster, Detective,* 1964; *Bobby Brewster's Potato,* Brockhampton Press, 1964; *Bobby Brewster and the Ghost,* 1966; *Bobby Brewster's Kite,* 1967; *Bobby Brewster's Scarecrow,* 1968; *Bobby Brewster's Torch,* 1969; *Bobby Brewster's Balloon Race,* 1970; *Bobby Brewster's Typewriter,* 1971; *Bobby Brewster's Bee,* 1972; *Bobby Brewster's Wishbone,* 1974; (with Val Biro) *The Sick Cow,* 1974; *Bobby Brewster's Bookmark,* 1975; (with Val Biro) *George the Fire Engine,* 1976; (with Val Biro) *Changing of the Guard,* in press.

Musical works: (With Capel Annand) *Blackbird Pie* (play for children), Boosey & Hawkes, 1956; five adult musical revues and ten children's musical programs produced by British Broadcasting Corp., 1949-57.

SIDELIGHTS: "I started as a teller of stories before any of my books were published, and telling stories remains my first love. I have told stories to all ages, races, colours and creeds in many countries, and broadcast both on radio and television on some thousands of occasions. In 1974 alone I gave over 1,200 sessions of storytelling and lecturing in schools, libraries, Colleges of Education, Universities and Teachers Centres throughout Britain, in the largest cities and most remote villages.

"My books are all (so far) about Bobby Brewster, a small boy nine years old who was three and a half thirty-five years ago when I started telling stories about him to my own sons. He is an ordinary boy who has the most extraordinary adventures with ordinary things. He has a round face, blue eyes, and a nose like a button—and he is part of me, part of my sons, and now part of the hundreds of thousands of children (girls as well as boys) who I meet every year. My books all contain about seven or eight self-contained short stories. I do not claim that they have great literary merit—but they are all real stories with a beginning, a middle, and an end. Children love a plot to end! I am often asked why I wrote only for children, and always reply that I have a mental age myself of eight and three-quarters, and am happy with it!

"My father told me stories when I was young—and I think that the exchanging of stories in a family or classroom, not only told to but also by children, is still one of the most useful and stimulating methods of communication which will never be replaced by mechanical means.

FOR MORE INFORMATION SEE: Children's Literature in Education/12, APS Publications, September, 1973; *The Guardian Miscellany,* January 29, 1975.

TURNER, Philip 1925-

PERSONAL: Born December 3, 1925, in Rossland, British Columbia, Canada; son of Christopher Edward (a clergyman) and Emma (Johnston) Turner; married Margaret Diane Samson, September 23, 1950; children: Simon, Stephen, Jane. *Education:* Worcester College, Oxford, B.A., 1950, M.A., 1962. *Agent:* Bolt and Watson, 8 Storey's Gate, London S.W.1, England.

PHILIP TURNER

CAREER: Ordained priest of Church of England, 1951; curate in Leeds, 1951-56; priest-in-charge, Crawley, Sussex, 1956-62; vicar of St. Matthews, Northampton, 1962-66; British Broadcasting Corp., Midland Region, Birmingham, religious broadcasting organizer, 1966-70; Briar Mill High School, Droitwich, Worcestershire, 1973-75; Eton College, Windsor, Berkshires, 1975—. Author of children's books and of plays. *Military service:* Royal Naval Volunteer Reserve, 1943-46; became sub-lieutenant. *Member:* Society of Authors. *Awards, honors:* Carnegie Medal of Library Association for best children's book published in United Kingdom in 1965, for *The Grange at High Force.*

WRITINGS—Children's books: *Colonel Sheperton's Clock,* Oxford University Press, 1964, World Publishing, 1966; *The Grange at High Force,* Oxford University Press, 1965, World Publishing, 1967; *Sea Peril,* Oxford University Press, 1966, World Publishing, 1968; *The Bible Story,* Oxford University Press, 1968; *Steam on the Line,* World Publishing, 1968; (author of text) *Brian Wildsmith's Illustrated Bible Stories,* F. Watts, 1969; *War on the Darnel,* World Publishing, 1969; *Wigwig and Homer,* Oxford University Press, 1969, World Publishing, 1970; *Devils Nob,* Hamish Hamilton, 1970, Thomas Nelson, 1973; *Powder Quay,* Hamish Hamilton, 1971; *Dunkirk Summer,* Hamish Hamilton, 1973.

Plays: *Christ in the Concrete City*, S.P.C.K., 1956; *Tell it with Trumpets*, S.P.C.K., 1959; *Cry Dawn in Dark Babylon*, S.P.C.K., 1959; *This is the Word in "Word Made Flesh,"* S.P.C.K., 1962; *Casey*, S.P.C.K., 1962; *So Long at the Fair*, Joint Board of Christian Education of Australia and New Zealand, 1966; *Men in Stone*, Baker Plays, 1966; *Cantata for Derelicts*, United Church Publishing House (Canada), 1967; *Madonna in Concrete*, S.P.C.K., 1971.

SIDELIGHTS: "I was born in Canada, but my family returned to England when I was six months old, and spent my childhood in the industrial north and the Midlands, Newcastle and the West Riding of Yorkshire and the Black Country. My father was a parson, who had been a railwayman and the son of a railwayman. I have strong memories of unemployment and malnutrition in the 1930's in the industrial parishes and, by way of contrast, holidays in the Yorkshire Dales.

"I sampled the whole range of possible education: State Council School, Grammar School, a private preparatory school and a Public School. I served in the war as an aircraft engineer in the Fleet Air Arm, and went to Worcester College, Oxford, in 1946 and read English.

"I went to Chichester Theological College and was ordained in 1951. Served in an artisan parish in Leeds, then went to Crawley New Town in Sussex and later was Vicar of St. Matthew's, Northampton, in 1962. In 1967, I took up an appointment as head of BBC Religious Programmes in the Midlands. I believe that the Church of England needs to be 'a lot less ecclesiastical and a lot more Christian, and a lot more concerned with the ordinary problems of ordinary people.'

"My main writing, before embarking on children's stories, was in the field of religious drama, and have several plays in print. My first children's story, *Colonel Sheperton's Clock*, was published in 1964."

HOBBIES AND OTHER INTERESTS: Collecting first editions of Walter Scott's novels, walking, carpentry and wine-making.

At the very top of the rise there was a signpost, a shabby signpost, and Peter propped Yellow Peril against it. ■ (From *The Grange at High Force* by Philip Turner. Illustrated by William Papas.)

FOR MORE INFORMATION SEE: Books and Bookmen, May, 1968.

VANCE, Eleanor Graham 1908-

PERSONAL: Born October 16, 1908, in Pittsburgh, Pa.; daughter of J. Paul and Margaret (Hargrave) Graham; married W. Silas Vance (a professor), November 22, 1945; children: Eleanor Margaret (Mrs. John Raders), Dale Lines. *Education:* Westminster College, New Wilmington, Pa., B.A., 1930; Northwestern University, M.A. in Journalism, 1931; additional study at University of Pittsburgh, Columbia University, and Middlebury College. *Home and office:* 109 Austin Blvd., Edinburg, Tex. 78539.

CAREER: Akron Typesetting Co., Akron, Ohio, proofreader, 1931-32; Pittsburgh Public Schools, Pittsburgh, Pa., teacher, 1933-37, 1939-43, organized home teaching of handicapped children, 1935-37; Colonial Williamsburg, Williamsburg, Va., member of research department, 1944-45; Northwestern State College, Alva, Okla., teacher, 1954-55. Freelance writer, 1931—; professional lecturer on literary and educational subjects, 1935—. Staff member for writers' conferences at West Texas State College, University of Oklahoma, Nebraska Wesleyan University. *Member:* Poetry Society of America, Authors Guild, Chi Omega, Delta Kappa Gamma (honorary). *Awards, honors:* Award of Merit

ELEANOR GRAHAM VANCE

Up and down the bank they leapt nimbly, their swords flashing in the sunlight and clanging with so much noise that all the birds flew away to the shelter of the forest. ■ (From *Adventures of Robin Hood* by Eleanor Graham Vance. Illustrated by Jay Hyde Barnum.)

of Northwestern University Alumni Association, 1938, for organizing home teaching of handicapped children in Pittsburgh; Litt.D., Westminster College, 1952; Achievement Award of Westminster College Alumni Association, 1956; George Washington Medal, Freedoms Foundation, 1958, for poem, "Jamestown."

WRITINGS: Christmas in Old England (operetta), Silver Burdett, 1938; *For These Moments* (poems), Stephen Daye Press, 1939; *A Musical Calendar,* Silver Burdett, 1940; *Canciones Pan-Americanas* (Latin-American folksongs), Silver Burdett, 1942; (author of introduction) Arthur Guiterman, *Brave Laughter,* Dutton, 1943; *Henry the Helicopter,* Albert Whitman, 1945; (adapter) *Famous Fairy Tales,* Wonder Books, 1946; (adapter) *Favorite Nursery Tales,* Wonder Books, 1946; (adapter) *Bedtime Stories,* Wonder Books, 1946; (adapter) Anna Sewell, *Black Beauty,* Random House, 1949.

Store in Your Heart (poems), Bookman Associates, 1950; (adapter) *Adventures of Robin Hood,* Random House, 1953; *The Story of Tweets, a Cat,* Twayne, 1956; *It Happens Every Day* (poems), Golden Quill, 1962; *Jonathan,* Follett, 1966; *Treasured Memories of Our Baby,* Gibson, 1970; (compiler) *From Little to Big* (poems), Follett, 1971; *The Everything Book,* Golden Press, 1974. Contributor of poems and articles to *Good Housekeeping, Saturday Evening Post, New Yorker, Ladies' Home Journal, Saturday Review, Parents', New York Times, New York Herald Tribune,* and to children's magazines.

WORK IN PROGRESS: Children's books; personal reminiscences.

SIDELIGHTS: "I write for children and for adults, and I guess I don't know the difference, because some of my books are for both—and I myself enjoy reading a good children's book just as much as (or sometimes more than) an adult book. I think I was thirteen when I read that Frances Hodgson Burnett had been first published at that age, and I felt backward because I had not. Now I feel backward because I haven't accomplished all that I hoped to by this time. I get my ideas from inside myself, from my own experiences and the experiences of people I see, and from reading. Even though I know I'm 'no great shakes,' I write because I *have* to, and I'm unhappy only when interruptions interfere too much with my writing. Last year when I was in the hospital, I asked my husband to bring me my diary. He didn't think I should be spending my energy on writing, and said so. I said (pitifully enough to get results!), 'But I don't even have a *pencil.*' So he gave me one and a scrap of paper. I wrote not a word, but I felt better because I had the paper and pencil.

"*The Everything Book* was the most fun (and I guess the most work, too) of any of my books, because it is full of people that I love (especially grandchildren) and things to make and do. When I was working on it, it seemed I would never be able to part with the manuscript and send it to the publisher, because I kept thinking of things to add."

HOBBIES AND OTHER INTERESTS: Reading, music, embroidery.

VAN TUYL, Barbara 1940-

PERSONAL: Surname rhymes with "style"; born November 26, 1940, in Brooklyn, N.Y.; daughter of Edgar Everett (a stockbroker) and Alexandra (a musician; maiden name, Tolkoff) Van Tuyl. *Education:* Attended public schools of Scarsdale, N.Y. *Home address:* P.O. Box 145, Clintondale, N.Y. 12515. *Agent:* Paul R. Reynolds, Inc., 12 East 41st St., New York, N.Y. 10017.

BARBARA VAN TUYL

CAREER: Scarsdale National Bank, Scarsdale, N.Y., teller, 1958-59; Lucky Leaf Stable, Port Chester, N.Y., working partner, 1959-62; International Business Machines (IBM), White Plains, N.Y., secretary, 1962-65; Kling Employment Agency, White Plains, N.Y., placement manager, 1965-66; Scarsdale Medical Center, Scarsdale, N.Y., secretary-assistant to doctors, 1966-67; Banbury Cross Riding Club, Rye, N.Y., working partner, 1969-71; writer, 1971—; breeding, training, schooling, showing, and racing horses.

WRITINGS: Select, Buy, Train, and Care For Your Own Horse, Grosset, 1969; (with Patricia H. Johnson) *The Sweet Running Filly* (juvenile), New American Library, 1971; (with Johnson) *A Horse Called Bonnie* (juvenile), New American Library, 1971; (contributor) Richard Glyn, editor, *The World's Finest Horses and Ponies,* Harrap, 1971; *How To Ride and Jump Your Best,* Grosset, 1973; *The Horseman's Handbook,* Prentice-Hall, 1973; *Sunbonnet: Filly of the Year* (juvenile), New American Library, 1973; *Bonnie and the Haunted Farm* (juvenile), New American Library, 1974; *Winning Ways at Horse Shows,* Grosset, 1975; *The Betrayal of Bonnie* (juvenile), New American Library, 1975. Contributor to *American Horseman.* Contributing editor of *Practical Horseman,* 1973—.

SIDELIGHTS: "My life has been dedicated to the extension of my knowledge of horses and to this end I have spent many years working with instructors, trainers, farm managers, veterinarians, farriers, grooms and the like in an effort to learn as much as I could about horses—thoroughbreds in particular. I was fortunate enough to own an American Horse Shows Association high score champion in 1958. This was my first horse and she was purchased by me with my life savings at the time which amounted to $425.00, and in gaining the annual championship in the Green Working Hunter division she had to beat horses worth anywhere from ten to thirty times her own purchase price. Her success story was in part the inspiration for my fiction series for NAL, although another mare I bought from a despicable junk dealer caused me to dream up the final plot for the first of the series. . . . I am on the verge of racing my first home-bred—a filly out of the junk dealer mare—and her training has been a wonderful education for me."

HOBBIES AND OTHER INTERESTS: Dogs, music.

VERRAL, Charles Spain   1904-
(George L. Eaton)

PERSONAL: Born November 7, 1904, in Highfield, Ontario, Canada; son of George William and Kate E. (Peacocke) Verral; married Jean Mithoefer, March 19, 1932; children: Charles Spain, Jr. *Education:* Attended Upper Canada College, 1919-23, and Ontario College of Art, 1923-26. *Religion:* Episcopalian. *Home:* 79 Jane St., New York, N.Y. 10014. *Office: Reader's Digest,* 380 Madison Ave., New York, N.Y. 10017.

CAREER: Free-lance commercial artist, New York, N.Y., 1927-30; Clayton Publications, New York, N.Y., an editor, 1930-33, art director, 1933-35; free-lance writer, New York, N.Y., 1935-62, with some editorial positions, including biographies editor for *Harper Encyclopedia of Science,* 1961-62; Reader's Digest Association, New York, N.Y., editor-writer for General Books, 1962—. *Member:* Mystery Writers of America, Authors League of America. *Awards, honors:* Bureau of Intercultural Education short story contest prize, 1947, for "The Miracle Quarterback."

WRITINGS: Captain of the Ice, Crowell, 1953; *Champion of the Court,* Crowell, 1954; *Men of Flight: Conquest of the Air,* Aladdin Books, 1954; *The King of the Diamond,* Crowell, 1955; *Mighty Men of Baseball,* Aladdin Books, 1955; *High Danger,* Sterling, 1955; *The Wonderful World Series,* Crowell, 1956; *Walt Disney's The Great Locomotive Chase,* Simon & Schuster, 1956; *Annie Oakley, Sharpshooter,* Simon & Schuster, 1957; *Lassie and the Daring Rescue,* Simon & Schuster, 1957; *Brave Eagle,* Simon & Schuster, 1957; *Broken Arrow,* Simon & Schuster, 1957; *The Lone Ranger and Tonto,* Simon & Schuster, 1957; *Rin-Tin-Tin and the Outlaw,* Simon & Schuster, 1957; *Lassie and Her Day in the Sun,* Simon & Schuster, 1958; *Cheyenne,* Simon & Schuster, 1958; *Walt Disney's Andy Burnett,* Simon & Schuster, 1958; *Play Ball,* Simon & Schuster, 1958; *Zorro,* Simon & Schuster, 1958; *Smoky the Bear,* Simon & Schuster, 1958; *Rin-Tin-Tin and the Hidden Treasure,* Simon & Schuster, 1959; *Zorro and the Secret Plan,* Simon & Schuster, 1959; *Walt Disney's The Shaggy Dog,* Simon & Schuster, 1959.

The Winning Quarterback, Crowell, 1960; *The Case of the Missing Message,* Golden Press, 1960; *Smoky the Bear and His Animal Friends,* Golden Press, 1960; *The Flying Car,* Golden Press, 1961; *Jets,* Prentice-Hall, 1962; *Go! The Story of Outer Space,* Prentice-Hall, 1962; *Robert Goddard: Father of the Space Age,* Prentice-Hall, 1963. Short stories anthologized in collections published by American Book Co., Harcourt, Holt, and Watts. Author of 25 book-length "Bill Barnes" air adventure stories in *Air Trails,* and some 150 short stories, novelettes and articles to *Boys' Life, Argosy, This Week, American Boy, Clues,* and other magazines, 1935-52. Continuity writer for national syndicated adventure newspaper strip, "Hap Hopper," 1941-47. Script writer for radio program, "Mandrake the Magician," 1940-41.

WORK IN PROGRESS: A juvenile mystery, for Golden Press.

HOBBIES AND OTHER INTERESTS: Amateur magician; cartooning and painting.

WALLOWER, Lucille

PERSONAL: Born in Waynesboro, Pa.; daughter of Roland C. (in advertising) and Nora Grace (Werdebaugh) Wallower. *Education:* Studied at Pennsylvania Museum School of Art and Traphagen School Fashion. *Home:* 828 Greenwood Ave., Jenkintown, Pa. 19046.

CAREER: Harrisburg Public Library, Harrisburg, Pa., school librarian, 1943-44, assistant children's librarian, 1944-46; fashion artist at Pomeroy's Inc., 1946-49, and at Bowman's Inc., 1949-52, in Harrisburg, Pa.; Abington Library, Jenkintown, Pa., children's librarian, 1959—, librarian, 1971-75; free-lance writer and illustrator, 1975—. Author and illustrator of children's books. Harrisburg Art Association Studio, director, 1943-48. *Member:* Pennsylvania Library Association, Historical Society of Pennsylvania, Philadelphia Children's Reading Roundtable, Old York Road Historical Society, Old York Road Art Guild.

LUCILLE WALLOWER

Ben was always busy . . . one of his wise sayings in Poor Richard's Almanac was: "Lost time is never found again." ■ (From *Your Pennsylvania* by Lucille Wallower. Illustrated by the author.)

WRITINGS—All self-illustrated except as indicated: *A Conch Shell for Molly* (Junior Literary Guild selection), McKay, 1940; *Chooky,* McKay, 1942; *The Roll of Drums,* Albert Whitman, 1945.

Your Pennsylvania, Penns Valley, 1953, 3rd edition, 1964; *The Pennsylvania Primer,* Penns Valley, 1954, 4th edition, 1972; *Indians of Pennsylvania,* Penns Valley, 1956, 2nd edition, 1965; *Old Satan,* McKay, 1956; *The Hippity Hopper,* McKay, 1957; *The Morning Star,* McKay, 1958; *All About Pennsylvania,* Penns Valley, 1958.

They Came to Pennsylvania, Penns Valley, 1960; *Your State: Pennsylvania,* Penns Valley, 1962; *Pennsylvania A B C,* Penns Valley, 1963; *The Lost Prince,* McKay, 1963; *My Book About Abraham Lincoln,* Penns Valley, 1967; *William Penn* (not self-illustrated), Follett, 1968; *Colonial Pennsylvania,* Nelson, 1969; *The Pennsylvania Dutch* (not self-illustrated), Penns Valley, 1971; *Introduction to Pennsylvania* (not self-illustrated), McRoberts, 1974; *Bicentennial Workshop,* Penns Valley, 1975; *Indians of Pennsylvania Workshop,* Penns Valley, 1976; *They Came to Pennsylvania Workshop,* Penns Valley, 1976.

Stories included in *Uncle Sam's Story Book,* McKay, 1944; *Stories from the East and North,* Silver Burdett, 1945; *With New Friends,* Silver Burdett, 1946; *Shining Hours,* Bobbs, 1961.

Illustrator: *Nanka of Old Bohemia,* A. Whitman, 1937; *The Treasure of Belden Place,* A. Whitman, 1938; *Ju Ju and His Friends,* A. Whitman, 1939; *Mystery Mountain,* A. Whitman, 1940; *Natalie,* A. Whitman, 1940; *Salute to the Flag,* A. Whitman, 1941; *Orange on Top,* Harcourt, 1945; *Their*

Way, A. Whitman, 1945; *How Many Friends?*, Judson, 1953; *Kindergarten Songs and Rhythms*, Judson, 1954; *My Bible Story Book*, Judson, 1955; *Mara of Old Babylon*, Abingdon, 1955; *Mara Journeys Home*, Abingdon, 1957.

WORK IN PROGRESS: Writing a Black history textbook.

SIDELIGHTS: "I was born in Waynesboro, Pennsylvania, and grew up, one of six children, in Harrisburg. After two years of art school, the depression caught up with our family. My first drawings were sold by writing stories to go with them for children's magazines. Then I began illustrating children's books. Soon I wrote my first picture book. The idea for this book about the Pennsylvania Canal, *A Conch Shell for Molly* was given to me by Miss Mary Rudy of the Harrisburg Public Library. It was the beginning of my writing about Pennsylvania. Because I love animals, I put my cat who liked hard boiled eggs and olives into the story. My second book, *Chooky*, was about my mother when she was little and her pet chicken. All my books are either fiction with an historical background or history texts of Pennsylvania.

"The uncertainties of a career as a writer-illustrator were bolstered at different times by various jobs. I received my library training in service at the Harrisburg Public Library. As children's librarian, I have given hundreds of picture book story hours together with my talking Dalmation puppy-dog puppet, Abbie.

"As a child, my favorite occupation was coloring the ladies in fashion catalogues, cutting them out and playing with them and other paper dolls. I still have them and add to my collection now and then. I also like to paint and to play the organ. My present cat is Nikki, a scraggly stray who turned into a beautiful Persian."

WATTS, Mabel Pizzey 1906-
(Patricia Lynn)

PERSONAL: Born May 20, 1906, in London, England; daughter of Ernest Henry and Edith (Elias) Pizzey; married William Watts; children: Stanley David McEtchin, Robert Lloyd McEtchin, Mrs. John F. Babcock. *Education:* Attended schools in London, England, and in Edmonton and Vancouver, Canada. *Home:* 1520 Ralston Ave., Burlingame, Calif.

CAREER: Worked in an office in Vancouver, British Columbia, Canada, for a time before marriage. Writer of children's books. *Member:* Burlingame Writers Club (president, 1962—).

WRITINGS: Dozens of Cousins, McGraw, 1950; (adapter) *Woody Woodpecker's Peck of Troubles*, Whitman, 1950; *Over the Hills to Ballybog*, Dutton, 1954; *The Patchwork Kilt*, Dutton, 1954; *Bedtime Stories*, Rand McNally, 1955; *Daniel, the Cocker Spaniel*, Rand McNally, 1955; *Goody-Naughty Book*, Rand McNally, 1956; *A Cow in the House* (Junior Literary Guild selection), Follett, 1956; *Hideaway Animals*, Rand McNally, 1957; *Feathered Friends*, Rand McNally, 1957; *Everyone Waits* (Junior Literary Guild selection), Abelard, 1959; *Helpful Henrietta*, Rand McNally, 1959; *Mailman Mike*, Rand McNally, 1959.

My Truck Book, Rand McNally, 1960; *Something for You, Something for Me*, Abelard, 1960; *Weeks and Weeks* (Junior Literary Guild selection), Abelard, 1961; *Famous Folk Tales to Read Aloud*, Grosset, 1961; *Read Aloud Horse Stories*, Grosset, 1961; *Where is the Keeper*, Whitman, 1961; *The Little Horseman*, Rand McNally, 1961; *Hildy's Hideaway*, Whitman, 1961; *The Lion and the Mouse*, Whitman, 1961; *Little Raccoon*, Rand McNally, 1961; *Funtime–to Read Aloud*, Grosset, 1961; *Little Fox*, Rand McNally, 1962; *Little Tiger*, Rand McNally, 1962; *A Little from Here, a Little for There*, Abelard, 1962; *The Bed of Thistledown*, Abelard, 1962; *Henrietta and the Hat*, Parents, 1962; *The Boy Who Listened to Everyone*, Parents, 1963; *Come Play With Me*, Whitman, 1963; *A New Suit for Henry*, Guild Press Books, 1963; *Little Camper*, Rand McNally, 1963; *Little Cub Scout*, Rand McNally, 1964; *The Day It Rained Watermelons*, Lantern, 1964; *The Light Across Piney Valley*, Abelard, 1965; *A Visit to Disneyland*, Whitman, 1965; *Read Aloud Storytime*, Grosset, 1965; *My Father Can Fix Anything*, Whitman, 1965; *Casey, the Clumsy Colt*, Whitman, 1965; *Douting Tomas*, Initial Teaching Alphabet Publishing (I.T.A.), 1965; *The Narrow Escapes of Solomon Smart*, Parents, 1966.

Under pseudonym Patricia Lynn: *Around and About on Buttercup Farm*, 1951, *Digger Dan*, 1953, *Handy Andy*, 1953, *Trumpet*, 1953, *Nobody's Puppy*, 1953, *Busy Bill*, 1954, *Farm A.B.C.*, 1954, *Getting Ready for Roddy*, 1955, *Ho-Hum!* 1957 (all published by Whitman).

"All through a rainstorm I stood, in my leaky old armor, protecting this castle," he said, while the bubble and squeak grew cold and limp. ▪ (From *Knights of the Square Table* by Mabel Watts. Illustrated by Haris Petie.)

SIDELIGHTS: "Born in London, England I started my schooling there. During World War I, I continued my schooling wherever my army father happened to be stationed, in the counties of Surrey, Hampshire, and Kent. In March, 1919 we sailed for Canada on the troopship, 'Minnedosa.' Outside Edmonton, Alberta, we settled in a two-room shack on the banks of the Saskatchewan River.

"After school I learned to swing an axe, and keep a good supply of wood for the fire. At school I found it rather hard to understand the Scotch-Canadian lingo of the other children. They, in turn, found my Cockney-London language rather difficult. A little practice in the woodshed soon remedied this, and I was soon rolling my 'R's' and sounding my 'H's' like a real Canuck.

"The next move was to Vancouver, British Columbia, where my parents ran a boarding house at English Bay. The next year we moved to North Lonsdale where we raised chickens, ducks and geese at the foot of Grouse Mountain. While attending North Vancouver High School, I did a lot of mountain-climbing, ice-skating, and bob-sledding.

"I now live in Burlingame, California, twenty miles down the Peninsula south of San Francisco. Have been an American citizen for thirty-two years. Have three grown children, and six grandchildren.

"It was quite by accident that I started writing for children. When my daughter Pat was four, she simply would not eat. 'Tell you what,' I said, one day, 'if you will eat, I will read you a story.' After that I made many visits to the library, read many picture books to Pat, and began writing them myself.

"Many of my books come from my British background. These include *The Story of Zachary Zween*, and *While the Horses Galloped to London*, which was a Caldecott nomination for 1974, and my favorite of all the many books I have written."

WAUGH, Dorothy

PERSONAL: Born in Burlington, Vt.; daughter of Frank Albert and (Mary) Alice (Vail) Waugh. *Education:* Studied at University of Massachusetts, Massachusetts School of Art, Art Institute of Chicago (graduate), Museum School of the Cleveland Museum of Art.

CAREER: Parsons School of Design, New York, N.Y., teacher; Cooper Union School of Art, New York, N.Y., teacher; Montclair Library, Montclair, N.J., former director of public relations; was public relations assistant to the mayor of Montclair. Commercial artist, decorator, designer and writer.

WRITINGS: (Self-illustrated) *Among the Leaves and Grasses,* Holt, 1931; (contributor) Shuler, Knight, and Fuller, editors, *Lady Editor,* Dutton, 1941; (self-illustrated) *Warm Earth,* Oxford University Press, 1943; (self-illustrated) *Muriel Saves String,* McKay, 1956; (self-illustrated) *A Handbook of Christmas Decoration,* Macmillan, 1958; (self-illustrated) *Festive Decoration of the Year Round,* Macmillan, 1962; *Emily Dickinson's Beloved, a Surmise,* Vantage, 1976. Verse in *American Mercury, Christian Sci-*

DOROTHY WAUGH

ence Monitor, Popular Gardening, Yankee, The Rotarian, Horticulture, Flower Grower, Cappers Weekly.

Illustrator: Frances Frost, *Innocent Summer,* Farrar, 1936; Inglis and Stewart, *Adventures in World Literature,* Harcourt, 1936; Van der Veer, *The River Pasture,* Longmans, 1936; Van der Veer, *Brown Hills,* Longmans, 1938; Dunham, *What's in the Sky,* Oxford University Press, 1941. Illustrations have appeared in her father's books and articles, a school reader for Lippincott, a book on drama for Row Peterson. Manager of the children's book department for Alfred A. Knopf, Inc. (1937-40) where she designed most of the department's books, several of which were cited by the American Institute of Graphic Arts among the "Fifty Books of the Year" selected annually for fine design. Designed festive decorations for *Family Circle, House Beautiful,* The Macmillan Company, *Horticulture, Popular Gardening, Flower Grower.* Also a dozen full-size travel posters and fifty stamp-size poster stickers in full color for The National Park Service.

WORK IN PROGRESS: Early history of Connecticut River Valley; biography of Emily Dickinson with emphasis on her environment.

SIDELIGHTS: "I started life as a city girl, born in Burlington, Vermont while my father was a professor at the University there; but when I was six he accepted an appointment to establish and head a division of horticulture at the Massachusetts Agricultural College, in Amherst, Massachusetts.

This was an exciting transition from a friendly little city neighborhood to an intellectually active village and a beautiful countryside.

"We lived in the heart of the campus, then a lovely, open, pastoral tract of several hundreds of acres of woodland, meadow, cultivated fields, orchards, vineyards and broad, varied terrain, including low flats with deveating brook, where a flock of crows that spent nights in the woods on the hill spent daytimes at work and play along the brookside. We children—my sister, four brothers, and I—learned to recognize some of these crows individually, and had names for them, for from the fields below, as we went for the family's milk from the herd of high-bred cows across the campus, we watched the daily flights, with one crow, the leader, cawing signals, and the ranks shifting in response.

"There were at that time only a very few buildings on the campus. Our only neighbors—and they not within sight or shouting distance—were the Dickinsons (related to Emily, though not closely), and the Brookses (who had lived for a dozen years in Japan). M A C (always known by its initials) had been one of the earliest, and was one of the finest, land-grant colleges; so, when the Imperial Government of Japan, in the late 1870's, had asked that a delegation be sent there to establish the first agricultural college in Japan, it was from M A C that men went out (headed by a friend of Emily Dickinson's; her father had been prominent in the founding of M A C, as her grandfather had been in the founding of Amherst College). Later William Penn Brooks, before he was our neighbor, had served as a professor, and then as president, of the Imperial Agricultural College of Japan.

"These various men, returning from Japan to Amherst, had brought back many specimens of fine plants not previously known in this country—new varieties of azalea, magnolia, clematis, dogwood, and so on. Three or four acres of the campus were set aside as an arboretum for these and later plantings. This wonderful garden became the playground of the six Waugh children and the haunt of many birds. I spent many happy summer hours alone there, before my sister and brothers awoke, for light always wakes me, so I am always the earliest up.

"There I found my first hummingbird's nest, saw a pair of verios raise a hungry brood in a firm nest of dried grasses and shreds of birch bark, and in general luxuriated in the out-of-doors at its finest.

"Meanwhile we were in the midst of the lively transition that by introducing scientific means, organization of administration, new machines and fertilizers was developing farming (then the country's and the world's chief occupation) to the stage that would make it possible for a much smaller proportion of the population to serve as farmers, freeing many to other occupations. As my father developed departments of forestry, floriculture, orcharding, vegetable culture, landscape gardening, and so on, we saw his students go out to serve as editors of garden magazines, park superintendents, foresters, landscape architects, tree surgeons, a director of the National Park Service, and leaders in many related fields. The departments my father had instituted at M A C had provided the most advanced and there-advancing movements in the wide field—and we children were in the very midst of the thrilling activities.

"My father was a prolific writer. During summers he took us children on weekly jaunts or gave us weekly assignments, providing notebooks in which we were to record our impressions. (I usually illustrated mine with pencil drawings.) All my four brothers became authors of published books. I believe we grew up thinking that everybody writes, as everybody breathes.

"My deep interests in the beauties of the out-of-doors, and in Emily Dickinson and her writings, have grown out, I am sure, of the influence of my early environment."

For seven years Dorothy Waugh conducted a commentary and interview program on radio station WVNJ.

FOR MORE INFORMATION SEE: Library Journal, June 1, 1948; Montclair, N.J. *Times,* April 8, 1965.

WEALES, Gerald (Clifford) 1925-

PERSONAL: Born June 12, 1925, in Connersville, Ind.; son of Frank and Mary (Burton) Weales. *Education:* Columbia University, A.B., 1948, A.M., 1949, Ph.D., 1958. *Office:* Department of English, University of Pennsylvania, Philadelphia, Pa. 19107.

CAREER: Georgia Institute of Technology, Atlanta, Ga., instructor in English, 1951-53; Newark College of Engineer-

GERALD WEALES

"How many times have I told you not to talk to me on the street?" said the cat. "I don't want everybody in Demmansville knowing that I can talk. I'd never have a minute to myself." ■ (From *Miss Grimsbee Is a Witch* by Gerald Weales. Illustrated by Lita Scheel.)

ing, Newark, N.J., instructor in English, 1953-55; Wayne State University, Detroit, Mich., instructor in English, 1955-56; Brown University, Providence, R.I., assistant professor of English, 1957-58; University of Pennsylvania, Philadelphia, 1958—, now professor of English. *Military service:* U.S. Army, 1943-46, became sergeant, received Bronze Star and Purple Heart. *Awards, honors:* George Jean Nathan award for drama criticism, 1965.

WRITINGS: Miss Grimsbee Is a Witch (juvenile), Little, 1957; *Tale for a Bluebird* (novel), Harcourt, 1960; *Religion in Modern English Drama*, University of Pennsylvania Press, 1961; *American Drama Since World War II*, Harcourt, 1962; (editor) *Five Edwardian Plays*, Hill & Wang, 1962; (editor) *Eleven Plays*, Norton, 1964; *A Play and Its Parts*, Basic Books, 1964; *Miss Grimsbee Takes a Vacation* (juvenile), Little, 1965; *Tennessee Williams*, University of Minnesota Press, 1965; (editor) *The Plays of William Wycherley*, Doubleday, 1966; (editor) Arthur Miller, *Death of a Salesman*, Viking, 1967; *The Jumping-Off Place, American Drama in the 1960's*, Macmillan, 1969; *Clifford Odets, Playwright*, Bobbs-Merrill/Pegasus, 1971; (editor) Arthur Miller, *The Crucible*, Viking, 1971. Contributor to magazines and newspapers.

WORK IN PROGRESS: A book on American film comedy in the 1930's.

SIDELIGHTS: "I wrote the first of the Miss Grimsbee books on a dare. I was teaching in Atlanta at the time and a friend of mine sent me the information about a contest in *Jack and Jill* and, added, write one. I did. I didn't win the contest, of course, because in those days (1952), fantasy would not have won first place in a one-man race. Still *Jack and Jill* liked it well enough to publish an abridgment, and several years later—after thirty-odd publishers had turned the book down—Atlantic Monthly Press published it and it sold modestly well until 1976, when it went out of print. It is now available only in an Italian edition.

"I was so pleased with the mail that I got from readers and with the requests for more Miss Grimsbee, that I finally got around to writing *Miss Grimsbee Takes a Vacation*.

"At the moment I seem to be a retired writer of juveniles. I wrote what I thought was a rather funny story about cows that gave ginger ale, but everyone hated it, so it has never seen the light of printed page.

"Unless I have another vision some evening (or another dare), I will remain in retirement—teaching, writing criticism, reading other people's juveniles and eating too much (as anyone who has read my books would guess)."

WEBSTER, David   1930-

PERSONAL: Born April 14, 1930, in Philadelphia, Pa.; son of Harold Shoemaker (an engineer) and Grace (Gourley) Webster; married Winifred Wightman, April 15, 1961; chil-

DAVID WEBSTER

Nobody likes mosquitoes. ■ (From *Let's Find Out About Mosquitoes* by David Webster. Illustrated by Arabelle Wheatley.)

dren: Douglas, Jocelyn. *Education:* Rutgers University, B.S., 1952; Harvard University, graduate student, 1958. *Politics:* Republican. *Religion:* Protestant. *Home:* Todd Pond Rd., Lincoln, Mass. 01773.

CAREER: Junior high school science teacher, Lebanon, N.H., 1955-57; director of science, Lincoln (Mass.) Public Schools, 1957-61; Elementary Science Study, Newton, Mass., staff writer; consultant in science education; writer. *Military service:* U.S. Army, 1952-54; became second lieutenant. *Awards, honors:* Future Scientists of America Star Award; New York Academy of Science honorable mention, 1973, for *Track Watching.*

WRITINGS—For young people: *Brain-Boosters,* Natural History Press, 1966; *Crossroad Puzzles,* Natural History Press, 1967; *Snow Stumpers,* Natural History Press, 1968; *Towers,* Natural History Press, 1971; *Track Watching,* Watts, 1972; *Photo-Fun,* Franklin-Watts, 1973; *More Brain-Boosters,* Doubleday, 1974; *First Book of Science Projects,* Watts, 1974; *First Book of Mosquitoes,* Watts, 1974. Wrote "Brain-Booster" column in *Nature and Science.* Contributed science activity articles to *Current Science and News, Ranger Ricks Nature Magazine,* and *Highlights for Children.* Has written several film loop programs at Ealing Corp. and developed activities for new Ginn Science Textbook Series, grades 1 through 8.

FOR MORE INFORMATION SEE: New York Times Book Review, November 5, 1967, November 3, 1968; *Horn Book,* August, 1969.

WEDDLE, Ethel H(arshbarger) 1897-

PERSONAL: Born September 6, 1897, in Girard, Ill.; daughter of Isaac Joseph (a farmer-preacher) and Martha (Brubaker) Harshbarger; married Lemon Talmage Weddle (a farmer), November 19, 1919; children: Edgar (deceased), Marzetta (Mrs. Oscar Rutherford, Jr.), Lois (Mrs. Henry L. Tipton), Leroy. *Education:* La Verne College, drama student, 1913-14; Illinois State Library extension courses in librarianship and writing. *Politics:* Republican. *Religion:* Protestant. *Home address:* 416 North 4th St., Girard, Ill. 62640.

CAREER: Girard Township Library, Girard, Ill., chief librarian, 1947-71. *Member:* Illinois State Historical Society, Macoupin County Historical Society, American Legion Auxiliary (Girard; historian, 1952-73), Girard Woman's Club (past president, three terms).

WRITINGS: Pleasant Hill, Brethren Publishing, 1956; (contributor) *Ginn Basic Reader,* Ginn, 1957; *Walter Chrysler, Boy Machinist,* Bobbs-Merrill, 1960; (contributor) *Brethren Trail Blazers,* Brethren Press, 1960; *Joel Chandler Harris, Young Storyteller,* Bobbs-Merrill, 1964; *Alvin C. York, Young Marksman,* Bobbs-Merrill, 1967; *A Brubaker Genealogy: The Descendants of Henry Brubaker, 1775-1848, of Salem, Virginia,* Brethren Press, 1970. Regular contributor of newspaper column "Library Window" to area newspapers. Stories in juvenile magazines and Sunday School papers.

WORK IN PROGRESS: Book chronicling the values of the district school in the development of America; youth story of growing up in the midwest in 1880's; *Let's Go Out and Play: Games for Children.*

ETHEL HARSHBARGER WEDDLE

"To be born on a farm in central Illinois was my good fortune. I could gather violets, spring beauties, daisies and apple blossoms to my hearts content. My pets were the big mother cats with their litters of cute, fluffy kittens; the clucking hens with their nests of downy chicks; the sleek horses in the long row of stalls in the great barn reaching over their feed boxes to let me stroke their velvety noses and give each of them six ears of yellow corn to eat.

"We rode to the big country church in our surrey with the fringe on top. In the summer we always wore starched, white dresses to church. In the winter papa buttoned side curtains on the surrey and we snuggled under plush robes and horse blankets to keep warm. When we returned home we stood over the big register and let the heat from the basement furnace blow our dresses out like balloons and make us cozy and warm.

"Unless it was terribly cold we always walked to the brick, district school. I loved school. Arithmetic was hard work and spelling was something to cry over. But the stories in the readers, the beautiful poems to memorize, the myths in the library books, the great men of our history, the peoples around the world were something special.

"I grew up past the years when I could hide in the top of an apple tree and read *One Thousand and One Arabian Nights,*

There was an air of suspense all around the clearing. Men, women, and children were watching. Would Alvin hit his mark? Would he miss? ■ (From *Alvin C. York: Young Marksman* by Ethel H. Weddle. Illustrated by Nathan Goldstein.)

hoping some one else would wash the dishes, but they never did. Then papa took the family to California and I was ready for high school. I was enrolled in the Academy of La Verne College and studied not only the required high school subjects, but elecution too. This gave me experience in public speaking, drama, and story-telling. The family came back to the farm in Illinois in time for me to graduate from our small town high school in 1915.

"After World War I, I married a young farmer who had served our country in France. We rented land and raised four children. I could not buy books and there were no public libraries in our area. There were the Reading Circle books during the school months but in the summer daddy drove us the thirty miles to Springfield to the Illinois State Library. We were allowed twelve books for one month. Planning a rest hour in our busy farm life, each day if possible, we spread a quilt on the grass under the maples and I read aloud. As I read I studied each author's style of work, plots and characterizations.

"All through the early years of our children's lives I told stories to them while doing the household work. One day the eldest, a boy of eleven, told me that I should write my stories because they were as good as any. I thought, 'Why not.' I began selling in 1935, short stories to juvenile magazines for quite a period of years. World War II came, that eleven-year-old boy left college, enlisted in the Air Corps and was lost in action. I turned to the study of writing books, at the same time working hard on the farm to help the other three children specialize in their educational choices.

"In 1947 I was offered the position of chief librarian in a library just being established in our home town. Neither the board nor I knew anything about this work. But I accepted the position and went to work on my training through the help of the Illinois State Library Extension Service. I remained with that library twenty-four years.

"It was a wide open opportunity to do research, to study the editors and their areas of publications. Although my first book was one based on local community history I had my eye on biographical writing for children. Through this interest came my three contributions to the 'Childhood of Famous Americans Series' published by Bobbs-Merrill.

"Like any writer, I received a large collection of rejection slips. Each rejection slip I considered a practice lesson.

"The United States with its wide, wonderful area was tied together by the railroads, and the ever greater engines and longer trains that traveled on them. Walter Chrysler did more than any one man to perfect the great steam-engines. And so I chose to write a book about him. Of all the writers of children's books I felt that Joel Chandler Harris had performed the most perfect task of preserving a great collection of folk-tales with their wisdom and humor. These tales had come to our country through our black population, thus tying us to some of the wisdom of the wide continent of Africa. Thus my next book was about the author of the Uncle Remus stories. Then while visiting in the Blue Ridge Mountains where my husband had been born and raised, I recalled that the great hero of World War I had been raised on the Kentucky side of these mountains. My third book was about that hero, Alvin C. York.

"I have files of researched material that would yield many other books but there has not been time. I have been happy in all the tangents of my contributions to the author's world. I continue in that work as I find time."

HOBBIES AND OTHER INTERESTS: Book reviews; public speaking; historical research; creative stitchery; collage art.

WEST, Betty 1921-
(Betty Morgan Bowen)

PERSONAL: Born August 9, 1921; daughter of William and Elma Bowen; married Gordon West (now managing director of family business), September 18, 1948; children: Andrea, William, Sally. *Education:* Antioch College, student, 1938-39; Swarthmore College, B.A., 1942; additional study at Pratt Institute School of Art, 1943-45, Haverford College, 1945-46; Saffron Walden College of Education, teaching diploma, 1967; University of London, B.A. Honors degree in English, 1972. *Home:* 8 West Rd., Saffron, Walden, Essex, England.

CAREER: Longmans, Green & Co. (publishers), New York, N.Y., secretary to junior books editor, 1944-45; Fort Ontario Emergency Refugee Camp, Oswego, N.Y., welfare worker, 1945-46; American Friends Service Committee, Aachen, Germany, relief worker, 1946-47; primary school teacher, 1964-65, 1967-69; Saffron Walden College of Education, lecturer in English, 1969—.

WRITINGS: Milo's New World, Longmans, Green, 1948; *Jan's Victory,* Longmans, Green, 1950; *One Against the Sea,* Longmans, Green, 1952; *Fly Away Home,* Burke, 1958; *For Love of a Donkey* (Junior Literary Guild selection), McKay, 1963; *Pride of Them All,* McKay, 1970. Contributor to British Broadcasting Corp. and to newspapers.

Illustrator: Morra Laverty, *Gold of Glanaree,* Longmans, 1945; Martha Barnhart Harper, *Red Silk Pantalettes,* Longmans, 1946.

SIDELIGHTS: "We lived during the wintertime in several places when I was young: Chicago, New Jersey, Tennessee, Washington, D.C. But during the summertime, every summer for twenty-one years, we were a family of seven cousins living in Grandma's summer house right on the beach of Long Island Sound, on the point described in *Pride of Them All.* I was the slow one at the end of the line, the dreamer who would rather sit cutting out magazine pictures or drawing rows of beautiful ladies than walking the bulkhead or crabbing up the creek. I made little books, sometimes embroidering their cloth covers, once burning out the title on heavy wooden covers.

"Once when I was sixteen, living with my parents and two sisters in Washington, D.C., I was lucky to survive a car crash and lay for three months in a darkened room, with the longing growing inside to write and illustrate children's books. Through the years at college and art college, through the year at Longmans, when I worked for an outstanding junior books editor and learned why so many manuscripts are rejected, the longing grew, and after working for a year as a volunteer in the emergency relief shelter for European refugees which President Roosevelt set up in old army barracks at Oswego, New York, I sat down to write *Milo's*

BETTY WEST

New World. Before it was finished I was on my way to do emergency relief work in Germany, and its illustrations had to be finished in a public library in London while the nine other volunteers and I waited to be sent to Quaker Relief teams at work in the bombed German cities.

"I have had to live my books before beginning to write them. *Jan's Victory* is about a Dutch family rebuilding their home after the war's devastation. *For Love of a Donkey* has woven into its story our exciting, distressing, saddening, inspiring experiences in Germany. *One Against the Sea* has under its current of action our own building of an Anglo-American family. I lived and worked in the Children's Village in Trogen, Switzerland before writing *Fly Away Home.*

"I am now caught in helping to set up a center for international education here in Saffron Walden, Essex. The quieter life of Yorkshire days, when we brought up our three children plus a winning little Nigerian girl, and when I dreamed stories while pouring the milk into the sugar basin, has had to be put aside. Up in the bedroom are five carton boxes of notes and pictures, and each box promises me when I look at it to become a book one day. There is no joy greater than making a whole book, the words and the pictures, even the jacket all by yourself!"

WILLIAMS, Barbara 1925-

PERSONAL: Born January 1, 1925, in Salt Lake City, Utah; daughter of Walter (a lawyer) and Emily (Jeremy) Wright; married J. D. Williams (a professor of political science), July 5, 1946; children: Kirk, Gil, Taylor, Kimberly.

Education: Banff School of Fine Arts, student, 1945; University of Utah, B.A., 1946, M.A., 1972; Boston University, graduate study, 1949-50. *Politics:* Democrat. *Home:* 3399 East Loren Von Dr., Salt Lake City, Utah 84117.

CAREER: Deseret News, Salt Lake City, Utah, occasional society reporter and columnist, 1944-50; Library of Congress, Washington, D.C., secretary, 1946-48, 1951; University of Utah, Salt Lake City, remedial English teacher, 1960-71; *Marriage,* St. Meinrad, Ind., children's book reviewer, 1972—. *Member:* Authors Guild, Mortar Board, Phi Beta Kappa, Phi Kappa Phi. *Awards, honors:* First place winner in Utah Fine Arts Writing Contest, 1965, for *William H. McGuffey: Boy Reading Genius,* and 1971, for *The Secret Name,* 1975, for *Desert Hunter; Albert's Toothache* was a

children's Book Showcase title, 1975, and listed as one of American Institute of Graphic Arts 50 Books of the Year.

WRITINGS—Juvenile, except as indicated: *Let's Go to an Indian Cliff Dwelling,* Putnam, 1965; *I Know a Policeman,* Putnam, 1966; *I Know a Fireman,* Putnam, 1967; *I Know a Mayor,* Putnam, 1967; *I Know a Garageman,* Putnam, 1968; *William H. McGuffey: Boy Reading Genius,* Bobbs-Merrill, 1968; *I Know a Bank Teller,* Putnam, 1968; *Twelve Steps to Better Exposition* (textbook), C. E. Merrill, 1968; *Boston: Seat of American History,* McGraw, 1969; *I Know a Weatherman,* Putnam, 1970; *The Well-Structured Paragraph* (textbook), C. E. Merrill, 1970; *The Secret Name,* Harcourt, 1972; *Gary and the Very Terrible Monster,* Childrens Press, 1973; *We Can Jump,* Childrens Press, 1973;

"You never believe me," whined Albert. "You believed Marybelle when she said she was the only girl in her class who didn't have a pair of black boots with zippers." ■ (From *Albert's Toothache* by Barbara Williams. Illustrated by Kay Chorao.)

BARBARA WILLIAMS

Albert's Toothache (Junior Literary Guild selection; ALA Notable Book), Dutton, 1974; *Kevin's Grandma*, Dutton, 1975; *Desert Hunter*, Harvey House, 1975; *Someday, Said Mitchell* (Junior Literary Guild Selection), Dutton, 1976; *Cornzapopping!*, Holt, 1976; *If He's My Brother*, Harvey House, 1976; *Never Hit a Porcupine*, Dutton, 1977; *26 Lively Letters* (adult), Taplinger, 1977; *Pins, Picks and Popsicle Sticks*, Holt, 1977; *Chester Chipmunk's Thanksgiving*, Dutton, in press; *Cookie Craft*, Holt, in press.

Plays: *Eternally Peggy* (three-act), Deseret News Press, 1957; *The Ghost of Black Jack* (one-act), Samuel French, 1961; *Just the Two of Us*, (one-act), Utah Printing, 1965.

SIDELIGHTS: "As I look back upon it, I feel sure I must have turned to pencils and typewriters in self-defense. The only non-athlete in the neighborhood (I failed courses in beginning swimming seven times, among other things), no captain ever chose me for his team; and I had to find *something* to do while all the other kids were playing football and baseball. As a result, I spent a good part of my childhood living in the realm of my imagination and setting down my ideas on an antique typewriter which I attacked with one finger. Each week I wrote two or three stories, an article or two, and an occasional poem—many of which were published in the children's section of the Salt Lake *Tribune*.

"Summers I wrote, directed, and costumed plays in which I could also have a starring role. This no doubt served to make up for the fact that I was never the lead in any school production. As the smallest girl in the class, I was invariably cast as the ingenue's little sister—a type casting which I eventually outgrew when I reached college and couldn't fool people any more. Then I turned to radio for a while and ap-

peared on a series of dramatic productions in the last days before television.

"Meanwhile, I was contributing regularly to all the school publications, writing both under my own name and ghosting stories and articles for students who were too lazy to write but wanted to see their names in print. At the university I served as the editor of our yearbook, the *Utonian*, and also wrote a weekly column about campus activities for *The Deseret News*, a downtown newspaper.

"The weekly column continued after I had graduated, married, and moved away from Salt Lake. While my husband was a graduate student at Harvard and I was a graduate student at Boston University, I continued to send articles back to Salt Lake for publication in *The Deseret News*.

"My first national sale didn't come until 1959, when my husband and I had moved back to Salt Lake and he was teaching at the University. This was a one-act play, *The Ghost of Black Jack*, published by Samuel French. It didn't exactly establish me as an instant success, but the play has been produced as far away as Weisbaden, Germany, and continues to provide me with tiny royalties each year.

"Like many other writers for children, I didn't turn to this genre until I had children of my own to read to and realized how interesting and how satisfying children's books could be. Although my college textbooks (which I wrote while I was teaching at the University of Utah) earn far more money than my children's books do, no reader of one of those books has ever sent me a 'thank you' letter. Children are the most appreciative readers in the world!

"In addition to being a political science professor, my husband is an erstwhile politician (unsuccessful candidate for the U.S. Senate in 1968) and tour director. In 1970 and 1972 the children and I accompanied him on college tours of Europe. In 1975 our family again spent the summer in Europe while he taught at a U.S. Air Force base."

FOR MORE INFORMATION SEE: Junior Literary Guild, September, 1974; *Horn Book*, April, 1975; *New York Times Book Review*, May 4, 1975.

WILLIAMS, Guy R. 1920-

PERSONAL: Born August 23, 1920, in Mold, North Wales; son of Owen Elias (a physician)) and Beatrice (Chadwick) Williams. *Education:* Attended St. Edward's School, Oxford, England, and several art schools; received art teacher's diploma, 1950. *Religion:* Church of England. *Home:* 8 The Mall, East Sheen, London S.W. 14, England. *Agent:* Anthony Sheil Associates, 52 Floral St., London W.C. 2, England. *Office:* 1A Earl Rd., East Sheen, London S.W. 14, England.

CAREER: Parmiter's School, London, England, master in charge of drama and careers, 1950—. Artist and illustrator, with work exhibited at Royal Academy, London, England, and at many galleries. *Awards, honors:* Saxon Barton Prize of Royal Cambrian Academy for an oil painting.

WRITINGS: Use Your Hands!, Chapman & Hall, 1956; *Use Your Eyes!*, Chapman & Hall, 1957; *Use Your Leisure!*, Chapman & Hall, 1958; *Use Your Head!*, Chapman & Hall,

GUY R. WILLIAMS

1959; *Instructions to Young Collectors,* Museum Press, 1959.

Use Your Spare Time!, Chapman & Hall, 1960; *Instructions to Young Model-Makers,* Museum Press, 1960; *Use Your Legs!,* Chapman & Hall, 1961; *Use Your Playtime!,* Chapman & Hall, 1962; *Woodworking,* Museum Press, 1962; *Drawing and Sketching,* Museum Press, 1962; *Use Your Ears!,* Chapman & Hall, 1963; *Sketching in Pencil,* Pitman, 1963; *Tackle Leatherwork This Way,* Stanley Paul, 1963; (editor) *Enjoy Painting in Oils,* Gollancz, 1963; *Instructions in Handicrafts,* Museum Press, 1964; *Making a Miniature House,* Oxford University Press, 1964; *Teach Your Child to be Handy,* Pearson, 1964; *Let's Look at Wales,* Museum Press, 1965; *Let's Look at London,* Museum Press, 1965; *Tackle Drawing and Painting This Way,* Stanley Paul, 1965; *Paint Now, Learn Later,* Emerson, 1966; *Indoor Hobbies,* Studio Vista, 1967; *Outdoor Hobbies,* Studio Vista, 1967; *Chester and the Northern Marches,* Longmans, 1968; *Oliver Twist* (adaptation), Macmillan, 1969; *Billy Budd* and *Moby Dick* (adaptations), Macmillan, 1969; *Making Mobiles,* Emerson, 1969; *The World of Model Trains,* Putnam, 1970; *The Doctor and the Devils* (adaptation), Macmillan, 1970; *The World of Model Ships and Boats,* Putnam, 1971; *David Copperfield* (adaptation), Macmillan, 1971; *Pip and the Convict* (adaptation from *Great Expectations*), Macmillan, 1971; *Taking Up Drawing and Painting,* Arthur Barker, 1971, Taplinger, 1973; *The World of Model Aircraft,* Putnam, 1973; *Nicholas Nickleby* (adaptation), Macmillan, 1973; *David and Goliath* and *The Burning Fiery Furnace,* Macmillan, 1975.

Editor of "Enjoying Home and Leisure" series, Gollancz. Regular contributor to *Children's Newspaper* and other periodicals.

WORK IN PROGRESS: The World of Model Cars for Andre Deutsch and Putnam.

SIDELIGHTS: "For many years I was in charge of the art teaching at Parmiter's School, and wrote books for young people—mainly, about hobbies and handicrafts—in my spare time. Then, I became increasingly interested in the pleasures (and problems) of play production, directing several Shakespearean and other presentations, editing the texts—where necessary—and designing the settings. Before long, I had started to give drama lessons as part of the normal school curriculum."

"Having become conscious of the need for play scripts that young people in schools and clubs would find valuable, I helped to establish, in the late 1960's, the 'Drama-Scripts Series' for Macmillan of London, and since then, have acted as the advisory editor of the series. I am heavily involved, now, in the youth drama situation in Britain—reviewing new productions, acting as stage director for big charity shows, and so on. From time to time I take teams of young actors and acrobats on tour round primary schools, which is enormous fun."

WOODBURN, John Henry   1914-

PERSONAL: Born July 17, 1914, in Marietta, Ohio; son of Henry B. and Elizabeth (Schram) Woodburn; married Ruth Biddison (a teacher), June 15, 1940; children: Charlene Sue. *Education:* Marietta College, A.B., 1935; Ohio State University, M.A., 1941; Michigan State University, Ph.D., 1952. *Home:* 9208 LeVelle Dr., Chevy Chase, Md.

JOHN HENRY WOODBURN

CAREER: High school teacher in Ohio, 1936-43; Michigan State University, East Lansing, assistant professor and member of board of examiners, 1946-49; Illinois State Normal University, assistant professor of science, 1949-52; National Science Teachers Association, assistant executive secretary, 1952-55; U.S. Office of Education, science specialist, 1955; Johns Hopkins University, Baltimore, Md., teacher training, 1956-59; high school chemistry teacher, Bethesda, Md., 1959-66; Woodward High School, Rockville, Md., chairman of science department, 1966—. *Military service:* U.S. Navy, air navigator, 1943-45, became lieutenant. *Member:* National Society for the Study of Education, National Association for Research in Science Teaching, National Science Teachers Association. *Awards, honors:* Gustav Ohaus—National Science Teachers Association Award, 1969, and achievement awards, 1971, 1975; Manufacturing Chemists Association National High School Chemistry Teacher Award, 1975.

WRITINGS: (With Robert H. Carleton) *Chemistry Activities,* Lippincott, 1952; (contributor) *The Challenge of Science Education,* Philosophical Library, 1959; *Nuclear Science Teaching Aids and Activities,* U.S. Department of Health, Education, and Welfare, 1959; (contributor) *Rethinking Science Education,* University of Chicago Press, 1960; (with William Haggerty) *Spacecraft,* Scholastic, 1961; *Radioisotopes,* Lippincott, 1962; *Cancer: The Search for Its Origins,* Holt, Rinehart & Winston, 1964; (with Ellsworth S. Obourn) *Teaching the Pursuit of Science,* Macmillan, 1965;

Excursions into Chemistry, Lippincott, 1965. Prepared vocational guidance film strips in several sciences, Scribner, 1958; *Know Your Skin,* Putnam, 1967; *Opportunities in the Chemical Sciences,* Vocational Guidance Manuals, 1971; (with Lewis R. Sanford and W. James Brawley, Jr.) *Demonstrations and Activities for High School Chemistry,* Parker, 1971; *The Whole Earth Energy Crisis* (Junior Literary Guild selection), Putnam, 1973; *Taking Things Apart and Putting Things Together,* American Chemical Society, 1976. Prepared vocational guidance film strips in several sciences, Scribner, 1958. Contributor to professional journals.

SIDELIGHTS: "Although working every day with the young people in my high school chemistry classes is great fun, to write books for young people adds another dimension to my desire to communicate with them. And to encourage them to talk back to me. Sometimes I feel that my peers wonder why I choose to work with high school age people rather than with professional chemists or at the college or university level. I guess the reason is that young people manage somehow to retain their enthusiasm and optimism so much better than do their more mature (chronologically) associates. And without the stimulation of matching wits with young people I don't know where I would find the wherewithal to write books."

FOR MORE INFORMATION SEE: Junior Literary Guild, September, 1973; *Horn Book,* August, 1974.

SOMETHING ABOUT THE AUTHOR

CUMULATIVE INDEXES, VOLUMES 1-11
Illustrations and Authors

ILLUSTRATIONS INDEX

(In the following index, the number of the volume in which an illustrator's work appears is given *before* the colon, and the page on which it appears is given *after* the colon. For example, a drawing by Adams, Adrienne appears in Volume 2 on page 6, another drawing by her appears in Volume 3 on page 80, and another drawing in Volume 8 on page 1.)

AUTHORS INDEX

(In the following index, the number of the volume in which an author's sketch appears is given *before* the colon, and the page on which it appears is given *after* the colon. For example, the sketch of Aardema, Verna, appears in Volume 4 on page 1).